## LAW, LEGAL EXPERTISE AND EU POLICY-MAKING

This edited collection examines the changing role of the legal profession as experts in the context of European Union policy-making. Drawing on theoretical and empirical research and the idea of law as a social and political practice, this socio-legal work brings together a group of legal scholars and political scientists to investigate how lawyers, through the deployment of their expertise and knowledge, act as experts in matters of EU related policy-making at the national, European and international levels. It provides new theoretical viewpoints and untold stories from legal experts themselves, promotes an evolving definition of what constitutes legal expertise and what shapes legal experts in a time when experts are in equal measure both revered and ignored, and introduces new critical voices in the field of EU socio-legal studies.

Emilia Korkea-aho is Professor of European Law and Legislative Studies at UEF Law School, and Academy of Finland Research Fellow, and Visiting Fellow at the Maastricht Centre for European Law. Her research interests cover EU institutional and constitutional law, and she has published in the areas of EU governance and soft law, lobbying and its regulation, and EU law methodologies. In 2020, she received the Academy of Finland Award for Social Impact for her work on lobbying and its regulation.

Päivi Leino-Sandberg is Professor of Transnational European Law and Director of the Master's Programme in Global Governance Law at the University of Helsinki. She is Deputy Director of the Erik Castrén Institute of International Law and Human Rights where she leads five international research projects in various areas of EU law. Before returning full time to the academia in 2015, she worked for over 10 years as a legal adviser for the Finnish government participating in numerous EU and international negotiations and Court cases.

# Law, Legal Expertise and EU Policy-Making

*Edited by*

EMILIA KORKEA-AHO
University of Eastern Finland

PÄIVI LEINO-SANDBERG
University of Helsinki

CAMBRIDGE
UNIVERSITY PRESS

CAMBRIDGE
UNIVERSITY PRESS

Shaftesbury Road, Cambridge CB2 8EA, United Kingdom

One Liberty Plaza, 20th Floor, New York, NY 10006, USA

477 Williamstown Road, Port Melbourne, VIC 3207, Australia

314–321, 3rd Floor, Plot 3, Splendor Forum, Jasola District Centre, New Delhi – 110025, India

103 Penang Road, #05–06/07, Visioncrest Commercial, Singapore 238467

Cambridge University Press is part of Cambridge University Press & Assessment, a department of the University of Cambridge.

We share the University's mission to contribute to society through the pursuit of education, learning and research at the highest international levels of excellence.

www.cambridge.org
Information on this title: www.cambridge.org/9781108821643

DOI: 10.1017/9781108909099



First published 2022
First paperback edition 2026

*A catalogue record for this publication is available from the British Library*

*Library of Congress Cataloging-in-Publication data*
NAMES: Korkea-aho, Emilia, editor. | Leino-Sandberg, Päivi, editor.
TITLE: Law, legal expertise and EU policy-making / edited by Emilia Korkea-aho, University of Eastern Finland; Päivi Leino-Sandberg, University of Helsinki.
DESCRIPTION: Cambridge, United Kingdom ; New York, NY : Cambridge University Press, 2022. | Includes bibliographical references and index.
IDENTIFIERS: LCCN 2021045485 (print) | LCCN 2021045486 (ebook) | ISBN 9781108830126 (hardback) | ISBN 9781108909099 (ebook)
SUBJECTS: LCSH: Policy sciences – European Union countries. | Expertise – Political aspects – European Union countries. | Government attorneys – European Union countries.
CLASSIFICATION: LCC KJE6428 .L39 2022 (print) | LCC KJE6428 (ebook) | DDC 341.242/2–dc23/eng/20211220
LC record available at https://lccn.loc.gov/2021045485
LC ebook record available at https://lccn.loc.gov/2021045486

ISBN 978-1-108-83012-6 Hardback
ISBN 978-1-108-82164-3 Paperback

# Contents

# Contributors

CAROLYN ABBOT, University of Manchester
LOLA AVRIL, European University Institute
ANU BRADFORD, Columbia Law School
PIERRE FRANCE, Université Paris 1-Sorbonne
CHRIS KIMURA, American University, Washington College of Law
JAN KLABBERS, University of Helsinki
EMILIA KORKEA-AHO, University of Eastern Finland
MARTTI KOSKENNIEMI, University of Helsinki
MARIA LEE, University College London
PÄIVI LEINO-SANDBERG, University of Helsinki
HANS-W. MICKLITZ, European University Institute
FERNANDA G. NICOLA, American University, Washington College of Law
MAXIMILIAN STEINBEIS, Verfassungsblog
ANTOINE VAUCHEZ, Université Paris 1-Sorbonne & Centre national de la recherche scientifique (CNRS)
MATTHEW WINDSOR, University of Nottingham
BENJAMIN YONG, Durham University

# Acknowledgements

This book has its roots in two research projects funded by the Academy of Finland. Both concerned the role and impact of advice provided by legal experts, with Päivi exploring these themes in the context of EU institutions and Emilia in the field of lobbying. They led us to reflect together on the role and effects of legal experts in relation to EU policy-making and to consider how they might be studied. Both of us presented our initial ideas at the W. G. Hart Legal Workshop on 'Valuing Expertise: Legal, Normative and Social Dimensions' organised by London University's Institute of Advanced Legal Studies in 2016. That event revealed that we were both particularly interested in the nature of legal expertise. We continued our discussions and methodological explorations in Helsinki and then came up with the idea of bringing together, for further reflection, a group of academics similarly interested in legal experts but whose approaches to the subject were somewhat different from our own.

Our plan to make this into a collective volume matured during a two-week writing retreat in Paris in April 2018 – the memory of which that has buoyed us up while bringing the project to completion during the pandemic! The contributions and overall plan were further developed through a conference on the subject of 'Legal Experts in Transnational Policy-Making' held at the Erik Castrén Institute of International Law and Human Rights (ECI) later that year. Antoine Buchet, Toni Malminen, Jo Shaw and Immi Tallgren took part in that conference, in addition to ourselves. Panu Minkkinen designed a poster for the event in accordance with our wishes. The conference received support from the Finnish Lawyers' Association and the UEF Law School, as well as from the Academy of Finland. The manuscript was completed in April 2020.

We thank Tapio Määttä, head of the UEF Law School at the time, for his encouragement, and Marja Kyllönen for managing our various projects so efficiently. Pinja Lindvall and Linda Sydänmaanlakka helped with the editing, and Katariina Flinck with the preparation of the index. Meg Morley translated the draft article by Pierre France and Antoine Vauchez. Anna van der Velde at ECI has supported us in every possible way during the realisation of the project. We also thank Katja Tukiainen for giving us permission to use her work *Lippujuhla* as the cover illustration for the book.

We dedicate the book to the legal experts whom we study, and to our families for their patience during the project and beyond.

# 1

# Law, Legal Expertise and EU Policy-Making: Introduction

Emilia Korkea-aho and Päivi Leino-Sandberg

## 1.1 INTRODUCTION

### 1.1.1 *The Thrust of the Book*

Experts increasingly play a more central role at all levels of public governance. As holders of expert knowledge, they are considered trustworthy providers of certainty and answers in the face of increased complexity, interdependence and the fast-changing pace of life.[1] The authoritative certainty to which they lay claim causes them to be frequently called upon and consulted by policy-makers. Their importance has increased as policy-making has become more complex and intense. Yet experts cannot be contained within a single definition. They constitute a highly heterogenous group and include in-house specialists, public interest stakeholders, lobbyists, and academics. This diverse group possesses specialised and technical knowledge across a wide range of policy fields and legislative instruments.

Expertise-driven policy-making is sometimes argued to be most noticeable in the European Union (EU). Not only does the EU rely on expertise, but it also nurtures the very expertise it relies on.[2] As Hans-W. Micklitz remarks in his contribution to this volume, '[t]he whole inner machinery of the EU is

[1] Peter M. Haas, 'Introduction: Epistemic Communities and International Policy Coordination' (1992) 46 *International Organization*, 1–37; Robert Dahl, 'Finding Competent Citizens: Improving Democracy' (1993) 351 *Current*, 23–30; Stephen Turner, 'What Is the Problem with Experts?' (2001) 31 *Social Studies of Science*, 123–149; Kevin M. Esterling, *The Political Economy of Expertise* (Ann Arbor: University of Michigan Press, 2004); Sean Gailmard and John W. Patty, *Learning While Governing: Expertise and Accountability in the Executive Branch* (Chicago: University of Chicago Press, 2013).

[2] For example, in 2011, the Commission responded to the call from a group of MEPs by establishing a financial programme to support the creation and running of two non-governmental organisations in the area of EU financial policy-making. In its press release, the Commission announced its support for 'the development of a *European centre of financial*

dependent on self-named and EU-certified experts'. However, research on the role of expertise in EU policy-making is predominantly interested in technical, scientific, organisational, or other non-legal forms of expertise, supplied by economists, engineers, and scientists. The discussion has overlooked legal experts, such as in-house legal advisors in national ministries or the European Parliament and legal professionals working in law firms, elsewhere in the private sector, academia, and not-for-profit non-governmental organisations (NGOs). At the level of international law, some studies have addressed the 'invisible college of international lawyers',[3] but primarily through the international lawyers' own lenses and personal histories.[4]

This collection of essays fulfils a twofold purpose. First, we bring together a group of legal scholars and sociologists to investigate how lawyers, through the deployment of their expertise and knowledge, act as experts in matters of EU-related policy-making at national, European, and international levels. Our investigations contribute to sketching the contours of a new space for studying legal expertise. Second, we draw on theoretical and empirical research and the idea of law as a social and political practice. As a socio-legal work, the book aims to contribute to the methodological enrichment of EU law by engaging in both an empirical and self-reflective study of what constitutes legal expertise. Although focusing on the EU, the ideas elaborated in this book can be further discussed in other national, international, and transnational contexts of law- and policy-making.

In this introductory chapter, we contextualise the subsequent chapters by describing and explaining what we mean by legal expertise and provide some ideas as to why legal and nonlegal research has sidelined legal expertise. We

*expertise* that would stimulate the involvement of consumers and non-industry stakeholders' (emphasis added). In other words, the Commission assisted NGOs in becoming experts. See EU Commission, 'EU Commission adopts proposal to help fund financial services NGOs', press release, 15 June 2016.

3 Oscar Schachter, 'The Invisible College of International Lawyers' (1977) 72(2) *Northwestern University Law Review*, 217–226, at 217. See also Santiago Villalpando, 'The "Invisible College of International Lawyers" Forty Years Later', ESIL 2013 5th Research Forum: International Law as a Profession, Conference Paper No. 5/2013 (4 December 2013), https://dx.doi.org/10.2139/ssrn.2363640.

4 See, e.g., *Collection of Essays by Legal Advisers of States, Legal Advisers of International Organizations and Practitioners in the Field of International Law* (New York: United Nations, 1999); F. D. Berman, 'The International Lawyer: Inside and Outside Foreign Ministries' in Christopher Hill and Pamela Beshoff (eds.), *Two Worlds of International Relations: Academics, Practitioners and the Trade in Ideas* (London: Routledge, 1994) pp. 79–92; Michael P. Scharf and Paul R. Williams, *Shaping Foreign Policy in Times of Crisis: The Role of International Law and the State Department Legal Adviser* (Cambridge: Cambridge University Press, 2010).

then discuss what we know about legal expertise in policy-making and reflect on the methodology of studying legal expertise and experts.

### 1.1.2 *Defining Legal Expertise and a Legal Expert*

There is no single definition of expertise or expert. For the purposes of the present collection, we understand expertise to mean a person's widely recognised knowledge, skill, or technical prowess which is accorded status and authority by her or his peers. Legal expertise accordingly refers to legal skills and knowledge of the law gained through a formal legal education and work experience. To be called a legal expert, a person typically requires a university degree providing its holder with an understanding of the legal system. Formal legal education is necessary, as it entails professional recognition and distinguishes a degree holder from lay people, who may have an interest in, and opinions about, law but lack the professional qualifications allowing them to make legal arguments.[5] Yet, a legal degree alone does not suffice, because the ins and outs of the profession are often learned in practice. The different contexts analysed by our authors are also visible in the definitions for legal expert that they use.

Does the EU have its own definition of a legal expert or a say in how to become one? While legal education has remained the prerogative of member states, the EU has had a role to play in the extent to which lawyers are able to offer legal services outside their home countries and become European legal experts.[6] Secondary legislation sets EU-wide rules which nonetheless leave the national legislator with much discretion to shape the conditions under which a lawyer from one member state is admitted to another member state's legal market.[7] In

5 Many fake lawyer scandals relate to cases where someone pretends to be qualified to represent clients in courts. Non-lawyers making legal arguments in politics or on Twitter rarely raise eyebrows.

6 In *Gebhard*, the ECJ required that 'Member States may not ignore the knowledge and qualifications already acquired by the person concerned in another Member State'. Case C-55/94 *Reinhard Gebhard* v. *Consiglio dell'Ordine degli Avvocati e Procuratori di Milano* [1995] EU:C:1995:411.

7 See Council Directive 77/249/EEC of 22 March 1977 to facilitate the effective exercise by lawyers of freedom to provide services, OJ 1977 No. L78, 26 March 1977, p. 17, last amended through Council Directive 2013/25/EU of 13 May 2013 adapting certain directives in the field of right of establishment and freedom to provide services, by reason of the accession of the Republic of Croatia, OJ 2013 No. L158, 10 June 2013, p. 368. See also Directive 98/5/EC of the European Parliament and of the Council of 16 February 1998 to facilitate practice of the profession of lawyer on a permanent basis in a Member State other than that in which the qualification was obtained, OJ 1998 No. L77, 14 March 1998, p. 36; Directive 2005/36/EC of the European Parliament and of the Council of 7 September 2005 on the recognition of professional qualifications, OJ 2005 L255, 30 September 2005, p. 22 (as amended).

practice, member states have considerable influence in determining who can be a legal expert in their markets, regardless of EU rules and procedures. Traditionally, the legal profession, in particular as far as practising lawyers are concerned, is regulated neither by the EU nor member states, but based on self-regulation. As professionals, members of the legal profession are given discretion to determine their own rules of conduct. In exchange for this privilege, lawyers are expected to abide by a set of professional values – competence, independence, and serving the public interest – which distinguishes them from purely commercial actors.[8]

The legal experts we study in this collection have gained their work experience in various contexts: as legal advisors in EU or national bureaucracies and non-governmental public interest organisations, as lawyer-lobbyists in private practice, or as legal academics in universities.[9] All possess legal expertise in EU-related policy-making gained through a legal education and practical experience. We understand 'EU-related policy-making' to mean the adoption and implementation of general decisions of political and social interest at European level by which we mean not only the level of EU institutions but also EU matters at national level and the EU's increasing external policy role. Recognising the importance of national matters as EU matters cuts across the chapters of this book.[10] Policy-making includes the legislative process, the adoption of regulatory policies or executive decisions, and the negotiation of international agreements.

8 Scott L. Cummings, 'What Good Are Lawyers?' in Scott L. Cummings (ed.), *The Paradox of Professionalism: Lawyers and the Possibility of Justice* (Cambridge: Cambridge University Press, 2011), p. 1.

9 We are leaving aside lawyers working in the context of adjudication and arbitration, since these questions are already covered in, e.g., Duncan Kennedy, *A Critique of Adjudication:* fin de siècle] (Cambridge, MA: Harvard University Press, 1997); Arman Sarvarian, *Professional Ethics at the International Bar* (Oxford: Oxford University Press, 2013); Gregory Shaffer, Manfred Elsig, and Sergio Puig, 'The Law and Politics of WTO Dispute Settlement' in Wayne Sandholtz and Christopher Whytock (eds.), *The Politics of International Law* (Oxford: Oxford University Press, 2016); Yves Dezalay and Bryant G. Garth, *Dealing in Virtue: International Commercial Arbitration and the Construction of a Transnational Legal Order* (Chicago: University of Chicago Press, 1996); Sergio Puig, 'Social Capital in the Arbitration Market' (2014) 25 *European Journal of International Law*, 387–424.

10 It also connects with what the EU itself expressed in its first Rule of Law Report: 'The EU is based on the rule of law. Threats to the rule of law challenge its legal, political and economic basis. *Deficiencies in one Member State impact other Member States and the EU as a whole.*' Communication from the Commission to the European Parliament, the Council, the European Economic and Social Committee and the Committee of the Regions 2020, 'Rule of Law Report: The rule of law situation in the European Union', COM (2020) 580 final, p. 2 (emphasis added).

### 1.1.3 *Researching (Legal) Expertise*

Expertise is a much-researched topic among social scientists, primarily sociologists and political scientists.[11] Lawyers have also studied the use of expertise and experts in various contexts of decision- and policy-making.[12] The standard approach to expertise in legal scholarship (to which, broadly speaking, the contributors to this volume belong) focuses on how judges deal with aspects of technical subjects of which they have limited mastery.[13] Particularly at national and EU levels, these studies typically question the capability of (lower court) judges to adjudicate on highly complex information in various fields of human life, such as in medical reports or toxicology documents.[14] Although such studies address the role of expertise in policy-making contexts, they focus exclusively on scientific and technical expertise.[15]

Legal research, but also research on expertise more generally, has ignored and overlooked what constitutes lawyers' 'own' expertise in policy-making. We believe that it has also left unexamined assumptions that underlie the nature of legal expertise ('technical', 'non-partisan', 'apolitical') and the conflicting expectations legal experts might encounter as to the role they should play. Despite the interest which scholars of international law have shown in the alleged 'neutrality' and 'invisibility' of expertise and in how experts frame discussions and influence policy choices and possible alternatives, there has

11 Harry Collins and Robert Evans, *Rethinking Expertise* (Chicago: University of Chicago Press, 2007); Sheila Jasanoff (ed.), *States of Knowledge: The Co-Production of Science and the Social Order* (London: Routledge, 2004). On the role of expertise in defining a profession, see Mike Saks, 'Defining a Profession: The Role of Knowledge and Expertise' (2012) 2(1) *Professions and Professionalism*, 1–10.

12 A representative example is Monika Ambrus, Karin Arts, Ellen Hey, and Helena Raulus (eds.), *The Role of 'Experts' in International and European Decision-Making Processes* (Cambridge: Cambridge University Press, 2014). See also, more recently, Vigjilenca Abazi, Johan Adriaensen, and Thomas Christiansen (eds.), *The Contestation of Expertise in the European Union* (Cham: Palgrave Macmillan, 2020).

13 E.g. Sheila Jasanoff, *Science at the Bar: Law, Science, and Technology in America* (Cambridge, MA: Harvard University Press, 1995).

14 E.g. Kenneth R. Foster and Peter W. Huber, *Judging Science: Scientific Knowledge and the Federal Courts* (Cambridge, MA: MIT Press, 1991); Maria Lee, 'Experts and Publics in EU Environmental Law' in Anthony Arnull (ed.), *The Oxford Handbook of EU Law* (Oxford: Oxford University Press, 2015), pp. 991–1041; Tiina Paloniitty and Mariolina Eliantonio, 'Scientific Knowledge in Environmental Judicial Review: Safeguarding Effective Judicial Protection in the EU Member States?' (2018) 27 *European Energy and Environmental Law Review*, 108–114.

15 For instance, none of the eighteen chapters in Ambrus et al., *The Role of 'Experts'* that concern environmental governance, human rights, and financial policy at international and EU levels discusses the role of legal experts.

been less interest in what constitutes the legal expertise of international lawyers.

We argue that as lawyers and legal scholars we have been slow at analysing our own expertise and whether our experience or conception of experts differs from those of other disciplines. However, this is not to suggest that lawyers have entirely avoided looking inwards up till now. The present collection is indebted to the attention given to the legal profession in the 'law and sociology' and 'sociology of law' literature. The central thrust of this literature is that the legal profession is believed to enjoy a unique role in society. Legal professionals are trusted to handle important matters and take professional responsibility for policymakers and clients' affairs, be they conducted in the public or private interest.[16] Studies internal to the profession are mostly centred on questions of professional independence as a governing principle of legal expertise. Studies on legal professionals as experts in policy-making are rarer and largely US-centred.[17]

The absence of studies on legal expertise as a defining feature of the legal profession is perhaps most striking in the EU context. Ever since the introduction of Cappelletti, Seccombe, and Weiler's 'Integration through Law' project,[18] few have doubted the centrality of law in the European integration

16 See, e.g., Richard L. Abel and Philip S. C. Lewis (eds.), *Lawyers in Society*, 3 vols. (Oakland: University of California Press, 1988–1989); Richard L. Abel, 'Comparative Sociology of Legal Professions: An Exploratory Essay' (1985) 10 *Law & Social Inquiry*, 1–79.; Terence C. Halliday, *Beyond Monopoly: Lawyers, State Crises, and Professional Empowerment* (Chicago: University of Chicago Press, 1987); Robert Dingwall and Philip Lewis (eds.), *The Sociology of the Professions: Lawyers, Doctors and Others* (New Orleans: Quid Pro Books, 2014).

17 William H. Simon, 'The Professional Responsibilities of the Public Official's Lawyer: A Case Study from the Clinton Era' (2002) 77 *Notre Dame Law Review*, 999–1022; Allan C. Hutchinson, '"In the Public Interest": The Responsibilities and Rights of Government Lawyers' (2008) 46(105) *Osgoode Hall Law Journal*, 105–129; W. Bradley Wendel, 'Government Lawyers, Democracy, and the Rule of Law' (2009) 77 *Fordham Law Review*, 1333–1362; Ann Southworth, Anthony Paik, and John P. Heinz, 'Lawyers in National Policymaking' in Scott L. Cummings (ed.), *The Paradox of Professionalism. Lawyers and the Possibility of Justice* (Cambridge: Cambridge University Press, 2011) pp. 220–242. France is an exception to the North American focus in the literature. In France, lawyers have tended to define themselves in political terms, and legal experts' professional identity has historically been constructed through explicitly rejecting market transactions and privileging a political definition of the profession as a collective. For a comparative view of the United States, Germany, and France, see Terence C. Halliday and Lucien Karpik (eds.), *Lawyers and the Rise of Western Political Liberalism: Europe and North America from the Eighteenth to Twentieth Centuries* (Oxford: Oxford University Press, 1997).

18 The 'Integration through Law' project began at the European University Institute, Florence, in 1978 and was directed by Mauro Cappelletti, Monica Seccombe, and Joseph H. H. Weiler. The *Florence Integration Through Law* series, edited by Cappelletti, Seccombe, and Weiler, was the result of this research project and comprises a number of volumes published in the

process. Despite this, EU law scholarship has been almost solely focused on the European Court of Justice as an epitome of legal expertise. Päivi Leino-Sandberg's monograph *The Politics of Legal Expertise in EU Policy-Making* (2021) is an exception in that it discusses the role of legal advisers working in the EU institutions. In EU law scholarship, research into lawyers as legal experts has been considered to require the regard of a neutral outsider and thus an external approach. Over the past twenty years, literature marked by a sociological, even everyday, perspective on this legal dimension of European integration has appeared,[19] building on earlier socio-historical analyses of law and lawyers as critical instruments in European integration.[20] Sociologists examining the legal profession from the outside have studied lawyers in various roles, including as lawmakers and bureaucrats in the EU. In these studies, recourse to legal expertise is seen as a part of promoting the European integrationist agenda. This, however, leaves aside much of the ordinary policy-making process – which this collection attempts to bring to light. By way of a bridge from that existing tradition, the collection nonetheless includes two chapters by sociologically oriented political scientists (Avril, France and Vauchez). Our hope is that, by bringing together lawyers and sociologists of law, the collection will examine the legal profession from both the inside and the outside.

## 1.2 LEGAL EXPERTISE IN POLICY-MAKING

Today, scholars interested in experts and expert governance are confronted with a dilemma. Policymakers turn to experts for advice to make the right decisions and communicate these to the general public. Yet, expertise is at the same time challenged more than ever by both policymakers and the general

1980s. See also Daniel Augenstein (ed.), *'Integration through Law' Revisited: The Making of the European Polity* (Farnham: Ashgate, 2012).

19 Antoine Vauchez and Bruno de Witte (eds.), *Lawyering Europe: European Law as a Transnational Social Field* (Oxford: Hart, 2013); Antoine Vauchez, *Brokering Europe: Euro-Lawyers and the Making of a Transnational Polity* (Cambridge: Cambridge University Press, 2015).

20 Antoine Vauchez, 'The Force of a Weak Field: Law and Lawyers in the Government of the European Union (For a Renewed Research Agenda)' (2008) 2 *International Political Sociology*, 128–144; Antonin Cohen and Antoine Vauchez, 'Les juristes et l'ordre politique européen' (2005) 26 *Critique internationale*, 97–99 and the articles that follow their introduction. See also Antonin Cohen and Antoine Vauchez, 'Introduction: Law, Lawyers, and Transnational Politics in the Production of Europe' (2007) 32 *Law & Social Inquiry*, 75–82 and the articles that follow their introduction; Yves Dezalay and David Sugarman (eds.), *Professional Competition and Professional Power: Lawyers, Accountants and the Social Construction of Markets* (London: Routledge, 1995).

public. Many recent elections and national consultations, including Brexit, have been seen as votes against expertise. For Sismondo, writing about post-truth, 'optimism about the coexistence of democracy and expertise may be misplaced'.[21]

The fact that politicians and the general public regard 'experts' and 'specialists' with suspicion also has repercussions on legal experts. We believe that discussions on who counts as an expert and what constitutes expertise should include legal experts and expertise. By initiating such a discussion, we do not claim that lawyers are 'special' or that their expertise is fundamentally different from other disciplines. Instead, we argue that legal scholarship must also take the distrust of experts seriously and treat it as a matter of concern for the legal profession. Can legal expertise maintain its authority in the post-truth policy-making process? This is a crucial question to ask, because lawyers' own understanding of their work relies on objectivity and neutrality.

Can lawyers uphold the values of objectivity and neutrality when facts are 'less influential in shaping public opinion than appeals to emotion and personal belief'?[22] Is there an emotional, demonstrative side to legal expertise and how does it fit the standard conception of legal expertise as content-oriented speech? Strong argues that 'conventional means of responding to legal and political misconceptions (i.e., content-oriented speech aimed at those who are believed to have simply failed to hear the relevant information)' no longer suffice.[23] Does suspicion towards experts concern all types of legal expertise, or are some better than others at ensuring their (epistemic) authority? Recognising the post-truth challenge to the contemporary policy-making process, this collection argues that distrust of (legal) experts is not only a political problem of policymakers and people questioning why and what experts are saying; it is also a legal problem implicating constitutional democratic governance.[24]

Scholars have long been preoccupied with the question of how professional and technical expertise fit into the governance process of a democratic society. The resulting literature is informed by the distinction between 'democratic politics' and 'policy'. The former 'describes the theory and practice of the power struggle between the players inside the polity'. The latter, on the other hand, is a concept that refers to activities that aim 'at the planned formation of

[21] Sergei Sismondo, 'Editorial: Post-truth?' (2017) 47 *Social Studies of Science*, 3–6, p. 4.

[22] See Oxford Languages, 'Word of the Year 2016', https://en.oxforddictionaries.com/word-of-the-year/word-of-the-year-2016.

[23] S. I. Strong, 'Alternative Facts and the Post-Truth Society: Meeting the Challenge' (2017) 165 *University of Pennsylvania Law Review*, 137–146.

[24] Sarah C. Haan, 'The Post-Truth First Amendment' (2019) 94 *Indiana Law Journal*, 1351–1406.

social domains such as economy, environment or education through collective binding decisions'.[25] For decades, students and practitioners of public law and administration have been taught that policy should not be driven by democratic politics and polls of the moment. Although politics set the tasks for policy, the power struggles of democratic processes are not supposed to interfere with administrative work, where government officials armed with technical expertise advance public interests.[26] The predominance of the administrative domain, with its scientific and technocratic modi operandi, is what is sometimes considered to characterise the administrative state.[27] However, the pendulum has swung the other way. Now the question is whether expert-driven policy-making with its scientific tendencies is a risk to politics, squeezing the life out of the democratic process.[28]

To date, scholarly inquiry into the relationship between policy and politics has identified two major positions, one building on separation and the other on politicisation.[29] As an illustration of the latter, critical international law (which is far ahead of EU law in discussing expertise) has held that the authority of experts in policy-making relies on the framing effect that expertise has. By shaping and reshaping issues, experts are able to (unduly) influence the domain of politics.[30] In other words, all expertise is political. David Kennedy, for instance, has argued that the 'background' work of experts has a framing effect, with an overt bearing on 'foreground' decision-making.[31] The

25 Gerhard Vowe, 'Politics, Policy, Polity' in Lynda Lee Kaid and Christina Holtz-Bacha (eds.), *Encyclopedia of Political Communication* (Thousand Oaks: Sage, 2008), sections 620–621.

26 David Rosenbloom, 'The Politics-Administration Dichotomy in U.S. Historical Context' (2008) 68 *Public Administration Review*, 57–60.

27 In the United States in particular, but also in the EU to a certain extent, the existence of the administrative state has been discussed with reference to administrative agencies. See, e.g., Adrian Vermeule, *Law's Abnegation: From Law's Empire to the Administrative State* (Cambridge, MA: Harvard University Press, 2016).

28 See, e.g., Frank Fischer, *Democracy and Expertise: Reorienting Policy Inquiry* (Oxford: Oxford University Press, 2009); Christine Boswell, *The Political Use of Knowledge: Immigration Policy and Social Research* (Cambridge: Cambridge University Press, 2009); Ray Pawson, *Evidence-Based Policy: A Realist Perspective* (London: Sage, 2007). See also, in the EU context, Åse Gornitzka and Ulf Sverdrup, 'Who Consults? The Configuration of Expert Groups in the European Union' (2008) 31 *West European Politics*, 725–750.

29 Tansun Demir, 'Politics and Administration: Three Schools, Three Approaches, and Three Suggestions' (2009) 31 *Administrative Theory and Praxis*, 503–532.

30 Revisiting the argument of how knowledge becomes power, David Kennedy, 'Law, Expertise, and Global Political Economy' (2018) 23 *Tilburg Law Review*, 109–120.

31 David Kennedy, *A World of Struggle: How Power, Law and Expertise Shape Global Political Economy* (Princeton: Princeton University Press, 2016). See also Ole Jacob Sending, *The Politics of Expertise: Competing for Authority in Global Governance* (Ann Arbor: University of Michigan University Press, 2017); Annabelle Littoz-Monnet (ed.), *The Politics of Expertise in International Organizations: How International Bureaucracies Produce and Mobilize*

present collection builds on the critical narrative with which international law scholars approach expertise in policy-making. The other approach, founded on separation, is instead concerned with the depoliticisation of the work of experts, focusing on how they mostly deal with technical and neutral questions in the spirit of craftmanship and administrative engineering. The holder of legal expertise is presumed to be 'apolitical' and 'neutral', and the advice given as legal expertise is projected as 'objective' and 'unquestionable'.[32] This corresponds to the perception legal experts have of themselves, although it often remains unexpressed and unexplored.

Despite taking the international law criticism of expert power seriously, neither of the above positions is – at least, in their pure versions – tenable. It would be an oversimplification to revert to the position that all expertise is political. Not only is this too easy as an explanation, but it overlooks the fact that an administration is driven by its own (bureaucratic) logic, which refuses to succumb to politics. This tension never disappears; it merely manifests itself differently in different cases. Equally unconvincing is the claim that the work of experts has no political influence on the choices and alternatives on the policymaker's table. The tasks experts deal with on a daily basis are about more than just implementing policies set by elected officials.

So, how to go on from here? We posit that the study of legal expertise offers a new take on this issue. First, it leads us to ask what role law assumes in the policy-politics (expertise-democracy) dichotomy, and in this way to help question the explanatory value of the dichotomy. Are legal experts like any other technical or 'professional policy' experts? Do legal experts try to go beyond the dichotomy by stressing the special nature of their expertise? How do they navigate the dichotomy in their daily tasks? Second, the literature on the relationship between expert administration and democratic politics has paid little attention to what France and Vauchez in this collection describe as 'the blurring of the public-private divide' and the 'spectacular rise of state expertise within private law firms'.

The provision of legal expertise in policy-making is not the prerogative of a governmental lawyer. This book introduces and develops the notions of in-house and external legal expertise. The expression 'in-house legal advice' is usually

*Knowledge* (London: Routledge, 2017); Holly Cullen, Catherine Renshaw, and Joanna Harrington (eds.), *Experts, Networks and International Law* (Cambridge: Cambridge University Press, 2017); Anna Leander and Tanja Aalberts, 'The Co-Constitution of Legal Expertise and International Security' (2013) 26 *Leiden Journal of International Law*, 783–792.

32 See, e.g., Jean-Paul Jacqué, 'The Role of Legal Services in the Elaboration of European Legislation' in Antoine Vauchez and Bruno de Witte (eds.), *Lawyering Europe: European Law as a Transnational Social Field* (Oxford: Hart, 2013), pp. 43–54.

reserved for legal advice provided by corporate legal counsels.[33] In the context of this collection, however, 'in-house legal expertise' refers to the expertise provided by insiders – that is, legal experts working within the policy-making process and legal advisors and counsellors working in the institutions, ministries, departments, and agencies concerned. Yet, as the collection shows, legal expertise can also be external, fed into the policy-making by outsiders – that is, legal advisors in NGOs, legal academics, or private sector lawyers as lobbyists for corporations and business associations. In many of the contributions to this collection, these two forms of legal expertise coexist, leading to the 'hybridisation' of legal expertise.

For present purposes, we prefer the terms 'internal' and 'external', as well as the notion of hybridisation, as the public-private dichotomy does not easily lend itself to explaining, for instance, the role of NGOs in offering legal advice (chapters by Lee and Abbot, or Korkea-aho), and their legal advisers hardly see themselves as 'private'. Although developed with reference to legal expertise, the notion of hybridisation of expertise suggests that the discussion on the role of experts in policy-making, be they economists, scientists, or engineers, needs to account for policymakers using expertise from various sources simultaneously. For instance, members of the European Parliament (MEPs) or national parliaments have learnt to benefit from this 'free market of legal advice', as shown by Leino-Sandberg and Yong in their contributions.

## 1.3 METHODOLOGY

Methodologically, the contributors to this collection not only investigate what legal expertise is in theory or at an abstract level, but also examine how legal experts see themselves and their influence. This requires approaches other than those traditionally used in doctrinal discussions.

Many of the contributions take a socio-legal approach by using interviews with experts to reveal individual and institutional worlds of legal expertise, thereby identifying patterns of practice across different contexts where legal experts operate (Avril, France and Vauchez, Kimura and Nicola, Korkea-aho, Lee and Abbott, Leino-Sandberg, Yong).[34] Other chapters are more explicitly normative in their outlook. However, these also push back the boundaries by developing new tools to theorise about legal expertise. Both Koskenniemi's performative analysis and Windsor's framing approach provide alternative, yet complementary, theoretical

33 See, e.g., Richard Moorhead, Steven Vaughan, and Cristina Godinho, *In-House Lawyers' Ethics: Institutional Logics, Legal Risk and the Tournament of Influence* (Oxford: Hart, 2018).

34 See also Emilia Korkea-aho and Päivi Leino, 'Interviewing Lawyers: A Critical Self-Reflection on Expert Interviews as a Method of EU Legal Research' (2019) *European Journal of Legal Studies*, Network of Legal Empirical Scholars (NoLesLaw) Special Issue, 17–47.

perspectives for investigating legal expertise. The collection's methodological uniqueness lies also in the self-critical manner in which contributors engage with their own role, expertise, and influence (e.g. Klabbers, Leino-Sandberg, Micklitz, Steinbeis). The volume also includes critical chapters by political scientists (political sociologists) who study the legal profession (Avril, France and Vauchez).

The approach adopted in this collection shows that both positions noted above (separation and politicisation) are deficient. They lack empirical insights into how the relationship between expertise and democratic decision-making is negotiated and settled on a daily basis. How do experts situate themselves in the politics-policy dichotomy in the current EU context? Is the dichotomy still relevant for their everyday activities or does it appear to be a relic of the past? Does this dichotomy meet the expectations of those to whom they provide advice? The contributions discuss not only what makes a legal expert but also how experts operate and influence policy-making through actual outcomes and how they themselves conceive their own role.

This socio-legal empirical orientation therefore departs from more conventional EU legal research focused on an analysis of case law and legal rules. Such research has shown less interest in what makes up the legal profession in the EU or in the use of socio-legal methods. For this reason, the collection builds on the emergence of sociological studies that have tried to understand lawyers in different roles, including as lawmakers and bureaucrats in the EU.[35] The present collection complements this scholarship by opening up everyday policy-making from the perspective of those inside. But it also departs from sociological scholarship by attempting to understand and envisage what legally oriented research of legal expertise might entail and how legal scholarship should conceptualise lawyers' expertise. The collection encourages methodological self-reflection and even the building of a certain tension between different approaches. By bringing all of these (to a certain extent, disharmonious) voices together, the editors want to contribute to a discussion about the possibilities and limits of the methodological tools we use to study legal experts.

## 1.4 BOOK OUTLINE

The book is divided into three parts. The contributions in Part I lay down the theoretical premises, which are then elaborated further in Part II and Part III.

35 See Vauchez and de Witte (eds.), *Lawyering Europe*; Vauchez, *Brokering Europe*. See also Tommaso Pavone, 'From Marx to Market: Lawyers, European Law, and the Contentious Transformation of the Port of Genoa' (2018) 53 *Law and Society Review*, 851–888.

Part I, comprising four chapters, provides an account of the general themes discussed in the book. Parts II and III respectively consist of four and five chapters deepening the discussion started in Part I.

All of the chapters in this collection revolve around four key questions: who are legal experts? How do legal experts frame and shape the issues they deal with? How do they interact with competing legal experts in situations of hybridisation of legal expertise? How do legal experts differ, if at all, from other persons providing professional policy expertise?

Part I, 'Theorising Legal Expertise', introduces and contextualises the main themes of the collection with respect to past and present theoretical debates in research on legal expertise. The opening piece by Martti Koskenniemi discusses how legal expertise is conceptualised in the area of international law and what EU law can and should learn from it. He argues that legal expertise is a performative expertise and that being a lawyer, especially a competent one, is a performance. In the following chapter, Matthew Windsor emphasises the performative nature of expertise as well, asking whether framing might serve as a pertinent concept to enrich our understanding of the politics of legal expertise. Attentiveness to framing effects would help expert advisers to become more reflexive about the metes and bounds of their approach. In the next chapter, Pierre France and Antoine Vauchez offer a new perspective from which to approach expertise by focusing on the blurring of the public-private divide that has accompanied the neoliberal turn in French policies over the past three decades. They narrate the development of the field of 'public affairs' in which law, law firms, and lawyers have come to play a central brokering role between the EU, states, and market actors. Finally, Hans-W. Micklitz discusses the link between legal expertise and the legal profession, and the future of legal expertise in the EU administrative state, enquiring whether there is a risk of deprofessionalisation of the legal profession and what would that entail.

The remaining chapters are divided into two parts, reflecting the idea that legal expertise can feed into the policy process either from outside or from within the process. Part II, 'In-House Legal Expertise', opens with Päivi Leino-Sandberg's discussion on legal experts in the European Parliament (EP). She paints a picture of the dynamics whereby legal expertise provided by the EPs' legal advisors regularly clashes with the political preferences of the MEPs. Benjamin Yong describes the production and use of legal expertise in the British parliament, arguing that the use of expertise by parliamentarians resembles what Eliot Friedson described as expert referral systems. Illustrated against the background of the United Kingdom's tumultuous politics following the Brexit vote, his contribution opens up important avenues of further inquiry on the transformation of legal expertise in contemporary decision-making environments moving from crisis to crisis. The last chapters of Part II take a global approach, reflecting the EU's increasing external role. First, building on the 'Brussels Effect' dynamic, Anu Bradford discusses the myriad ways in which the Commission leverages its legal, economic, and technical expertise outside the EU and how actors outside the EU strategically use legal and regulatory experts within Europe. Finally, Chris Kimura and Fernanda Nicola analyse trade experts in free trade negotiations. They argue that the politicisation of legal expertise in FTAs offers an external response geared towards the media and civil society.

Part III, 'External Legal Expertise', the focus moves to legal experts who try to influence the policy process from outside. First, Lola Avril offers a fascinating historical account of how lawyers have expanded the traditional limits of their legal expertise and become powerful intermediaries between companies and European institutions, transnational Euro-lawyers. Emilia Korkea-aho looks at the role of legal advisors in environmental and human rights NGOs and ponders the increasing significance of legal expertise in lobbying. She shows how, as a legal expert, the NGO lawyer has to defuse the tension that exists in cause lawyering between political commitment and technical professionalism, between being a rock star and a guitar technician. Maria Lee and Carolyn Abbot continue the discussion on NGO legal experts, arguing that, notwithstanding some clear weaknesses in the general place of legal expertise in the UK environmental groups, environmental NGOs impressively brought their legal expertise to bear in advocacy around Brexit. Despite this outcome, they express the worry that the contributions of NGO legal experts may be overlooked by the NGO community, with the result that legal experts are never called upon and their absence never noted.

Academics consider matters of principle and policy as well, exercising significant influence on a government's choices. Academics may also engage with the policy-making processes in less obvious ways, including through research, teaching, and participation in government-funded projects. Jan Klabbers discusses these and shows that legal academics can influence the political process in a multitude of ways, which usually go unnoticed. They exercise authority in academia by epistemic means: though their writings and the classroom. A great deal of current debates in relation to policy-making takes place on social media. In these debates, legal expertise (or the lack of it) matters, as, for example, the Brexit discussion clearly demonstrates. In the final chapter, using *Verfassungsblog* as an example, Maximilian Steinbeis and the editors provide an account of how legal expertise can be created and fed into the policy-making process through blogs and social media, and how this new form of legal expertise compares with legal expertise residing in the policy-making process.

The twofold account of in-house and external legal experts brings forward new questions not previously articulated but now considered, for the first time, in the contributions of this collection. What is the role and responsibility of academics as legal experts? How does their legal expertise shape policy-making processes? How do social media change or impact building and facilitating legal expertise?[36] Does the legal advisor in the EP or the Commission have a client? Does the NGO legal advisor have one? Are the issues faced by 'in-house' legal advisors similar to those in in-house corporate counselling? In Weberian thinking, one may argue that civil servants 'adopt an attitude of neutrality by which they may serve as an instrument of their political master (government) and thereby loyally work to implement political goals'.[37] But how loyal are MEPs or national parliamentarians to legal experts, or do they shop around for legal expertise, and how does this affect the role of a legal expert? The analysis of legal experts through this twofold account shows how legal experts operate on a continuum rather than in fixed positions. Legal advisors working in the EU institutions or in national parliaments can be placed at one end, as they are on the inside of the policy process, whereas those legal experts who use social media, such as *Verfassungsblog*, to gain attention are on the outside. Yet, as the chapters demonstrate, legal experts continuously reposition themselves in relation to the policy-making process.

In our Afterword, we map the relationship between legal expertise and policy-making and review the emerging themes of the book.

***

When selecting the cover of this book we browsed through the artwork used by the publisher for the series. We did numerous searches on 'law', 'lawyer', 'expert', 'negotiation', 'European Union', 'international organisation' and other relevant key words. What emerged on our screens were a number of dark depictions of lawyers, who were all white men in suits or gowns. This is not the vision of legal experts that we wish to convey. For the cover of this volume we have selected a painting called *Lippujuhla* by a Finnish female artist of our own generation, Katja Tukiainen. To us, it symbolises the reason

36 Antoine Duval, 'Publish (Tweets and Blogs) or Perish? Legal Academia in Times of Social Media' (2018) 23 *Tilburg Law Review*, 91–108. Outside the context of legal expertise, for an analysis of public contestation and expansion of expertise on Twitter in the context of COVID-19, see Esa Väliverronen, Salla-Maria Laaksonen, Mikko Jauho, and Piia Jallinoja, 'Liberalists and Data-Solutionists: Redefining Expertise in Twitter Debates on Coronavirus in Finland' (2020) 19 *Journal of Science Communication*, 1–21.

37 See Peter Triantafillou, 'The Politics of Neutrality and the Changing Role of Expertise in Public Administration' (2015) 37 *Administrative Theory and Praxis*, 174–187, p. 176.

why we wanted to write and edit this book. Legal experts are more numerous and more diverse than typically thought, and they work in transnational pockets of power reaching beyond those of any nation-state. But there is something else we wish to convey through the painting. Its bright colours suggest that our interest in legal experts and their impact on policy-making is emphatically sincere, not sinister. Studies of experts often portray them as unaccountable power-wielders, tucked away at the end of long corridors in key-card-operated buildings. We hope that we manage to make legal experts and their impact on policy-making more visible by giving them a voice too.

# PART I

# THEORISING LEGAL EXPERTISE

# 2

# Performing Legal Expertise: Reflections on the Construction of Transnational Authority

Martti Koskenniemi

## 2.1 WHAT IS LEGAL EXPERTISE?

What is it that law schools teach? Rules or practices? Doctrines, systems, ways of thinking 'like a lawyer'? Probably all such things to a varying extent, with varying success. Legal theorists have had much to say about what 'law' is, and what, we may assume, it is to be a legal expert. But jurisprudence has never set the expectations about what lawyering is or should be nearly as efficiently as popular novels or TV series. Major law schools may have learned to advertise themselves as conveyors of 'leadership' and 'innovation', 'excellence in ideas' and 'intellectual exchange'. 'Vision' and 'values' stand high on the list of things promised for prospective students in today's managerial law school. Whatever such language may mean to deans, rectors, funding institutions, education authorities, it fails to pay any regard to the fact that to appear as a competent 'lawyer', a judge, legal adviser or an academic is the outcome of a *performance*. A graduate without some idea of how to act or write as a competent lawyer would have no chance on the labour market. And most do eventually learn to perform as lawyers, a little hesitantly at first, but then, through practice, with increasing confidence – until the day when the intimate sense that one is 'performing' is no longer felt at all. The person and performance have become one, a solid and reliable part of an institutional structure, for better or for worse.

In the following pages I will discuss the way legal expertise is performed in the sphere of transnational law – the multiplicity of legal institutions and rules systems that reach beyond the single state. Of these, the European Union is perhaps the most intense example. My sense is that while this type of expertise in many ways resembles domestic lawyering, there are also differences that have to do with the closeness of transnational law to global regimes of scientific knowledge. Both share the view that a competent legal performance is ideologically neutral. A legal performance that turns out to be ideological advocacy would fail. 'Learning to think like a lawyer means learning to leave one's personal and political views behind, to think analytically about the fit between facts and rules'.[1] Apparently, at least in US law schools, politically committed students tend to give up their activism in the course of learning to 'think like lawyers'.[2] I think the matter is more complicated in the world of transnational law, where legal expertise is closely connected with knowledge regimes that also embody ideological projects. 'Learning to think like a lawyer' would also involve thinking of oneself as an activist for a cause.[3]

I would like to examine this by giving a new twist to the old idea of law as a science, a *Rechtswissenschaft*. Today's pragmatic, interpretative jurisprudence has little sympathy for that idea. I find it useful, however, to think about the nature of the legal expertise that participates in transnational governance. We are familiar with the movement to think of law as science within the nineteenth-century historical school of jurists, who depicted the legal expert, the academic jurist, as someone who, after years of meticulous study, gives voice to the spirit of 'the people'.[4] To treat law as a science – instead of an interpretative craft about 'justice' – is to suggest that legal expertise is work with (true) knowledge about some aspect of the world. I think this is what many experts in transnational law think to contrast what they do against the volatile and equivocal world of ideology. By appearing as a set of conclusions borne out of scientific knowledge, legal expertise partakes of what Sheila Jasanoff has called 'politics of demonstration', intended to create an impression of ideological neutrality that will cause its audience to consider it a legal necessity.[5]

In this essay, I will present transnational legal expertise as the translation of scientific knowledge into institutional policy or a decision. But instead of seeing that knowledge itself as a firm datum about the world, I will highlight the multiplicity of regimes of knowledge and the active role of law in

1 Stuart A. Scheingold and Austin Sarat, *Something to Believe In: Politics, Professionalism, and Cause Lawyering* (Stanford: Stanford University Press, 2004), p. 51.
2 Ibid., pp. 54–60.
3 On cause lawyering and activism, see Korkea-aho in this volume.
4 Friedrich Carl von Savigny, *Vom Beruf unserer Zeit für Gesetzgebung und Rechtswissenschaft* (Heidelberg: Mohr, 1840; republished Hildesheim: Olms, 2013).
5 Sheila Jasanoff, *Science and Public Reason* (London: Routledge, 2012), pp. 1–4. I have elaborated on this in 'Is Legal Science Possible?' in Gralf-Peter Calliess and Lorenz Kähler (eds.), *Theorien im Recht/Theorien über das Recht* (ARSP Beiheft 155, Stuttgart: Steiner, 2018), pp. 31–43. On the use of shifting ideas about science in international law, see Anne Orford, 'Scientific Reason and International Law' (2014) 25 *European Journal of International Law*, 369–85.

articulating and giving effect to the ideological projects that they embody.[6] The fact that lawyers may disagree with each other does not call their competence into question, because they are all equally distanced from the contrasting or conflicting regimes of knowledge at the service of which they perform.

In communicating what it suggests as true knowledge about the world, law is an intensely linguistic affair.[7] As they learn a new lexicon and a set of professional idioms, first-year students often possess a vivid sense of law's linguistic aspect. Trying these out on their non-lawyer friends and relatives at home gives them an ambivalently pleasurable sensation about what it is to grow up and be taken as an expert. In due course, they will also learn a grammar, a professional way of joining legal words into complex sentences that both create and represent expertise in their chosen specialism (contract law, administrative law, European law, international law, and so on). Gradually, the sense of wonder about the power of those words vanishes as students enter the *habitus* of the legal expert, ready to receive the benefits that come from learning to 'think like a lawyer'.

Examining the way legal expertise is performed means exploring the linguistic techniques through which scientific evidence is translated into forms of legality that – precisely because it reflects true knowledge – may claim to be independent of the political ideologies targeting the transnational world. I will pay especial regard to three linguistic trajectories: conceptualism; policy orientation; and balancing. Today's transnational law is a pragmatic mixture of different idioms, representing what sociologically oriented lawyers call 'pluralism', where several normative projects coincide and different types of legal expert performance claim authority.[8] If lawyers disagree, but their competence remains unquestioned, that is because the transnational world embraces conflicting ideological projects, all of which can be supported by different variants of scientific knowledge.[9]

6 David Kennedy has written on the power of experts in terms of such articulation in *A World of Struggle: How Power, Law and Expertise Shape Global Political Economy* (Princeton: Princeton University Press, 2017), pp. 135–67.

7 A recent work with a broadly similar perspective is Justin Desautels-Stein, *The Jurisprudence of Style: A Structuralist History of American Pragmatism and Liberal Legal Thought* (Cambridge: Cambridge University Press, 2018).

8 I still find systems theory the most impressive perspective on the operation of a pluralist (transnational) system. For a summary of Teubner's works on that theme, see Gunther Teubner, *Constitutional Fragments: Societal Constitutionalism and Globalization* (Oxford: Oxford University Press, 2012).

9 One way of acknowledging this is to follow Moyn and conclude that there is presently no unifying or leading theory to make sense of today's legal world, 'no successful *Zeitgeist* now, only remainders of contest and failure'. See Samuel Moyn, 'Legal Theory among the Ruins' in

I will start by showing how law and specific types of legality may be created by the making and unmaking of conceptual distinctions that open the way to opposing avenues of legal argument. I will then show how, in the field of the legalities thus created, lawyers have learned to stabilise contrasting views by making further conceptual distinctions between rules and exceptions, principles and counter-principles. Because such distinctions remain unstable at a purely conceptual level, lawyers have learned to manage them by referring to 'policies' supposedly underlying them. But as the 'policies' themselves have turned out to be in conflict, legal expertise has developed into a practice of balancing and seeking reasonable accommodations between them. In the end, if a sense of legal necessity is created, it emerges and is sustained through the cohesion of the legal profession itself, the collegial solidarity lawyers working in the transnational space feel towards each other. This lessens their ontological insecurity, but alienates lay audiences who have drawn from lawyers' constant disagreement the conclusion that legal expertise is just a species of elite opinion.

## 2.2 MAKE A DISTINCTION! (OR DENY IT)

Law starts with the performance of a distinction. An early example would be the justification of private property by the leading Catholic intellectuals of the sixteenth century, the Spanish Dominican theologians. The arrival of the silver ships from the Indies boosted the expansion of commerce across Europe, consolidating claims of private ownership and wealth accumulation that clashed with traditional religious views. How could those practices be justified? According to the theologians, property was an expression of human dominion over the world. The problem was that, as stated in Genesis, God granted such dominion to humans under natural law and in common: *Deus fecit omnia communia omnibus*.[10] Natural law was eternal and absolutely binding. Was private property sinful, then? Well, no, the theologians argued. Although natural law remained unchanged, it no longer always took the form of a command (*praeceptio*), but instead often expressed itself in the form of permission (*concessio*). From the fact that natural law provided for common ownership it did not follow that it prohibited the contrary.[11] Justifying property

Justin Desautels-Stein and Christopher Tomlins (eds.), *Searching for Contemporary Legal Thought* (Cambridge: Cambridge University Press, 2017), p. 101.

10 Francisco de Vitoria, *Comentarios a la Secunda secundae de Santo Tomás*, ed. Vicente Beltrán de Heredia (Salamanca, 1934/1952), Q. 62 A 1 n 18 (74).

11 Ibid., Q. 62 A 1 n. 20 (77): 'Concedimus ergo quod nullius fuit praeceptum quod omnia essent communia, sed solum fuit concession.' On the early canon law origins of this argument, see

by drawing a distinction between two kinds of natural precept – command and permission – enabled the Church to view the events in the surrounding world with realism. Civil lawyers in the late Middle Ages had made a similar distinction. In the fourteenth century Bartolus of Sassoferrato distinguished between *de iure* and *de facto* to explain that the emperor's status as *Dominus mundi* was entirely compatible with the territorial overlordship ('sovereignty') of the North Italian city states. Both had their legal force.[12] His student Baldus of Ubaldi elaborated on this position by quite ingeniously adding that the religiously compelling dictum that the emperor ruled universally did not mean that he ruled every particular as well.[13]

I give these early examples of scholastic distinction making to illustrate not only its historical centrality as a type of performing law but also its political force in justifying equally important, though contradictory, aspects of the world. Property is both shared and private; the world is both united and split into separate sovereigns. Distinctions help to manage the complexity of experience: humankind is one but its distribution in rival groups is all right. Further distinctions made by the law of nations between Christians and pagans, the civilised and the uncivilised, the developed and the developing world continue to help us to believe in our ideals and operate in a reality in contradiction with them.

The idea that the world is united but that nations are entitled to go their separate ways receives powerful expression in the relationship between the binding force of the United Nations Charter and the principles of sovereign equality and domestic jurisdiction (Articles 2(1) and 2(7)). States are simultaneously bound and free. As a result, when someone today suggests that we need to 'take back control' and reaffirm sovereignty in face of the faceless bureaucracy of Brussels, others will retort that joining the European Union is precisely an act of sovereign power without which we could not attain the benefits that allow us to be masters of our lives.[14] Distinguishing between the

Brian Tierney, 'Permissive Natural Law and Property: Gratian to Kant' (2001) 62 *Journal of the History of Ideas*, 384–88.

12 Cecil N. Sidney Woolf, *Bartolus of Sassoferrato: His Position in the History of Medieval Political Thought* (Cambridge: Cambridge University Press, 1913), pp. 23–5.

13 In detail, see Joseph Canning, *The Political Thought of Baldus de Ubaldis* (Cambridge: Cambridge University Press, 1987), pp. 104–58.

14 It was this antinomy that stood at the heart of the *Austro-German Customs Union* case in 1933. While the Allied Powers argued that by joining the union Austria was violating the independence it had promised to uphold in the Treaty of Saint-Germain of 1922, the Austrian side retorted that if it were unable to do this, it could not really be held to be independent. See PCIJ Rep. Series A/B No. 41 and the parties' arguments at Series C No. 53, pp. 119–52 (France) and pp. 94–101 (Austria).

two sides of international institutions like the European Union – one for constraint, the other for freedom – is a key aspect of legal competence that allows jurists to argue both ways. By distinguishing between membership as being bound and as being sovereign allows lawyers to explain constraint as a result of sovereign choice and sovereignty as a status granted by membership.

Distinction making has in recent years greatly assisted the rise of new legal regimes and institutions with expanding claims of autonomy and jurisdiction. Human rights law arose in the 1970s and 1980s from the convergence between the work of human and civil rights activists and the neoliberal turn in Western politics.[15] Eventually, the European Court of Human Rights would mark a clear separation from the past. There was 'a fundamental difference in the role and purpose of the separate tribunals [which] provides a compelling basis for distinguishing Convention practice from that of the International Court'.[16] Under an apparently technical point, the distinction affirmed the validity and power of a large ideological project that the Court had already discussed a few years earlier – namely, that, 'unlike international treaties of the classic kind, the [European] Convention comprises more than merely reciprocal engagements between Contracting States. It creates, over and above a network of mutual, bilateral relationships, objective obligations.'[17]

This was perhaps inspired by the earlier moment when a group of European lawyers created their own professional world as in contradistinction to public international law. The judges in *Costa* v. *ENEL* famously held that the treaty on the European Economic Community had been concluded in 'contrast with ordinary Treaties [so that] the EEC Treaty [had] created its own legal system which, on the entry into force of the Treaty, became an integral part of the legal systems of the Member States'.[18] The notions of direct effect and superiority were nowhere to be found in the Treaties themselves but emerged from bold distinctions performed by a group of lawyers with an integrationist

15 On the burgeoning literature on the history of human rights, see Pamela Slotte and Miia Halme-Tuomisaari, *Revisiting the Origins of Human Rights* (Cambridge: Cambridge University Press, 2015). See also Jessica Whyte, *The Morals of the Market. Human Rights and the Rise of Neoliberalism* (London: Verso, 2019).

16 *Loizidou* v. *Turkey* (Preliminary Objections), Judgment of 23 March 1995, (1995) Series A No. 310, pp. 26–7, paras. 70–2 and p. 29, paras. 84–5.

17 *Ireland* v. *United Kingdom*, Judgment of 18 January 1978, (1978) Series A No. 25, p. 90, para. 239. Likewise, Inter-American Court of Human Rights, *Effect of Reservations on the Entry into force of the Inter-American Convention on Human Rights (Arts. 74 and 75)*, Advisory Opinion OC-2/82. 24 September 1982, Series A No. 2, pp. 14–16, paras. 29–33; Inter-American Court of Human Rights, *Restrictions to the Death Penalty*, Advisory Opinion OC-3/83, 8 September 1983, Series A No. 3, pp. 76–7, para. 50.

18 Case 6/64, *Costa* v. *ENEL*, Judgment of 15 July 1964, [1964] ECR 585, p. 593.

bias and an ordoliberal agenda.[19] As they explained, without its special nature, the obligations 'would not be unconditional, but merely contingent if they could be called into question by subsequent legislative acts'.[20] Although this could be said about all public international law, the distinction stuck owing to the skilful use of legal diplomacy at the right moment.[21] In a famous text from 1981, Eric Stein from Michigan – himself an active legal entrepreneur – cited the case law of the European Court of Justice as an object lesson on how to create a legal system by repeated performances of a distinct type of legal knowledge.[22]

The emergence in recent decades of legal regimes on international environmental law, international trade law, international criminal law and so on has been not only strengthened but achieved through the performance of parallel distinctions. For each field, the lawyers specialising in it have devised rules and set up institutions to reflect its special character. For example, the well-known story of the making of a distinction between a state's responsibility under international criminal law and under public international law for acts of paramilitaries in another country (the contrast between *Nicaragua* and *Tadić*) highlights the efforts made by activists in the fight against impunity (especially Antonio Cassese) to strengthen the field's stance against dubious military operations supported by states outside their boundaries.[23] Legal practice in

[19] For the collective biographies of the first European judges and advocates general, see Antonin Cohen and Mikael Rask Madsen, 'Cold War Law: Legal Entrepreneurs and the Emergence of a European Legal Field (1945–1965)' in David Nelken and Volkmar Gessner (eds.), *European Ways of Law: Towards a European Sociology of Law* (Oxford: Hart, 2007), pp. 190–7; see also pp. 187–8 (on Teitgen and Reuter). On Reuter, see also Martti Koskenniemi, *The Gentle Civilizer of Nations: The Rise and Fall of International Law 1870–1960* (Cambridge: Cambridge University Press, 2002), pp. 345–7.

[20] *Costa* v. *ENEL*, p. 594. Both *Van Gend en Loos* and *Costa* v. *ENEL* had been staged by activist jurists using the technique of preliminary rulings in cases of low-level political significance. Their followers could then reference the constitutional nature of those cases with the effect that the principles they inaugurated could no longer be contested as the correct view about EU law. See Antoine Vauchez, *Brokering Europe: Euro-Lawyers and the Making of a Transnational Polity* (Cambridge: Cambridge University Press, 2015), pp. 116–46.

[21] I borrow the term 'legal diplomacy' from Madsen's discussion of the strategies used by the judges of the European Court of Human Rights in its early cases to 'placate[] the member state and underline[] that it was receptive to the complexities of interior politics'. See Mikael Rask Madsen, 'International Human Rights and the Transformation of European Society: From "Free Europe" to the Europe of Human Rights' in Mikael Rask Madsen and Chris Thornhill (eds.), *Law and the Formation of Modern Europe* (Cambridge: Cambridge University Press, 2014), p. 258.

[22] Eric Stein, 'Lawyers, Judges, and the Making of a Transnational Constitution' (1981) 75 *American Journal of International Law*, 1–27.

[23] International Criminal Tribunal for the former Yugoslavia, *Prosecutor* v. *Duško Tadić*, Judgment of 15 July 1999, Case No. IT-94-1-A, A.Ch., (1999) 38 ILM 1518, pp. 1540–6, paras. 115, 116–45.

the different fields is characterised by techniques to distinguish them from old international law, perceived as too weak and ineffective to advance the objectives activist lawyers wish to advance by distinguishing their field as something 'special'.[24]

The above examples of distinction making have to do with empowering someone or something (a property owner, a sovereign, an institution, a legal regime) against a larger, earlier or general item. They are performances by legal entrepreneurs designed to support some new knowledge or authority by persuading an audience – perhaps a court or committee, or the readership of a law journal – of the great value of that new legal sphere brought into existence by the distinction. For those who disagree, a performance in the opposite direction is usually available. The claim by the European Court of Human Rights that reservations to human rights treaties should be assessed differently from reservations under the Vienna Convention on the Law of Treaties was immediately opposed by traditionalists as an unjustified departure from old law's consensual principles.[25] As soon as activist lawyers argued that something like an international environmental law had come into existence, traditionalists would retort that the new instruments were simply part of 'old' international law applied in a new subject area.

Rhetorical performances in support of a new law need not always take place by distinguishing, especially where the law may prove too weak or controversial to survive separately. When the first advisors in international law were appointed to foreign ministries and the first professorships in the field created in law faculties towards the end of the nineteenth century and in the early years of the twentieth century, the argument was often made that the field was sufficiently analogous to domestic law to warrant those types of institutional recognition.[26] Were not multilateral treaties comparable to domestic legislation; arbitration, and possibly the Permanent Court of International Justice, assimilable to domestic courts; and

[24] These techniques are discussed at great length in ILC, 'Fragmentation of International Law: Difficulties Arising from the Diversification and Expansion of International Law Report of the Study Group of the International Law Commission, Finalized by Martti Koskenniemi, UN Doc. A/CN.4/L.682 (2006).

[25] See the long discussion on the so-called severability doctrine, the proposition that a human rights treaty body might 'sever' a reservation considered incompatible with the object and purpose of the treaty, in apparent contradiction with general treaty law, in ILC, 'Text of the Guide to Practice on Reservations to Treaties, adopted by the Commission at its sixty-third session', *Yearbook of the International Law Commission 2011*, vol. II/3, pp. 232–7.

[26] 'International legislators are *all* legislators who deal with questions of the relations of men as members of different states; International Courts are *all* courts which take to cognizance the like problems; and International Sanctions are *all* sanctions which enforce the decisions of these courts.' T. A. Walker, *The Science of International Law* (London: Clay, 1893), p. 50.

international institutions functionally equivalent to domestic administration? The argument about the League of Nations Covenant being higher law, analogous to a domestic constitution, would eventually be made in relation to the UN Charter and then gradually in relation to the leading texts in the ever-expanding corpus of international instruments. The argument about international law's 'constitutionalisation', prevalent in juristic debates on global governance in the past decade, relies wholly on a domestic analogy.[27]

All such performances have been both endorsed and challenged. Sometimes, the claim is made that the new treaty or institution is actually regulated by the old law – after all, for it to have validity, it had to be created by the old procedures! Although the WTO treaties of 1995 were negotiated by trade experts,[28] insistent on not creating an institution of the traditional legal type, as soon as the Appellate Body (significantly not labelled a 'court' or a 'tribunal') started functioning, it made a note that those treaties are 'not to be read in clinical isolation from public international law'.[29] The stakes were obvious: would the preferences of the 'old' law still have validity, or must they now be replaced by new ones? The prevailing tendency was towards compromise. Many felt that the ILC debate on the 'fragmentation of international law' (2002–6) was titled too negatively. At issue was not the breaking apart of a legal system but its healthy 'expansion and diversification'.[30] It was quite possible, they noted, to affirm the binding quality of both general law and those special branches – just as it had been possible for late medieval civil lawyers to affirm the universal power of the emperor and the autonomy of individual republics. There are innumerable instances of judicial dialogue and accommodation across institutional boundaries.[31] Academic

27 Hersch Lauterpacht, 'The Covenant as Higher Law' (1954) 17 *British Yearbook of International Law*, 54–65. On the present debates, see, e.g., Jan Klabbers, Anne Peters and Geir Ulfstein, *The Constitutionalization of International Law* (Oxford: Oxford University Press, 2009); Christine E. J. Schwöbel, *Global Constitutionalism in International Legal Perspective* (Leiden: Nijhoff, 2011).

28 See Kimura and Nicola in this volume.

29 *United States – Standards of Reformulated and Conventional Gasoline*, AB-1996-1, Report of the Appellate Body, WT/DS2/AB/R, 29 April 1966, p. 17. For a spirited defence of the view that the WTO treaties were not intended to be binding like regular rules of international law, see Judith W. Bello, 'The WTO Dispute Settlement Understanding: Less Is More', (1996) 90 *American Journal of International Law*, 416–17.

30 For a recent, detailed study, see Tullio Treves, 'The Expansion of International Law. General Course on Public International Law', *Collected Courses of the Hague Academy on International Law*, vol. 398 (2019), especially pp. 339–73.

31 The basic argument was in Anne-Marie Slaughter, *The New World Order* (Princeton: Princeton University Press, 2004). With reference to co-operation and accommodation between judges in the European institutions, see Nico Krisch, *Beyond Constitutionalism: The Pluralist Structure of Postnational Law* (Oxford: Oxford University Press, 2010), pp. 109–43.

lawyers transferred the language of legal pluralism from the domestic to the international context, and practitioners began to speak of a 'principle of systemic integration' supplanting the notion of harmony of interests that had received a bad reputation in the inter-war period with a more scientific-sounding rhetoric.[32] Over and over again, lawyers have assured the emperor and the prince that the law is able to give both what they wish. Whether or not they were persuaded, lawyers have usually received their fees.

## 2.3 BETWEEN RULES AND EXCEPTIONS, AND FROM POLICIES TO BALANCING

Drawing distinctions and making analogies are routine legal performances that create space for something new to become 'law', either in opposition to or as part of an older legality. Once that legality has been created, it will then offer space for further performances with the materials it contains. These performances consist of certain basic linguistic and intellectual manoeuvres with which competent lawyers seek to inspire in their audience that feeling of legal necessity they are expected to achieve. I follow Duncan Kennedy and identify three basic modes of argument that have been developed in Western law between the demise of naturalism in the late nineteenth century and the present: conceptualism (legal formalism); policy-oriented jurisprudence; and balancing (pragmatism).[33] Historically, conceptual jurisprudence arose with the consolidation of sovereign statehood and the market in the liberal West through the positing of 'will' (of the people, of the contract partner) as the heart of jurisprudence. Socially oriented law focused on solidarity and interdependence and took a functional view of law as social engineering. This leaves contemporary law as a melange of tropes drawn from conceptual deduction-induction and policy in an effort to seek a reasonable'(proportionate) balance between conflicting considerations. The key point about contemporary law lies in its lack of distinctiveness and its pragmatic orientation within specialist (functional) legal regimes –something often labelled its pluralism'.[34] I will now go on to illustrate

[32] See Campbell McLachlan, 'The Principle of Systemic Integration and Article 31(3)(c) of the Vienna Convention' (2005) 54 *International and Comparative Law Quarterly*, 279–319; ILC, 'Fragmentation of International Law', pp. 206–13.

[33] Duncan Kennedy, 'Three Globalizations of Law and Legal Thought: 1850–2000' in David M. Trubek and Alvaro Santos, *The New Law and Development: A Critical Appraisal* (Cambridge: Cambridge University Press, 2006), pp. 19–73.

[34] Kennedy's threefold distinction and especially his characterisation of 'contemporary law' have been usefully discussed in the many essays in Desautels-Stein and Tomlins (eds.), *Searching for Contemporary Legal Thought*.

the way i.e. what – moves from each of the three modes structure the grammar of competent performance in various fields of transnational law.

Conceptual jurisprudence operates with legal rules, which it understands as outcomes of conscious rule-making activity, to implement justice in a tangible way. But, owing to the complexity of the world, rules might themselves became sources of injustice (because they are either over- or under-inclusive). This is why they are supplemented by exceptions.[35] The fact that there is no firm indication (such as another rule, for example) of when a situation calls for the application of the rule and when the exception opens conceptual jurisprudence up to contrasting performances. An unexceptional prohibition of war in the UN Charter, for example, would only benefit the aggressor.[36] At least in self-defence, war must therefore be allowed. Because the exception threatens the rule itself, its use is subjected to a strict criterion – 'if an armed attack occurs' (Article 51 of the UN Charter). And yet, because that criterion is too limitative, its users have derived from the policy inspiring it – protecting the state – the right to take preventive action even against an imminent attack.[37] In three simple and very common legal performances, the rule has first been shown as insufficient and supplemented by an exception, and the operation of the rule-exception scheme has then been subordinated to a policy. But what does that policy (to protect the state) mean (after all, disputing states would each plead the need to protect themselves) and how should it fare in relation to alternative policies (of peaceful settlement or human rights, say)? In the 1990s and thereafter, liberal internationalists began to advocate reading the sovereignty that the Charter was to safeguard functionally in the sense of the 'responsibility to protect' the state's own population. Lawyers on all sides produced competent performances, some arguing from the supposedly original and 'limited' provisions of the Charter, others insisting on the need to read it in the light of present-day humanitarian sensibilities. In the end, the rapidly transformed political context prevented the emergence of the kind of executive authority that lay on the horizon

35 See Frederick Schauer, *Playing by the Rules; A Philosophical Examination of Rule-Based Decision-Making in Law and in Life* (Oxford: Clarendon, 1991), pp. 31–7, 47–52.

36 This was the conclusion that the drafters of the UN Charter drew from the collapse of the unexceptional nature of the prohibition on going to war in the League Covenant.

37 Here again, lawyers make what appears a crucial, though utterly open-ended, distinction between prevention (allowed under the Webster formula) and pre-emption, forbidden as illicit use of force. Here, as elsewhere, the choice between opposite positions is mitigated by (again open-ended) notions of imminence, necessity and proportionality. See, e.g., James Crawford, *Brownlie's Principles of Public International Law*, 8th ed. (Oxford: Oxford University Press, 2008), pp. 747–9, 750–2.

during the debate; each actor preserved their freedom to act in the way they saw best.[38]

The insufficiency of conceptual analysis was brought forth in the 1920s and 1930s by a group of French-trained jurists using the Durkheimian notion of social solidarity to define international law as a 'dynamic instrument' that was to reflect the laws of interdependence that tied together members of a community of nations.[39] But the introduction of policy analysis in twentieth century international jurisprudence owes perhaps more to the combined influence of legal realism and the rise of the international relations discipline in the United States.[40] In addition to the Yale school from the 1950s, policy-based legal thinking came also from specialists in political science, who began to situate international law within its political context and to develop a functional perspective on it.[41] In an influential intervention in 1964, Wolfgang Friedmann considered new developments in the law to be part of a general move from co-existence to co-operation. The thaw in Cold War relations and increased technological and economic interdependence, he argued, had expanded international law 'to the growing number of fields in which all parts of the family of nations co-operate for purposes of international welfare'.[42] Expansion called for specialisation in international constitutional law, international labour law, international criminal law, international commercial law, international economic development law, international corporation law, international anti-trust law and international tax law.[43] Regional developments in integration and human rights were also a part of this

[38] The best account is Anne Orford, *International Authority and the Responsibility to Protect* (Cambridge: Cambridge University Press, 2011).

[39] Well-known names in the French sociological school were Georges Scelle, Alejandro Alvarez and Nicolas Politis. Much has been written on each, but for a general treatment, see Koskenniemi, *Gentle Civilizer*, pp. 266–352. See, further, Hubert Thierry, 'The Thought of Georges Scelle' (1990) 1 *European Journal of International Law*, 193–209; Emmanuelle Jouannet, 'A Century of French International Law Scholarship' (2009) 61 *Maine Law Review*, 94–9.

[40] See Koskenniemi, *Gentle Civilizer*, pp. 413–509.

[41] For an early programmatic statement from the Yale school, see Myres McDougal, 'International law, Power and Policy: A Contemporary Conception', *Collected Courses of the Hague Academy on International Law*, vol. 82 (1953). See, further, Morton Kaplan and Nicholas Katzenbach, *The Political Foundations of International Law* (New York: Wiley, 1961); William D. Coplin, *The Functions of International law: An Introduction to the Role of International Law in the Contemporary World* (Chicago: Chicago University Press, 1966); Wesley Gould and Michael Barkun, *International Law and the Social Sciences* (Princeton: Princeton University Press, 1970).

[42] Wolfgang Friedmann, *The Changing Structure of International Law* (New York; Columbia University Press, 1964), p. 68.

[43] Ibid., pp. 152–87.

transformation of the law from mere co-ordination of inter-sovereign relations to the expression of a 'universal community of interests'.[44]

Rule-oriented conceptualism is a way to safeguard the interests of sovereigns; only rules that express their will bind them. Should there be no rules, then, according to the Lotus principle the sovereign will remain free. Policy-orientation and functionalism, as already outlined by Friedmann in the 1960s, looks beyond state will and interest to common objectives in particular regimes such as trade law, environmental law, human rights law, humanitarian law, international investment law, international criminal law and so on. They may not have reached the same degree of intensity as European integration, but they, too, are ideological projects designed not just to co-ordinate state actions or settle disputes but to advance free trade, to attain a clean environment, to protect the rights of human groups, to safeguard the legitimate expectations of foreign investors or to end the culture of impunity. Expert performances within those regimes are expected to show commitment to their purposes that would become visible in anti-formal readings of the relevant instruments designed to optimally advance the interests that they have been designed to protect.[45] But, of course, those regimes and those policies do not exist alone in hermetic isolation; they constantly confront countervailing policies and objectives, and this gives rise to the ruling mode of contemporary law – namely, balancing.

Two policies that expanded widely in the 1990s were those of free trade and the protection of foreign investment. The WTO treaties, on the one hand, and the beginning of the efforts, first at a multilateral and then bilateral level, of safeguarding the rights of foreign investors, on the other hand, were both inspired by neoliberal ideas about separating economic relations from the volatile world of domestic politics. The new trade and investment regimes were both initially inspired by the effort to limit the regulatory powers of states. This was something new. In the 1950s and 1960s, GATT was aimed at the stabilisation of international economic relations through deference to domestic social and labour policies. By contrast, in the 1980s and 1990s GATT panels and trade lawyers began to advance a widening understanding of when domestic regulation might count as prohibited discrimination. A limited view of the scope of the GATT Article XX exceptions was adopted.[46] Cases

44 Ibid., p. 68.

45 I have discussed the deformalised approach of legal expertise within specialist regimes in 'The Fate of International Law: Between Technique and Politics' (2007) 70 *Modern Law Review*, 9–19.

46 'The starting-point for any discussion of policy for the international economic system today', wrote John Jackson in 1997, a prominent trade law expert at the time, 'is the notion of "liberal trade", meaning the goal to minimize the amount of interference of governments in trade

regarding asbestos, tobacco and the protection of dolphins demonstrated that a regulation would be prohibited only if it had an effect on competition.[47] Advancing private trade became the principal objective of the system.

In the early 2000s, however, a backlash against the WTO within civil society and by a number of governments suggested that free trade did not have a monopoly as the objective of global governance. Despite the prevalence among trade lawyers of the view that WTO law was autonomous from the rest of international law, the case of US legislation to protect turtles gave occasion for the Appellate Body to consider the 'conservation of exhaustible natural resources' under GATT Article XX(g) and treaties on the protection of endangered species.[48] The subsequent debate on 'trade and . . . ' issues brought to light the ubiquitous conflicts between free trade and other priorities and turned the attention of legal experts to balancing. But how could a balance be sought without an overriding standpoint from the perspective of which the conflicting policies could be set against each other? The academic debates of recent years on regime interaction have been precisely about the need for specialist lawyers to co-ordinate the policies of parallel legal regimes, thus initiating endless debate about transparency and participation that ultimately cloaks the topic to be dealt with in the political science jargon of legitimacy.[49]

A similar development may be observed with respect to investment law, a field of specialisation whose popularity with students nowadays surpasses that of human rights or environmental law. Data on the expansion of bilateral investment treaties (BITs) and investor-state dispute settlement is well known.[50] The overriding policy goal of the field has been the expansion of foreign investment by ensuring that the host state does not violate the rights of the foreign investor. Conflict between the host state and the foreign investor would be 'depoliticised' by lifting them into the international realm.[51] As

flows that cross national borders.' John H. Jackson, *The World Trading System: Law and Policy of International Economic Relations* (Cambridge MA: MIT Press, 2000), p. 11.

47 Andrew Lang, *World Trade Law after Neoliberalism: Re-Imagining the Global Economic Order* (Oxford: Oxford University Press, 2011), pp. 221–72.

48 *United States – Import Prohibition of Certain Shrimp and Shrimp Products*, AB-1998-4, Report of the Appellate Body, WT/DS58/AB/R, adopted 6 November 1998.

49 For a detailed effort to respond to the problems of legitimacy occasioned by the turn to increasing expert negotiations as a response to regime conflict, see Margaret Young, *Trading Fish, Saving Fish: The Interaction between Regimes in International Law* (Cambridge: Cambridge University Press, 2011), pp. 271–87.

50 A recent UNCTAD reports lists 707 concluded and 347 pending cases of ICSID arbitration by July 2020.

51 For a review of this argument, see Martins Paparinskis, 'The Limits of Depoliticisation in Contemporary Investor-State Arbitration' in James Crawford and Sarah Nouwen (eds.), *Select Proceedings of the European Society of International Law*, vol. 3 (Oxford: Hart, 2010).

a result of a series of early interpretations by tribunals of the non-discrimination and fair and equitable treatment standards, the policy space of host states was significantly diminished.[52] A civil society backlash ensued: in a public consultation by the European Commission in 2015, more than 90 per cent of participants showed themselves willing to give up the system because of concerns over domestic labour, health and environmental powers. A debate has now begun on whether investor-state dispute settlement could endorse other objectives alongside investment protection. One suggestion is that it might work as a technique for boosting good governance in the host state – but there is little evidence of this in practice, and it smacks of civilising paternalism.[53] But it is unclear whether the ongoing negotiations within the UN Commission on International Trade Law on a multilateral investment treaty may, as has been suggested, be used to strengthen the duties of transnational companies.[54] In any case, it is unrealistic to think that a key problem of globalisation – that of moving significant domestic policy choices to international experts – could be usefully tackled by consultations among those experts, meeting at international locations and planning a new multilateral treaty with an international court. The balancing that such a body would conduct would be just another facet of the development of international legal expertise into a technique of global governance.[55]

Pluralism, policy conflict, regime interaction … The language of legal expertise in global governance is penetrated by technical and procedural

52 The tendency towards expansive views on investor rights against the state in investment cases is expounded and discussed in Gus van Harten, *Sovereign Choices and Sovereign Constraints. Judicial Restraint in Investor-State Arbitration* (Oxford: Oxford University Press, 2013).

53 For a critical empirical analysis of the suggestion that BITs might operate as good governance instruments, see Mavluda Sattorova, *The Impact of Investment Treaty Law on Host States: Enabling Good Governance?* (Oxford: Hart, 2018).

54 See, e.g., UNCTAD, 'Taking Stock of IIA Reform: Recent Developments', *IIA Issues Note*, Issue 3 (June 2019); see also, e.g., Anthea Roberts, 'UNCITRAL and ISDS Reforms: Agenda-Widening and Paradigm-Shifting', www.ejiltalk/org. For some scepticism about the effort to create balanced treaties on the basis of experiences during 2004–8, see also M. Sornarajah, *Resistance and Change in the International Law on Foreign Investment* (Cambridge: Cambridge University Press, 2015), pp. 400–4, 418–20. The CETA Treaty between EU and Canada now contains a reaffirmation by the parties of 'their right to regulate … to achieve legitimate policy objectives, such as the protection of public health, safety, the environment or public morals, social or consumer protection or the promotion and protection of cultural diversity'. A mere legislative change or a refusal to renew or maintain a subsidy that would have negative effect on the investor would not as such amount to a breach. Article 8.9, paras. 1–3. See https://data.consilium.europa.eu/doc/document/ST-10973-2016-INIT/en/pdf.

55 For an overview of this, see Martti Koskenniemi, 'International Law as "Global Governance"' in Desautels-Stein and Tomlins (eds.), *Searching for Contemporary Legal Thought*, pp. 199–218.

idioms. Most multilateral environmental treaties in the last three decades have been formulated in terms of flexible and open-ended standards that set up regimes of scientific co-operation, monitoring, negotiation and consultation, as well as financial arrangements. Law does not reside in rules but in larger policies, technical guidelines and phasing-out schedules. The story of the search for responsibility for transboundary environmental damage is typical. From the early effort to give teeth to state responsibility and liability as laid out in the Stockholm Declaration on the Human Environment in 1972, the item has been translated into economic adjustments between public and private actors under the scheme of 'allocation of loss in the case of transboundary harm arising out of hazardous activities'.[56] With the climate change treaty regime, specialist performance in environmental law collapsed into cost-benefit analyses, reviews of technical standards and the management of 'flexibility mechanisms' that seek to fit commitments with capabilities through individualised emission limitations.[57] While law turns into an endless negotiation process, the objective of that process can never be put to question. Fleur Johns has described how in the field of climate change law the periodic reports of the International Panel on Climate Change (IPCC) have attained the quality of a kind of supra-legality; climate change law is simply about the implementation of the autonomous normativity of its findings.[58]

It is normal to think of human rights as an antidote to the impersonal exercise of expert power. As I have elsewhere argued, human rights arose in the late 1960s and the 1970s precisely to oppose the deformalisation of modern law and administration – the flexibility of administering open-ended (Keynesian) policies. The call to take rights seriously aimed to empower individuals and excluded groups vis-à-vis public authorities. 'It is my life! Who are you to tell me how I should live!' The power of this (liberal) argument led to its expansion in the 1980s and 1990s as an increasing number of preferences were re-described as 'rights' of their holders. Freedom-rights collided with rights of security of others. Rights against the state were supplemented by social, economic and cultural rights that required states to adopt

[56] ILC, 'Draft Principles on Allocation of Loss in the Case of Transboundary Harm Arising Out of Hazardous Activities', *Yearbook of the International Law Commission 2006*, vol. II/2, pp. 59–90. See, further, Katja Creutz, *State Responsibility in the International Legal Order: A Critical Appraisal* (Cambridge: Cambridge University Press, 2020), pp. 163–7, 248–51.

[57] Ian H. Rowlands 'Atmosphere and Outer Space' in Daniel Bodansky, Jutta Brunnée and Ellen Hey (eds.), *The Oxford Handbook of International Environmental Law* (Oxford: Oxford University Press, 2007), pp. 330–2.

[58] Fleur Johns, *Non-Legality in International Law: Unruly Law* (Cambridge: Cambridge University Press, 2013), pp. 164, 170 and generally 158–84 (pointing out the significant fact that the IPCC is itself a creation of international law).

specific policies; rights of communities to their identity were supplemented by rights of members of those communities to liberate themselves from it; and so on. By the end of the century, rights had become ubiquitous in Western administrations and international institutions.[59]

Initially, this did not seem too worrying. Did it not just mean that human rights were becoming increasingly powerful? But as more and more groups began to dress their claims in terms of rights, increasing amounts of social conflict began to appear as rights conflicts. In the absence of a litmus test to differentiate between genuine and fake rights claims, the arguments began to lose their power. The practice of human rights changed from applying a right to balancing between conflicting rights. But where was a policy to be found that would allow two rights to be measured against each other? How does the right of freedom of speech (Article 10 ECHR) fare against the right of privacy (Article 8 ECHR) or the right of religious beliefs (Article 9 ECHR)? What about the claim that someone's social rights are impinged upon by another's use of their right of property? Even a cursory glance at the case law of the European Court of Human Rights shows that rights work depends on choices over the meaning and limits given to individual rights and their relationship to each other. What does it mean that a right may be limited to the extent such limitation is 'necessary in a democratic society'? Where are the limits to the 'margin of appreciation' that a state is said to have in deciding what rights policy to follow? In a well-known 2003 case, the Grand Chamber of the ECtHR associated the noise caused by increases of flights at Heathrow airport with recurrent problems regarding environmentally harmful but economically useful activities. 'In both contexts regard must be had to the fair balance that has to be struck between the competing interests of the individual and of the community as a whole.'[60] In order to find that balance, some criterion ought to be found that is independent of the rights to be balanced, so as to assess them and put them in a hierarchical order in a neutral way. But here, as in many other cases, the Court found no such criterion or policy. Instead, it once again stated that 'in both contexts the State enjoys a certain margin of appreciation in determining the steps to be taken to ensure compliance with the Convention'.[61] Although rights once arose as a limitation on policy, what they mean and how they should be assessed against each other can be determined only by . . . policy. And that policy is likely to be whatever the institution

59 I have further discussed this in 'The Effect of Rights on Political Culture' in Philip Alston (ed.), *The European Union and Human Rights* (Oxford: Oxford University Press, 1999), pp. 99–116.

60 *Hatton* v. *UK*, App. No. 36022/97, Judgment of 8 July 2003, para. 98.

61 Ibid.

enjoying such discretion considers to be the purpose of its activity. It did not take long for the European Court of Justice to articulate the freedoms under its constituent treaties as the fundamental rights of European citizens, but also to add that those rights were 'not absolute and their exercise may be subject to restrictions justified by objectives of general interest pursued by the Community'.[62]

Transnational legal expertise appears sometimes as policy-oriented work within a knowledge regime, sometimes as conceptual distinction making around rules and rights. In the conflicts between policies and between countervailing rules and rights, the legal expert picks up from the lexicon ambiguous metaphors about balancing and proportionality – such as the 'fair and equitable treatment' used by investment tribunals – to stabilise the relationship between clashing ideas. The more complex the argument, the more the conclusion will appear both necessary and random – necessary in view of the time and the exhaustion of pro and con arguments, random from the perspective of the infinite regress of the premises from which the arguments were derived or on the basis of which they could be evaluated. For a lawyer with a project, no existential crisis need emerge from what inevitably appears as a strategic accommodation. For the audience, the result's incomprehensibility can only appear as either a reflection of the immense complexity of the task of global governance or further evidence that expertise is nothing but glorified opinion.

## 2.4 PERFORMING LEGAL EXPERTISE: WORLD MAKING AND ADVOCACY

Law and lawyers are everywhere in transnational governance. They have jobs at international and European institutions, civil society organisations, international businesses, corporate law firms, think-tanks, universities and in state departments managing a country's international relations. Since the 1970s and 1980s, law has attained a position in the West and in the transnational world that it had never had before.[63] Legitimacy collapsed into legality as human rights, constitutionalism and the ubiquitous rhetoric of the rule of law penetrated the public realm. Notions of contract and increasingly complex ideas of

62 Case 44/79, *Hauer* [1979] ECR 3747.

63 A full treatment of this process ends Marcel Gauchet's massive four-volume history of democracy, *L'avènement de la démocratie*, vol. IV, *Le nouveau monde* (Paris: Gallimard, 2017), pp. 487–632. On the spread of legalisation into the transnational realm, see Judith Goldstein, Miles Kahler, Robert Keohane and Anne-Marie Slaughter, *Legalization in World Politics* (Cambridge MA: MIT Press, 2001).

property consolidated the expansion of the market. Law would become both an ideology and a privileged technique for organising complex social relations. Everywhere, it was accompanied by judicialisation, increasing use of courts as ultimate managers of social conflict. As Ian Hurd observes: 'In the global environment today, the mode of confrontation is legal. Legitimacy is the prize over which states compete, and it is won and lost through adherence to law – which is to say, skilful deployment of legal resources.'[64]

These resources are managed by legal experts. Many still take on classical roles as judges, legal advisers, activists and academics, but an increasing number work as corporate lawyers and lobbyists, managers and directors, officials in international and domestic institutions. They are trained as lawyers and engage in the most varied kinds of regulatory, policy-making and operative tasks.[65] In these capacities, they contribute to imagining a world consisting of the separate realms of politics and management; situating themselves firmly on its technical and non-political side; 'invoking science, or more accurately, public imagination of science, in support of the . . . planned action';[66] arguing that a given regulation was/was not in accordance with the principle of fair and equitable treatment, that an instance of limitation of freedom of speech was/was not proportionate, that a particular use of the river was/was not in accordance with the principle of equitable utilization and so on. The choices are both professionally justified and utterly open-ended. At the same time, they frame the worlds of economic development, political freedom and sustainable uses of the environment in particular idioms, through which problems are delineated, agency is distributed and policy is called upon when adjudicating specific claims.[67]

Transnational law has produced an image of the world as an object of global governance, full of themes and problems that can be dealt with only through *global* action and the organised conduct of adversity between *global* projects and systems of preference. Earlier in the twentieth century, similar ambition was displayed by public international lawyers. The results of public diplomacy – treaties and the constitutions of international institutions – were presented as aspects of a progressive project towards world peace and co-operation. Modern

64 Ian Hurd, *How to Do Things with International Law* (Princeton: Princeton University Press, 2017), p. 131.

65 For the many types of regulatory, administrative and operational interactions in which internationally trained lawyers are involved, see Jeffrey Dunoff, 'A New Approach to Regime Interaction' in Margaret Young (ed.), *Regime Interaction in International Law: Facing Fragmentation* (New York: Cambridge University Press, 2012), pp. 158–73.

66 Jasanoff, *Science and Public Reason*, p. 11.

67 See Windsor in this volume.

sovereignty bore the seeds of an increasingly international future. This assumption stabilised both colonial trusteeship and the political antagonism between east and west. But then lawyers began to imagine a different world. Wolfgang Friedmann's world in the mid-1960s was populated by all kinds of new actors and objectives, changing the way statehood and the international world were understood. Until that time, there had been no great distance between European and international law, with the same person teaching both in law schools, for example. But then European law began to present itself as more than just a common market.[68] The intensification of the human rights system, the conclusion of the WTO treaties in 1995, work to set up processes in climate change and international criminal law – all that emerged from a new kind of background thinking about the world. Students would eagerly take up European law, engage in human rights work, specialise in environmental or international business law. They would see themselves as experts in cyber law, post-conflict governance and minority protection. Courses on 'public international law' at US law schools began to be replaced by foreign relations law, national security law, human rights and international business transactions.[69]

Law translated new types of specialised knowledge – truly global in character – into legal rules and institutional policies.[70] That made it seem up to date and attractive as a career choice. There would be much legal work *inside* the knowledge regimes to make them more effective. Environmental and investment lawyers would intensely debate the means whereby a pristine environment or a well-working investment regime could be attained. They might disagree about the policy implications of the latest biological diversity report or the effects of bilateral investment treaties on the economies of developing states. But they would emphatically agree that those are the relevant questions. They would also agree that answers to global problems cannot consist of uniform action across the world. Instead, broad principles and standards were needed to accommodate local conditions and new information. And for this purpose, expert systems or a court – that is, more global governance – would be required.[71]

68 The standard account is Joseph Weiler, 'The Transformation of Europe' (1991) 100 *Yale Law Review* 2403–83.

69 See Anthea Roberts, *Is International Law International?* (Oxford: Oxford University Press, 2017), pp. 104–5. See also the report of her shock when she entered the US world of international law and found that much of what they called international law was unrecognisable as such to her; ibid., pp. xviii–xix.

70 On the expansive and ultimately global expansion of cognitive-normative systems, see also Niklas Luhmann, *Law as a Social System* (Oxford: Oxford University Press, 2004), pp. 468–9.

71 I have discussed international law's deformalisation and the turn to management in many places; see, e.g., 'The Fate of International Law: Between Technique and Politics' (2007) 70 *Modern Law Review*, 1–32; 'International Law as "Global Governance"'.

This then would occasion the clash of expert knowledges. Is this a human rights problem or a regular issue of treaty interpretation? Does this subject concern health or free trade, development or human rights? Is it a domestic, European or transnational problem? Each view would point to a distinct body as competent to deal with it. Suspected emissions of nuclear materials in the Irish Sea occasioned a conflict between the North Sea environment regime (OSPAR), the regime of the UN Convention on the Law of the Sea and the regime of European law.[72] Margaret Young's detailed study of the global fisheries problem illustrates how that problem engaged three rival systems of knowledge and action – those of trade (WTO), protection of endangered species (CITES) and food safety (FAO).[73] This was the point that sparked the debate about 'fragmentation' two decades ago. In a clash of legal expert regimes, who will have the last word?

No doubt, what Andrew Lang has called the 'principles of vision' of each such way of framing the world may ignore the larger context in which the problems have arisen and the collateral damage caused by the single-minded pursuit of one objective.[74] Nevertheless, recent studies conducted on 'fragmentation' have shown that in fact legal experts are quite capable of co-operating and even of accommodating each other's views. Horizontal coordination is frequent and authors highlight the synergies arising from co-operation and division of labour.[75] The relative openness of scientific knowledge has been stressed, as have principles of subsidiarity and complementarity. Many have suggested using the insights developed within private international law to deal with potential conflicts, and a massive effort has been made to apply principles of constitutionalism and administrative law in order to bring order to the world of transnational regimes.[76] None of this is really surprising. Co-ordination is part

72 The MOX Plant cases refer to three sets of litigation instituted under the OSPAR Convention, the UN Convention on the Law of the Sea and with reference to the European Union.

73 Young, *Trading Fish, Saving Fish.*

74 Andrew Lang, 'Legal Regimes and Professional Knowledges: The Internal Politics of Regime Definition' in Young (ed.), *Regime Interaction*, pp. 32–5. This is the point of Johns's critique of climate change law in *Non-Legality*, pp. 181–8. It is discussed in terms of the problems of bureaucratic rationality (with special reference to the actions of the International Criminal Court in Africa) in Touko Piiparinen, 'Law vs. Bureaucratic Coherence: The Case of the ICC and the Transparency of Instrumental Rationality' in Jan Klabbers and Touko Piiparinen (eds.), *Normative Pluralism and International Law: Exploring Global Governance* (Cambridge: Cambridge University Press, 2013), pp. 251–82.

75 See, e.g., Sebastian Oberthür, 'Regime-Interplay Management' in Kerstin Blome et al. (eds.), *Contested Regime Collisions: Norm-Fragmentation in World Society* (Cambridge: Cambridge University Press, 2016), pp. 90–9.

76 The literature is really too large to be properly referenced here. Suffice to note that global constitutionalism is really the European, and markedly German, approach to regime conflict,

of the transnational expert culture where participants from academic backgrounds appreciate each other's work and tend to be in agreement that 'it would be hazardous to leave the horizontal coordination of different legal orders to political negotiation' as this would mean that 'the imponderables of happenstance, opportunity and capture could possibly reign'.[77]

As a result, the gap between the world of global governance, the culture of transnational expertise, and the local world of political contestation deepens. Law frames, limits and empowers. By maintaining the idea that legal expertise is neutral, transnational law relegates the world-creating and distributive aspects of institutional power to men and women whose experiences and normative expectations are geared in a particular way and whose bargaining takes place far away from political constituencies. The recent backlash against expert power and international elites revels in the image of highly educated and well-paid, expert bureaucrats sitting at meetings in Brussels, Geneva, Beijing or New York, taking advantage of the synergies of their respective projects, with little sense of the contested character of their power and their suggested projects. It is trite to suggest that transnational governance ought to be controlled by domestic governments – 'taking back control'. The regimes of knowledge underlying legitimate rulership have penetrated statehood itself, such that modern government often resembles a local version of an international negotiation. The environment minister represents thoroughly global environmental knowledge; the finance ministry is a kind of local bureau of the World Bank, DG ECFIN or the Economic and Financial Committee; and the justice minister never ceases reminding everyone of the protections from the human rights treaty system. Corporate lawyers, activists in domestic NGOs and professors of civil and constitutional law argue in a wholly transnational idiom. Domestic politics are already colonised by systems of knowledge that have nothing domestic about them.

Expert governance is inescapable. Every politician worth their salt has an expert by their side to formulate the chosen policy in terms of its scientific (economic, technical) necessity. But perhaps something could be done about understanding expert knowledge itself. Expertise is a kind of politics, it is often

while the effort to extend principles of administrative law to the global level has been especially well developed under the auspices of New York University School of Law. The former perspective is well displayed in the volume by Klabbers, Peters and Ulfstein, *Constitutionalization*, and the latter in Benedict Kingsbury, Nico Krisch, Richard B. Stewart and Jonathan B. Wiener (eds.), 'The Emergence of Global Administrative Law' (2005) 68 *Law and Contemporary Problems*, Special Issue.

77 Lars Viellechner, 'Responsive Legal Pluralism: The Emergence of Transnational Conflicts Law' in Blome et al. (eds.), *Contested Regime Collisions*, p. 120.

said. What is meant by this is not only that expertise is power but that it is open-ended and contestable, like a country's politics – divided between those in the government and those in opposition, the Left and the Right, and normatively positioned against other types of expertise.[78] Although experts are aware of the inner hierarchies in their field and the distance between their way of seeing the world and that of other people, insufficient attention is given in training to such relationships. Nor is the world-framing and distributive work highlighted as part of becoming an expert.

I began this piece with comments on legal expertise. Let me end with four theses about what the above reflexions suggest about education in transnational legal expertise.

First, students of transnational law ought to have a clearer view that the expertise they acquire is a linguistic competence, the possession of a specific lexicon and a set of idioms and grammar that allows the making of distinctions that frame the world in a specific way. That framing has a history and it contrasts with other ways of carving up the world. As a way of world making, transnational expertise allocates resources, powers and vulnerabilities between human groups. It creates and denies agency and directs people to think about the world in a specific way – that there are states and markets in which some types of behaviour are normal and other types of behaviour deviant.[79]

Second, students of transnational law should learn that the linguistic competence conveyed to them frames what really are choices as if they were necessary aspects of the world. The legal grammar directs them to conceptual work with rules and exceptions, principles and counter-principles, as well as to policies and teleologies with which their conceptual distinctions are stabilised in typically patterned or path-dependent ways.[80] They should learn that those patterns have a history and that they co-exist with alternative patterns. The expertise they learn – their 'field' – organises them in hierarchical relations: there are mainstream and heterodox ways of thinking about the patterns.

Thirdly, they should learn that transnational law is not just a tool for the management of global problems but as a world-framing devise singles out some issues as 'problems' and sets other aside as a commonsense from which

78 Kennedy, *World of Struggle*, pp. 135–67.

79 The ways in which legal expertise distributes benefits, competencies and vulnerabilities among human groups by laying out the background conditions of normality/deviation is well presented in Kennedy, *World of Struggle*, pp. 171–217.

80 The significance of path dependency for creating the sense of legal necessity is usefully discussed in Duncan Kennedy, 'A Social Psychological Interpretation of the Hermeneutic of Suspicion in Contemporary American Legal Thought' in Desautels-Stein and Tomlins, *Searching for Contemporary Legal Thought*, pp. 374–9.

legal work starts and which it suggests are not problematic at all. They should learn that, rather than being one technical instrument among others, transnational law penetrates all social relations by drawing boundaries between powers, competencies, and vulnerabilities of human groups that other fields of expertise such as politics, economics or other governance technologies take as their starting points. The way law draws distinctions between what is public and what is private, for instance, conditions much about how people see the alternatives for development.

Finally, teaching and research in transnational law ought not to take place by imitation of practical assignments in rule interpretation or policy formation. Both can be undertaken in different ways depending on how the interpretative or policy-making context is presented. Students ought to ask neither 'What is the right interpretation of this rule or policy?' nor 'What policy might be the best way to attain a social objective?' Instead, they should be taught to ask 'What should I believe in order to think this is the right interpretation or the best policy?' That is to say, instead of asking a technical and instrumental question about the subject of their expertise – how they could best perform the tasks they are given by their (imagined) clients or supervisors – they should ask an interpretative or critical question about the assumptions about the world that condition work in transnational law.[81] This would enable them not only to think better and argue more sharply about the rules and policies in question but also to reflect on the contingency of the way their expertise frames the world – the *ideology* of their expertise, in other words.

81 I have discussed this contrast of framing legal research questions in 'What Is Critical Research in International Law? Celebrating Structuralism' (2016) 29 *Leiden Journal of International Law*, 727–35.

# 3

# Expertise As Framing

Matthew Windsor

What matters is the shape-making impulse.
Seamus Heaney

## 3.1 INTRODUCTION

This chapter explores the pertinence of framing as a concept that might enrich our understanding of the politics of legal expertise. As the legal content and context of public administration has become increasingly complex, the need for policymakers to draw on the expertise of legal advisers has assumed significance. However, exactly what occurs when expert knowledge meets political power in the advisory context has been understudied.[1] Framing – the idea that the way a problem is presented can impact how that problem is understood and resolved – is a constructive heuristic in this regard.

Rather than exploring policy framing solely in the context of the European Union,[2] the present contribution unpacks the dynamics of framing and its contribution to 'epistemic governance' at a higher level of

For helpful suggestions, I am grateful to Immi Tallgren, Anna Leander, Chris Hilson and participants at the 'Politics of Legal Expertise' workshop at the University of Helsinki and the 'Paths of Change in International Law' workshop at the Graduate Institute of International and Development Studies.

1 See, generally, Monika Ambrus, Karin Arts, Ellen Hey and Helena Raulus (eds.), *The Role of 'Experts' in International and European Decision-Making Processes* (Cambridge: Cambridge University Press, 2014).

2 Falk Daviter, 'Policy Framing in the European Union' (2007) 14(4) *Journal of European Public Policy*, 654; Heike Klüver, Christine Mahoney and Marc Opper, 'Framing in Context: How Interest Groups Employ Framing to Lobby the European Commission' (2015) 22(4) *Journal of European Public Policy*, 481; Ece Özlem Atikcan, *Framing the European Union: The Power of Political Arguments in Shaping European Integration* (Cambridge: Cambridge University Press, 2015); Daniel Rasch, *Lobbying Success in the European Union: The Role of Information and Frames* (New York: Routledge, 2018).

abstraction.[3] It is intended as a cross-cutting reflection on the role of legal expertise in policy-making, introducing some general themes to which other contributions return. Section 3.2 offers a brief snapshot of framing's invocation in a range of disciplinary fields. Section 3.3 interrogates how legal experts deploy framing to influence policy choice in the advisory process. Section 3.4 discusses issues of frame contestation and change, drawing on convention theory developed by the French sociologist Luc Boltanski. Given the recent erosion of civic discourse in political life and the supplanting of human expertise by algorithmic governance and regulation, Section 3.5 concludes with a reflection on the future of framing. If Peter Goodrich is right in opining that modern lawyers are not always adequately schooled in the 'critical apprehension of the visible',[4] the analysis of framing herein is offered as a generative response.

## 3.2 FRAMING 101

References to framing are ubiquitous across the social sciences and humanities. In some disciplinary contexts, the language of framing plays a central role in theorising – complete with elaborate definitional taxonomies – whereas in others it is little more than a rhetorical flourish.[5] An initial distinction can be drawn between equivalence framing (focusing on variations in *how* a given piece of information is presented to audiences), and emphasis framing (focusing on variations in *what* is being communicated). Equivalence framing is famously associated with the work of psychologists Amos Tversky and Daniel Kahneman, who revealed how preferences shift when the same issue is framed in different ways.[6] On the other hand, emphasis framing understands the frame in terms of the selection of one set of facts or arguments over another. Emerging from a sociological tradition preoccupied with meaning making,

3 Pertti Alasuutari and Ali Qadir, 'Epistemic Governance: An Approach to the Politics of Policy-Making' (2014) 1(1) *European Journal of Cultural and Political Sociology*, 67. For an application of framing to EU and transnational governance, see Koskenniemi's chapter in this volume.

4 Peter Goodrich, *Legal Emblems and the Art of Law: Obiter Depicta as the Vision of Governance* (Cambridge: Cambridge University Press, 2014).

5 Robert Entman, 'Framing: Toward Clarification of a Fractured Paradigm' (1993) 43(4) *Journal of Communication*, 51 (describing framing as a 'scattered conceptualization', a 'potential research paradigm that remains fractured' and 'often defined casually, with much left to an assumed tacit understanding of reader and researcher').

6 Amos Tversky and Daniel Kahneman, 'The Framing of Decisions and the Psychology of Choice' (1981) 211 *Science*, 453 (discussing the appetite for risk when outcomes are presented as 'gains' or 'losses').

Erving Goffman posited a distinction between the 'content of a current perception and the reality status we give to what is thus enclosed or bracketed within perception'.[7] For Goffman, we frame reality to 'negotiate it, manage it, comprehend it, and choose appropriate repertories of cognition and action'.[8]

Political analysis has benefited from the insights offered by framing in numerous areas, including cognitive linguistics,[9] media studies,[10] social movement theory[11] and scholarship concerning interest representation.[12] In the context of political communication, frames have been likened to 'recipes ... advice from experts on how citizens should cook up their opinions'.[13] Constructivist international relations scholars Michael Barnett and Martha Finnemore observed that:

> Actors use frames to situate events and to interpret problems, to fashion a shared understanding of the world, to galvanize sentiments as a way to mobilize and guide social action, and to suggest possible resolutions to current plights. Events, in short, do not have an objective meaning but must be made meaningful by actors, and actors compete to affix meaning to these events because doing so creates boundaries of acceptable action.[14]

A number of theorists in the humanities have focused their attention on the exclusionary character of the frame's boundaries, including Martin Heidegger's treatment of enframing in the context of modern technology,[15]

7 Erving Goffman, *Frame Analysis: An Essay on the Organization of Experience* (Boston MA: Northeastern University Press, 1986), p. 3.

8 Ibid.

9 George Lakoff, *Don't Think of an Elephant: Know Your Values and Frame the Debate* (White River Junction VT: Chelsea Green, 2004).

10 Robert Entman, *Projections of Power: Framing News, Public Opinion, and US Foreign Policy* (Chicago: University of Chicago Press, 2004). For a critique of the 'added value' of emphasis frames in the media context, see Michael Cacciatore, Dietram A. Scheufele and Shanto Iyengar, 'The End of Framing as We Know It ... and the Future of Media Effects' (2016) 19(1) *Mass Communication and Society*, 7 (discussing schemas, scripts, priming and agenda-setting).

11 Robert Benford and David Snow, 'Framing Processes and Social Movements: An Overview and Assessment' (2000) 26 *Annual Review of Sociology*, 611. See also Korkea-aho's discussion in this volume.

12 Daviter, 'Policy Framing'; Klüver, Mahoney and Opper, 'Framing in Context'; Atikcan, *Framing the European Union*; Rasch, *Lobbying Success*.

13 Donald R. Kinder, 'Curmudgeonly Advice' (2007) 57(1) *Journal of Communication*, 155–56. See also James N. Druckmann, 'Political Preference Formation: Competition, Deliberation and the (Ir)relevance of Framing Effects' (2004) 98 *American Political Science Review*, 671.

14 Michael Barnett and Martha Finnemore, *Rules for the World: International Organizations in Global Politics* (Ithaca NY: Cornell University Press, 2004), p. 33.

15 Martin Heidegger, *The Question Concerning Technology and Other Essays* (New York: Harper and Row, 1977).

Susan Sontag's analysis of the representation of atrocity in photography[16] and Jacques Derrida's deconstruction of aesthetic accounts of framing.[17] Nancy Fraser has explored the phenomenon of misframing, asserting that where political space is 'unjustly framed, the result is the denial of political voice to those who are cast outside the universe of those who count'.[18] Because the 'question of the frame' is a 'question of justice',[19] misframing gives rise to a pressing need to 'democratize the process of frame-setting'.[20]

For those interested in the power and potential of framing, not only the substantive content of the frame but also framing activities themselves must be scrutinised.[21] In his actor-network theory, Bruno Latour rejected 'settl[ing] scale in advance' by insisting on 'one absolute frame of reference'; instead, he memorably argued that such 'zoom effects' must be called into question.[22] This requires sensitivity to the power of occlusion: 'the capacity to pre-empt both that which gets seen and the terms of discussion through what gets seen is described'.[23]

## 3.3 LEGAL EXPERTISE, ADVISING AND FRAMING

The legal adviser is frequently described as having a crucial role to play in effecting state compliance with international and European Union law.[24] As a 'custodian and exponent of international law for the foreign ministry',[25] the legal adviser is thought to perceive international law as capable of both

16 Susan Sontag, *Regarding the Pain of Others* (New York: Picador, 2003), p. 46.

17 Jacques Derrida, *The Truth in Painting* (Chicago: University of Chicago Press, 1987).

18 Kate Nash and Vikki Bell, 'The Politics of Framing: An Interview with Nancy Fraser' (2007) 24 (4) *Theory, Culture & Society*, 73, 77.

19 Ibid.

20 Nancy Fraser, *Scales of Justice: Reimagining Political Space in a Globalizing World* (New York: Columbia University Press, 2010), p. 22. To counter misframing, Fraser proposes the substitution of the 'membership principle', which regards nationality as the relevant criterion to define subjects of justice in a given polity, with the 'all-subjected principle', where 'all those who are subjected to a given governance structure have moral standing as subjects of justice in relation to it' (ibid., p. 65).

21 Judith Butler, *Frames of War: When Is Life Grievable?* (London: Verso, 2016).

22 Bruno Latour, *Reassembling the Social: An Introduction to Actor-Network Theory* (Oxford: Oxford University Press, 2005), p. 186.

23 David Jenkins and Steven Lukes, 'The Power of Occlusion' (2017) 10(1) *Journal of Political Power*, 6, 22.

24 Matthew Windsor, 'Consigliere or Conscience? The Role of the Government Legal Adviser' in Jean d'Aspremont, Tarcisio Gazzini, André Nollkaemper and Wouter Werner (eds.), *International Law as a Profession* (Cambridge: Cambridge University Press, 2017), p. 355, p. 375–78.

25 Ronald St. J. MacDonald, 'The Role of the Legal Adviser of Ministries of Foreign Affairs', *Collected Courses of the Hague Academy of International Law*, vol. 156 (1977), 377, 387.

clarifying and constraining the policy options available to government. Attentiveness to framing helps illuminate how advisers speak legal expertise to power, permeating policy-making in the process.[26] In his account of the juridical field, Pierre Bourdieu noted that lawyers 'create the need for their own services by redefining problems expressed in ordinary language as legal problems, translating them into the language of the law'.[27] Legal rhetoric thus has a 'coercive aspect', to the extent it 'structures sensibility and vision'.[28]

In a recent contribution to the 'jurisprudence of form', Pierre Schlag and Amy Griffin explore framing in the specific context of how legal doctrine is applied to the facts.[29] They discuss a range of different aspects of framing:[30] entry-framing;[31] broad vs narrow time frames; segmented vs continuous transactions; action vs omission; the level of abstraction;[32] and exit-framing.[33] For Schlag and Griffin, the selection of a frame 'influence[s] what doctrines can be engaged, what kinds of legal arguments can be advanced, and what legal issues can be raised'.[34]

When a legal issue reaches a policymaker for determination, the expert adviser has typically framed the issue in a specific way.[35] The way in which advisers set up policy choices for decision-makers and frame the alternatives has an ineradicable

26 In the context of public international law, see Anne van Aaken and Jan-Philip Elm, 'Framing in and Through Public International Law' in Andrea Bianchi and Moshe Hirsch (eds.), *International Law's Invisible Frames* (Oxford: Oxford University Press, 2021) (discussing international negotiations, international adjudication, global performance indicators and norm framing).

27 Pierre Bourdieu, 'The Force of Law: Toward a Sociology of the Juridical Field' (1987) 38 *Hastings Law Journal*, 805, 833.

28 James Boyd White, *The Legal Imagination* (Chicago: University of Chicago Press, 1973), p. xiii.

29 Pierre Schlag and Amy J. Griffin, *How to Do Things with Legal Doctrine* (Chicago: University of Chicago Press, 2020), p. 4.

30 Schlag and Griffin draw extensively on Mark Kelman, 'Interpretive Construction in the Substantive Criminal Law' (1981) 33(4) *Stanford Law Review*, 591.

31 Kelman, 'Interpretive Construction', 33 (described as the 'performative installation of views and commitments' in the audience).

32 In the EU context, see Gerard Conway, 'Levels of Generality in the Legal Reasoning of the European Court of Justice' (2008) 14(6) *European Law Journal*, 787.

33 Kelman, 'Interpretive Construction', 51 (described as the 'frame the author leaves with the reader or the audience').

34 Ibid., 32. On the choice of a narrative frame, see Paul Kahn, *Making the Case: The Art of the Judicial Opinion* (New Haven CT: Yale University Press, 2016), p. 24.

35 David Fontana, 'Executive Branch Legalisms' (2012) 126 *Harvard Law Review Forum*, 21, 42; Martin Wählisch, 'Cognitive Frames of Interpretation in International Law' in Andrea Bianchi, Daniel Peat and Matthew Windsor (eds.), *Interpretation in International Law* (Oxford: Oxford University Press, 2015), p. 332 (frames are 'frequently oriented by strategic policy aims that impact on the use of vocabulary and the direction of interpretation').

influence on policy outcomes.[36] Recalling his role as legal adviser to the US State Department, Harold Koh recalled how '[y]ou may not be able to herd cats, but you can move their food . . . chang[ing] incentives and restructur[ing] situations'.[37] In this way, advisers acquire 'control over the way in which the law is applied . . . over and above their function of finding and explaining the law'.[38]

If it is correct that the choice of the frame helps determine the decision,[39] we must zero in on the knowledge practices of legal advisers tasked with frame construction and entrenchment. In his elegant cartography of legal expertise, David Kennedy argued that insufficient attention is paid to the way that political decision-making is shaped by experts such as legal advisers acting in the 'background'.[40] In other words, a myopic focus on the moment of decision detracts from the assiduous efforts of experts to 'frame and influence the front of the stage'.[41] For that reason, in the context of EU law, Antoine Vauchez endorsed a holistic appraisal of the space in which a 'case has been debated and framed', rather than articulating 'a priori boundaries'.[42]

In a legal environment characterised by regime proliferation, expert advisers are typically engaged in a competition for semantic authority.[43] The advisers who win the 'framing contest' have a consequential role in setting the terms of subsequent debate.[44] The oft-discussed fragmentation of

36 Dennis Thompson, 'Ascribing Responsibility to Advisers in Government' (1983) 93(3) *Ethics*, 546. In the EU context, see Päivi Leino-Sandberg, *The Politics of Legal Expertise in EU Policymaking* (Cambridge: Cambridge University Press, 2021).

37 Harold Koh, 'The State Department Legal Adviser's Office: Eight Decades in Peace and War' (2012) 100 *Georgetown Law Journal*, 1747, 1773.

38 Franklin Berman, 'The International Lawyer, Inside and Outside Foreign Ministries' in Christopher Hill and Pamela Beshoff (eds.), *Two Worlds of International Relations: Academics, Practitioners and the Trade in Ideas* (London: Routledge, 1994), p. 79, p. 85.

39 Martti Koskenniemi, 'The Fate of Public International Law: Between Technique and Politics' (2007) 70(1) *Modern Law Review*, 1, 6.

40 David Kennedy, *A World of Struggle: How Power, Law, and Expertise Shape Global Political Economy* (Princeton: Princeton University Press, 2016), pp. 110–16.

41 Samuel Moyn, 'Knowledge and Politics in International Law' (2016) 129 *Harvard Law Review*, 2164, 2172 (reviewing *A World of Struggle*). See also David Kennedy, 'Challenging Expert Rule: The Politics of Global Governance' (2005) 27 *Sydney Law Review*, 5, 9 (it is the expert who 'stands between the foreground *prince* and the lay *context*, advising and informing the prince, implementing and interpreting his decisions for laymen').

42 Antoine Vauchez, 'EU Law Classics in the Making' in Fernanda Nicola and Bill Davies (eds.), *EU Law Stories: Contextual and Critical Histories of European Jurisprudence* (Cambridge: Cambridge University Press, 2017), p. 21, p. 31.

43 Ingo Venzke, *How Interpretation Makes International Law* (Oxford: Oxford University Press, 2012), pp. 62–64. See, generally, Ole Jacob Sending, *The Politics of Expertise: Competing for Authority in Global Governance* (Ann Arbor: University of Michigan Press, 2017).

44 Neta Crawford, *Argument and Change in World Politics* (Cambridge: Cambridge University Press, 2002), p. 22. See also the chapters by Leino-Sandberg and Yong in this volume.

international law gives rise to strategic framing activities, involving the 'description and re-description of aspects of the world . . . to make them fall under the jurisdiction of particular institutions'.[45] In the process, experts frequently draw 'frame-consistent inferences' in their interactions with other expert groups.[46]

However, the boundary work undertaken by legal advisers is not only intra-disciplinary in orientation. Indeed, an exclusive focus on the deployment of 'legal' frames in the study of legal mobilisation would be to engage in selection bias. To avoid this bias, one must also study the way in which 'non-legal' frames are strategically deployed in legal mobilisation.[47] The spectre of systems theory looms large here, where law is normatively bounded but structurally coupled with other social systems like politics and the economy.[48] Social change depends on whether the expert adviser's frames can be brought into alignment with other discourses and agendas.[49] But how exactly do frames change?[50]

## 3.4 HOW FRAMES CHANGE

Although it does not explicitly use the vocabulary of framing, convention theory relevantly explores how individuals produce justifications for their actions in social interaction and critique those of other actors.[51] In *On Justification*, Luc Boltanski and Laurent Thévenot argued that there are six major regimes of justification (or 'orders of worth').[52] The orders of worth are

45 Koskenniemi, 'Fate of Public International Law', 7. For a useful example, see Margaret Young, *Trading Fish, Saving Fish: The Interaction between Regimes in International Law* (Cambridge: Cambridge University Press, 2011), pp. 227–29.

46 Anthea Roberts, 'Clash of Paradigms: Actors and Analogies Shaping the Investment Treaty System' (2013) 107(1) *American Journal of International Law*, 45, 56.

47 I am grateful to Chris Hilson for this insight.

48 Niklas Luhmann, *Law as a Social System* (Oxford: Oxford University Press, 2004).

49 David Snow, Burke Rochford, Steven Worden and Robert Benford, 'Frame Alignment Processes, Micromobilization, and Movement Participation' (1986) 51(4) *American Sociological Review*, 464.

50 Ingo Venzke, 'Cracking the Frame? On the Prospects of Change in a World of Struggle' (2016) 27(3) *European Journal of International Law*, 831 (on the need for an 'account of transitions').

51 Luc Boltanski and Laurent Thévenot, *On Justification: Economies of Worth* (Princeton: Princeton University Press, 2006); Luc Boltanski and Laurent Thévenot, 'The Sociology of Critical Capacity' (1999) 2(3) *European Journal of Social Theory*, 359; Luc Boltanski and Laurent Thévenot, 'The Reality of Moral Expectations: A Sociology of Situated Judgement' (2000) 3(3) *Philosophical Explorations*, 208.

52 To explicate the orders of worth, convention theory combines empirical data collected in fieldwork with hermeneutic excavations of intellectual paradigms and political philosophies. Each order of worth is exemplified by a particular author: the market order (Adam Smith); the civic order (Rousseau); the industrial order (Saint-Simon); the domestic order (Bossuet); the inspiration order (Augustine); and the fame order (Hobbes).

an attempt to articulate the 'culturally embedded central grammars' that provide 'legitimate social bonds in democratic societies'.[53] Each order of worth contains an interpretation of the common good and involves a distinct attribution of value. Convention theory proceeds to explore how these orders of worth conflict as individuals compete to legitimise their view in disputes ('test situations'). Disputes typically involve the invocation of an order of worth that is different from the one on which other participants are fixated in their justificatory activity. Social interaction involves navigation between these orders and the striking of compromises, where the 'situation remains composite but a clash is averted'.[54]

Convention theory was developed by Boltanski as a marked departure from the critical sociology of Pierre Bourdieu, his erstwhile teacher and mentor.[55] According to Boltanski, critical sociology failed to give due consideration to the critical capacities of everyday social actors and the reflexive structure of social practice. Boltanski's sociology of critique acknowledges that society is replete with its own forms of justification, critique and evaluation, which inevitably come into conflict. For Boltanski, the social world is not a 'site of domination, endured passively and unconsciously', but rather a 'space shot through by a multiplicity of disputes, critiques, disagreements and attempts to re-establish locally agreements that are always fragile'.[56]

The difference in orientation between Bourdieu's critical sociology and Boltanski's sociology of critique cashes out on the issue of change. Critical sociology largely privileges social reproduction and structural determinism,[57] with the habitus significantly restricting the horizon of possibilities open to agents.[58] In the sociology of critique, a focus on social reproduction is replaced

53 Frank Gadinger, 'On Justification and Critique: Luc Boltanski's Pragmatic Sociology and International Relations' (2016) 10 *International Political Sociology*, 187, 193.

54 Boltanski and Thévenot, *On Justification*, p. 277.

55 See, generally, Robin Celikates, 'From Critical Social Theory to a Social Theory of Critique: On the Critique of Ideology After the Pragmatic Turn' (2006) 13(1) *Constellations*, 21; Thomas Bénatouïl, 'A Tale of Two Sociologies: The Critical and the Pragmatic Stance in Contemporary French Sociology' (1999) 2(3) *European Journal of Social Theory*, 37. More recently, Boltanski has set out to develop a framework that makes it possible to reconcile the antagonistic approaches: *On Critique: A Sociology of Emancipation* (Cambridge: Polity Press, 2011).

56 Boltanski, *On Critique*, p. 27.

57 Christian Bueger and Frank Gadinger, *International Practice Theory: New Perspectives* (Basingstoke: Palgrave Macmillan, 2014), p. 28 (describing the emphasis of Bourdieu's praxeology on the 'stability, regularity and reproduction of practices and less on subversion and renewal').

58 Robin Celikates, *Critique as Social Practice: Critical Theory and Social Self-Understanding* (London: Rowman & Littlefield, 2018), p. 38. Cf. Anna Leander, 'The Promises, Problems, and Potentials of a Bourdieu-Inspired Staging of International Relations' (2011) 5 *International*

by an overt effort to contribute to a theory of social change.[59] It emphasises the creative effort of actors to change and adapt their practices of justification and critique in situations of conflict. In *The New Spirit of Capitalism*, Boltanski and Ève Chiapello produced an explicit model of ideational change, exploring how new orders of worth emerge and become institutionalised at a societal level.[60] The idea was to enable greater understanding of how the ideologies associated with economic activity can be modified.[61] They charted how a new spirit of capitalism emerged in the mid-1970s in response to anti-capitalist contestation, abandoning Fordist hierarchies in favour of the network as the organising principle of social relations at work. By internalising critiques of industrial alienation and disempowerment, the new spirit of capitalism ushered in a new order of worth, ostensibly predicated on worker autonomy and flexibility. The resulting institutional changes here were intimately connected to changes at the level of justificatory discourse.

Bourdieu's critical sociology has dominated international and EU legal scholarship as far as the 'turn to practice' is concerned.[62] For Bourdieu, it was fundamentally important to escape the 'neutralising and naturalising discourse' of the professionals under examination.[63] In a discipline where the 'scholarly styles of serving or aspiring government legal advisers . . . dominate the field,[64] Bourdieu's analytic tools have certainly offered a welcome

*Political Sociology*, 294, 298 (arguing that the notion of fields, 'far from constructing unchangeable monoliths, leaves scope for struggle and change').

59 Hans Joas and Wolfgang Knobl, *Social Theory: Twenty Introductory Lectures* (Cambridge: Cambridge University Press, 2009), p. 541.

60 Luc Boltanski and Ève Chiapello, *The New Spirit of Capitalism* (London: Verso, 2005). For useful discussion, see Paul Du Gay and Glenn Morgan (eds.), *New Spirits of Capitalism? Crises, Justifications and Dynamics* (Oxford: Oxford University Press, 2014).

61 Luc Boltanski and Ève Chiapello, 'The Role of Criticism in the Dynamics of Capitalism: Social Criticism versus Artistic Criticism' in Max Miller (ed.), *Worlds of Capitalism: Institutions, Governance and Economic Change in the Era of Globalization* (London: Routledge, 2005), p. 237, p. 265.

62 See Martti Koskenniemi, 'Between Commitment and Cynicism: Outline for a Theory of International Law as Practice' in Jean D'Aspremont, Tarcisio Gazzini, André Nollkaemper and Wouter Werner (eds.), *International Law as a Profession* (Cambridge: Cambridge University Press, 2017); Yves Dezalay and Bryant Garth, *Dealing in Virtue: Transnational Commercial Arbitration and the Construction of a Transnational Legal Order* (Chicago: University of Chicago Press, 1996); Antoine Vauchez, *Brokering Europe: Euro-Lawyers and the Making of a Transnational Polity* (Cambridge: Cambridge University Press, 2015). In international relations, see Rebecca Adler-Nissen (ed.), *Bourdieu in International Relations: Rethinking Key Concepts in IR* (London: Routledge, 2013).

63 Yves Dezalay and Mikael Rask Madsen, 'The Force of Law and Lawyers: Pierre Bourdieu and the Reflexive Sociology of Law' (2012) 8 *Annual Review of Law and Social Science*, 433, 447.

64 Benedict Kingsbury, 'The International Legal Order' in Peter Cane and Mark Tushnet (eds.), *Oxford Handbook of Legal Studies* (Oxford: Oxford University Press, 2005), p. 289.

corrective.[65] Indeed, Bourdieu's work has provided a fertile research agenda for the sociology of international law, with a number of scholars deploying habitus and field to different transnational contexts to interrogate the political capital of lawyers and the social conditions that make the force of law possible. Yet, it has been suggested that the widespread reliance on Bourdieu is the main reason why international practice theory, more generally, has struggled with the question of change.

While convention theory has been widely analysed in sociological circles,[66] the discussion of Boltanski in international relations scholarship largely takes the form of prefiguring future research possibilities.[67] Anna Leander has effectively demonstrated how Bourdieu's critical sociology might be bolstered productively with insights from Boltanski.[68] More recently, Frank Gadinger has argued that Boltanski provides an illuminating research methodology and conceptual framework to study the normative dimension of international practices in disputes, particularly how normative claims emerge, stabilise and change in practices of justification.[69]

It is no great leap to discern how the conceptual apparatus of convention theory might productively bolster an account of frame contestation and change amongst legal experts. Like analyses of framing, convention theory challenges monistic assumptions of political order that conceal the plurality of legitimations used by actors.[70] Competing frames can readily be understood as distinct orders of worth or regimes of justification.[71] In a similar vein, David Kennedy has observed how it is a 'quality of professional disputation to frame one's claim in an ostensibly general language', offering reasons based on 'common ideas about justice or equality', rather than asserting one's interests directly.[72] Of particular relevance to EU policy-making is the way in which convention theory

65 Matthew Windsor, 'Consigliere or Conscience', pp. 368–69.

66 See Simon Susen and Bryan S. Turner (eds.), *The Spirit of Luc Boltanski: Essays on the 'Pragmatic Sociology of Critique'* (London: Anthem Press, 2014); Paul Blokker, 'Pragmatic Sociology: Theoretical Evolvement and Empirical Application' (2011) 14(3) *European Journal of Social Theory*, 251.

67 See, generally, Sebastian Schindler and Tobias Wille, 'How Can We Criticize International Practices?' (2019) 63(4) *International Studies Quarterly*, 1014.

68 Leander, 'Promises, Problems, and Potentials'.

69 Gadinger, 'On Justification and Critique', 187.

70 Paul Blokker and Andrea Brigenthi, 'Politics between Justification and Defiance' (2011) 14(3) *European Journal of Social Theory*, 283.

71 There is no need to transpose the specific 'orders of worth' in *On Justification*, which 'blatantly reflect the preferences of the authors who were educated in the French philosophical tradition': Axel Honneth, 'Dissolutions of the Social: On the Social Theory of Luc Boltanski and Laurent Thévenot' (2010) 17(3) *Constellations*, 376, 381.

72 Kennedy, A *World of Struggle*, p. 189.

forces one to confront the 'capacity of regimes of economic power to assert themselves successfully in coherent normative, political and philosophical terms', explaining the resilience of dominant frames in the process.[73]

## 3.5 THE FUTURE OF THE FRAME

Ben Lerner's recent novel *The Topeka School* offers a deep dive into the language games of competitive high school debating in the 1990s, with its protagonist Adam Gordon attempting a 'genealogy of his speech, its theaters and extremes'.[74] In policy debate, Adam is a master of 'the spread': a strategic effort to 'make more arguments, marshal more evidence than the other team can respond to within the allotted time', on the understanding that a 'dropped argument' is conceded.[75] When one debater is asked to 'account for the *value* of the spread', a range of arguments are canvassed, including the quixotic notion that 'speaking at the far end of intelligibility was actually about inclusivity'.[76] An alternative style of debate termed 'extemp' emphasised improvisation, where 'style and presentation remained primary'.[77] Fledgling debaters interested in the 'niceties of speech' were steered away from 'the spread' in favour of 'extemp'.

On its release, *The Topeka School* was billed as a 'startling prehistory of the present', canvassing the 'collapse of public speech' and the 'tyranny of trolls and the new right'. As the novel proceeds, Adam begins to perceive a 'fearful symmetry between the ideological compartmentalisation of high school debate and what passed for the national political discourse'.[78] Relatedly, the novel contains cautionary – if elliptical – lessons about the future of expertise and framing, in a world where liberal aspirations of communicative action are undermined[79] and performance is pre-eminent.[80] When he rejects 'linguistic overkill' and defends a more 'human scale of exchange',[81] Adam loses the final debate of his career.

The erosion of egalitarian exchange depicted in *The Topeka School* is not the only way in which the future of framing is imperilled. Automation and

73 William Davies, *The Limits of Neoliberalism: Authority, Sovereignty and the Logic of Competition* (Los Angeles: SAGE, 2017), p. 194. See also Bradford's contribution to this volume.

74 Ben Lerner, *The Topeka School* (London: Granta, 2019), p. 143.

75 Ibid., p. 22.

76 Ibid., p. 213.

77 Ibid., p. 136.

78 Ibid.

79 Raymond Geuss, 'A Republic of Discussion: Habermas at Ninety' *The Point* (18 June 2019).

80 For a discussion of the performative dimensions of expertise, see Koskenniemi's contribution to this volume.

81 Lerner, *The Topeka School*, p. 214.

machine learning is rapidly ushering in fundamental alterations in the way that specialist expertise is delivered, with the need for human professionals in the delivery of legal services in steady decline.[82] Legal automation has the potential to advance efficient administration, with machines increasingly producing better results because they are scrupulously unbiased in their recommendations. However, legal automation may have a deleterious impact on the deliberative aspects of decision-making, privileging some rule of law values (such as consistency) over others (such as reasoned elaboration).[83]

Given the increased adoption of algorithmic tools in the provision of legal advice, algorithmic accountability has assumed significance. The essential attribute of algorithms is that they 'afford greater degrees of recognition and value to some features of a scene than they do to others'.[84] For that reason, much depends on the 'predisposition of the algorithm designers and on the specific data the machines use in their learning process'.[85] Yet – concerningly – algorithmic governance is often carried out by individuals with a negligible claim to expertise.[86] In an account that has suggestive synergies with framing analysis, Louise Amoore likens algorithms themselves to 'aperture instruments', involved in 'condensing plural possible pathways to a single output'.[87] A critical response to algorithmic enframing thus involves 'trac[ing] the other durations that continue to beat in the discarded data, the multiple other potential pathways that could be mapped between fragments'.[88] Whether the future of policy-making is largely driven by humans or machines, a sensitivity to the dynamics of framing continues to engender (in the words of Sheila Jasanoff) an awareness of the 'contingency of social responses and the partiality of the imaginative space that is carved out for political action in any society'.[89]

82 Richard Susskind and Daniel Susskind, *The Future of the Professions: How Technology Will Transform the Work of Human Experts* (Oxford: Oxford University Press, 2016).

83 Monika Zalnieriute, Lyria Bennett Moses and George Williams, 'The Rule of Law and Automation of Government Decision-Making' (2019) 82(3) *Modern Law Review*, 425. See also Frank Pasquale, *New Laws of Robotics: Defending Human Expertise in the Age of AI* (Cambridge MA: Harvard University Press, 2020).

84 Louise Amoore, *Cloud Ethics: Algorithms and the Attributes of Ourselves and Others* (Durham NC: Duke University Press, 2020), p. 8.

85 Eyal Benvenisti, 'Upholding Democracy Amid the Challenges of New Technology: What Role for the Law of Global Governance?' (2018) 29(1) *European Journal of International Law*, 9, 58.

86 Fleur Johns, 'Data, Detection and the Redistribution of the Sensible in International Law' (2017) 111(1) *American Journal of International Law*, 57.

87 Amoore, *Cloud Ethics*, p. 17.

88 Ibid., pp. 17–18.

89 Sheila Jasanoff, *Designs on Nature: Science and Democracy in Europe and the United States* (Princeton: Princeton University Press, 2011), p. 24.

# 4

# Lawyers, Revolving Doors and the Public-Private Foundations of the French Regulatory State

Pierre France and Antoine Vauchez

## 4.1 INTRODUCTION

Over the past two decades, the borders between government, law and business have been profoundly transformed in France.[1] While this transformation had long remained hardly visible to the naked eye, a single case suddenly brought the new reality to the foreground. In 2010, articles in the press revealed that Jean-François Copé, leader of the majority party in the French National Assembly and a former finance minister, was concurrently acting as of counsel with the leading French law firm Gide. Figures emerged indicating that his income from the law firm was close to 20,000 euros a month[2] – more than twice what he earned as a member of parliament. As Gide frequently handles matters related to some of the highest-value contracts in France and Europe, including contracts to which the French state is a party, a public debate arose in France around the 'revolving door'[3] and the related issues of conflicts of interest and the moralisation of politics.[4] As it turned out, Jean-François Copé was the first in a series of similar cases reported in the press; it transpired that quite a few politicians, on both the Left and the Right, had for years also been practising as lawyers. On the Left, the names included two candidates in the

[1] The authors wish to thank Meg Morley for the translation, as well as Emilia Korkea-aho and Päivi Leino for their useful remarks on an earlier version of the text. For a detailed presentation of the underlying research, we refer readers to Antoine Vauchez and Pierre France, *The Neoliberal Republic: Corporate Lawyers, Statecraft and the Making of Public-Private France* (Ithaca: Cornell University Press, 2020).

[2] In his 'Declaration of Interests' statement submitted to the Haute Autorité pour la transparence de la vie publique, Copé reported that his law earnings were €313,702 in 2012 and €184,734 in 2013. The Haute Autorité was created in 2013 to collect, monitor and publish the income and assets statements of public officials.

[3] Timothy M. LaPira and Herschel F. Thomas, *Revolving Door Lobbying: Public Service, Private Influence, and the Unequal Representation of Interests* (Lawrence: University Press of Kansas, 2017).

[4] Éric Phélippeau, *L'argent de la politique* (Paris: Presses de Science Po, 2018).

presidential primary, Ségolène Royal and Dominique Strauss-Kahn, as well as the future president François Hollande (president of France from 2012 to 2017). On the Right, a roster of former ministers, including Rachida Dati (former minister of justice), Dominique de Villepin (former prime minister) and François Baroin (former minister of the economy), had been pursuing careers in the legal profession without attracting attention before the Copé case came to light.

These moves from public office to private legal practice are intriguing in many respects. Firstly, their sheer number leads us to address the cases not individually but globally, as a systemic phenomenon rather than a series of individual cases and anecdotes. The wide political spectrum involved is also telling. We find not only members of the presidential staff and cabinet of Nicolas Sarkozy (president from 2007 to 2012) but also left-wing politicians from the Socialist party. Finally, their timing is also intriguing, as the first cases date back to the early 1990s.

Even more crucially, this mobility between government and the Bar also involves leading civil servants. This is partly due to the fact that high-level civil service and top political careers are fundamentally intertwined in France,[5] giving rise to a body called the 'politico-administrative elite'. But it also indicates that this is not merely a political phenomenon. Behind Jean-François Copé and a few other politicians we find a cohort of individuals whose names are not known to the general public, but who have held some of the highest posts in public administration – a former director of the department of fiscal legislation, a former director-general in the fiscal administration, etc. These other figures remain less visible, not attracting the spotlight of the specialist business and legal press, for example, in the same way as MPs and ministers. Those who have entered the legal profession include members of the prestigious Conseil d'État; several general secretaries of the office of the president (the Élysée); members of the prime minister's cabinet (Matignon); high-level civil servants from the ministry of the economy and other cabinet offices; and officers from various public bodies responsible for market regulation. At a time of intense competition on the market of corporate legal advice,[6]

[5] Most notably, they are trained at the same institution, the École nationale d'administration (ENA).

[6] Anne Boigeol and Laurent Willemez, 'Fighting for Monopoly: Unification, Differentiation and Representation of the French Bar' in William Felstiner (ed.), *Organization and Resistance: Legal Professions Confront a Changing World* (Oxford: Hart, 2006), pp. 41–65. See also Christian Bessy and Benoit Bastard, 'France. The Reconfiguration of a Profession' in Richard L. Abel et al (eds), *Lawyers in 21st-Century Societies. Volume 1: National Reports* (Oxford: Hart, 2021), pp. 193–208.

the Paris Bar welcomes them and prides itself on attracting such prestigious names that in turn add lustre to its reputation.

Several aspects of this circulatory movement deserve attention. Firstly, it is a phenomenon that began at a time when, between the early 1990s and 2010, few members of parliament or ministers were lawyers and the influx from the legal profession, once seen as a stepping-stone to elite posts in politics or government administration, appeared to have run dry.[7] Secondly, it should be distinguished from the traditional forms of *pantouflage*, a term that coined to express the mobility of high-level civil servants transitioning into the private sector. Traditionally, *pantouflage* involved banking and finance but rarely law firms. Thirdly, it is intriguing that the proximity with the Bar went unnoticed for so long. When it caught the public eye in 2010, little was known about the legal careers of politicians and/or civil servants; next to nothing was known about the Paris law firms where they practised and the *dossiers* that these public-servants-turned-lawyers handled. Even more remarkable, the French state had not yet recognised this phenomenon as significant; there was no discussion within the state about what this new type of mobility might mean, and no talk of the possible need to regulate such movement. Interestingly, the European Union served as a springboard for this new type of mobility, as can be seen from early examples of transition from a civil service position to a law firm, such as Antoine Winckler, a former ENA graduate who in the late 1980s became a leading practitioner in EU law competition at Cleary Gottlieb in Brussels, or Jean-Pierre Jouyet, head of cabinet to Jacques Delors between 1993 and 1995 during the latter's final years at the head of the Commission, who moved to the law firm Jeantet & Associés immediately upon leaving the Commission.

The weakly structured field of EU law offered opportunities that were not traditionally open to French political and administrative elites to bring their government experience to bear in the private sector.[8] This was all the more so as lawyers and law firms had carved out for themselves a key role at the centre of EU core policies, not least competition.[9] A new circuit opened for French officials in Brussels – be they commissioners, EU civil servants or members of

7 Laurent Willemez, 'La "République des avocats" 1848: Le mythe, le modèle et son endossement' in Michel Offerlé (ed.), *La profession politique* (Paris: Belin, 1999), pp. 201–229.

8 On the looseness of EU law and the circulation it allows, see Antoine Vauchez, *Brokering Europe: Euro-Lawyers and the Making of a Transnational Polity* (Cambridge: Cambridge University Press, 2015).

9 See the chapter by Lola Avril in this volume; Emilia Korkea-aho, 'Legal Lobbying: The Evolving (but Hidden) Role of Lawyers and Law Firms in the EU Public Affairs Market' (2021) 22 *German Law Journal*, 65–84.

France's permanent representation – which has remained very active ever since, as confirmed by the recent case of Pierre Sellal, a seasoned French diplomat, who joined the Paris law firm August & Debouzy in 2018 after being France's permanent representative in Brussels for a decade.

In investigating this topic, the present study relies on both qualitative and quantitative research. Through a close reading of the national press and more narrowly focused professional sources (rosters of administrative personnel, legal press, etc.), we identified 217 public officials who had moved into the legal profession during the period running from the early 1990s to 2017. The database furnishes classic statistical information on the social backgrounds of the individuals concerned and highlights the range of professional positions and institutions that are frequently traversed before and after a period in legal practice. Rather than using a regression model to test the importance of each variable, we have taken all variables together, so as to demonstrate the emergence of a social space marked by shifting boundary lines between public service and the private sector. To supplement this database, we conducted comprehensive interviews with nineteen of these 'in and outers', covering the details of their backgrounds and careers. They provide an entry point into the motivations and justifications that underpin this mobility. Our findings lead to fundamental questions regarding the new boundaries between the public and private sectors, and the implications for a regulatory state in France and beyond. Our research shows how the realms of the law and the field of legal practice have become a 'crossroads' or third sector between the public and private sectors and a favoured point of passage between these two poles. By underscoring the systemic muddling of the public and private that characterises this border zone, this study casts new light on contemporary debate concerning the deployment of (legal) expertise in public decision-making, the prevention of conflicts of interest and the moralisation of public life.

## 4.2 FROM PUBLIC OFFICE TO LAW FIRMS: THE RISE OF A NEW CIRCULATION PATHWAY

Our story begins at a pivotal moment in the history of French legal practice. On 27 November 1991, a year after a profound reform that merged the professions of *avocat* (a lawyer who pleads in court) and *conseil juridique* (legal advisers, especially in the field of tax law),[10] a decree was adopted that opened up a new career path for 'category A' (i.e. high-rank) civil servants (or

[10] On the importance of this merger, see Lucien Karpik, *French Lawyers: A Study in Collective Action, 1274–1994* (Oxford: Oxford University Press, 2000).

persons assimilated into this category) who have practised 'juridical activities' in this capacity for a period of at least eight years in a government department, public service or international organisation', who were henceforth permitted to join the Bar without passing the entrance examination or completing an internship (though they were still required to hold a law degree).[11] As subsequently interpreted by the Paris Bar, this decree has over the years considerably transformed conditions of access to the legal profession. In its interpretation of the decree, the Paris Bar has assimilated parliamentarians to so-called category A civil servants (top civil servants) and held that the exercise of a parliamentary mandate or ministerial functions counts as twelve years of 'juridical activity' on the ground that it entails 'participation in law-making'. Furthermore, the Bar has adopted a flexible definition of the type of 'law degree' required for simplified access to the Bar, thus opening it up to a broad range of candidates.[12] Interestingly, though, the Paris Bar recently introduced a restriction by preventing an EU civil servant from benefitting from this exceptional form of access on the ground that the eight years of 'juridical activity' had not been in the field of national law – a decision subsequently upheld by the Court of Justice of the European Union.[13] Nevertheless, thanks to its broad interpretation of the possibilities of accessing the legal profession, the Paris Bar has become a focal point for converting governmental and political experience into marketable professional capital, all the more so as the profession of lawyer traditionally offers the advantage of a fluid title with great flexibility, capable of accommodating a diverse range of statuses – of counsel, partner, associate, full- or part-time, etc. – and allowing these to be

[11] This measure came on top of the dispensation traditionally accorded to judges from the ordinary, administrative and financial courts (decree of June 1972), who are exempted not only from the Bar exam and from having to undertake an internship, but also from the requirement to hold a law degree (Article 97). Judges rarely took advantage of this possibility, however.

[12] The decree of 15 April 2013 established a new dispensatory measure benefitting 'the assistants of deputies and senators who provide evidence of juridical activity at managerial level as their principal function for a period of at least eight years'.

[13] In a preliminary ruling delivered on 17 December 2020, the CJEU interpreted EU law as 'not precluding national legislation which makes such an exemption contingent on the person concerned having performed legal work in the field of national law, and excluding from the scope of that exemption officials, members or former members of the EU civil service who have performed legal work in that capacity, in one or more fields of EU law, provided that that national legislation does not exclude account from being taken of legal work involving the practice of national law'. See Case C-218/19, *Adina Onofrei* v. *Conseil de l'ordre des avocats au barreau de Paris and Others*, EU:C:2020:1034. We would like to thank the editors of the volume for bringing this to our attention.

combined with other positions (notably, parliamentary office) while ensuring all-important confidentiality.

The decree of 27 November 1991 is just one manifestation of the big bang in the legal profession that led French firms to reorganise along the lines of British and American law firms and the French market to open up to these 'Anglo-Saxon' firms and the increasingly international nature of legal practice.[14] Whereas the recruitment of new partners is aimed at attracting 'business developers' who will bring new clients to the firm, the snapping-up of civil servants and politicians is driven by a different sort of strategy. There, the goal is to prepare for the opening of new markets by acquiring the knowledge of state mechanisms needed to compete in them. But there is also a need to build a distinct reputation, as law firms are now increasingly having to publicise their activity and develop a brand image.[15]

This narrative of law firms intersects with another historical development, this time within the French state, where the playing field of professional venues and careers has been redrawn in the wake of successive waves of privatisation from the mid-1980s, which put an end to the 'golden age' of the *dirigiste* state.[16] As an example of this change, graduates of France's École nationale d'administration (ENA), where, traditionally, most top civil servants and many EU officials receive their training, now increasingly look to the private sector for employment. As early as 1984, an advertisement in the daily newspaper *Le Monde* was enticingly captioned 'Offrez-vous un énarque' ('Gift yourself a graduate of ENA'). This appeal illustrated the extent of the structural change in administrative spheres in France. As the state's neoliberal transformation got under way, career opportunities within the public sector

14 Yves Dezalay, *Marchands de droit* (Paris: Fayard, 1992). For a recent and updated account: Christian Bessy and Benoit Bastard, 'France. The Reconfiguration of a Profession' in Richard L. Abel et al (eds), *Lawyers in 21st-Century Societies. Volume 1: National Reports* (Oxford: Hart, 2021), pp. 193–208.

15 From the point of view of methodology, this study has happily, and paradoxically, benefitted from the consequences of this new orientation. We look at new publications, in addition to material that had earlier gone unnoticed due to its professional and sectoral nature and publication in journals read only by professionals in the field. Starting in the 1990s, law firms, which had traditionally kept a low profile in France, began to communicate publicly about their activities, holding events, creating cross-disciplinary organisations, and instituting awards. To address this new reality, law firms have resorted to the services of communication professionals, who in turn have created new professional journals with titles like *legalnews*, *Le monde du droit* [The World of Law], *La Lettre des juristes d affaires* [The Business Lawyers' Newsletter], which are quite openly dedicated to reporting on the movements of lawyers within and between firms. Since the 1990s it has been of prime importance for firms to show how attractive they are for professionals from other domains, and so they readily reveal their hires.

16 Pierre Birnbaum, *Les sommets de l'État: Essai sur l'élite du pouvoir en France* (Paris: Seuil, 1994; first published 1977); Ezra Suleiman and Guillaume Courty, *L'âge d'or de l'État* (Paris: Seuil, 2007).

progressively shrank, making it harder for ENA graduates to attain the most prestigious posts in government. At the same time, the gap was widening between salaries in the public and private sectors. The difference between the average pay of the top 1 per cent of earners in the public and private sectors doubled between 1980 and 1990[17] and has steadily increased since.[18] The state, for its part, was not retreating but engaging in a process of redeployment through the proliferation of independent regulatory agencies. As recourse to at-will employment increased and, later, a para-state sector responsible for public oversight of markets sprung up, new career opportunities started to emerge.

## 4.3 IN AND OUTERS: A GROUP PORTRAIT

What are the profiles and backgrounds of the individuals who took advantage of this decree between 1991 and 2017 and whose careers coincide with these structural changes? The first salient finding drawn from the database is gender: of 217 individuals, only 13 per cent are women. This finding indicates a social bias that has already been noted in earlier studies on the phenomenon of *pantouflage* – namely, the existence of a glass ceiling when it comes to the outward mobility of women belonging to the elite state corps.[19] Unlike their male counterparts with the same social background, women rarely cross from the public to the private sector. Likewise, they rarely occupy more than one post at a time, whereas interlocking relations are precisely a feature of the outwardly mobile elite.[20]

Another surprising finding is the age of the individuals. The subjects in our survey became lawyers between the ages of twenty-five and seventy-eight, with the average age being forty-seven. In the group, 59 per cent joined the Bar before the age of fifty, and close to one-third (29 per cent) before the age of

17 Marie-Christine Kessler, 'L'évasion des membres du Conseil d'État vers le secteur privé' in CURAPP (ed.), *Le Droit administratif en mutation* (Paris: PUF, 1993), pp. 122–138.

18 Eva Baradji, Dorothée Olivier and Erwan Pouliquen, 'L'encadrement supérieur et dirigeant dans les trois versants de la fonction publique' (Point Stat No. 17, DGAFP, February 2015).

19 Olivia Bui-Xuan, *Les Femmes au Conseil d'État* (Paris: L'Harmattan, 2001); Luc Rouban, 'L'accès des femmes aux postes dirigeants de l'État' (2013) 1 *Revue française d'administration publique*, 89–108.

20 The composition of the elite corps also mirrors the social stratification that is specific to the legal profession in France. Although women graduates from law schools in France outnumber men, they remain confined to certain kinds of practice, such as family law, and their careers are limited to subordinate positions in law firms. They rarely become partners. The legal specialisations and positions of the 'in and outers' we have studied are precisely those that in most cases are not readily accessible to women. See *Le Bulletin du Barreau de Paris*, Special Issue 'Femmes au Barreau' (March 2013).

forty. The under-forties group has become larger over time. The career of former prime minister Édouard Philippe (prime minister from 2017 to 2020) is typical in this respect. After graduating from ENA, Philippe joined the Conseil d'État in 1997. A few years later he was elected mayor of Le Havre, a medium-sized city, and also became the director-general of the main conservative party, UMP. In 2005, at the age of thirty-five, he joined an American law firm, Debevoise & Plimpton LLP, as counsel, and remained with the firm until 2007. He spent the next three years of his career with Areva, a French public sector undertaking in the energy industry. Thereafter, he returned to local and national public office until, in 2017, he was appointed prime minister. This back-and-forth (*pantouflage*, followed by *retro-pantouflage* back into government) between the private sector and public office is noteworthy; it is characteristic of many of the career paths we have studied and is typified by that of Édouard Philippe, who has continuously moved in and out of public (Conseil d'État, mayor, prime minister) and private (lawyer at Debevoise & Plimpton LLP, lobbyist for French multinational Areva, board member of French IT multinational Atos) positions. The subjects in our survey have increasingly fashioned their careers on this in-and-out basis.

Outwardly, this pattern is reminiscent of the earlier part of France's Fifth Republic (established under the constitution of 1958), when the careers of high-level civil servants often included stints in the state corporations spawned by mixed economy capitalism. The 1980s and 1990s saw waves of privatisation, and some of the corporations created at the time, like Areva (nuclear energy company), are still in existence.[21] Yet, beyond this similarity, the more recent 'in and outers' play by a new book incorporating features of a strand of old-style *pantouflage* that traditionally involved members of the Inspection des finances, one of the most elite corps of the state, along with those of the Conseil d'État and the Cour des comptes. Members of this corps are frequently recruited by banks and financial institutions at a young age.[22] Not only do these movements occur at an early point in their administrative careers, but they also offer the possibility of switching back and forth between the public and private sectors. None other than the current president of France,

[21] *Pantouflage* is in other cases a second career, just before or after retirement. In these cases, the switch to the private sector is backed up by the legitimacy acquired by high-level civil servants in the course of a long career in which they have held key positions. Several of the subjects in our survey followed this type of path, including eleven *préfets* (representatives of the interior ministry at departmental level in France) who became lawyers following their administrative careers.

[22] These recruits do not pass through law firms, and hence are absent from our database. Luc Rouban, 'L'Inspection générale des finances, 1958–2008: Pantouflage et renouveau des stratégies élitaires' (2010) 21 *Sociologies pratiques*, 19–34.

Emmanuel Macron, incarnates this type of profile. An ENA graduate, he joined the Inspection des finances in 2004, and four years later, aged thirty-one, moved to Banque Rothschild, becoming the youngest partner at the bank in 2010. Even by the standards of *pantouflage* as habitually practised by members of the Inspection des finances, thirty-one is an exceptionally young age at which to move into the private sector. And yet, in 2012 Emmanuel Macron returned to the public sector, which seemed to suggest that a spell in the private sector was no longer seen as a handicap but, on the contrary, conferred legitimacy and acted as a powerful lever for pursuing a prestigious career in public office. His return was via one of the foremost positions in the French Republic, deputy secretary-general of the office of the president, after which he was appointed minister of finance and ultimately elected president of the country in 2017. In other words, time spent in the private sector would appear to serve in acquiring legitimacy for high positions that previously would have been accessible only after a long career in the public sector.

Emmanuel Macron and Édouard Philippe both illustrate the search for legitimacy, through an increasingly visible and publicised stint in the private sector, that civil servants and politicians alike have progressively been pursuing as a way to bolster their careers in public service or office. The 'private' sector in which they navigate is a somewhat deceptive façade, a *trompe-l'oeil*, as it is largely composed of corporations that were formerly public undertakings and of major banks and blue-chip listed companies whose size and the scale of whose operations puts them more on a par with government ministries and administrations (with whom they often work) than with small and medium-sized businesses in the French economy. This passage through the private sector now also takes in the field of public-private mediation and advisory services, as evidenced by the law firm careers that are the particular focus of this study. These intermediate structures in the economy now emerge as privileged passageways serving as a source of legitimacy, so much so that moving back and forth between sectors has become an integral part of the new career paths sought by ENA graduates.

At first sight, 217 profiles might seem to be a fairly small sample, compared to the 8,000 top civil servants listed by the Haute Autorité pour la transparence de la vie publique or the yearly total of 150–250 moves by partners in Paris law firms. Qualitatively, however, the database is highly material. It is not by chance that it includes a former prime minister, as well as many examples of the 'elite of the elite' that have been instrumental in redrawing the contours of the state and public careers.

One segment of the sample is made up of individuals (mainly men) who originate from the top echelon of France's elite civil-service corps. Over half

(53 per cent) are ENA graduates. In addition, most followed a common path, as 88 per cent graduated from both ENA and Science-Po Paris, another prestigious Paris institution considered as the royal road to ENA. Furthermore, 45 per cent of the group were the top students of their class – known as *la botte* – which is a passport to employment in one of France's most elite corps of civil servants. These prized positions represent about 20 per cent of jobs obtained immediately upon graduation from ENA.[23] The Conseil d'État is an opening particularly sought after and one of the institutions that most often appeared in the careers we studied.

These top positions feature even more as careers develop. At some point, 60 per cent of these ENA graduates held jobs in a government ministry, which is double the average for their class as a whole, and most often they held key positions in cabinet offices. Whether due to the prominence of their posts (often chiefs of staff) or of their ministry or cabinet office (e.g. that of the president, the prime minister or finance ministry), the members of this group clearly constitute a highly elite stratum of the French civil service. Besides being closely connected to the political sphere, the members of this super-elite also have links with the private sector: some 20 per cent had spent time in major listed companies or former public corporations, which is twice the proportion for the other individuals in the database. Their profiles correspond to those of the most senior partners in law firms, rated as 'leading lawyers' in the 'top tear' by annual professional rankings. Such firms, many of which are French (e.g. Gide, Jeantet, August & Debouzy), are typically housed at some of the most prestigious addresses in Paris, close to the ministries and public institutions.

The profiles of the members of this super-elite confirm that their mobility towards law firms intersects with the summit of the state and its most prominent positions of power, and for this reason it is significant. It does not stop there, however, but extends to other areas of government administration, and to the political sphere as well. These facets, too, are of interest and indicative of the overall significance of the phenomenon. Two other typical pathways also stand out. Not surprisingly, the first of these is directly linked to work in a political capacity, as an elected official or member of an elected official's staff (e.g. a parliamentary aide). Secondly, we find career paths built on the accumulation of governmental and technical expertise, nurtured by the state's role as regulator. For the first category, experience of elected office or in a parliamentary assembly is more important than having attended ENA or worked in a cabinet ministry (of those individuals, 56 per cent are

[23] Rouban, 'L'accès des femmes'.

non-énarques). For the second category, what is important is to have held a technical position in government administration, or a quasi-governmental body or agency.

This class of public administrators consists not so much of professional politicians, but rather of civil service technocrats: 31.3 per cent had never held elective office, nor a position in a ministerial cabinet or as a political staff member. This is a group of public policy specialists, whose activities cover taxation, public procurement, competition policy, regulated sectors (telecommunications, transportation, energy, etc.) and strategic matters (defence, international contracts, etc.). Be they ENA graduates or not, these administrators (who more often than not are women – the proportion of women in this group being twice as high as the average across the entire database) are more likely to display their professional skills at various levels state regulatory activity.

Last point, experience in regulatory agencies is common to both ENA graduates and those who have not passed through ENA. A similar proportion of each (18 per cent of ENA graduates and 17 per cent of those who have not passed through ENA) had taken this route, which was made possible by the emergence of such bodies that have typified the regulatory state since the 1990s. The Autorité de la concurrence, the Autorité des marchés financiers and a host of sectoral agencies are most representative of these new career routes and the new delineation of the public and private sectors. In some careers a stint working in one of these institutions had been combined with a spell of varying duration at the venerable Conseil d'État, which shows that the state is present, both in its traditional forms and its more recent avatars.

## 4.4 THE PUBLIC-PRIVATE FOUNDATIONS OF THE FRENCH REGULATORY STATE

To properly understand public-private crossovers in career paths, we must look at the phenomenon in a fresh light. Although it typically remains below the radar of analysis, there is a need for elucidation. It might, for instance, be thought that the phenomenon is not new. In the late nineteenth and early twentieth centuries, at a time when the French Republic was branded a *République des avocats*,[24] the legal profession after all served as a prime

[24] In 1912, 30 per cent of *députés* were lawyers. After World War II the percentage fell considerably. An average of 12.8 per cent of parliamentarians were lawyers during the years 1945–1958, 7 per cent in the 1960s, and the proportion dropped to as low as 6 per cent in 1986. On this point, the classic reference is Mattei Dogan, 'Les professions propices à la carrière politique: Osmose, filières, viviers' in Michel Offerlé (ed.), *La profession politique: XIX*[e]*–XXI*[e] *siècles*

breeding ground for future politicians. However, political science traditionally views the relationship between the legal profession and the political and governmental spheres during that period in linear terms, as a one-way road, with the profession of lawyer being seen as a route of access to political office. But such a view does not account for the in and out movement that characterises the more recent crossover phenomenon. For one thing, most crossovers are in the opposite direction, as they involve people who have moved from politics or government into the legal sphere. Further, the highly mediatised transitions of Jean-François Copé and Dominique de Villepin are but the tip of an iceberg that likely comprises the entire body of high-level civil servants.

Just as the expressions 'breeding ground' and 'route of access' fail to capture the many forms of circulation between sectors, the term *pantouflage*, which traditionally refers to the 'departure' of top civil servants into the private sector, is an inadequate and somewhat eccentric term to use for this new mobility. The new in and out movement appears in the careers of people who are relatively young and it works both ways, into and out of the private sector. Unlike *pantouflage*, it is not confined to the civil servants of the tax inspectorate, and it designates more than merely high-level civil servants moving from one powerful position to another. It applies also to more ordinary career paths, to less prominent positions, to technicians and behind-the-scenes staff who turn the wheels of the state's regulatory apparatus and whose professional lives take them, quite naturally, from governmental bodies and public agencies to law firms at various stages in their careers or lead them to work on a daily basis with law firms.

It is clear that we are no longer in the era of hard separations between domains, and that we must devise new conceptual tools accordingly. To apprehend the different facets of the crossover phenomenon, it is more useful to think in terms of a circulatory space and of careers comprising cumulative activities. These new careers are shaped by the postmodern state,[25] that in the course of the past two decades has emerged at the very heart as well as on the fringes of the French Republic. At the same time as New Public Management policies were being adopted and a regulatory apparatus put in place, France's core institutions (the Élysée, Matignon, the Conseil d'État, the ministry of the economy, etc.) underwent modernisation, resulting in the emergence of a border zone in which the public and private sectors intersect. The public institutions involved in the regulation of the economy have not only

(Paris: Belin, 1999), pp. 171–199; see also Gilles Le Beguec, *La République des avocats* (Paris: Armand Colin, 2003).

25 Jacques Chevalier, *L'État post-moderne*, 3rd ed. (Paris: LDGI, 2014).

undergone internal change, they also increasingly turn to the services of financial and legal intermediaries from the private sector – consultants, bankers, business lawyers – to handle major contracts under public-private partnership arrangements and financial and banking transactions. This has in effect created a private sector market for advisory services to the state.[26] Conversely, companies have discovered the crucial market importance of vetting and approval procedures, compliance certification, market authorisation for products. and the protection of free competition. These procedures are supervised not only by the state's economic and fiscal authorities, but also by the numerous regulatory agencies which have been created over the past twenty years. These various procedures generally involve law firms, which act as privileged intermediaries in all sectors of the economy. This 'crossroads' is highly relevant to our understanding of the crossover phenomenon. Thus, a trend that in the early 1990s initially appeared to be limited to fiscal law and to involve just a few civil servants with a family background in law has since unceasingly expanded into new areas of legal practice (arbitration, competition law, public procurement, financial transactions, public affairs, etc.). During the past two decades, the transformation of the state has not simply renewed tools and procedures, it has also spawned new relationships between the public and private sectors. As a consequence, brand new career paths have opened up and new actors have come to the fore.

## 4.5 THE NEW BROKERING ROLE OF LAW IN-BETWEEN STATE AND MARKETS

At a time when the state's role as producer was diminishing – a downsizing that, for the elite in public administration, heralded severely reduced career opportunities within major nationalised companies – this new opening brought fresh possibilities for a career conversion. Initial cases of civil servants moving to law firms in the 1990s did not have any untoward consequences for the protagonists, which encouraged others to embark on this hitherto unexplored pathway. Indeed, in some instances those pioneers became recruiters for the next generation. Such examples refreshed ideas about what is possible and feasible in the course of a career, intensifying the attractivity dynamic and drawing new recruits.

The intersecting border space that has gradually formed between public law in business affairs (*droit public des affaires*) and the realm of 'public affairs' (lobbying, consulting, etc.) constitutes a new area of attraction. Thus, as the

[26] 'Le Conseil de l'État' (2012) 193–194 *Actes de la recherche en sciences sociales.*

state's role as regulator has grown in importance, so too has a politico-administrative elite, small in size but powerful due to its strategic position between the public service elites, the field of regulators, consultancy firms specialising in public affairs and major corporations in the private sector. This new elite is the standard-bearer of a new definition of the general interest.[27]

These public managers-turned-lawyers have in effect imposed themselves as pivotal brokers in control of this new border space where the public and private sectors come together. They are frequently called upon by administrative bodies to serve as experts on ministerial commissions or in working groups advising regulatory agencies or in informal consultations, and they continue to have privileged relationships with their former employers in the public sector. Indeed, many of them consider their new positions to be a continuation of their public service, though in another form. One of those we interviewed, an ENA graduate from an elite governmental corps, told us that he felt he was 'defending the general interest in the private sector'. Another example is the now dissolved firm Bruno Kern & Associés, whose then website touted its 'experience in high-level public administration, in Parliament and in Local authorities', to the point that the firm's associates parrot the jargon of administrative law to define their 'activity as lawyer as that of "auxiliaries in Public service"' in that in their advisory capacity they put the emphasis on their role as an 'aid to public decision-making'. In the words of one member of the Conseil d'État, it is as if they 'continue to advise the state, but more effectively', and indeed, this time according to Olivier Debouzy, 'as lobbyist in Brussels in fact fulfil a public service function'.[28]

It would be a mistake to dismiss this discourse as mere strategic self-promotion or an exercise in bad faith. Such a view would fail to take into account the existence of a third sector, now consolidated into a space encompassing public–private practices, which has generated its own norms, standards and models of excellence, distinct from the norms of each of the other two sectors, and has left its mark in novel institutional forms, events, publications, etc. Our concern here is not to suggest that in the private sector the former state employees do 'exactly the opposite of what they were paid to do in the public sector' (i.e. 'shield the company from eventual enquiries'),[29] or that they sell access to their address book, but to reveal the existence of this third sector where new beliefs in the mutual benefits of public-private partnerships now flourish. These benefits are said to be administrative effectiveness, better

[27] See also Avril in this volume.
[28] Olivier Debouzy, 'Lobbying: *The French Way*' (2003) 54 *Les notes de l'Ifri*, 5–23, p. 6.
[29] Service central de la prévention de la corruption, *Rapport annuel* (1990), p. 43.

career management for the elite corps of civil servants, fresh air for public service, etc. All the signs point to continuity. Frédéric Salat-Barroux, for example, who was the equivalent of the chief of staff to President Jacques Chirac, is part of the practice area described as 'French Public Law and Government Affairs' at the firm Weil, Gotshal & Manges LLP. Laurent Deruy, former auditor at the Cour des comptes, spent many years in Gide's 'Government & Public Sector' department, where he advised French and foreign public institutions and private corporations (Caisse des dépôts et consignations, SNCF, Voies navigables de France, etc.) and represented them in court. The phenomenon has grown broader and deeper and has picked up speed. Compare, for instance, the statement by a former tax department employee in 2014 that he was 'regularly and discreetly' consulted by his former office with the revelation four years later, in 2018, that a parliamentary bill had been written entirely by a law firm (which charged for its work). The public law partner concerned was of course a graduate of ENA, which caused a scandal among civil servants.[30]

This last case is the ultimate manifestation of the growing power of the public law, compliance, regulatory law and competition departments that have proliferated in Paris law firms over the past twenty years. It highlights the fact that in such firms these new 'in and outers' are carrying over functions and attributions that they previously held in the public sector, going even so far as to continue to draft legislation. In this context, their experience in the state apparatus is an integral part of their identity, and, tellingly, their business cards sometimes continue to vaunt this experience with wording such as 'Avocat à la cour – Diplômé de l'ENA', 'former minister', etc. These 'in and outers' portray the contours of lobbying *à la française*, characterized by the privileged access former civil servants have, officially or otherwise, to information and decision-making in the public sector and, even more significantly, the intimate knowledge of the everyday operation of government which constitutes their bureaucratic capital.[31] Here, we observe, on the one hand, law firms as new power brokers of relations between the public and private sectors[32] and, on the other, the emergence of novel career paths built around crossover mobility between the two.

30 *Le Monde* (29 November 2018).

31 Pierre Bourdieu, *On the State* (New York: Polity, 2015).

32 Talcott Parsons, *Essays in Sociological Theory* (New York: Free Press, 1964), pp. 370–385 (ch. 18, 'A Sociologist Looks at the Legal Profession'); Wright Mills, *The Power Elite* (1st ed., 1956; Oxford: Oxford University Press, 2000), pp. 288–289; Mark Miller, *The High Priests of American Politics: The Role of Lawyers in American Political Institutions* (Knoxville: University of Tennessee Press, 1995).

This trend is neither a step in a larger process of privatisation nor part of a process of state capture. Indeed, removing the border between the public and private sectors would not be in the interest of these former civil servants, for it is precisely to their advantage. The process at play here is rather one of consolidating the in-between space they have collectively shaped than ensuring the triumph of the private over public. The border is more than just a boundary line between the public and the private sectors, with some crossover points under their guard; In itself, it forms a hybrid and evolving space. The pertinence of our research is not to point to a hidden stage in the privatisation of the state and the transfer of public prerogatives to the private sector, and even less to explore just one aspect of the proximity of the public sector to lawyers and legal practice. Our data and observations reveal something else: an intermediary zone fashioned as a distinct and enduring social world, the fabric of which is woven of careers, discourses and institutions. Three decades of public/private rapprochement and liberalisation of the public sector have given birth to this third sector, a hybrid space on the confines between the public and private sectors which is becoming increasingly autonomous.

In sum, this chapter has shown how the neoliberal turn in French policies over the past three decades has profoundly blurred the public-private divide through its numerous manifestations: the formation of new circuits of *pantouflage* in-and-out of the state and in and out of the EU; the spectacular rise of state expertise within private law firms as they increasingly seize the new opportunities offered the emergence of the French regulatory state; and the development of an area of professional activity labelled 'public affairs', in which the law, law firms and lawyers have come to play a central brokering role between the EU, states and market players and whose force of attraction and transformative influence is increasingly felt on both sides of public-private divide in law firms, large companies, regulatory agencies, Commission DGs, etc.

While recognising the political risks a border zone of this type poses to democracy, our intention here is not to enter into the normative discussion such risks necessarily occasion.[33] Rather, the aim of the foregoing exploration is to draw attention to a hitherto neglected phenomenon, with a view to informing the contemporary debate on the deployment of (legal) expertise in decision-making, the prevention of conflicts of interest and the so-called moralisation of public life. Far from being a manifestation of institutional dysfunction and/or personal failing, the blurring of the lines between the

[33] For further developments, see Vauchez and France, *The Neoliberal Republic* as well as Antoine Vauchez, *Public* (Anamosa, 2022).

public and private sectors is now central to the normal workings of the state, especially in the context of its economic activity. In pointing to the shifting tectonic plates that underlie the public and private domains, this sociological and topographical survey underscores the systemic, as opposed to individual, nature of conflicts of interest. The prevention of such situations calls for thinking that goes well beyond the classical debate on the ethics of professions and professionals and must instead be directed towards a resolutely political reflection on the conditions underlying the proper functioning of democracy.[34]

[34] See Michael Walzer, 'Liberalism and the Art of Separation' (1984) 12(3) *Political Theory*, 315–330. For a general discussion of these issues we refer readers to the last chapter of our book *The Neoliberal Republic*.

# 5

# Legal Professionalism and (Legal) Expertise in EU Lawmaking

Hans-W. Micklitz

Two souls, alas, exist in my breast, one separated from another:
One, with its crude love of life, just clings to the world, tenaciously, grips tight,
The other soars powerfully above the dust into the far ancestral height

*J.-W. Goethe*[1]

## 5.1 . . . AND NOW THE LEGAL PROFESSION

The quote is not just for decorative purposes but expresses a personal dilemma. I feel torn between the sympathy for using law to initiate societal change, for improving society, and a growing concern for the long-lasting effect the instrumentalisation of law has on the legal profession, legal scholarship, and the law. My position is deeply rooted in my educational training and the rediscovery of the political dimension of the law in the late 1960s. My formative years as a law student left deep traces in my way of thinking, first in the theoretically grounded conviction that instrumentalising the law for social purposes is 'good', later in my awakening to question the over-instrumentalisation of the law and the reduction of the 'political'.[2] After my

I would like to thank Evgenia Ralli, PhD researcher at the EUI, for her constant support in the research, Thomas Roethe for clarifying the notion of legal professionalism, and Emilia Korkea-aho, Päivi Leino-Sandberg and the participants of the Helsinki conference for their comments and critique which allowed me to improve the paper. The usual disclaimer applies.

1 Johann Wolfgang von Goethe, 'Zwei Seelen wohnen, ach! in meiner Brust, die eine will sich von der andern trennen: Die eine hält in derber Liebeslust sich an die Welt mit klammernden Organen; die andre hebt gewaltsam sich vom Dust zu den Gefilden hoher Ahnen', www.iowagrandmaster.org/Books%20in%20pdf/Faust.pdf.

2 Stefano Bartolini, *The Political* (Colchester: European Consortium for Political Research, 2018); Hans-W.Micklitz, 'The Transformative Politics of European Private Law' in Poul Kjaer (ed.), *The Law of Political Economy* (Cambridge: Cambridge University Press, 2020), pp. 205–27.

studies, I spent much of my professional life developing and promoting social private law first at the national level, later at the European Union (EU) and international levels. My conviction was twofold: writing academic articles and books on social private law, whilst not losing contact with people and various civil society groups that support social justice causes and place their trust in public interest litigation. In Milosz's[3] well-known distinction between Alpha the Moralist, Beta the Disappointed Lover, Gamma the Slave of History, and Delta the Troubadour, I would probably classify myself then as a moralist. I believe(d) in the good cause of creating a better and more just German legal order, and later in the opportunities of building a European legal order with a social face.

In retrospect, two events influenced my self-understanding. The first was academic: a 1988 conference in Bremen on 'Critical Legal Thought',[4] where Bremen Law School proponents met critical legal studies scholars from US Ivy League law schools. The discussions on what role legal theory should play irritated my belief in the transformative power of law. The second event was political. At the beginning of the new millennium, the EU took three measures which changed its 'constitution'. In 2000, the Lisbon Summit made economic efficiency the key parameter of European integration; in 2001, the White Paper on Governance substituted integration through law with integration through governance; and in 2000, the Declaration of Fundamental Rights established a safety net to balance economic efficiency through constitutionalisation.[5]

From the turn of the century onwards, I have been increasingly concerned that the law's ability to initiate change through European integration has moved from social integration to focus on economic efficiency. All of the suggested transformations that worry me are not, of course, triggered by the EU but constitute part of a much larger, ongoing change in our economies, our societies, and our legal systems. The roots of this threefold transformation can be first traced back to the establishment of an international economic order in the aftermath of World War II, without which the legal design of the Treaty of Rome is hardly understandable. The development has continued leading to the decline of the welfare state and the rise of social regulation in the EU against the backdrop of the fall of the Berlin Wall, the collapse of the Soviet Empire, and the Eastern enlargement of the EU. Last but not least, the

3 Czeslaw Milosz, *The Captive Mind* (New York: Vintage, 1953).

4 Christian Joerges and David Trubek, 'Critical Legal Thought: An American-German Debate' (1989) 11 *Schriftenreihe des Zentrums für Europäische Rechtspolitik*, republished in a special issue: (2011) 12 *German Law Journal* 1–33.

5 Hans-W.Micklitz, *The Politics of Justice in European Private Law, Social Justice, Access Justice and Societal Justice* (Cambridge: Cambridge University Press, 2018), p. 180.

rise of neoliberalism in various forms has challenged social regulation and, more recently, information technology has begun redesigning the international economic order.[6] These economic, political, and social transformations have impacted the legal profession. In this professional upheaval, the EU serves as a catalyst and as an instigator. And I have turned from a moralist into a troubadour.

The present chapter, which looks at the effects of these transformations on the legal profession, is part of my studies on the impact of European integration and European law on legal methodology,[7] European legal scholarship,[8] European legal education,[9] European legal research,[10] and the integrity of the law.[11] There is a common denominator to their findings: the transformations should not only be understood as a threat but also as an opportunity for rethinking the role of law, not only EU law but also beyond. But in line with the focus of the edited collection, the present focus is on the EU. Do opportunities exist for the Europeanisation of the legal profession? Is the EU deconstructing and substituting the legal profession through legal expertise? Or is the suggested deconstruction, if there is any, paving new paths for a reconfigured legal profession? This chapter focuses on the lawmaking exercise, discussing the role of lawyers in EU lawmaking. It deliberately sets aside the role of lawyers in law enforcement, be it through the European Court of Justice (ECJ), the European Commission, or the European agencies. However, only the making and the enforcement of law together can provide a full picture of the transformation of the legal profession.[12]

[6] Richard Baldwin, *The Great Convergence: Information Technology and the New Globalisation* (Cambridge, MA: Harvard University Press, 2017).

[7] Hans-W. Micklitz with Rob Van Gestel, 'Why Methods Matter in European Legal Scholarship' (2014) 20(3) *European Law Journal* 292–316.

[8] Hans-W. Micklitz, 'A European Advantage in Legal Scholarship?' in Rob van Gestel, H.-W. Micklitz, and Ed Rubin (eds.), *Rethinking Legal Scholarship: A Transatlantic Dialogue* (Cambridge: Cambridge University Press, 2017), pp. 262–309.

[9] Hans-W. Micklitz, 'The Bifurcation of Legal Education: National vs Transnational' in Christopher Gane and Robin Huang (eds.), *Legal Education in the Global Context: Opportunities and Challenges* (Farnham: Ashgate, 2016), pp. 43–60.

[10] Hans-W. Micklitz with A. Villanueva, 'REFIT or Rethink: The Politics of EU Research: A Grand Misunderstanding?' in Esther van Schagen and Stephen Weatherill (eds.), *Better Regulation in EU Contract Law: The Fitness Check and the New Deal for Consumers* (Oxford: Hart Publishing, 2019), pp. 37–59.

[11] Hans-W. Micklitz, 'The Measuring of the Law through EU Politics', to be published in Marija Bartl et al. (eds.), *Beyond Methods: The Politics of Legal Research* (Cheltenham: Edward Elgar, 2021).

[12] The complementary analysis will be published in the *Festschrift for Stephen Weatherill* with Oxford University Press in 2023.

## 5.2 SOCIAL CHANGE, THE LEGAL PROFESSION, AND LEGAL EXPERTISE

My analysis begins with the adoption of the Single European Act (SEA) in 1986. The SEA constituted a breaking point in the development of the EU. It integrated social regulation into the EU legal order and enabled majority decision-making. The revised treaty paved the way for the elaboration of a significant amount of secondary EU law, not only but also in the field of social regulation, labour law, non-discrimination law, and consumer law. European legislation is today estimated to consist of 170,000 pages, of which over 100,000 pages have been produced in the last ten years.[13] This shows that the EU institutions have turned into one of the most important legislators around the world, interfering with ever broader areas of the economy and the society.

The sheer amount of rules seems to suggest that the role of law and the legal profession has increased since 1986. However, in line with sociological research on the importance of the legal profession within the administrative state, it is hypothesised that the role of law and the legal profession has declined over the years.[14] More importantly, the EU, maybe much more than the nation state, advances the transformation of the legal profession through governance and the promotion of European integration 'without law'.[15] The EU's extensive reliance on experts and expertise in the lawmaking process has no doubt accelerated this process. Is Gamma – the slave of history – the archetype of the expert needed for this purpose, being the slave of the unquestioned need for ever-further European integration?

### 5.2.1 *Legal Scholarship and Legal Professionalism*

In 'An Advantage for European Legal Scholarship' I argued that there is a direct line from the attempt to transform society through law in the aftermath of 1968 towards the instrumentalisation of law in building a Europe beyond the market after the adoption of the Single European Act in 1986. I focused on

13 In their call for the MIREL 2018 workshop which is on file with the author, what the convenors call the Luxembourg Logic for AI Summit (LuxLogAI 2018), which took place on 17–26 September 2018, see https://luxlogai.uni.lu/.

14 Ole Hammerslev and Mikael Rask Madsen, 'The Return of Sociology in Danish Socio-Legal Studies: A Survey of Recent Trends' (2014) 10(3) *International Journal of Law in Context* at 403.

15 Christian Joerges, From Integration through Law to the De-legalisation of Europe: An Exercise in Sociological Jurisprudence and Economic Sociology, paper presented at the Conference on EU Constitutional Imagination: Between Ideology and Utopia, iCourts, University of Copenhagen, 1–2 November 2018 (on file with the author).

the rise of 'the Social', as Duncan Kennedy[16] calls it, and the role and function of law in the context of the European welfare state. I addressed specifically how EU Member States passed the bucket when the welfare state project began to run into difficulties. I argued against Reimann[17] that there is a distinct European legal advantage, which is a result of the openness of the European legal order and its experimental character. The latter is visible in the promotion of modes of governance that allow the EU to implement 'the Social' beyond the nation state through 'access justice' and 'societal justice'.[18]

I will use this analysis as a background to obtain a better understanding of the economic and political transformations and the key role that law played in them. These transformations influenced and still impact the legal profession. A clarification of what is meant by the legal profession is a necessary condition, to have a benchmark against which the transformation of the legal profession can be measured. There is a whole subsection in sociology that discusses what constitutes a profession, what might be understood by professionalism, and what these developments mean for the legal profession.[19] This is certainly not the place to delve deeper into the controversies and the lack of a common understanding. My take in the present context is influenced by the collaboration I have had with Thomas Roethe, with whom I conducted various socio-legal research projects,[20] and who in turn was inspired by Oevermann.[21]

Oevermann's critique of the sociological theories of professions is to argue not from the historical development of professions but from the problems arising with regard to an individual and collective life practice. There are crises to overcome and decisions to be taken even when sufficient justifications for them cannot be given. The need to make decisions in the absence of justifications is

16 Duncan Kennedy, 'Three Globalizations of Law and Legal Thought: 1850–2000' in David M. Trubek and Alavaro Santos (eds.), *The New Law and Economic Development: A Critical Appraisal* (New York: Cambridge University Press, 2006), pp. 19–73.

17 Matthias Reimann, 'The American Advantage in Global Lawyering' (2014) 1 *Rabels Zeitschrift für Ausländisches und Internationales Privatrecht* 1–36.

18 Micklitz, *The Politics of Justice in European Private Law, Access Justice, Social Justice and Societal Justice*.

19 For a useful overview on the sociology of professions, stressing the usefulness of Max Weber against taxonomic approaches, see Mike Saks, 'Defining a Profession: The Role of Knowledge and Expertise' (2012) 2(1) *Professions and Professionalism* 1–10.

20 Hans-W. Micklitz, Thomas Roethe, and Stephen Weatherill (eds.), *Federalism and Responsibility: A Study on Product Safety Law and Practice in the European Community* (London: Graham & Trotmann, 1994).

21 More generally see Ulrich Oevermann, *Strukturprobleme supervisorischer Praxis. Eine objektiv hermeneutische Sequenzanalyse zur Überprüfung der Professionalisierungstheorie* (Frankfurt: Humanities Online, 2010). The paragraph is the result of a discussion I had with Thomas Roethe on how to define and to explain the particularities of the legal profession.

the topos that has given rise to the evolution of professionalised professions – priests, lawyers, and physicians. In other words, professionalised action is the social place of the mediation of theory and practice under conditions of scientific rationality, that is, under the conditions of scientifically justified practical problem-solving. At the same time, professional action denotes a severe loss of personal autonomy of clients and reminds us that professional action occurs in situations that have rendered clients helpless. Professionals are brought in to find solutions for the client's problems.[22] Consequently, professionalised crisis resolution in systematic case reconstruction generates something new, since the previously workable routine is no longer effective. Professionalised action is therefore always innovative, by adding knowledge gained from case reconstruction to the existing knowledge. Social action by professionals simultaneously addresses the validity question of the decisions taken and leaves them for further examination, as has always been the case in human history. The structural logic of professionalised action is thus ultimately rooted in the independent and future-looking processing of validity questions.

Professionalised action of the three classical professions refers to three areas: 'law and justice', 'bodily and psychosocial integrity', as well as the 'methodically explicit examination of questions of validity and claims under the regulative idea of truth'.[23] Clients turn to the professional when they realise that they are about to lose their personal autonomy. This can be illustrated by the classical and immediately obvious example of the physician whom the patient asks for help. The physician is primarily concerned with diagnosis, then with aetiology, procuring therapy, and aftercare. The physician has to act even if there is no routine rule and no certified knowledge available. The same applies to lawyers. Social change constantly generates new problematic constellations for which predetermined legal rules and certified legal knowledge are not available. The legal profession is mandated to solve the conflict between a case and the rule to re-establish the client's personal autonomy in consent with society. In a sense, legal professional action compares to problem-solving therapy in a normative reality. At the same time, the singular case solution results in a gain for the profession.

In addition to the professions discussed, there are two other special forms of 'professionalised professions': scientists and artists whose client is society as a whole. I will leave aside artists with their claim to truth and instead focus on

22 For the importance of the client for professionals, see also Yong, Chapter 7 in this volume.

23 Ulrich Oevermann, 'Theoretische Skizze einer revidierten Theorie professionalisierten Handelns' in Arno Combe and Werner Helsper (eds.), *Pädagogische Professionalität* (Frankfurt am Main: Suhrkamp 1996), pp. 70–183.

science with the same mandate. In scientific action – for present purposes, legal scholarship – legal scientists are supposed to apply the rule-governed verification methods of general legal knowledge that is subject to scrutiny by the whole legal academic community. This is not to claim that there is one objective truth or to defend legal positivism.[24] Rather the point is that legal scholarship or legal scientific action in the language of sociologists is submitted to a constant and ongoing verification and self-affirmation process within the scientific community.[25] Society funds science to eliminate false certainties such as superstitions (lightning and thunder as an expression of the wrath of the gods) and encourage permanent criticism in a bid to check and falsify again and again all scientific results worked out so far.[26] Progressive knowledge, establishing provisional certainty, is documented in new theories.[27] Society as a client is provided with new knowledge to revise the way of life. Revised collective life practices create new problematic situations requiring constant questioning. This applies to both natural and social sciences, and therefore also to the law as legal scientific action.[28]

### 5.2.2 *The Need for a 'Different' Lawyer*

Whatever understanding one might have of the legal profession, there is overall agreement in scholarship that the rise of the administrative state (here used as a synonym for the welfare state) requires a 'different' lawyer with 'different' knowledge and 'managerial skills'.[29] This different lawyer is not

[24] Duncan Kennedy, 'The Hermeneutics of Suspicion in Contemporary American Legal Thought' (2014) 25 *Law and Critique* 91–139.

[25] Josef Esser, *Vorverständnis und Methodenwahl in der Rechtsfinding* 1970 (Frankfurt on main: Suhrkamp, 1970). On Esser in particular, see Stefan Grundmann, 'The Inside and the Outside of the Law' in Stefan Grundmann, Hans-W. Micklitz, and Moritz Renner (eds.), *New Private Law Theory: A Pluralist Approach* (Cambridge: Cambridge University Press, 2020), p. 35.

[26] Karl Popper, 'A Note on Tarski's Definition of Truth' (1955) 64 *Mind*; Pavel Tichý, 'On Popper's definitions of verisimilitude' (1974) 25(2) *The British Journal for the Philosophy of Science* 155–60; David Miller, 'Popper's Qualitative Theory of Verisimilitude' (1974) 25(2) *The British Journal for the Philosophy of Science* 166–77.

[27] Thomas Kuhn, *The Structure of Scientific Revolutions* (Chicago: University of Chicago Press, 1962).

[28] In a similar direction David Kennedy, 'Law, Expertise and Global Political Economy' (2018) 23(1) *Tilburg Law Review* 116.

[29] John Flood and Peter D. Lederer, 'Becoming a Cosmopolitan Lawyer' (2012) 80 *Fordham Law Review* at 2513; Michael Martinek, 'Der Eurojurist: Zum Paradigmenwechsel in der deutschen Juristenausbildung vom national-staatlichen Justizjuristen zum kosmopolitischen Rechtsmanager' (2013) 30 *Ritsumeikan Law Review* at 203.

the practising lawyer applying rules to cases such as the judge or the attorney-at -law. When sketching the contours of this new lawyer type, one should keep in mind the description of legal scholarship and legal scientists. Their client is, as noted, society. Moreover, these legal scientists need to have specialised knowledge in fragmented fields of the law and managerial skills outside of the legal profession and the traditional legal education, which favours the generalist. The managerial competence that the administrative state seems to call for favours the integration of business administration into legal education and law.

In the administrative state, legal drafting is done by ministries and, at the European level within their functional equivalents, the various general directorates of the European Commission. This chapter is not the place to evaluate the history of the administrative state and the role and changing function of lawyers and the legal profession. As a shorthand, I rely on recent sociological research.[30] This research has analysed the decline of the legal profession, which goes hand in hand with the involvement of other scientific disciplines.

Research in the United States serves as a helpful starting point. Across the Atlantic, lawyers have to struggle for their position and accept that a law degree is no longer a guarantee for an outstanding position in interdisciplinary committees and working groups.[31] Lawyers are just like any other expert. The emergence of big law firms has also changed the landscape. Lawyers who are looking for a job have the choice between Scilla und Charybdis, between meeting the requirements of the administrative state or meeting similar requirements in big law firms. According to US research, law firms are moving away from classical politics of professionalism towards a new business culture, where lawyers turn into the 'handmaiden' or the consigliere of 'economic efficiency'.[32] The result is the de-professionalisation of legal practice and a loss of professional autonomy.[33] In the process, they lose their

30 Hammerslev and Madsen, 'The Return of Sociology in Danish Socio-Legal Studies: A Survey of Recent Trends' at 403.

31 See with regard to intra-company structures, Martin Heidenreich, 'Berufskonstruktion und Professionalisierung: Erträge der soziologischen Forschung' in Hans Jürgen Apel, Klaus-Peter Horn, Peter Lundgreen, and Uwe Sandfuchs (eds.), *Professionalisierung pädagogischer Berufe im historischen Prozess* (Bad Heilbrunn: Klinkhart, 1999), pp. 35–58.

32 Hammerslev and Madsen, 'The Return of Sociology in Danish Socio-Legal Studies: A Survey of Recent Trends' at 406; Lederer and Flood, 'Becoming a Cosmopolitan Lawyer' at 19–20.

33 Nick Frost, 'Professionalism and Social Change: The Implications of Social Change for the Reflective Practitioner' in Helen Bradbury, Nick Frost, Sue Kilminster, and Miriam Zukas (eds.), *Beyond Reflective Practice: New Approaches to Professional Lifelong Learning* (Abingdon: Routledge, 2010), who stresses that changes must be placed in the wider context of globalisation, informationalisation, networking, and managerialism. The results, among

capacity to act as problem-solving therapists, as Oevermann would describe them, and to find consensus in that process. Lawyers working in big US firms abandon their roles as intermediaries between state and society.[34] The price for the high salaries is dissatisfaction with the type of work entrusted to them.[35]

To my knowledge, there is no similar empirical research on the transformation of the legal profession through the administrative state at the Member State level or through the EU being understood as a quasi-administrative state. In light of the above findings, one might, however, assume that similar transformations of the legal profession are occurring within the EU more generally, and particularly within the European Commission.[36] Today's EU lawyers compete with other disciplines for the same position in internal administrative committees or working groups. This competition with other experts has led to the situation where the legal profession – in order to do well in competition – forfeits its autonomy in the dialectically contradictory unity of case and rule. The hypothesis then is that the legal scholars working in and for the EU administration are no longer abiding by Oevermann's standards of professionalised professions. Assuming that this consideration is correct, it would necessarily lead to the de-professionalisation of lawyers that transforms them into 'experts'. Lawyers that have traditionally assumed the role of mediators of case and rule are being transformed into experts who have special knowledge of rules in this or that question, but must, or indeed are required to fail in the perception of social reality to obey with the political agenda of the administration. The legal experts in the administrative state are bound to the respective European political agenda, nowadays the claimed neoliberal agenda of the Lisbon Summit. One might therefore hypothesise that the EU administration could be compared to big US law firms.

### 5.2.3 *The European Commission Rules on Expertise*

The gateway to transforming the legal profession has been the establishment of the EU expert as a genuine European figure. There is abundant literature on what counts as an expert and how the rise of expertise is jeopardising

others, include the loss of professional autonomy, as well as being inspected and checked all the time and needing to update skills and expertise constantly.

34 Larry E. Ribstein, 'The Death of Big Law' (2010) 749 *Wisconsin Law Review*, discussing de-professionalisation at 767, see also Robert A. Brooks, *Cheaper by the Hour: Temporary and the Deprofessionalisation of the Law* (Philadelphia: Temple University Press, 2013); Dana A. Remus, 'Out of Practice: The Twenty-First-Century Legal Profession' (2014) 63 *Duke Law Journal* 1243.

35 Alex M. Johnson Jr., 'Think Like a Lawyer, Work Like a Machine: The Dissonance between Law School and Law Practice' (1991) 64 *Southern California Law Review* 1231.

36 See Bradford, Chapter 8 in this volume.

democracy. For instance, Tannelie Blom distinguishes between the different disciplines and their contribution to the study of experts and expertise: sociologists (expertness as ascribed quality), cognitive scientists (domain specific experience), decision-making researchers (expertise as politics), political scientists (focus on the use of expertise), and social psychologists (hidden profiles paradigm with a focus on shared instead of unshared information).[37] The legal scholarship's contribution is missing. She advocates for an information-based processing approach following a fivefold differentiation: (1) subject matter expertise, (2) political expertise, (3) procedural expertise, (4) policy expertise, and (5) expertise on experts.[38] In her approach, there is no differentiation between expertise and legal expertise. Instead, legal expertise is just one possible competence that is integrated into the information-based processing approach. As shown below, her fivefold distinction fits the way in which the European Commission has institutionalised expertise through procedural rules and substantive requirements.

Although difficult to empirically prove, it has been claimed that expert groups were part of the European Commission from its founding.[39] Over time, the system of experts has been extended, which is evident in the increasing number of expert groups in the European Commission.[40] Experts and expert groups form the largest organised information system in the EU.[41] Of particular relevance for today's understanding of the existing European rules on expertise are two documents from the European Commission both adopted in 2016: a framework for European expert groups[42] and the decision on their creation and operation.[43] The former explains the policy shift which goes back to political struggles between the European Commission, the European Parliament, and the

37 Tannelie Blom, 'Conceptualising the Role of Expertise in EU Policy-Making' in Vigjilenca Abazi, Johan Adriaensen, and Thomas Christiansen (eds.), *The Contestation of Expertise in the European Union* (Cham: Palgrave Macmillan, 2021), p. 21.

38 Ibid., pp. 35–6.

39 Julia Metz, *The European Commission, Expert Groups, and the Policy Process: Demystifying Technocratic Governance* (New York: Palgrave Macmillan, 2015).

40 Gornitzka and Sverdrup report a rise from 537 (in 1975) to 1237 (in 2007). See Åse Gornitzka and Ulf Sverdrup, 'Who Consults? Expert Groups in the European Union', Working Paper, No. 12, August 2007, www.sv.uio.no/arena/english/research/publications/arena-working-papers/2001-2010/2007/wp07_12.pdf, p. 13.

41 Ibid.

42 The current chapter will not discuss the role of experts and expertise within the European Parliament but will focus on the European Commission communication dated 30 May 2016, http://ec.europa.eu/transparency/regexpert/PDF/C_2016_3300_F1_COMMUNICATION_TO_COMMISSION_EN.pdf.

43 See http://ec.europa.eu/transparency/regexpert/PDF/C_2016_3301_F1_COMMISSION_DECISION_PLUS_ANNEXES_EN.pdf; http://europa.eu/rapid/press-release_IP-16-1923_en.htm.

European Ombudsman.[44] The latter defines the application, the selection procedure and criteria, and lays down a code of conduct for experts.[45] There is a website titled 'Become an Expert for the European Commission'[46] for scholars who would like to participate in the tendering. There is even a European Union of Experts – 'an association of former staff of the European Commission and other EU Institutions',[47] – and a model contract for experts who assist the EU in evaluating and monitoring EU funding programmes.[48]

There is no certification procedure but instead a registration procedure[49] or in some cases an application procedure. In the case of the registration procedure, an online portal exists under which a person (natural or legal) can create a profile. The profile is evaluated by the Commission that informs registrants by email whether they are selected for an assignment as an expert. The contracting process is entirely electronic via the 'Expert Area' on the participant portal.[50] The Commission departments may also open an application procedure through a specific call and make use of different types of application procedures such as various online platforms,[51] or even applications sent to a specific email address. The European Commission has created an entirely new 'field' of 'expertise': a club of 'experts', which supports it in the completion of tasks. These experts build a genuine community, the community of European experts, a microcosmos in itself. Not being an expert and not being registered means being excluded from the EU bureaucracy, whatever the field or the subject matter might be.

Despite the amount of rules on the different types of expert groups and different types of classification,[52] it is not easy to find substantive criteria of what constitutes an expert. The Commission decision on the creation and operation of Commission expert groups requires in Article 10 (5):

> When selecting the members of groups, Commission departments shall aim at ensuring, as far as possible, a high level of expertise, a geographical

44 Metz, *The European Commission, Expert Groups, and the Policy Process: Demystifying Technocratic Governance*.

45 See http://ec.europa.eu/research/participants/data/ref/h2020/experts_manual/h2020-experts-mono-contract_en.pdf. The code of conduct forms part of the model rules.

46 See https://ec.europa.eu/info/funding-tenders/become-expert-commission_en.

47 See www.euexperts.eu.

48 See http://ec.europa.eu/research/participants/data/ref/h2020/experts_manual/h2020-experts-mono-contract_en.pdf#page=27.

49 See http://ec.europa.eu/research/participants/portal/desktop/en/experts/index.html.

50 See https://ec.europa.eu/research/participants/portal/desktop/en/support/faqs/faq-369.html.

51 See http://ec.europa.eu/justice/grants1/priamos/index_en.htm.

52 See http://ec.europa.eu/transparency/regexpert/PDF/C_2016_3301_F1_COMMISSION_DECISION_PLUS_ANNEXES_EN.pdf, art. 25.

balance, as well as a balanced representation of relevant know how and areas of interest, taking into account the specific tasks of the expert group, the type of expertise required and the response received to calls for application.

Annex II is more elaborate: 'Proven and relevant competence and experience, including at European and/or international level, in areas relevant to . . . Proven capacity to represent effectively the position shared by stakeholders . . ..' The Code of Conduct in the Annex to the Model Rules clarifies how the work has to be performed:

> the expert must work independently, in a personal capacity, in the public interest and not on behalf of any organisation . . . perform his/her work to the best of his/her abilities, professional skills, knowledge and applying the highest ethical and moral standard.[53]

The rules are not made for legal experts, but for experts as such. Lawyers compete with other disciplines under the overall heading of 'expertise'. No discipline is excluded and all are treated equally. The EU rules do not specify what should be understood by 'professional skills', 'experience' and 'knowledge'. Read together, the rules suggest a distinction between 'the expert' and 'the professional'. An expert is a broader concept, which encompasses the professional. The examples provided for 'professionals'[54] (physicians, nurses, architects, engineers and lawyers), indicate that the profession is separated/detached from a specific policy area. Those who are no longer active professionals or members of the profession can still be registered and contracted as an expert.[55] Likewise, being considered a professional by educational standards does not mean that he or she is automatically regarded as an 'expert'. Expertise is bound to specific policy areas. The requirements for expertise are subject- and policy-bound, not education-bound. Through its call for expertise, the European Commission defines the policy field. The whole inner machinery of the EU is dependent on self-named and EU-certified experts. Each and everybody can name themselves an expert subject to evidence requirements. Through its selection process, the European Commission provides the 'expert' with a status.

In the above description, at least four out of Blom's five parameters are met, perhaps with the exception of expertise on experts. Experts need to demonstrate that they know the subject matter, and should have political expertise on

53 See http://ec.europa.eu/research/participants/data/ref/h2020/experts_manual/h2020-experts-mono-contract_en.pdf, the code of conduct forms part of the model rules.

54 See http://ec.europa.eu/transparency/regexpert/PDF/C_2016_3301_F1_COMMISSION_DECISION_PLUS_ANNEXES_EN.pdf, p. 20.

55 See https://ec.europa.eu/research/participants/portal/desktop/en/support/faqs/faq-367.html.

the role and function of the Commission, they should also have managerial competence which is what Blom understands as procedural expertise, and last but not least, they need to have policy expertise. Experts are not only nominated because of their knowledge of the field, but rather, should be able to take politics and policies into consideration. Expertise on experts, Blom's fifth parameter, does not feature in the Commission rules. Yet, one might easily imagine that such expertise is equally required, be it informally when it comes to communicating with the outside world or tendering procedures to find and nominate the experts in the field who could contribute to the execution of a study.

## 5.3 VARIATIONS OF PROFESSIONAL TRANSFORMATION

The following section of the chapter is meant to provide evidence for the claimed transformation of legal professionalism into legal expertise in European lawmaking. Subject-wise, the findings concern European Economic Law and European Private Law, but the findings are claimed to be paradigmatic for lawmaking in other legal and policy fields, too. Methodologically speaking, the findings combine oral history and empirical, mostly qualitative, research. The variations are linked to my personal experience and involvement in the European integration process as a scholar of EU lawmaking. This way it is a living history and bears a subjective character, which is conditioned to the control of the scientific community.

The overall claim is that the rise of legal expertise downgrades the legal profession to a service provider within the European lawmaking machinery under the guidance of the European Commission. Until the new millennium, the role of law, lawyers and legal expertise remained by and large uncontested. As noted above, this changed at the beginning of the new millennium with the three key documents, the Lisbon Summit, the White Paper on Governance and the Charter for Fundamental Rights. The transformation of legal professionalism (and the legal profession) to legal expertise (and experts) in lawmaking has to be understood as being part of this much larger process, which changed the constitutional outlook of the EU as a whole.

### 5.3.1 *The Self-Understanding of Legal Scholarship in EU Lawmaking*

The personal element of what I discuss below calls for critical self-reflection on the role and function that the European legal scholarship played in the European integration process right from the beginning. Walter Hallstein famously and influentially stated in 1969: 'The European Community is a remarkable legal phenomenon. It is a creation of law; it is a source of law; and it is a legal system'.[56] The formula underlines the key role of law and of the legal profession. Hallstein had in mind the Treaty of Rome and the European Court of Justice that turned a supranational treaty into an autonomous legal order based on supremacy and direct effect.[57] This second generation of EU lega scholars (to which I belong) entered the European legal field exactly at a moment in time when the national welfare states were on the decline, and when the EU took over the 'Social' from the Member States through the Single European Act. Law was perceived as a means to establish a better and more just society. The search for the optimistic spirit of this generation of European lawyers who devoted their career to promote European integration through social regulation takes us to the 1960s and the 1970s. The epistemic community was driven by the enthusiasm and the strong belief in what J. H. Weiler has called the EU DNA, that is, Europe's messianism;[58] the conviction that European integration is 'good' for the citizens and the European people, not only for peace through trade but also for building Europe with a 'social face'. This was the language used to legitimate the Single European Act in 1986.[59] What kind of impact did that spirit have on legal professionalism and the legal profession in general?

In June 2017, I organised a conference at the European University Institute in Florence on the 'Mothers and Fathers of Consumer Law and Policy'.[60] The participants were all heavily involved in building national consumer law in their home countries and later in the establishment of consumer law in the EU. The spirit of the times is well-documented by the following statement of Thierry Bourgoignie made in June 2017. He draws a parallel between the years 1968 and 1986, and the use of consumer law for the building of a better society:[61]

[56] Walter Hallstein, *Europe in the Making* (originally published in German under the title *Der unvollendete Bundesstaat* (ECON, 1969)) (London: George Allen & Unwin Ltd., 1972), p. 30.

[57] Eric Stein, 'Lawyers, Judges and the Making of a Transnational Constitution' (1981) 75 *American Journal of International Law* 1–27.

[58] Joseph H. H. Weiler, 'Deciphering the Political and Legal DNA of European Integration: An Exploratory Essay' in Juliet Dickson and Pavlos Eleftheriadis (eds.), *Philosophical Foundations of European Union Law* (Oxford: Oxford University Press, 2012), pp. 137–58.

[59] More generally on the role of Euro-lawyers, Antoine Vauchez, *Brokering Europe, Euro-Lawyers and the Making of a Transnational Polity* (Cambridge: Cambridge University Press, 2015).

[60] Hans-W. Micklitz, Ewoud Hondius, Thom van Mierlo and Thomas Roethe (eds.), *The Mothers and Fathers of Consumer Law and Policy in Europe, The Foundational Years 1950–1980* (Florence: EUI, 2019), available at http://hdl.handle.net/1814/63766.

[61] Thierry Bourgoignie in Micklitz, Hondius, van Mierlo and Roethe (eds.), *The Mothers and Fathers of Consumer Law and Policy in Europe*, p. 55.

> In fighting for consumer policy both at national level and at the EU level I think you mentioned this distinction between protecting consumers against market forces or protecting consumers through market forces. That for me is a very right way to reflect the different objective we have been following. Personally, when I started I really wanted to fight against market forces. There is a radical approach in my thesis in 1988.[62] I had been criticized by many as being too leftish and too radical with a Marxist analysis of the market operation and for me that was the goal. That was the ultimate goal. Trying to correct markets failures for me was a very reformist approach; why to make the market better operating if the market exploits or cheats consumers? Let's change the paradigma so for me there is a link with the student movement. I was politically very much engaged in the student movement . . .

He continues,

> Remember at that time there is also a Vietnam war. So this was a kind of Anti-Americanism. Not to import into Europe the same capitalism that was in the US. I was educated on consumer law in the US. I was at Yale and this is where I studied consumer law. When I decided to come back to Europe I was absolutely decided not to see in Europe the same type of capitalism as it was there so this was behind all the investment. The same in the EU. When I see the EU started developing the internal market I had exactly the same approach, I said we have to fight so that this internal market is not the predominant, is not the only, is not the exclusive objective of all EU integration process. We will have to harmonize all because there is not internal market if there is no harmonization. So we have to fight as lawyers so that harmonization is among the highest denominators and so that consumer protection policy is not just a byproduct of the internal market policy which it was.

The anchoring of consumer law and policy in the national legal order and even more at the European level was regarded as a political project. Law should tame the market power and provide for the rights of the weaker parties that were by that time mostly the workers and consumers. Whilst some of the more theoretical conceptual theories bore an anti-capitalist undertone, in essence the political project of European integration through social regulation was one of social democratisation as F. Scharpf[63] has termed it. The second generation EU lawyers were deeply involved in promoting European

62 Thierry Bourgoignie, *Éléments pour une théorie du droit de la consommation. Au regard des développements du droit belge et du droit de la Communauté économique Européenne, Collection Droit et Consommation* (Brussels: Story Scientia, 1988).

63 Fritz W. Scharpf, *Governing in Europe: Effective and Democratic?* (Oxford and New York: Oxford University Press, 1999).

integration through social regulation, united in the belief for the good cause. Over time this spirit has been lost. The failure of the two grand projects that were meant to transform the EU into a quasi-state – the European Constitution and the European Civil Code in 2004/2008 – served as a wake-up call for many to distance themselves from the European integration project, not least because of its 'justice deficit', both with and without a question mark.[64] Much of the fundamental critique comes close to the strong language Thierry Bourgoignie is using, blaming the overtly strong focus on the internal market to the detriment of the citizens, on market integration instead of social integration.[65]

What then is the relationship between the 1968/1986 spirit and the transformation of the legal profession? Has the input that lawyers provided to European lawmaking in the belief of creating a better and more social Europe eroded legal professionalism and paved the way for the rise of the expert? Is there a contradiction between legal professionalism and fighting for a good cause? Oevermann's answer would be that as long as legal scientists – legal scholars – abide by the rules of legal professionalism, these rules being the constant need for rule-governed verification of general knowledge, such danger does not exist. In Milosz's language, the only role that lawyers could play is that of a troubadour, a role that I personally have also come to assume. In my perspective, and relying on theories of professionalism and professions, the real test is, however, autonomy. The legal profession may voluntarily give up its autonomy, or it may be squeezed into the rationality of the EU administration. One might therefore suggest that autonomy requires mutual respect for the boundaries and the different responsibilities on both sides, the 1968/1986 epistemic community and the EU administration.

In what follows I will discuss the interaction in lawmaking between the epistemic community of legal scholars with the European Commission. The chosen example demonstrates the shift from a spirit of cooperation towards the model of service providers, hand in hand with the decline of legal professionalism and the rise of legal expertise. A similar story could be told from the way in which the European Commission transformed the organisation of legal

64 The different voices are very well presented in Dimitry Kochenov, Gráinne de Búrca and Andrew Williams (eds.), *Europe's Justice Deficit?* (Oxford: Hart Publishing, 2015). The question mark goes back to Gráinne de Búrca as is spelt out by the editors in the introduction.

65 Gareth Davies, 'Freedom of Contract and the Horizontal Effect of Free Movement Law' in Dorota Leczykiewicz and Stephen Weatherill (eds.), *The Involvement of EU Law in Private Law Relationships* (Oxford: Hart Publishing, 2013), pp. 53–70; Marija Bartl, 'Internal Market Rationality, Private Law and the Direction of the Union: Resuscitating the Market as the Object of the Political' (2015) 21 *European Law Journal* 572–98.

research into a scientific element in lawmaking process. The complex tendering process removed research institutions and universities out of the cooperative relationship with the European Commission to the benefit of consultancy firms as service providers. Legal professionalism is substituted through (legal) expertise.[66]

### 5.3.2 *Cooperation, Legal Professionalism and EU Lawmaking: The Example of ECLG*

In 2014, Sophie Jacquot investigated the merger of two legal expert groups – gender equality and non-discrimination, using four parameters for getting to grips with the changing functions of expert groups of the European Commission.[67] These four are: (1) instrumental – in strengthening its capacity to act, (2) legitimising – in increasing its legitimacy through the reliance on external legal expertise, (3) substantive – in using legal expertise strategically to justify and inform its texts and (4) evangelising – in carrying the European mission into national contexts, and participating in the acculturation and acceptance of expertise. She compares the four functions with regard to before and after the merger. Her conclusion is that the merger affected the four functions heavily, with each of them decreasing through the merger. Her conclusion is that the merger transformed former partners into service providers. This finding can easily be supported by similar developments in the field of consumer law, to which we turn now as an example for the changing role of lawyers in EU lawmaking.

The European Consumer Law Group (ECLG) was established in 1977. The European Commission provided financial support to finance the biannual meetings in Brussels. The members worked pro bono. The ECLG brought together two representatives per Member State, a representative from academia and one from national consumer organisations. The group was not limited to Member States. Prospective Member State representatives who joined the EU later – such as Greece, Finland, Portugal and Sweden – also participated, as did the representatives from non-EU countries like Switzerland. The authors and contributors of the series edited by N. Reich

66 I have analysed the transformative change elsewhere, see Micklitz with Villanueva, 'REFIT or Rethink – The Politics of EU Research – A Grand Misunderstanding?', pp. 37–59; Hans-W. Micklitz, 'The Intellectual Community of Consumer Law and Policy in the EU' in Hans-W. Micklitz (ed.), *The Making of Consumer Law and Policy in Europe* (Oxford: Hart Publishing, 2021).

67 Sophie Jacquot, 'Small Decisions? The European Commission and the Transformation of the Role of Legal Expert Groups: The Case of Gender Equality and Non-Discrimination' (2020) 58(3) *Journal of Common Market Studies* 1–17.

on 'Consumer Protection Law in the Nine Member States', formed the academic core of the ECLG.[68] Until the mid-1980s, English and French were the working languages of the ECLG.

The ECLG had no status in the lawmaking procedure. It was a non-institution: there was no 'inaugurational decree' nor was it a registered association; it had no bylaws and was not appointed as an 'expert group'. Its power, if there was any at all, resulted from arguments and from the knowledge on national consumer laws collected through the participation in the research studies initiated by the European Commission. The key to understanding the ECLG is the exceptional symbiosis between Commission officials and legal scholars as experts. The ECLG was involved in the drafting procedure of consumer legislation, prior to the publication of a proposal in the Official Journal and prior to official hearings being organised by the Assembly and the European and Economic Social Committee. The intellectual exchange worked ad persona, through mutual trust and recognition of divergent positions. Key figures of the European Commission participated in the biannual meetings held in Brussels, oftentimes together with the Commission official in charge of elaborating the first draft. The size of the group, fifteen to twenty people, allowed for an open exchange notwithstanding the status of the members and their country of origin. Academics and practitioners did not speak with one voice. There was no 'us' (the national representatives) against 'them' (the European Commission). The practice came close to the domination free discourse (*herrschaftsfreier Diskurs*) Habermas had in mind.[69] In Jacquot's terminology, the ECLG and the European Commission cooperated on an equal level, with mutual respect and for a common cause.

It is hard to find evidence that allows evaluation of what happened over the years; whether the European Commission got corrupted like Steindorff seemed to suggest when he spoke pejoratively of 'the consumer circles'.[70] This would imply that the European Commission had taken over the ECLG positions, especially those that were advocating for the primacy of social regulation over market integration. As a group, the ECLG operated through 'opinions' to be agreed on between its members. Fortunately, the Centre de Droit de la Consommation in Louvain-la-Neuve had published the opinions of the ECLG in two reports, from 1977 to 1984 and 1986 to 1997.[71] A careful

68 Norbert Reich and Hans-W. Micklitz, *Consumer Legislation in the EC Countries – A Comparative Analysis* (New York: Van Nostrand Reynolds, 1980).

69 Jürgen Habermas, *Theorie des kommunikativen* (Frankfurt: Suhrkamp, 1981).

70 Ernst Steindorff, *EG-Vertrag und Privatrecht* (Baden-Baden: Nomos, 1996).

71 European Consumer Law Group, Reports and Opinions, September 1977–March 1984 Rapports et avis Septembre 1997–March 1984, Centre de Droit de La Consommation

reading reveals that the first part of the opinions was produced far ahead of the legislative measures. This changed over the years of the ECLG's work. The modus operandi of the ECLG changed from ex-ante consultation to ex-post reaction and criticism. The latter does not reflect the cooperation mode anymore, but neither does the change to ex-post commenting endanger the group's autonomy. Whether the exceptional symbiosis is in itself to be seen as a form of lost autonomy remains for the scientific community to decide. The end of the symbiosis, however, initiated a new relationship between external expertise and the European Commission.

In a first step, the European Commission stopped the institutional funding of the ECLG as an autonomous body, which combined professional lawyers and national practitioners. The group collapsed. The European Consumer Organisation (BEUC) managed to get funding from the European Commission, no longer to provide input into the lawmaking but to improve the enforcement of consumer law.[72] The European Commission reduced the input of consumer organisations and consumer lawyers in lawmaking by establishing a formal consultative body, the European Consumer Policy Advocacy Group,[73] formerly the Consumer Consultative Committee.[74] Here the abovementioned rules on the appointment on experts and expert groups apply.

The Consumer Policy Advisory Group is composed of fifty-five Members. These include (1) six to eight EU level consumer organisations and other entities representing relevant consumer, civil society or special interest groups, such as the elderly, disabled, youth, educators, users or regulators of financial,

(Brussels: E. Story-Scientia, 1986); European Consumer Law Group, Reports and Opinions, Rapport et Avis 1986–1997 (Brussels: E. Story-Scientia, 1997).

72 Geraint Howells and Hans-W. Micklitz, 'Consumer Law Enforcement Forum Project, Guidelines for Consumer Organisations on Enforcement and Collective Redress', September 2009, available at www.mpo.cz/assets/dokumenty/40585/45442/550298/prilohaoo1.pdf. Consumer Justice Enforcement Forum, prepared with the support of Geraint Howells and H.-W. Micklitz, 'Guidelines for Enforcement on Consumer Rights', 2013, Consumer Justice Enforcement Forum prepared with the support of Evelyn Terryn, Geraint Howells and Hans-W. Micklitz, 'Enforcement of Consumer Rights: Strategies and Recommendations' 2016, available at www.beuc.eu/publications/beuc-x-2016-051_cojef_ii-enforcement_of_consumer_rights.pdf.

73 73/306/EEC: Commission Decision of 25 September 1973 relating to the setting up of a Consumers' Consultative Committee OJ L 283, 10.10.1973, pp. 18–19, which brought together representatives from four different branches at the European level: consumer organisations, family organisations, cooperatives and trade unions, see Ludwig Krämer, *EWG-Verbraucherrecht*, Vol. 118 (Baden-Baden: Nomos 1985), see https://ec.europa.eu/info/policies/consumers/consumer-protection/our-partners-consumer-issues/european-consumer-consultative-group-eccg_en.

74 See www.mpo.cz/assets/en/consumer-protection/information-for-consumer-organisations/consumer-consultative-committee/2021/1/Open-call-for-applications–Consumer-Policy-Advisory-Group.pdf.

telecommunication, energy or other services or sectors with public service aspect (e.g. transport), local and community initiatives; (2) one consumer organisation per each Member State, chosen to hold an adequate level of experience and expertise, able to perform an advisory role to the Commission; (3) ten to twelve industry associations and organisations representing European businesses and other economic operators with commercial activities directly interacting with European consumers and accounting for an important part of EU private consumption; and (4) four to six experts, professionals or members of academia with suitable/relevant expertise. The agenda is determined by the respective action plans of the European Commission. The European Commission appoints the members, in line with the above-mentioned recruitment rules. Legal expertise is not a mandatory requirement. In addition to the Advisory Group, there are three special expert groups, dealing with safety, non-food products and finance.[75] Membership varies in line with the particular design of the expert group. Experts can be scholars, practitioners, and the group can be mixed bringing together different stakeholders or focusing just on enforcement authorities, like in the consumer safety group. These special expert groups are institutionally and functionally different from the former ECLG. They are interdisciplinary service providers, not cooperative partners, inculcated in the values of (legal) professionalism.

## 5.4 IS THERE A BRIGHT SIDE TO THE TRANSFORMATION?

The analysis seems to suggest both theoretically and empirically that the European integration has not only created but has also accelerated the transformation of the legal profession in EU lawmaking. I belong to the second (older) generation of lawyers educated at a turning point of legal education in the late 1960s in Europe. Thus, I have the two souls in my breast: my training as a professionalised professional observes the downgrading of the legal profession and the rise of (legal) expertise in lawmaking with concern; my commitment to the 'Social' and my scepticism against legal positivism supports the use of the law for establishing a better and more just society.

My inner conflict leads me to the following question: Is there something good in the transformation of the legal profession in lawmaking, the loss of its outstanding role in European integration through law, in the rise of political science and economics, in the growing importance of interdisciplinarity in expert groups and working committees? Katharina Pistor concludes her book *The Code of Capital*

75 See https://ec.europa.eu/info/policies/consumers/consumer-protection/our-partners-consumer-issues/consumer-expert-groups_en.

with preliminary thoughts on what a coding of the law could look like. The future law should avoid the pitfalls she convincingly describes and which are caught in the subtitle of the book: *How the Law Creates Wealth and Inequality*.[76] In my context, the subtitle would portray the creation of a European law that deepens the gulf between market integration and social regulation and further drives inequality in the EU. Is there anything to be done about the deepening of the gulf? In my view, integrating economics, politics and psychology into EU lawmaking provides for an opportunity to develop European law and a European lawyer who takes the power of wealth creation and inequality through law seriously. But what does it mean for 'law' and 'the society' if the lawyer as the professionalised professional ceases to exist in the lawmaking process? It appears as if the effects can be studied already today in the way in which EU law is drafted. This holds true for primary EU law but even more so for secondary EU law.[77] The regulations and directives, in particular in the regulated markets, quite often look more like policy programmes that provide little guidance for the administrative authorities who have to apply the law, let alone for European Courts.

This contribution has deliberately not discussed whether and to what extent the claimed transformation of the legal profession in lawmaking and the rise of legal expertise affects the European judiciary, attorneys and administrative authorities. The search for the new generation of lawyers might very well require a nuanced answer, distinguishing between lawmaking and law enforcement, between the role for lawyers in the making and in the application of EU law, between 'legal experts' and 'legal professionals' in law application. However, a word of caution is needed. EU law provides ample evidence of how the borderline between the making and the enforcement of law is getting blurred. European agencies tend to mix rule-making and enforcement, and European courts may turn into lawmakers in public interest litigation.[78] A more nuanced analysis is needed. But it will not be an easy exercise.

76 Katharina Pistor, *The Code of Capital: How the Law Creates Wealth and Inequality* (Princeton: Princeton University Press, 2019).

77 See the early concern of Ernst-Joachim Mestmäcker, 'Auf dem Wege zu einer Ordnungspolitik für Europa' in Ernst-Joachim Mestmäcker, Hans Möller and Hans Peter Schwartz (eds.), *Eine Ordnungspolitik für Europa. Festschrift für Hans von der Groeben* (Baden-Baden: Nomos, 1987), pp. 9–49 with regard to the different language in the Single European Act in comparison to the Rome Treaty, on the policy character of the secondary law of the Banking Union see Hans-W. Micklitz, 'The Internal Market and the Banking Union' in Stefan Grundmann and Hans-W. Micklitz (eds.), *The European Banking Union and Constitution – Beacon for Advanced Integration or Death-Knell for Democracy* (Hart Publishing, 2018), pp. 267–91.

78 Hans-W. Micklitz, 'The Transformation of Enforcement in EU Private Law: Preliminary Considerations' (2015) 23(4) *European Review of Private Law* 491–524.

# PART II

# IN-HOUSE LEGAL EXPERTISE

# 6

# WANTED: A Creative Lawyer with Great Technical Skills for Demanding Work in the European Parliament

Päivi Leino-Sandberg

## 6.1 INTRODUCTION

An old joke, often told by policy-makers venting their frustrations, divides lawyers into two categories. The first kind of lawyer outlines why something absolutely cannot be done. The second type of lawyer explains how to do it. It is not difficult to guess which type of lawyers policy-makers tend to prefer. Beneath the rather tired joke, there lies an important question of the role of legal advisers in public policy-making institutions. How should the obligation to serve the employers' agenda be combined with the perceived objectivity of legal advice and the law's integrity? Is it even possible for legal advice given as part of a political process to remain technical and unbiased by value judgment?

This chapter studies these questions in the context of EU decision-making where such decisions are almost completely detached from any political mandate gained from the electorate.[1] Legislation is usually drafted by politicians and generalists without a formal training in legislative techniques. The chapter discusses the function of legal advice in the European Parliament (EP), focusing in particular on its Legal Service, which 'may deliver opinions in connection with legislative procedures, especially where it perceives a serious risk that a legal dispute may subsequently arise'.[2] The use of legal

Thanks to Daniel Wyatt for research assistance and Hans Micklitz, Tuomas Saarenheimo, Jo Shaw, Bruno de Witte and Ben Yong for comments on an earlier draft and Richard Crowe and Luca Visaggio for discussions on legal advice in the European Parliament. A first version of the Chapter was presented at the 'Annual Conference: The Contribution of the Legal Services of the European Institutions to European Union Law' at the Max Planck Institute for European Legal History in Frankfurt in June 2019. I thank all participants, in particular Gregorio Carzón Clariana, Christian Pennera and Sigfrido Ramírez Pérez, for the discussion.

1 For this in a national context, see Stephen Laws, 'Giving Effect to Policy in Legislation: How to Avoid Missing the Point' (2011) 32(1) *Statute Law Review* 1–16 at 3.

2 Article 5(1), see European Parliament, 'Decision on the Consultation of the Legal Service, Bureau Decision of 28 January 2004'.

expertise in parliaments in general, and in the European Parliament in particular, remains largely uncovered territory.[3] Apart from a number of historical and sociological studies, to the extent that legal advisers working in the public sector have been studied, the focus has been on government legal advisers working in other areas than EU decision-making.[4] Existing studies emphasise the difficulty of producing a coherent account of the influence of legal advisers: much of their work is confidential and thus hidden from public sight.[5]

This chapter approaches the issue from two particular perspectives: of a legal adviser and of a client, the Member of the European Parliament (MEP). Its ambition is mostly descriptive.[6] It aims to increase the understanding of how legal arguments are used in EP decision-making and what constitutes the EP lawyers' legal expertise for the purpose of enabling its critical examination. It draws on a unique set of sixty-three interviews with Members of the Parliament and of its Legal Service, policy advisers, Secretariat staff and with policy-makers and legal advisers working in other EU institutions.[7] The respondents have been anonymised while leaving their function and institutional context visible.[8] The interviews illustrate how legal advice in the EP is often motivated by the aim of protecting the Parliament's institutional prerogatives. MEPs frequently consult their own sources of legal advice

[3] See Päivi Leino-Sandberg, *The Politics of Legal Expertise in EU Policy Making* (Cambridge: Cambridge University Press, 2021). However, some literature exists in relation to the UK, see Ben Yong, Greg Davies and Cristina Leston-Bandeira, 'Tacticians, Stewards and Professionals: The Politics of Publishing Select Committee Legal Advice' (2019) 46 *Journal of Law and Society* 367–95; Edward C. Page, 'Their Word Is Law: Parliamentary Counsel and Creative Policy Analysis' (2009) *Public Law* 790–811, as well as Yong, Chapter 7 in this volume. See also Bruno Latour, *The Making of law. An Etnography of the Conseil d'État* (Cambridge: Polity Press, 2010).

[4] See, e.g., Ben Yong, *Risk Management: Government Lawyers and the Provision of Legal Advice within Whitehall* (London: The Constitution Society, 2013); Matthew Windsor, 'Consigliere or Conscience? The Role of the Government Legal Adviser' in Jean D'Aspremont, Tarcisio Gazzini, Andre Nollkaemper and Wouter Werner (eds.), *International Law as a Profession* (Cambridge: Cambridge University Press, 2017); W. Bradley Wendel, 'Government Lawyers, Democracy, and the Rule of Law' (2009) 77 *Fordham Law Review* 1333–62. Overall, 'systematic research on lawyers' political roles is sparse'. Ann Southworth, Anthony Paik and John P.Heinz, 'Lawyers in National Policymaking' in Scott L. Cummings (ed.), *The Paradox of Professionalism: Lawyers and the Possibility of Justice* (Cambridge: Cambridge University Press, 2011), p. 220.

[5] Page, 'Their Word Is Law', 805.

[6] For discussion of description as research objective, see Anne Orford, 'In Praise of Description' (2012) 25 *Leiden Journal of International Law* 609–25.

[7] While only a selection of these interviews is used in this chapter, they are referred to with their original numbering. As for pronouns, I have opted for 'her' and 'she' regardless of actual gender. Extracts from interviews have at times been lightly edited for clarity and linguistic correctness.

[8] The method is further explained in Leino-Sandberg, *The Politics of Legal Expertise in EU Policy Making*.

(hybridisation of legal expertise). The interviews also demonstrate how legal advice becomes subject to numerous political compromises, with the effect that legal questions are often blurred. This institutional setting offers avenues for political accountability:[9] as a result of various rounds of negotiation, in the end legal advice, even when openly offered and publicly available, risks becoming entirely invisible. But if legal advice is always geared towards finding political compromise between MEPs, can it still remain objective? Are legal advisers offering this advice accountable to someone, and should they be?

This chapter will first sketch the working environment of the EP legal adviser and outline the development of its Legal Service, the evolution of its role through defending the Parliament's prerogatives primarily through litigation, and its relationship with the Parliament's Legal Affairs (JURI) Committee. Section 6.4 describes how EP legal advisers work and how they see their own function – it presents the legal advisers' perspective. Section 6.5 will outline the MEP perspective. Does legal advice have any influence on political choice in the Parliament?

## 6.2 EP LEGAL ADVISER AS A LEGAL EXPERT: SETTING THE SCENE

In EU institutions, lawyers are everywhere. Many work as case handlers or administrators. All EU institutions also have a designated Legal Service that has the specific task of providing legal analysis for the purposes of institutional decision-making.[10] The Legal Service of the European Parliament is one of them. The legal professional capacity of its members is aimed at keeping the European Parliament in 'good working order'.[11] Members of the Legal Services of the EU institutions are European civil servants and as such they are subject to staff rules.[12] Under the EU Staff Regulations,

9 On this in the US context, see 'Rethinking the Professional Responsibilities of Federal Agency Lawyers' (2002) 115 *Harvard Law Review* 1170–92 at 1170.

10 See the Rules of Procedure of each EU institution in Leino-Sandberg, *The Politics of Legal Expertise in EU Policy Making*.

11 See W. Bradley Wendel, *Lawyers and Fidelity to Law* (Princeton: Princeton University Press, 2010), p. 7, p. 208.

12 See Regulation No. 31 (EEC), 11 (EAEC), laying down the Staff Regulations of Officials and the Conditions of Employment of Other Servants of the European Economic Community and the European Atomic Energy Community. OJ 1962 No. P 45 14 June 1962, 1385. See also Päivi Leino-Sandberg, 'Enchantment and Critical Distance in EU Legal Scholarship: What Role for Institutional Lawyers?', European Law Open 2/2022.

> An official shall carry out his duties and conduct himself solely with the interests of the Union in mind. He shall neither seek nor take instructions from any government, authority, organisation or person outside his institution. He shall carry out the duties assigned to him objectively, impartially and in keeping with his duty of loyalty to the Union.[13]

This obligation of objectivity is customary in the civil service, which generally invokes neutrality in serving the political master and loyalty in implementing its goals.[14] Bureaucrats are expected to 'set aside all their possible qualms, disagreements and personal interests and employ their technical skills to implement policy goals in the most effective way'.[15] Apart from the general staff regulations and soft law guidance provided by the Commission for members of its own Legal Service,[16] there are no instruments or guidelines that would guide the work of institutional legal advisers in particular. Instead, they rely on institutional practices and their legal professional ethics[17] – irrespective of whether they are members of a bar or other legal professional community.

The key tasks of institutional legal advisers are threefold. They act as *counsellors* trying to prevent unconstitutional or illegal actions; as *advisers* assisting in drafting and explaining legislative technique; and as *advocates* in EU Courts. As counsellors, their focus is often on questions of the applicable legal basis and EU competence.[18] The choice of legal basis is, based on established Court jurisprudence, to be made on objective grounds which are amenable to judicial review.[19] Other legal questions frequently addressed by legal advisers involve subsidiarity, and the use of and borderline between delegated acts and implementing acts.[20] As advisers, the Legal Services engage

[13] Regulation No. 31 (EEC), 11 (EAEC), laying down the Staff Regulations of Officials and the Conditions of Employment of Other Servants of the European Economic Community and the European Atomic Energy Community, Art. 11(1).

[14] On this also Page, 'Their Word Is Law', 811.

[15] Peter Triantafillou, 'The Politics of Neutrality and the Changing Role of Expertise in Public Administration' (2015) 37(3) *Administrative Theory and Praxis* 174–87 at 176.

[16] See Leino-Sandberg, *The Politics of Legal Expertise in EU Policy Making*, Chapter 5.

[17] On such values, see also Scott L. Cummings, 'What Good Are Lawyers?' in Scott L. Cummings (ed.), *The Paradox of Professionalism. Lawyers and the Possibility of Justice* (Cambridge: Cambridge University Press, 2011), p. 1.

[18] Interview with members of the Council Legal Service (Respondents 7 and 8).

[19] See also Interinstitutional Agreement between the European Parliament, the Council of the European Union and the European Commission on Better Law-Making, OJ 2016 No. L 123, 12 May 2016, p. 1, para. 25.

[20] Interview with legal advisers working at a Member State Permanent EU Representation (Respondents 11 and 12).

with procedural questions[21] and the quality of legislation.[22] Sometimes the work involves the need to 'fight some positions and explain' . . .

> but that's part of the job of legal advice. It's not saying yes to everything the other person is saying, it's trying to give a concrete and objective answer. Knowing that you have to know the implications, if you go on this path then . . . we might end up in court, we might end up having something very unpleasant.[23]

Interinstitutional negotiations often touch upon technical legal issues that may be delegated to the Legal Services to discuss and agree on a position,[24] to be subsequently approved by each of the three institutions in accordance with their own internal procedures.[25] As the Court has confirmed, the 'Legal Services act under a mandate and with the aim of reaching an agreement. They thus simultaneously act as negotiators and advisers with regard to legal matters'.[26] Finally, in the EU institutions, the Legal Services act as advocates and enjoy a strong monopoly over litigation since their members represent their institution before the EU Courts as agents and enjoy a broad discretion when pleading before the Court.[27]

In contrast to national settings no politically elected government or opposition exists in the EU. The EP is fragmented in composition. The 751 MEPs, representing hundreds of political parties, are organised in seven European political groups. These political groups are the main players in various political power games though, due to their ideological heterogeneity, less relevant in formulating actual political positions in the EP. The adoption of legislative acts is a process where a great amount of material is digested through amendments, first in specialised Committees led by rapporteurs and finally in the plenary where the positions of political groups are decisive. The programmes of the EP political groups lack the depth and detail to be helpful in forming

21 Interview with a legal adviser working at a Member State Permanent EU Representation (Respondent 12).

22 Interinstitutional Agreement of 22 December 1998 on common guidelines for the quality of drafting of Community legislation, OJ 1999 No. C 73, 17 March 1999, 1.

23 Interview with a member of the European Parliament's Legal Service (Respondent 3). On how a lawyer's job is in general to offer a reliable prediction of how the law (courts, specifically) will respond, see Brian Z. Tamanaha, 'A Socio-Legal Methodology for the Internal/External Distinction: Jurisprudential Implications' (2006) 75 *Fordham Law Review* 1255–74 at 1269. On the force of such evaluation in the UK context, see Page, 'Their Word Is Law', at 810.

24 Interview with members of the EP Legal Service (Respondents 2 and 5).

25 Case T-755/14, *Herbert Smith Freehills LLP* v. *Commission* [2016] EU:T:2016:482, 30.

26 Case T-755/14, *Herbert Smith Freehills LLP* v. *European Commission*, para. 59.

27 On this, see Leino-Sandberg, *The Politics of Legal Expertise in EU Policy Making*, Chapter 3.1.3.

positions on particular files, leaving a lot of power in the hands of the rapporteur. In the end, MEPs nevertheless tend to vote with their group and, hence, the political groups are decisive for the Parliament's positions. A director in the EP's Legal Service explains how the Parliament's fragmentation makes its unpredictable. It lacks political identity and voting discipline, which 'makes constant negotiation unavoidable with no result being ever guaranteed, no matter who the rapporteur or other protagonist of the decision making process are or whichever the political commitments of one or other political group'.[28]

Amendments as such are a normal parliamentary working method. The sheer number of them sets the European Parliament apart from other parliaments. The right to propose amendments is not limited to political groups but is also available to individual MEPs, who use this as a way to leave their fingerprints on the legislation. As a result, amendments often number in the thousands. They are traded against each other to build an acceptable compromise, and eventually voted on one by one. Internal consistency and clarity of legislation have little weight in this process.[29] What matters is achieving a sufficient majority to approve the compromise,[30] either based on a majority on the left or on the right. Yet, on major questions one might also try to gain a compromise with all big groups.[31] The rapporteur needs to determine her own priority items, and trade away less important ones. In this work, policy advisers' help is irreplaceable.[32]

Unlike its counterparts in particular in the Commission, the EP Legal Service has no monopoly in advising the MEPs, but has to operate in a highly competitive marketplace.[33] The EP is essentially a free market of legal advice. Legal advice flows not only from the EP Legal Service and the JURI Committee and its Secretariat. In addition, MEPs have sporadic access to the advice of the Council Legal Service, the Commission Legal Service, from Member States, and from other sources including stakeholders who all hold opinions about what is legally possible. Parliament bodies sometimes make even formal requests to gain access to legal advice by the Council Legal

[28] Maria José Martínez Iglesias, 'The Accidental Democracy: A European Model' in Sascha Garben, Inge Govaere and Paul Nemitz (eds.), *Critical Reflections on Constitutional Democracy in the European Union* (Oxford: Hart Publishing, 2019), pp. 202–03.

[29] Interview with an MEP (Respondent 40); interview with a policy adviser to a political group and former adviser to an MEP (Respondent 43).

[30] Interview with an MEP (Respondent 40).

[31] Interview with a former MEP (Respondent 46).

[32] Ibid.

[33] Interview with a member of the EP Legal Service (Respondent 2).

Service.[34] As a result, the Parliament's Legal Service is considered institutionally weaker than its siblings in other Union institutions.

Legal functions at the European Parliament are divided between officials and politicians. Questions relating to the verification of the legal basis are defined as falling under a political body, the Legal Affairs (JURI) Committee,[35] the members of which are selected on the basis of the general rules on the composition of parliamentary committees[36] rather than knowledge that could be characterised as 'legal expertise'. The Committee exercises political judgement on legal matters and may issue opinions either at the request of other Committees or on its own initiative.[37] The JURI Committee employs administrators with legal training who provide the Committee (especially the chairman and rapporteur) with legal advice, in much the same way as the Parliament's Legal Service.[38] Committees, especially the JURI Committee, often decide legal matters themselves and 'think that they are the best lawyers, so they do not need legal advice'.[39] Many lawyers work as administrators in the Committees,[40] and if they have the confidence of influential Members they can have a broad margin of manoeuvre.[41]

34 For a Council reply to such a request, see Council of the European Union, 'Request for access to Council Legal Service Opinion on the Commission's Proposal for an Inter-Institutional Agreement on a Mandatory Transparency Register', Doc. No. A 004042, 11 April 2017.

35 Rules of Procedure of the European Parliament, 8th parliamentary term – September 2015, Rule 39 and Annex V: Powers and responsibilities of standing committees; XVI. In addition, the JURI Committee is responsible for the substance of EU legislation in a number of policy areas. For an example of its legislative work, see, e.g., Björn Lindberg, 'Are Political Parties Controlling Legislative Decision-Making in the European Parliament? The Case of the Services Directive' (2008) 15(8) *Journal of European Public Policy* 1184–204.

36 Rules of Procedure of the European Parliament, 8th parliamentary term – September 2015, Rule 199. However, previous research demonstrates that lawyers and those with an attachment to human rights organisations are more likely to become members of the Legal Affairs Committee. Shaun Bowler and David M. Ferrell, 'The Organizing of the European Parliament: Committees, Specialization and Co-ordination' (1995) 25 *British Journal of Political Science* 219–43 at 231; Nikoleta Yordanova, 'The Rationale behind Committee Assignment in the European Parliament' (2009) 10(2) *West European Politics* 253–280 at 272.

37 Rule 39, Rules of Procedure of the European Parliament, 8th parliamentary term – September 2015.

38 Interview with a former Member of the EP Legal Service (Respondent 19).

39 Interview with a Member of the Commission Legal Service (Respondent 17).

40 Interview with a Member of the EP Legal Service (Respondent 2).

41 On this, see Olivier Costa, 'Administrer le Parlement Européen: Les Paradoxes d'un Secrètariat Général incontournable, mais faible' (2003) 3 *Politique Européenne* 143–61. See also Thomas Winzen, 'Technical or Political? An Exploration of the Work of Officials in the Committees of the European Parliament' (2011) 17 *Journal of Legislative Studies* 1, 27–44; Christine Neuhold and Mathias J. Dobbels, 'Paper-Keepers or Policy Shapers? The Role of Unelected Officials in the European Parliament' (2015) 13(5) *Comparative European Politics* 577.

As far as legal basis questions are concerned, Rule 39 in the Parliament's Rules of Procedure 'establishes a complex procedure, whose objective is primarily to guarantee that the question of legal basis is settled in full knowledge of the facts'.[42] In case the leading committee disputes the validity or the appropriateness of the legal basis, it must engage the JURI Committee in the matter and request its opinion. The JURI Committee may also take up legal basis questions on its own initiative. It

> always cooperates closely with the competent committees and hears the advice of Parliament's Legal Service before making a recommendation. Furthermore, the committee nearly always proceeds unanimously in exercising its duties in respect of legal basis and contentious matters, with the rapporteurship rotating twice a year between the political groups. This practice of 'standing rapporteurs' has arguably reinforced the authoritative effect of its opinions within and indeed outside the institution.[43]

In practice, the Legal Service prepares a note on the issue to the Committee's Standing Rapporteur, whose opinion goes to a vote in the Committee, where it is either approved without amendments or rejected. If the Committee decides to dispute the legal basis, it reports its conclusions to Parliament, which votes on this question before voting on the substance of the proposal.

Other legal advisers working in Brussels have a certain degree of sympathy for their colleagues in the Parliament, whose advice seems easy to bypass through the political inclinations of MEPs:[44] After all, 'the MEPs are not very interested in what is possible and what is not, at least when you read the documents you get the impression that quite often what they are suggesting is notoriously legally totally impossible'.[45] The Parliament Legal Service is 'something that we just never come across';[46] 'they're totally an invisible animal';[47] and fairly insignificant because lawyers are generally seen to have little prominence in the Parliament.[48] On the whole, 'I would say so that the

[42] María José Martínez Iglesias, 'The Lisbon Treaty's Competence Arrangement Viewed by the European Parliament', in Sascha Garben and Inge Govare (eds.), *The Division of Competences between the EU and the Member States. Reflections on the Past, the Present and the Future* (Oxford: Hart Publishing, 2017), p. 199.

[43] European Parliament Committee on Legal Affairs, *Stocktaking of Parliamentary Committee Activities During the 7th Legislature* (8 December 2014) at 90–91.

[44] Interview with a member of the Council Legal Service (Respondent 13).

[45] Interview with a former legal adviser at a Member State Permanent Representation in Brussels (Respondent 1).

[46] Interview with a legal adviser at a Member State Permanent Representation in Brussels (Respondent 22).

[47] Ibid.

[48] Ibid.

legal advisers working in the Parliament ... have to be much more innovative'.[49] While the Commission tends to be guided towards the more integrationist approach, the European Parliament is seen to always opt for the legal basis that maximises its own influence. This political motivation tends to override any legal considerations, thus further limiting the relevance of the EP Legal Service.[50]

## 6.3 THE EVOLUTION OF THE EP LEGAL SERVICE: FROM IDEOLOGICAL TO PROFESSIONAL LEGAL EXPERTISE

In principle, in an environment characterised by political confrontations, the Legal Service could be expected to stand for 'non-partisan advice of an independent administrative service'.[51] This indeed is the impression given by the Parliament's website: the 'Legal Service has a leading role in a Union primarily based on democracy, the rule of law and respect for fundamental rights. It advises Parliament on legal questions and represents it in legal cases'.[52] The extent to which it in fact can serve such a role is debatable. As described above, the MEPs have no duty to consult the Legal Service. The only binding consultation of the Legal Service in the Parliament relates to certain categories of administrative documents on which the Legal Service 'must' be consulted.[53] This setting is fundamentally different from that in the Commission or the Council. The Commission Rules of Procedure oblige officials always to consult colleagues in the Legal Service,[54] whose advice is almost impossible to bypass.[55] As to the Council, even without a formal obligation to consult the Legal Service, the Council routinely does, and most of the people meeting in different formations work in national administrations, and 'they have the instinct to know that if your lawyers tell you that

49 Interview with a former member of the Commission Legal Service (Respondent 44).

50 Interview with a member of the Commission Legal Service (Respondent 16).

51 Interview with a former member of the EP Legal Service (Respondent 19).

52 European Parliament Secretary General, 'Legal Service', available at www.europarl.europa.eu/the-secretary-general/en/organisation/legal-service.

53 See Annex to the Bureau decision, supra. Article 3.

54 Article 23(4) of the Commission Rules of Procedure. Commission decision of 24 February 2010 amending its Rules of Procedure (2010/138/EU, Euratom). OJ No. L 55/60, 5 March 2010, pp. 60–67.

55 Under Article 12 of the Rules of Procedure of the Commission, written procedure can be used to gain the 'agreement of the Members of the Commission to a draft text from one or more of its Members'; however, the use of this procedure presumes 'that the approval of the Legal Service and the agreement of the departments consulted in accordance with Article 23 of these Rules of Procedure has been obtained'.

something is legally problematic, you take it seriously'.[56] In contrast, since there is no obligation to consult the EP Legal Service, often it is easier not to. In fact, it is doubtful whether MEPs can be understood as 'clients' of the Legal Service: in most cases there is no relationship between the two.

For the European Parliament, the most salient legal issues concern institutional questions, such as the choice of legal basis or comitology procedure. Matters regarding its prerogatives act 'as a strong incentive to contest the legal basis'.[57] Where a legislative proposal concerns matters of institutional design, the two are inextricably linked.[58] The Parliament's Legal Service was born and evolved on such institutional battlegrounds. It has been instrumental in creating and defending the Parliament's institutional prerogatives,[59] many of which have been subsequently consolidated through Treaty reforms. The Legal Service was set up as a part of the Parliament's Secretariat in January 1986, largely in anticipation that the Court would recognise the Parliament's right to participate in institutional litigation.[60] The Council was strongly opposed to such a development, but its arguments were dismissed by the Court.[61] The Court confirmed in *Les Verts* the possibility of bringing annulment proceedings against the Parliament,[62] and in *Chernobyl*, as regards proceedings brought by Parliament.[63] A number of early cases also concerned the Parliament's right to be consulted[64] or to regulate its own seat and working places.[65] The early legal basis discussions were not straightforward. In various instances the advice of the JURI Committee was ignored when forming the

56 Interview with a Member of the Council Legal Service (Respondent 30).

57 Iglesias, 'The Lisbon Treaty's Competence Arrangement Viewed by the European Parliament', 198–209 at 201.

58 Interview with a former Member of the EP Legal Service (Respondent 19).

59 Ibid.

60 Ibid. Relating to the early case law, see Kieran St. Clair Bradley, 'Maintaining the Balance: The Role of the Court of Justice in Defining the Institutional Position of the European Parliament' (1987) 24 *Common Market Law Review* 41–64; Kieran St. Clair Bradley, 'The Variable Evolution of the Standing of the European Parliament in Proceedings before the Court of Justice' (1988) *Yearbook of European Law* 27–57. On the development of the legal service and its functions, see also Gregorio Carzón Clariana, 'Building a role for the jurisconsult of the European Parliament and the legal service', contribution to the Max Planck Institute Workshop in June 2019 (in file with author).

61 Case 138/79, *SA Roquette Frères* v. *Council* [1980] ECR 3333, paras 19, 21.

62 Case 294/83 *Parti écologiste 'Les Verts'* v. *European Parliament* [1986] ECR 1339 (paras. 24–25).

63 Case C-70/88 *European Parliament* v. *Council* [1990] ECR I 2041. The development has been outlined in Christian Pennera, 'La Cour de Justice et le Parlement europeen' in A. Rosas, Egils Levits and Yves Bot (eds.), *The Court of Justice and the Construction of Europe: Analyses and Perspectives on Sixty Years of Case-law* (The Hague: T.M.C. Asser Press, 2013), 121–39.

64 Case 138/79, *SA Roquette Frères* v. *Council*, para. 33.

65 See Kieran St. Clair Bradley, 'Legal Developments in the European Parliament' (1990) *Yearbook of European Law* 367–405 at 388–92.

Parliament's position, which again was ignored by the Council. Yet few of these disputes led to legal proceedings.[66] While selectively used, the European Parliament saw legal basis litigation as 'a potentially useful tool in advancing wider political aims designed to expand, or to confirm, their own powers' and part of 'a political strategy to maximize power and influence'.[67]

In its early days, the Legal Service consisted of three or four legal advisers who all had significant personal responsibility for formulating the Parliament's positions in the institutional battles.[68] There was some initial reluctance in the Court to allow the European Parliament to take Court action in case 'this new, irresponsible, very active institution would flood the Court with dozens of cases every year'.[69] This turned out to be an ungrounded fear, since in practice the EP Legal Service proved to be a relatively cautious litigator.[70] One of the first legal advisers notes how during these times they were often guided by an ideological understanding of 'what is right is what goes in the line of the European construction, in ... ever closer union, etcetera'.[71] The legal advisers pursued their work in the context of an ideology: 'in a way we tried to reach these political objectives so, but they were not seen as political by ourselves'.[72] Today the EP legal advisers take pride in independence and neutrality: 'we are more professional'.[73]

After the entry into force of the Treaty of Lisbon and with it the dominant position of the ordinary legislative procedure, the choice of legal basis has become less contested.[74] Instead of bringing annulment actions, the Parliament today often acts as co-defendant in actions questioning the validity

66 Bradley, 'Legal Developments in the European Parliament' at 375–80. One example was the setting up of the European Environmental Agency. Council Regulation (EEC) No. 1210/90 of 7 May 1990 on the establishment of the European Environment Agency and the European Environment Information and Observation Network, OJ No. L 120, 11 May 1990, p. 1. See also Case C-295/90 *Parliament* v. *Council* [1992] ECR I 4193.

67 Holly Cullen and Andrew Charlesworth, 'Diplomacy by Other Means: The Use of Legal Basis Litigation as a Political Strategy by the European Parliament and Member States' (1999) 36 *Common Market Law Review* 1243, at 1243.

68 Interview with a former Member of the EP Legal Service (Respondent 19).

69 Ibid.

70 Ibid.

71 Interview with a Member of the EP Legal Service (Respondent 2).

72 Ibid.

73 Ibid.

74 Päivi Leino, 'The Politics of Efficient Compromise in the Adoption of EU Legal Acts' in M. Cremona and C. Kilpatrick (eds.), *EU Legal Acts: Challenges and Transformations* (Oxford: Oxford University Press, 2018), pp. 30–69; Päivi Leino, 'EU Competence As a Framework for Argumentation' in Sascha Garben and Inge Govare (eds.), *The Division of Competencies in the EU Legal Order: A Post-Lisbon Assessment* (Oxford: Hart Publishing, 2017), pp. 210–31.

of acts.[75] This means that by and large its role has changed from that of the challenger to that of a co-legislature in most policy areas, with shared responsibility for producing solid legal acts that will stand up in the Court. Overall, the Parliament can have 'imaginative little things here and there', perhaps adopt a resolution asking for impossible things. However, 'in legislation in general, I think they have [a] responsible approach'.[76] Interinstitutional litigation has continued in areas where the Parliament's prerogatives remain more limited: in the area of external relations (Article 218 TFEU)[77] and the use of and choice between delegated acts and comitology.[78]

Today, the main tasks of the Parliament's Legal Service consist of providing legal assistance for the Parliament's political bodies[79] and for its Secretariat, as well as helping the EP Committees with their legislative work and representing the European Parliament in European and national courts.[80] There are no Parliament-specific professional rules for the work of their legal advisers. There is a unit in the Legal Service in charge of legislative and judicial coordination, which provides interpretations of for example the Rules of Procedure of the Parliament for internal use.[81] The Legal Service falls under the Parliament's Secretary General. A former Parliament Jurisconsult explains how he 'always took very seriously the principle that the members of the Legal Service worked under my authority and not under the authority of someone else'. However, he admits that 'independence is not only a question of the courage of the Jurisconsult or of the members of its Service. In practice, this principle also depends on the understanding by the political authorities and the Secretary-General of the specific mission of the Legal Service'.[82]

The Legal Service is organised based on parliamentary committees and in three directorates: A for institutional, budgetary and staff affairs; B for

75 European Parliament Committee on Legal Affairs, *Stocktaking of Parliamentary Committee Activities During the 7th Legislature* (8 December 2014) at 85.

76 Interview with a Member of the EP Legal Service (Respondent 2).

77 See, e.g., Christina Eckes, *EU Powers Under External Pressure. How the EU's External Actions Alter Its Internal Structures* (Oxford: Oxford University Press, 2019), pp. 185–222.

78 Many of these cases are explained in European Parliament Committee on Legal Affairs, *Stocktaking of Parliamentary Committee Activities During the 7th Legislature* (8 December 2014).

79 These include the President, the Bureau, the Conference of Presidents, the Conference of Committee Chairmen, the Conference of Delegation Chairmen, the College of Quaestors and the committees.

80 European Parliament Secretary General – Legal Service. For details see www.europarl.europa.eu/the-secretary-general/en/organisation/legal-service.

81 Interview with a Member of the EP Legal Service (Respondent 2).

82 Clariana, 'Building Role for the Jurisconsult of the European Parliament and the Legal Service' at 11.

legislative affairs; and C for parliamentary and financial affairs. Each directorate is led by a Head of Unit, and is responsible directly to the Jurisconsult (Director General).[83] Formal consultations are initiated in writing, signed by the committee president, and will be responded to with a formal written legal opinion. The Legal Service also produces 'legal notes' and 'legal opinions', which are all treated as legal advice. Recent questions or not yet settled case law of the CJEU are addressed in 'notes for reflection'.[84] The Jurisconsult can require modifications to the draft opinion, though in practice matters have been discussed before the opinion has been finalised and disagreement is rare.[85] Action by the Legal Service is collective: legal advice is provided by the Parliament's Legal Service *qua* the administrative unit of the Secretariat, and under the authority of the Jurisconsult, signed or countersigned by him or, under his authority, by one of the Directors.[86] Coordination takes place within and between Legal Service units,[87] as a result of which many horizontal, frequently surfacing matters are clearly aligned within the Legal Service and are thus easy to react to. Others might be more complicated,[88] especially when legal advice is required on the spot.[89]

In the early days, the Legal Service only expressed its views formally, as a legal opinion. However, today members of the Legal Service 'are everywhere'. Much of the advice is informal and given orally,[90] even though 'the views expressed by members of the Legal Service shall not necessarily reflect the official views of the Legal Service, save where those views are confirmed in writing'.[91] Members of the Legal Service are also present in bilateral meetings and in trilogues,[92] 'we are always there, always'.[93] Overall, even as far as formal consultation is concerned, it is difficult to evaluate how actively committees engage the Legal Service, since there is no comprehensive public information on the matter. The Legal Service often prefers providing oral briefings behind

83 Interview with a Member of the EP Legal Service (Respondent 2).
84 G. Garzón Clariana, 'The Work of the Legal Adviser of International Organisations, with Special Reference to the European Union' in C. Jimenez Piernes (ed.), *The Legal Practice in International Law and European Community Law – A Spanish Perspective* (Leiden: Brill Nijhoff, 2007), pp. 239–54 at p. 243.
85 Interview with a former Member of the EP Legal Service (Respondent 19).
86 Article 1(2), European Parliament, 'Decision on the Consultation of the Legal Service, Bureau Decision of 28 January 2004'.
87 Interview with a Member of the EP Legal Service (Respondent 2).
88 Ibid.
89 Interview with a former Member of the EP Legal Service (Respondent 19).
90 Interview with a Member of the EP Legal Service (Respondent 2).
91 Article 5(2), European Parliament, 'Decision on the Consultation of the Legal Service, Bureau Decision of 28 January 2004'.
92 Interview with a Member of the EP Legal Service (Respondent 2).
93 Ibid.

closed doors. A legal and policy adviser in the Parliament explains that if a Committee wishes to have the view of the Legal Service on a particular issue, the first suggestion will always be an oral briefing in camera in a coordinators' meeting.[94] Legal advisers feel that informality sometimes creates challenges for maintaining the distance required by professional ethics: 'We try . . . to keep our role limited also. So . . . to maintain this authority we have to make ourselves scarce somewhere and well it's a difficult balance.'[95]

In principle, each legislative file has an allocated project team including the Secretariat, the Legal Service and a lawyer-linguist. There seems little awareness of the availability of legal assistance among MEPs and policy advisers. EP Legal Service members respond to questions, but unless those questions are asked, there will be no particular follow up.[96] Each Committee has a few members in the Legal Service who follow its files and are available for consultation if needed. However, each rapporteur chooses freely whether to engage with the Legal Service, and practices vary. The stance of the Legal Service is passive rather than active: 'if I have questions that need answers, I will get them, but I will not be actively approached by the Legal Service'.[97] A policy adviser explains that most of the legal advice in the Parliament is technical. Thus, the Legal Service has remained faceless, its members seem busy, and mainly comment on nuances and choices between individual words.[98]

The Legal Service can also be engaged with a file directly. In cases of formal consultation, the Parliament's Bureau has laid down rules governing the right to refer questions to the Legal Service. Committees may request opinions without restrictions, but individual members may only do so if the Committee concerned agrees.[99] A Committee will in practice always request an opinion if the rapporteur or a sufficient number of members wish to have one.[100] These

94 Interview with a legal and policy adviser to a Vice-President of the European Parliament (Respondent 54).

95 Interview with a Member of the EP Legal Service (Respondent 2). On distance, see Philip Lewis, 'Aspects of Professionalism. Constructing the Lawyer-Client Relationship', in Scott L. Cummings (ed.) *The Paradox of Professionalism. Lawyers and the Possibility of Justice* (Cambridge University Press: Cambridge, 2011), p. 150.

96 Interview with a policy adviser to a political group; former adviser to an MEP (Respondent 43).

97 Ibid.

98 Ibid.

99 See European Parliament, 'Decision on the Consultation of the Legal Service, Bureau Decision of 28 January 2004', available at www.europarl.europa.eu/RegData/publications/notes/2004/0001/EP-PE_NT(2004)339484_XL.pdf, which lists the persons and/or bodies that may submit a written request for the drawing up of a legal opinion.

100 Interview with a former Member of the EP Legal Service (Respondent 19).

choices are also political in nature: 'Committees should of course be aware that once they ask for an opinion, they have no influence on its content, which may not in the end suit their political views; there's no putting the toothpaste back into the tube.'[101] Political tensions are also visible: a former legal adviser could recollect two instances where 'members, or even committee chairmen, verbally [attacked] the bearer of bad legal news in the course of a public committee meeting', indicating that the 'legal advice contradicts the viability of the chairman's, or a member's, pet project'. The webcasting of committee meetings has reduced this problem.[102]

It is traditional for EU legal advisers to think that impartiality and objectivity require high levels of confidentiality.[103] However, unlike the Legal Services of the Commission and the Council, the Parliament's Legal Service often needs to defend its opinions in public:

> I don't think we are that cautious, but on occasion we have to be quite prudent because anything we say will probably end up in Court. If we [...] say the Commission got it wrong or the Council's got it wrong, it'll end up in Court. It's not automatic, but it happens quite a lot.[104]

So while Legal Service opinions in the EP are formally not public, they are in practice in relatively free circulation within the Parliament. They are requested by committees that make them public in sessions where the other institutions tend to present and take note of what the EP Legal Service says: 'So we've sort of laid our cards on the table before we ever get to Court, but that's the way Parliament works, it's much more open.'[105] This may, in part, be out of pragmatism, since in the Parliament nothing remains permanently confidential.[106]

Opposing the publicity of legal advice has been a big issue for the Legal Services of the Council and the Commission.[107] The Parliament is generally interested in getting its hands on legal advice provided by the Legal Services of other institutions.[108] As a political institution, the Parliament has placed the political emphasis on how 'opinions of the institutions' legal services must, in

101 Ibid.
102 Ibid.
103 Deirdre Curtin and Päivi Leino, 'In Search of Transparency for EU Law-Making: Trilogues on the Cusp of Dawn' (2017) 54(6) *Common Market Law Review* 1673–712.
104 Interview with a former Member of the EP Legal Service (Respondent 19).
105 Ibid.
106 Interview with a legal and policy adviser to a Vice-President of the European Parliament (Respondent 54).
107 Curtin and Leino, 'In Search of Transparency for EU Law-Making'.
108 Examples of this are the cases brought by Turco and In't Veld, both MEPs.

principle, be disclosed',[109] and MEPs have challenged the Council's secretive practices in this regard.[110] Yet, the EP's own public register of documents contains very few entries for Legal Service opinions,[111] making it difficult to evaluate how many opinions the Legal Service effectively issues and how many of them are registered and made publicly available. For example, the opinion of the Parliament's Legal Service on the international Anti-Counterfeiting Trade Agreement (ACTA) – where the EP exercised hard pressure on the Commission and the Council to make more of their documents publicly available,[112] and finally rejected the agreement – is publicly available only to a very limited extent. Most of the substantive parts are blanked out.[113] The Parliament also has particular sensitivities when it comes to its institutional and Members' prerogatives. In its 2018 Annual Report, the Parliament observes an increased public interest in legal advice given to its Bureau and raises concern of the effect of this on its continued ability to seek legal advice:

> Publication might lead to the services involved in their drafting to refrain from setting out in such notes certain views and knowledge that could be used to undermine the decisions to be taken. Indeed, this kind of self-censorship would deprive the Bureau from useful arguments and legal opinions enabling it to exercise its prerogatives in the interests of the Parliament and undermine its ability to take informed decisions.[114]

Pleading for the Parliament in Court is the only area of legal work where members of the EP Legal Service have a monopoly.[115] Even there, the JURI

[109] Public access to documents 2011–2013, European Parliament resolution of 11 March 2014 on public access to documents (Rule 104(7)) for the years 2011–2013 (2013/2155(INI)) P7_TA-PROV(2014)0203, para. 38.

[110] Joined cases C-39/05 P and C-52/05 P *Sweden and Turco* v. *Council* and C-350/12 P *Sophie In't Veld* [2008] ECR I-4723.

[111] This search was made in the Parliament's document register on 15 March 2019 and gave the following results: 2018 (1); 2017 (2); 2016 (1); 2015 (8); 2014 (7); 2013 (3); 2012 (2); 2011 (5); 2010 (6); 2009 (1); 2006 (3); 2005 (1); 2004 (1); 2002 (1); 1993 (1); 1988 (3), about half of which are documents relating to litigation.

[112] See, e.g., European Parliament resolution of 10 March 2010 on the transparency and state of play of the ACTA negotiations, P7_TA(2010)0058.

[113] See the Legal Opinion on Anti-Counterfeiting Trade Agreement (ACTA) (5 October 2011), SJ-0501/11. OJ C147/1, 5 June 2010, 1–13.

[114] European Parliament's Annual Report – Public Access to Documents 2018, March 2019, at 14. One of the cases that engaged the Bureau in 2018 related to the Parliament's suspicious additional pensions scheme. N. Nielsen, 'EU Taxpayers Risk Bailing out MEP Pension Scheme', *EU Observer*, 20 February 2018. For a critical assessment of confidentiality in the legal services, see Leino-Sandberg, *The Politics of Legal Expertise in EU Policy Making*, Chapter 4.

[115] Interview with a former member of the EP Legal Service (Respondent 19).

Committee and its lawyer administrators take the lead on settling whether or not litigation is in the interests of the Parliament. Its report builds on work done in the Legal Service, but goes through two political decision-making stages, focusing on public interest such as the breach of fundamental rights or the Parliament's prerogatives. In these discussions, the Legal Service is seldom proactive.[116] In practice, legal basis cases are almost always purely about interinstitutional prerogatives.[117] While the Legal Service always provides advice on whether or not the case is likely to be successful, the decision to initiate legal proceedings is significantly influenced by considerations of political opportunity; Parliament has initiated proceedings when they were deemed hopeless by the Legal Service, as well as refused to initiate proceedings when advised that they had every chance of success.[118]

Irrespective of earlier advice, the Legal Service officials – usually the same individual who has previously worked on the file – will defend Parliament's position before the Court, which for the legal adviser 'provides a sharp incentive to get it right the first time'.[119] The actual litigation seems to be the only clear monopoly of the Legal Service, which it conducts largely without the direct involvement of the JURI Committee, based on the mandate given.[120] This suggests that pleading is considered a specialised kind of legal expertise where political considerations might become secondary to the secret arts of litigation. As a result, the pleadings of the Parliament or other parties are neither distributed nor discussed within the Committee. This may result in the Parliament's positions as presented in Court not being in line with the political positions it has expressed in other fora. The Court itself has drawn attention to it, indicating that such inconsistencies weaken the Parliament's argumentation.[121] In the context of litigation, the client of the Legal Service is clear: it defends the institutional interest of the European Parliament, and enjoys broad discretion to determine how that interest is best served.

116 Ibid. One example of this could be the case relating to the Schengen Borders Code, Case C-355/10, *European Parliament* v. *Council* [2012].

117 An example often named are the PNR cases, C-317/04, *European Parliament* v. *Council* and C-318/04, *Commission* [2006] ECR I-04721, often seen as a case where the Parliament acted strongly to defend fundamental rights and privacy. However, the case also had a strong element of *ultra vires* action.

118 Interview with a former Member of the EP Legal Service (Respondent 19).

119 Ibid.

120 Ibid.

121 Case T-540/15, *Emilio De Capitani* v. *the European Parliament* (ECLI:EU:T:2018:167) e.g. at para. 110.

## 6.4 HOW DO EP LEGAL ADVISERS SHAPE THE ISSUES?

In Parliamentary Committees, members of the Legal Service are the only officials in the Parliament who may take the floor during a debate.[122] Performance and delivery count a great deal: 'if it's more than two minutes no one listens, you have to be very focused'.[123] In general, 'my role is to be helpful to the members and if I am saying all the time that I cannot answer, [then] I think I am really not helpful to them'.[124] In the debates, legal advice often gets hybridised or, as a legal adviser working for the Council explains, 'let's say, nuanced or somehow watered down'. This adviser further explains how '[f]rankly I don't envy them in the Legal Service in the Parliament, because they have 751 bosses who all think that law is like one of many other factors that somehow come into the game'.[125] For a lawyer, this is clearly wrong: law needs to be special and maintain its integrity. And yet, it never does: 'no matter what point of view you express in the Parliament, you will always have somebody against it'.[126]

In the European Parliament, as in any political environment, legal arguments tend to get politically weaponised, and hence legal advice needs to be carefully framed as non-partisan. Members of the Legal Service need to remain 'whiter than white'.[127] Objectivity and impartiality is 'something that we take very strongly and it's very much dear to our position'.[128] The same services need to be offered to all groups and MEPs:

> my main function as a legal advisor in Parliament has always been the provision of independent legal advice, i.e., the law as I saw it, unencumbered by considerations of party political or personal advantage. Party political, obviously, because if you favour one political group or tendency, you will inevitably displease all the others, and in any case it is up to the politicians to decide on political matters. Personal, because it is dishonest to provide a legal opinion simply to please the crowd.[129]

EP legal advisers serve multiple clients within the legislature.[130] For this,

122 Interview with a Member of the EP Legal Service (Respondent 2).
123 Interview with a Member of the EP Legal Service (Respondent 4).
124 Interview with a Member of the EP Legal Service (Respondent 5).
125 Interview with a Member of the Council Legal Service (Respondent 30).
126 Interview with a former Member of the EP Legal Service (Respondent 19).
127 Ibid.
128 Interview with a member of the EP Legal Service (Respondent 3). In relation to these presumptions more generally, see, e.g., Wendel, *Lawyers and Fidelity to Law*, at 6.
129 Interview with a former Member of the EP Legal Service (Respondent 19). This could also be seen as an example of framing, further discussed by Windsor, Chapter 3 in this volume.
130 On this, see also Yong et al., 'Tacticians, Stewards and Professionals'.

> I am trying really not to sound that I am in favour of this or that political position or this or that political group. Of course sometimes what I am saying will help the Greens, sometimes what I am saying will help the ECR, yes, this is much more rare I think, but it's like what at least I am trying really not to be a friend of anyone, at least not like openly.[131]

Among legal advisers, there is a feeling that, for some groups, legal questions matter more than for others. And while certain groups tend to be more critical of the Legal Service opinions, they still trust and acknowledge its position, which the advisers see as a sign of 'the good health of our corporate reputation'.[132] MEPs 'expect us to be neutral and they expect us to give our position and I think that's the most gratifying thing is when you have people from different political groups turning to you and asking you'.[133] This represents trust[134] and 'it really makes our day'.[135] Legal advice is forceful only if taken up by one of the political groups.[136] Unlike in the Council, national positions are seldom relevant[137] except in agriculture or fisheries,[138] or in patent law, which is 'everybody against Spain and Spain against everybody'.[139] Since the matter was litigated in Spanish,[140] Spaniards dealt with the case in the Legal Service. However, 'this is a clear example of neutrality, complete neutrality'.[141]

MEPs often dislike having too many options and prefer a single solution. If more than one option remains on the table, 'immediately it will be this typical comment about . . . five lawyers five different opinions'.[142] But a preference for one option is also tied to the fragmented composition of the Parliament: group support will likely be divided between the alternatives.[143] While some politicians 'are really eager to fight', others are mainly geared at wrapping up things, and seem prepared to fight for any solution that the Legal Service suggests.[144]

131 Interview with a Member of the EP Legal Service (Respondent 5).
132 Interview with a Member of the EP Legal Service (Respondent 2).
133 Interview with a Member of the EP Legal Service (Respondent 3).
134 Interview with a Member of the EP Legal Service (Respondent 2).
135 Interview with a Member of the EP Legal Service (Respondent 3).
136 Ibid.
137 See also more generally in relation to EP officials, Morten Egeberg, Åse Gornitzka, Jarle Trondal and Mathias Johannessen, 'Parliament Staff: Unpacking the Behaviour of Officials in the European Parliament' (2013) 20(4) *Journal of European Public Policy* 495–514, at 510.
138 Interview with a Member of the EP Legal Service (Respondent 4).
139 Interview with a Member of the EP Legal Service (Respondent 2).
140 See Case C-146/13 *Spain* v. *Parliament and Council* (ECLI:EU:C:2015:298).
141 Interview with a Member of the EP Legal Service (Respondent 2).
142 Ibid.
143 Interview with a former Member of the EP Legal Service (Respondent 19).
144 Interview with a Member of the EP Legal Service (Respondent 3).

Legal advisers have an understanding of this dynamic. An MEP deals with numerous issues each day; she might be the rapporteur on one file or ten files, and may just wish for one solution, which for the legal adviser might not always be easy to offer.[145] Yet, MEPs wish for certainty and the answer needs to be framed that way.[146] A clear answer provides a safety net and the assurance needed.[147]

Few questions can be answered with a simple 'yes' or 'no'. Often the Legal Service engages with the MEPs with a view to finding a good way of drafting or another way of reaching a particular goal.[148] Helping out involves asking additional questions to clarify the objective.[149] The difficulty of keeping the role of a neutral expert is that the legal solutions an expert offers often end up shaping the political objectives as well.[150] EU legal advisers tend to believe that the two can be kept separate.[151] Yet, the distinction between legal questions (the legal advisers' territory) and political questions (which legal advisers strongly feel they should stay clear of)[152] often becomes difficult to maintain. Legal advisers receive questions that are not very legal, or are asked to provide solutions that are not necessarily a choice between the 'legal' and the 'illegal', but rather indicate a preference.[153] When a legal adviser clearly indicates that 'by the way the last sentence is a purely political one, it's not a legal assessment and they'll often say, "but that's good, I liked it."'[154] The legal adviser explains this with reference to time constraints, 'the nature of today's politicians . . . not

[145] Interview with a Member of the EP Legal Service (Respondent 4).

[146] On this, see Koskenniemi, Chapter 2 and Windsor, Chapter 3 in this volume.

[147] Interview with a Member of the EP Legal Service (Respondent 3).

[148] Interview with a member of the European Parliament's Legal Service (Respondent 4). In 'Risk Management: Government Lawyers and the Provision of Legal Advice' Ben Yong calls this the 'coorporate approach', where lawyers are encouraged to work closely with administrators (Section 3.10). See also Laws, 'Giving Effect to Policy in Legislation: How to Avoid Missing the Point', 1–16.

[149] Interview with a Member of the EP Legal Service (Respondent 5). On this, see also Jean-Paul Jacqué, 'The Role of Legal Services in the Elaboration of European Legislation' in Antoine Vauchez and Bruno de Witte (eds.), *Lawyering Europe. European Law as a Transnational Social Field* (Oxford: Hart Publishing, 2013), p. 49.

[150] Triantafillou, 'The Politics of Neutrality and the Changing Role of Expertise in Public Administration', 174–87, at 183.

[151] Jacqué, 'The Role of Legal Services in the Elaboration of European Legislation', at 49.

[152] On this, see also Page, 'Their Word Is Law', at 83.

[153] Interview with a member of the European Parliament's Legal Service (Respondent 4). Yong notes in his study 'Risk Management: Government Lawyers and the Provision of Legal Advice' that Whitehall legal advisers were often drawn into issues which are not strictly or purely 'legal': to comment and give their opinion on cases, operational matters, implementation (legislative or non-legislative), and the legal implications of proposed government action, but also issues of practicality, prudence and 'handling', para. 3.3.

[154] Interview with a Member of the EP Legal Service (Respondent 3).

to lose too much time with questioning and with debates' but rather 'have precise orientation and go for it'.[155] The political is built into the context in which legal advisers work. Legislating is a political process, which influences the work of legal advisers, also making it difficult to distinguish between the legal and the political. Yet, 'when it just goes too far I've always said this: here are your choices, you choose, I cannot do it for you'.[156] Sometimes when MEPs do not 'know how to solve a particular problem they are tempted to ask an innocent expert in this room'.[157] Then of course it would be the legal advisers' job to assist with the legal questions, but 'if it's purely political I think we should be honest and tell it to them'.[158] Most EP legal advisers feel that it is not only imperative but also possible to avoid solving political questions:

> I receive all of the time questions that are of a political nature but then I am simply telling the members that this is where my advice finishes and from this point on there is a political choice.[159]

Even in these cases, it is the legal adviser's job to alert to possible consequences of different alternatives.[160] While politics penetrates law in many ways, legal advisers seem to feel that they know where the line between legal and political questions is. Some also stress how political choices involve political responsibility, which should always stay with the MEPs.[161] Politicians are under no duty to follow the legal advice received. Under the principle of non-accountability generally attached to lawyers, legal advisers are not considered accountable for their client's actions.[162]

In negotiations, a legal adviser's job is to assist the negotiators 'to find solutions which were legally viable and would facilitate agreement'.[163] When negotiating with the other institutions, legal advisers do not receive political instructions regarding the legal advice they are to provide.[164] A legal adviser is expected to state the law as it stands. To receive political instructions on legal matters would be 'somewhat contradictory': 'If a Legal Service were to be instrumentalised in

155 Ibid.
156 Interview with a Member of the EP Legal Service (Respondent 4).
157 Interview with a Member of the EP Legal Service (Respondent 5).
158 Ibid.
159 Ibid.
160 Ibid. This is a key element also in Yong, 'Risk Management: Government Lawyers and the Provision of Legal Advice'.
161 Interview with a member of the EP Legal Service (Respondent 3). See also Lewis, 'Aspects of Professionalism', 132–52 at 151.
162 Andrew Boon, *Lawyers' Ethics and Professional Responsibility* (Oxford: Hart Publishing, 2015), p. 113.
163 Interview with a former member of the EP Legal Service (Respondent 19).
164 Ibid.

this fashion, the resulting analysis would be devoid of legal credibility, and would just become another element in the morass of political considerations being bandied about'.[165] The Parliament's delegation will have a predefined political position, and the legal adviser may be asked to assist in appreciating whether a particular compromise solution departs from this position.[166] Whatever advice the EP legal advisers give is likely to be mirrored against and challenged by the legal advisers of the other institutions who also participate in these negotiations. Legal Service positions often take the form: proposal X is possible, if this, this and that is taken into account in the manner required by the Treaties.[167] This formulation is useful in particular in case of strong political will to promote the proposal in question but the matter is legally problematic. Formulating a 'conditional but cautiously positive' opinion avoids the need to issue a negative opinion. However, when the opinion enters the political arena conditions are easily forgotten: 'we checked with the Legal Service, and the Legal Service says that X is fine'.[168]

The fragmented composition of the Parliament increases the need to find compromises on legal issues. The focus of EP legal advisers is on offering solutions, often through imaginative or alternative means. This is essential for maintaining one's usefulness in an environment where they need to justify their existence. Lawyers defending legality and the Treaties tend to be conservative.[169] In the EP, both legal and diplomatic skills are needed:

> if they see that we are providing them with helpful expertise and . . . we have shown that we have been helpful then . . . the more they try to take our opinion into account but, of course, it depends also on their political agenda and on what they want to achieve. Sometimes what we are saying can be in the way of what they want to achieve.[170]

For some, maintaining law's integrity in this viciously instrumentalised environment becomes too much. A respondent forcefully indicated how this environment 'where law makes no difference' makes it impossible to fulfil the lawyer's task of standing for the integrity of the law.[171] It is a constant struggle for authority and recognition. While the Council Legal Service may, due to its strong institutional position, speak like an oracle and still be listened to, the

165 Ibid.

166 Ibid.

167 Interview with a legal and policy adviser to a Vice-President of the European Parliament (Respondent 54).

168 Ibid.

169 Interview with a member of the EP Legal Service (Respondent 2).

170 Interview with a member of the EP Legal Service (Respondent 5).

171 Interview with a member of Commission Services (Respondent 47).

environment in which the EP Legal Service operates forces it to be persuasive. This setting is unusual for a group of professionals, who tend to play a dominant role in any professional-client relationship.[172] In the Parliament, what you say will affect how much attention will be given to your advice. If you are too much of a lawyer, you are not helpful. If you object too much, 'they will tell you that you are crazy. Well, it's not easy'.[173]

## 6.5 THE CLIENTS' WISH LIST

Few MEPs seem to believe much in the objectivity of law. 'Five lawyers, five opinions' is a quote often repeated in interviews. Every lawyer has a different opinion, and there is always the choice of deciding which one to follow. MEPs also pay attention to how the Council and EP Legal Service often disagree on points of law.[174] An adviser to a political group notes how it is 'quite funny' in trilogues when the Council and the EP Legal Service disagree on so many issues. 'So you notice that they are politicians as well.'[175] For this reason, 'I think we should see that on most issues, lawyers are likely to disagree.'[176] Instead of demonstrating faith in the objectivity of law, MEPs appreciate creativity in applying it:

> What I have learned here is that there is no one lawyer or one objective interpretation; when it comes to the Parliament's lawyers it is always a matter of who you ask especially when it comes to questions of competence. Some are very cautious and always rather think that there is no competence. But then there are those who are more creative, and who start comparing and digging and end up identifying many cases that a competence claim could be built on.[177]

MEPs never work in isolation. Whatever advice is given is scrutinised many times in different committees and shadow meetings. An experienced MEP explains how she never trusts only one opinion, except when it is a perfect match with her own. And even then it might not be wise to trust it, because it is certain that someone else will have found another lawyer who says something different and it is clever to know in advance how this other person will

172 Richard Wasserstrom, 'Lawyers As Professionals: Some Moral Issues' (1975) *Human Rights* 1–24 at 18.

173 Interview with a Member of the EP Legal Service (Respondent 2).

174 Interview with a policy adviser to a political group; former adviser to an MEP (Respondent 43).

175 Ibid.

176 Interview with an MEP (Respondent 41).

177 Ibid. This often happens in EU legislative negotiations. See Leino, 'EU Competence As a Framework for Argumentation'.

argue.[178] Politicians have little wish to be constrained by law or a legal service. 'My job is to legislate, and this presumes creativity, and I often know clearly what I want. But I am not a lawyer, nor am I an expert in EU law, even though I do have some understanding of it', says an MEP.[179] Legal expertise may also be held by others than lawyers in general, or EU legal advisers in particular. For this reason, the interviewed MEP would not check everything with legal experts presuming that she knows what the law says. However, with new issues or matters requiring more far reaching interpretation, she would.[180]

Overall, the interview data suggests a lack of awareness regarding legal questions among the MEPs[181] who see competence questions as an irritating constraint which cannot be totally ignored: if I do not cover my back there will be somebody else coming with that legal argument. Responsible rapporteurs are also responsive to legal issues. Competence is largely approached as a political question, not a legal one. If political support exists competence will be found as part of a compromise. This is fundamentally not a legal or technical question, and cannot be defined in just one way.[182] For this reason, an MEP explains that using legal argumentation in parliamentary discussions

> makes me furious. As a politician, I may hold any opinion that I like; that the EU should be shut down, or that it holds this particular competence. Law should never be a ground for limiting political opinions. I may hold the opinion that the EU must offer minimum social security to everyone, and will then be told by a lawyer that I cannot demand this because there is no competence. But I may hold any political demands that I see fit.[183]

These demands may also stretch to matters where the EU has no competence: 'I think the EU should start legislating also on matters that fall under national competence ... leaving matters in national hands often means that nobody is dealing with them.'[184] Possibility of litigation may come up during parliamentary discussions, but it is not necessarily enough to dissuade MEPs from taking a particular course of action.[185] Recently the Court has addressed two cases where EP Legal Service opinions have been invoked to demonstrate that the European Parliament had ignored the opinion of its legal advisers. In *Donnici*, a legal opinion addressed to the JURI committee was used as

[178] Interview with an MEP (Respondent 41).
[179] Ibid.
[180] Ibid.
[181] On this, see also Yong et al., 'Tacticians, Stewards and Professionals'.
[182] Interview with an MEP (Respondent 41).
[183] Ibid.
[184] Ibid.
[185] Interview with a former political adviser to an MEP (Respondent 42).

evidence by MEP Beniamino Donnici to challenge the Parliament's decision on the verification of credentials.[186] A similar type of dispute emerged when Hungary challenged the European Parliament's resolution on Article 7(1) TEU on the existence of a clear risk of a serious breach by Hungary of EU values with reference to an opinion of the Legal Service, addressed to its President.[187] In both cases the Parliament argued that the opinion was an internal and confidential document,[188] which the Court accepted. This setting is, however, different from public access to legal opinions given in the legislative context, which the Court has been called to address several times in relation to Council and Commission Legal Service opinions and where the Court has consistently underlined the need to ensure broad public access.

Does law have any role in the European Parliament then? For MEPs, knowledge of the law is tied to credibility:

> Those who have been longer in this business understand that you will appear as an idiot if you make silly proposals. This will affect your future chances; people will think that that person cannot be trusted with anything serious since she has no understanding of how the system works and what the EU competences are.[189]

Notwithstanding the general scepticism towards the objectivity of law, Treaty limits still matter. If there is a general conviction than a proposal would require Treaty amendment, then it is not considered worth the trouble.[190] An MEP explains how, prior to making proposals on competence, for example, she checks the ground with not only the EP's own lawyers, but also the Commission and their lawyers[191] with a view to clarifying whether it is possible to do what she wishes to do:

> I recently had the experience that what I wished to do could not be done because it affected the Treaties and competence. So how can I write such a report when people will think I'm a jerk who proposes things that are not

[186] Joined cases C-393/07 and C-9/08 *Italian Republic* v. *Beniamino Donnici* v. *European Parliament*, Order of the Court of 29 January 2009.

[187] Case C-650/18 *Hungary* v. *Parliament*. More recently on public access to legal service opinions given in the legislative context, see Cases C-156/21 *Hungary v. Parliament and Council*, paras. 36–64, and C-157/21 *Poland v. Parliament and Council*, paras. 33–61, concerning the budget conditionality mechanism.

[188] Order of the Court of 14 May 2019, paras. 3–5.

[189] Interview with an MEP (Respondent 41).

[190] Ibid.

[191] Relying on the Commission's line of argumentation is common also among EP officials, who are often attracted by the European agenda of a supranational institution. Egeberg et al., 'Parliament Staff: Unpacking the Behaviour of Officials in the European Parliament', at 510.

> legally possible? So I needed to propose things that were legally possible; of course that matters.[192]

Even though better regulation always figures high on the institutional Legal Services' task lists, the way the Parliament conducts its legislative work is arranged so as to make it virtually impossible. The Parliament's working methods place emphasis on the rapporteur. Much of EU legislation is detailed regulation. There is seldom a political position on every detail within the group; instead, it is the rapporteur who is trusted to sort out such matters, especially if she is known as a reliable MEP who does not overdo her own agenda.[193] MEPs' political advisers often act instead of the MEP and may have significant responsibility and freedom.[194] The Legal Service seems to have effectively sidetracked these debates. An MEP notes how '[n]ever in a million years have I seen the Legal Service participate in these discussions. I may engage them to consider how the Treaty should be interpreted on a particular question, but they are not involved in drafting compromises; this takes place between rapporteurs, shadow rapporteurs and their assistants and the Committee Secretariat'.[195] When the Parliament votes on amendments, often opposing or inconsistent amendments win and are subsequently included in the Parliament's position to be later sorted out in trilogues.[196] Often, there is confusion about how to vote about packages that contain conflicting elements,[197] something that the Legal Service could have dealt with already at the Committee level. Instead, the incoherent Parliament position is left for the Secretariat to sort out, without amending the voting result.[198]

What does legal expertise then mean in the European Parliament? Does such a thing even exist? And what are lawyers needed for?

The interviews illustrate the desire for a creative lawyer whose function comes close to that of a quasi-politician.[199] The 'ideal' lawyer needs to be a free European spirit with a great deal of imagination and courage to actively propose solutions. Overall, lawyers are seen as conservative, without much vision.[200] Yet, the Treaties include endless possibilities for creative solutions,

192 Interview with an MEP (Respondent 41).
193 Interview with a policy adviser to a political group; former adviser to an MEP (Respondent 43).
194 Ibid.
195 Interview with an MEP (Respondent 40).
196 Ibid.
197 Interview with a former MEP (Respondent 46).
198 Interview with an MEP (Respondent 40).
199 See Wendel, *Lawyers and Fidelity to Law*, at 11.
200 On this, see also Stephen Laws, 'Legislation and Politics' in David Feldman (ed.), *Law in Politics, Politics in Law* (Hart: Oxford 2015), pp. 93–5.

which lawyers should be eager to offer, and which indeed can often be found: 'If for example taxation is not an EU competence and tax evasion cannot be controlled that way, how about treating this as money laundering and immediately EU competence emerges.'[201] Creativity is the key:

> this kind of lawyers is exactly what I need and this Parliament needs so very urgently as the co-legislature. This kind of skill is what lawyers should have because I think the lawyers have too big a tendency to explain how things are, and see as a starting point that they cannot be much different from what they are now.[202]

Often questions are less about legality and more about turning political ideas into reality: Legal assistance is needed in the instrumentalist sense: with 'drafting or using the right provisions or the right case law or the right precedents'.[203] So from the MEP perspective,

> if I am the average politician, I write a political statement that this is what I want. And they tell me that she may want all that she wants but this falls outside the scope. And that's when I need this creative lawyer who has the guts to start creating this legislation and would take as starting point that this is what I want; if these matters were included in scope, what needs amending.[204]

There is also a need for an 'amoral technician whose peculiar skills and knowledge in respect to the law' are for the use of her clients.[205] Lawyers are needed for their knowledge of legislative technique. An MEP explains how in her thinking, the specific expertise required from legal advisers is primarily technical in character. As a politician, an MEP would not know how to change legislation or competence, 'what paragraphs and how and what grounds I could change them', what other legislation or existing case law might need to be amended. Being told that doing what I wish to do is not possible is 'so frustrating'.[206] Rather than being a power player in the Parliament, the Legal Service is an enabling tool.[207]

201 Interview with an MEP (Respondent 41). This kind of creativity is often used as a legislative technique in EU lawmaking. See Leino, 'The Politics of Efficient Compromise in the Adoption of EU Legal Acts'.

202 Interview with a policy adviser to a political group; former adviser to an MEP (Respondent 43).

203 Interview with a Member of the EP Legal Service (Respondent 45).

204 Interview with an MEP (Respondent 41). On creativity, see also Jacqué, 'The Role of Legal Services in the Elaboration of European Legislation', p. 46. David Howarth, *Law as Engineering – Thinking About What Lawyers Do* (Cheltenham: Edward Elgar Publishing, 2013).

205 Wasserstrom, 'Lawyers As Professionals: Some Moral Issues', at 6.

206 Interview with an MEP (Respondent 41).

207 Interview with a policy adviser to a political group; former adviser to an MEP (Respondent 43).

Nevertheless, legal advisers feel that their opinions are 'very often' taken into account.[208] They feel that their role is relevant; it builds on the authority that is founded in the opinion being based on facts.[209] Being seen as impartial and objective brings with it some expectations as well. A legal adviser remembers how she during negotiations spotted a problem, which she pointed out to one of the policy advisers: 'and the policy advisor said yes I know, but you have the authority to go there to the MEP and say what you're saying is basically bullshit almost, and I can't because it's my boss and you have the authority of the Legal Service so you can go there and say that, so please do it'.[210] Overall, the key job of the EP Legal Service is to enable the realisation of the political ideas that the Parliament produces, not to oppose everything, or question them.[211] A parliamentarian does not wish to be

> inhibited by [law as a] limiting factor. This makes them difficult to deal with, frankly, because they don't have that legal instinct, and well, if we don't like the law we just change the law, if we don't like the Treaties, we just disobey the Treaties.[212]

## 6.6 CONCLUSIONS

In the European Parliament, there is no single authority responsible for legal interpretation. MEPs can and do shop around in a free market for legal advice, and the market often provides a substantial variety of opinions. Faced with a choice of legal interpretations, a parliamentarian tends to opt for the one that best serves his or her political objectives. Law certainly does not rule. At best, it is seen as a servant, an instrument for promoting political objectives. Many times, it looks more like an adversary and irritant.

Legal work in a political environment is always a balancing act, but in the EP, matters are further complicated by the weak institutional status of its Legal Service and the competition from other sources of legal advice. The inhouse legal advisers are under pressure to calibrate their message and delivery so as to stay relevant and in demand. But they also need to remain conscious of their independence and their need to provide an objective view.[213] In such a setting,

208 Interview with a member of the EP Legal Service (Respondent 2).

209 Interview with a member of the EP Legal Service (Respondent 3).

210 Ibid.

211 Interview with a policy adviser to a political group; former adviser to an MEP (Respondent 43).

212 Interview with a member of the Council Legal Service (Respondent 30).

213 Lewis, 'Aspects of Professionalism', at 150.

even with the best of intentions, defending the integrity of law becomes difficult. The obvious risk is that legal advice becomes subordinated to the political agenda and loses its claim to objectivity, a central premise of its power. 'If the law comes to be seen merely as politics by other means then public decision-making . . . is deprived of a dimension that is otherwise liable to improve its quality, efficiency and even its effectiveness.'[214]

In the quest for a more democratic and more accountable decision-making in the European Union, the European Parliament serves a critical role as its main forum of political contestation. Law provides a frame for that political contestation and needs to facilitate proper translation of electoral voices into political action. The law is 'worthy of being taken seriously, interpreted in good faith with due regard to its meaning, and not simply to be seen as an obstacle standing in the way of the client's goals'.[215] This requires intelligent and, no doubt, sometimes creative reading of the Treaties. But law is also meant to constrain, and to protect the careful balance of powers that underlies the European construction. A Union that is seen to be careless about the limits of its powers will quickly lose its legitimacy. In this quest, the job of lawyers is to act as guardians of the EU's constitutional and institutional structure, and to mediate the tension between political will and the rule of law. As lawyers in general, Parliament's legal advisers 'must respect the scheme of rights and duties established by the law, and not seek to work around the law because either they or their clients believe the law to be unjust, inefficient, stupid or simply inconvenient'.[216] This is what the European Parliament lawyers try to do in their institution. Considering the weak standing of law and its proponents in the Parliament, this is an unenviable task. In the European Parliament, there is little space for the Legal Service to control political choice beyond identifying possible solutions.

But maybe this is as it should be. In the Council and the Commission, Legal Services often act as power players and effectively limit political choice with their readings of what the law allows as a solution to any political problem. In the Parliament, lawyers' proper role may be to make sure that procedures are roughly followed and the institution remains broadly within its powers, subject to appropriate mechanisms of judicial and political accountability. After all, regardless of its depressingly underdeveloped institutional and constitutional underpinnings, the European Parliament is what the Union has for a place of political contestation.

214 Philip Allott, 'The International Lawyer in Government Service: Ontology and Deontology' (2005) 23(13) *Wis. Int'l L. J.* at 17–18.

215 Wendel, *Lawyers and Fidelity to Law*, at 8.

216 Ibid., 49.

# 7

# The Politics of Legal Expertise at Westminster in Times of Crisis

Ben Yong

## 7.1 INTRODUCTION

How is legal expertise deployed in an intensely political environment like the Westminster Parliament? Certainly what has marked out the period since the 2016 referendum on leaving the EU ('Brexit') has been a marked use of law and legal expertise by parliamentarians as a political instrument – or at least, a marked awareness of the importance of legal expertise for Brexit-related issues. Both *Miller* cases,[1] for instance, had Parliament at centre stage: *Miller I* concerned the role of Parliament in notifying the EU of the UK's intention to leave the EU; *Miller II* dealt with the question of whether or not the prorogation of Parliament was lawful.

Inside Parliament, there have been several occasions in which legal advice has been used in political argument. Various governments have made use of the Law Officers (ministers in the executive responsible for legal advice) in Parliament to bolster various positions on Brexit, with limited and sometimes unexpected effects: for instance, the May government was forced to publish the Attorney-General's legal advice on the effect of the Withdrawal Agreement's Protocol, following a Commons vote that ministers were in contempt of Parliament for refusing to do so.[2] Select committees have shown an increased willingness to publish legal advice

[1] *R (Miller)* v. *Secretary of State for Exiting the European Union* [2017] UKSC 5 ('*Miller I*') and *R (Miller)* v. *The Prime Minister and Cherry* v. *Advocate General for Scotland* [2019] UKSC 41 ('*Miller II*').

[2] The House of Lords Library has a useful briefing on this incident, and other attempts to force the government to publish government legal advice: see House of Lords Library, 'Publishing Government Legal Advice' (2018), https://researchbriefings.files.parliament.uk/documents/LLN-2018-0115/LLN-2018-0115.pdf.

provided by the in-house lawyers of the Houses of Parliament;[3] but there have also been leaks.[4]

And yet, some parliamentarians have felt dissatisfied with the adequacy of legal support available. We can get a sense of this from an older debate on the Chilcot Report on the Iraq War.[5] Graham Allen MP complained of the difficulties that parliamentarians had in getting legal advice at the time:

> We raised collectively a series of issues about how the House works, one of which was the question of legal advice to Members of Parliament. … The then Clerk of the House said, 'Yes, Mr Allen, I will get you some legal advice.' … I was sent off to the lawyer that the House employs to deal with health and safety matters … That was not of great help, although that was not the lawyer's fault. The House and Members should have had legal advice, just as the Government had legal advice.[6]

Similarly, Margaret Hodge, a Labour MP, has publicly discussed her attempt to gain 'heavyweight' legal support from the House of Commons when chair of the powerful Public Accounts Committee (PAC). Goldman Sachs, which had engaged in a tax-avoidance scheme, had struck a deal with the UK Revenue and Customs department (HMRC) to pay its taxes, but not the interest. When questioned by PAC, HMRC and the National Audit Office (NAO) both refused to disclose information on the deal on basis of confidentiality; and backed up their claims citing legal advice. Hodge argued:

> As both the [NAO] and HMRC had legal advice backing them, we wanted to obtain our own legal advice to challenge them. However, when I asked for this to be arranged I was told that there was no money available. The House of Commons has a £200 million budget, but the powers that be could not find the money we needed to test our view with the lawyers. That decision had, I thought, more to do with the system conspiring against us than with the finances of Parliament. If select committees are to hold the government to account effectively, we need to be able to access all the advice and support

3 Ben Yong, Greg Davies and Cristina Leston-Bandeira, 'Tacticians, Stewards and Professionals: The Politics of Publishing Select Committee Legal Advice' (2019) 46(3) *Journal of Law and Society* 367.

4 'Leaked Commons legal analysis of Brexit deal vindicates Trump, contradicts May and adds to Brexiteers' concerns', *Brexit Central* (2 December 2018), https://brexitcentral.com/leaked-commons-legal-analysis-brexit-deal-vindicates-trump-contradicts-may-adds-brexiteers-concerns/.

5 The Chilcot Inquiry was established in 2009 to consider events between 2001 and 2009 regarding the UK's involvement in the Iraq; and set out what happened and what lessons could be learned. The report was published in 2016 and can be found here: https://webarchive.nationalarchives.gov.uk/20171123123237/http://www.iraqinquiry.org.uk/.

6 HC Deb 14 July 2016 Volume 613 Col. 478.

> necessary to help us to do our work. It is simply not on to permit public money to be used to fund advice to officials, but to deny the facility to politicians.[7]

These comments suggest parliamentarians, who are at the centre of the law-making process, appear to have limited provision or access to legal expertise. If true, this would be unfortunate: one study argues that 'effective [parliamentary] scrutiny is more tied to legal expertise than is usually acknowledged'.[8] But we should be wary in reaching such a conclusion too hastily. We should interrogate the meaning of legal expertise; and examine the processes by which parliamentarians seek and receive advice about legal issues.[9]

In this chapter we use the broad term 'legal support' to refer to legal expertise. Legal support is best understood as different kinds of knowledge about legal issues from those trained in the law. There is legal advice, legal opinion and legal information. *Legal advice* is a formal written opinion to a client setting out the law, and its cautious application to a certain set of facts. This is what is commonly imagined when one talks of legal advice – and one suspects what Graham Allen MP was after. There is *legal opinion*, which has no identifiable client, and is perhaps less cautious and emphasises application of the law to facts. And finally there is *legal information*: a matter-of-fact statement of how the law works, but with no or very limited discussion of how it might apply.

This chapter uses Eliot Freidson's model of lay and professional referral systems to explain how legal expertise is understood and made use of at Westminster. Parliamentarians do have access to a vast array of sources from which they can get legal support. But parliamentarians – like all laypeople – will first tend to make use of known networks to understand legal issues. They may seek help from in-house support, but this varies on what is being asked for, and only rarely will they seek legal advice – primarily, within select committees. The ultimate argument of the chapter is that the processes of seeking out and receiving legal support in Parliament operate similarly to the way that legal advice or professional advice is sought and received in society more broadly. There is much ignorance of the law; much self-help; with only the educated or the highly motivated seeking (and perhaps needing) 'legal advice'.

This chapter draws on data from a Leverhulme Trust-funded project examining the provision and reception of legal support in the four legislatures of the

7 Margaret Hodge, *Called to Account: How Corporate Bad Behaviour and Government Waste Combine to Cost Us Millions* (London: Little, Brown, 2016), p. 71.

8 Carolyn Evans and Simon Evans, 'Messages from the Front Line: Parliamentarians' Perspectives on Rights Protection' in Tom Campbell, Keith D. Ewing, and Adam Tomkins (eds.), *The Legal Protection of Human Rights: Sceptical Rssays* (Oxford: Oxford University Press, 2011), pp. 329 and 346.

9 For elaboration of the issue at the EU level, see Leino-Sandberg, Chapter 6 in this volume.

TABLE 7.1 *Interviews at Westminster*

| Actor | Number |
|---|---|
| MPs | 3 |
| Peers | 6* |
| Clerks | 11 |
| Parliamentary lawyers | 11 |
| Research staff | 7 |
| Third parties | 5 |
| TOTAL | 43 |

* One of these peers was a former MP.

UK.[10] The primary research method was semi-structured elite interviews conducted over 2017–18 just after the Brexit vote. The interviews aimed to capture a variety of actors to map the process of provision and reception of legal advice in the legislature: parliamentarians, in-house parliamentary lawyers, clerks, researchers[11] and third parties (i.e. lobbyists and private lawyers) – see Table 7.1. A total of eighty-five people were interviewed, but in this chapter, we shall only make use of interviews done at Westminster.

We begin this chapter by discussing how legal expertise and the legal profession has been understood in literature on the sociology of the legal profession, and Freidson's model of the lay referral system and its counterpart, the professional referral system. We then briefly discuss the Westminster Parliament and its organisation. We suggest that the process of seeking legal support is primarily client-driven, and given the nature of Parliament, what we end up seeing is something similar to what Freidson described in relation to medical expertise: the operation of a lay referral system, and a professional referral system.

## 7.2 THE SOCIOLOGY OF PROFESSIONS

We begin with some brief comments on the sociology of the legal profession, which may shed light on the nature and use of expertise. Like the sociology of the professions more generally,[12] much of the early research on the legal

10 'Legal advice to legislatures – supporting a professionalising legislature' (RPG-2016–388).

11 This refers to permanent, non-partisan staff, rather than those staff employed and under the control of members themselves.

12 Julia Evetts, 'The Sociology of Professional Groups: New Directions' (2006) 54 *Current Sociology* 133; and Elizabeth H. Gorman and Rebecca L. Sandefur, '"Golden Age" Quiescence, and Revival How the Sociology of Professions Became the Study of Knowledge-Based Work' (2011) 38 *Work and Occupations* 275.

profession initially focused on definitional issues – how the profession differed from other occupations, and the question of control.[13] Amongst other matters, a profession is marked by its claim to possess a particular expertise, which laypeople do not and cannot share. Possession of this expertise points to another marker of a profession: control over its own work, and therefore autonomy from the client. Part of this autonomy is the capacity of the profession to determine what the appropriate boundaries of their expertise are. Moreover, since the client lacks this particular expertise, they are in a position of weakness relative to the profession. The potential for abuse of this position is offset by a final characteristic of professions: a normative orientation towards the service of their clients and more generally the public.

However, a major theme of the sociology of the legal profession is that in practice individual professionals, the structure of the profession as a whole – and therefore the use of legal expertise – has been and remains profoundly shaped by the client. Heinz et al. showed, for instance, in a number of classic works that the legal profession is organised into two hemispheres: those with large corporate clients and those with small clients.[14] This inverted the traditional view that a key marker of the legal profession is its relative autonomy from the client – instead, it is the client who organises lawyers. Later studies suggested that in practice the relationship between lawyer and client is not one of dominance and submission, but rather a negotiated relationship.[15]

If anything, the fundamental importance of the client for professionals, lawyers or otherwise, has only become more apparent in recent years. The sociology of the professions has arguably become the study of knowledge-based work, reflecting changes in the professions themselves. Whereas many (perhaps most) professions were previously self-employed, general practitioners, many now work within large complex organisations.[16] Professionals are now in a much more precarious position, subject to the demands and norms of their employers. They are also under pressure because of the emergence of other occupations who also offer services based on expert

[13] See generally Richard Moorhead, 'Lawyers and Other Legal Service Providers' in Peter Cane and Herbert Kritzer (eds.), *The Oxford Handbook of Empirical Legal Research* (Oxford: Oxford University Press, 2010), p. 785.

[14] John Heinz and Edward Laumann, *Chicago Lawyers: The Social Structure of the Bar* (revised ed., Illinois: Northwestern University Press and American Bar Foundation, 1994); and John Heinz, Robert Nelson, Rebecca Sandefur and Edward Laumann, *Urban Lawyers: The New Social Structure of the Bar* (Chicago and London: University of Chicago Press, 2005).

[15] Austin Sarat and William Felstiner, *Divorce Lawyers and Their Clients: Power and Meaning in the Legal Process* (Oxford: Oxford University Press, 1995).

[16] Gorman and Sandefur, '"Golden Age," Quiescence, and Revival How the Sociology of Professions Became the Study of Knowledge-Based Work'.

knowledge; and more recently, from the explosion of freely available information on the internet and moves towards automation.[17] All this weakens the ability of professionals to maintain control over what has traditionally been seen as 'their' bodies of knowledge. They no longer have a monopoly over their expertise.[18]

But the importance of the client has other implications. Lewis suggests that what matters is the client's perception of expertise (legal or not). Expertise is therefore to some extent constructed.[19] As Moorhead has argued:

> [C]lients' problems are embedded in the social: problems are ultimately defined in the clients' language and should be solved in their world. Clients may want the lawyers to speak their language and empathize ... More fundamentally, this emphasis on the social (clients as the organizing construct), over the professional (a neutral body of specialist knowledge) casts some doubt on the objective value of legal knowledge.[20]

Eliot Freidson's research sits squarely within the sociology of professions. In a number of works, Freidson developed a model to understand the process by which illness is understood and diagnosed in a community, and more broadly, the role of the medical profession and the use of medical expertise.[21] And although he focused on the medical profession, Freidson did think his work could be more widely applied.[22] Freidson argued that professions cannot be understood without reference to their clients. Clients often have ideas about what they want and need which are different from that of the professions, or practitioners. To understand professions, therefore, they must be located in local communities of prospective clients.

In broad terms, Freidson posited two ideal referral systems (although in practice there may be several such referral systems coexisting at any one time): the lay referral system, and the professional referral system. A layperson exhibiting symptoms of an illness is likely to first self-diagnose. When this self-diagnosis fails, she then seeks out friends and family – what Freidson calls

17 See also Micklitz, Chapter 5 in this volume.

18 Gorman and Sandefur '"Golden Age," Quiescence, and Revival How the Sociology of Professions Became the Study of Knowledge-Based Work'.

19 Philip Lewis, 'Aspects of Professionalism: Constructing the Lawyer-Client Relationship' in Scott Cummings (ed.), *The Paradox of Professionalism: Lawyers and the Possibility of Justice* (Cambridge: Cambridge University Press, 2012), p. 132.

20 Moorhead, 'Lawyers and Other Legal Service Providers' 785, at 788.

21 Eliot Freidson, 'Client Control and Medical Practice' (1960) 65(4) *American Journal of Sociology* 374; and Eliot Freidson, *Profession of Medicine: A Study of the Sociology of Applied Knowledge* (revised ed., Chicago: University of Chicago Press, 1988).

22 See, e.g., Freidson, *Profession of Medicine: A Study of the Sociology of Applied Knowledge*, p. 300.

'consultants' – for further diagnosis and potential remedies. This casual process of exploring diagnoses when drawn out takes the form of referrals, moving from the close to the successively more distant. This is the lay referral system. At a certain point, however, a professional physician – the general practitioner (GP) – is finally consulted. It is at this point that the patient may enter the professional referral system, if the GP cannot herself diagnose and provide a cure for the patient's illness. Thereafter, depending on the nature of the illness, the patient may then be moved through the professional referral system (in the UK, the NHS – the National Health Service).

This process is not as tidy or deliberate as presented, of course. One of the characteristics of the lay referral system is its untidiness: this is because it is *the patient* who is in control and determines if she is 'sick' and when and if she seeks help. By contrast, the professional referral system is relatively regimented and structured. In this system, the layperson may be referred to other professionals, but he or she has limited say in the matter – it is primarily at the discretion of the professional they are seeing at the time.

Freidson's model fits most people's experience of sickness. If we have symptoms of illness, we tend to self-diagnose first: is this something we have had before, and have managed ourselves? Is this just a rash brought on by spring pollen, or something more? If our symptoms continue or become more serious, we may only then seek the advice of friends and family – those we think are more knowledgeable than ourselves. If their suggested diagnoses and/or remedies do not work, we might ask a friend who is a retired doctor or nurse. Failing that, we might only then call our GP clinic for an appointment. We often avoid seeking professional advice unless we have to, for various reasons: because we do not even recognise we are sick; because we think we are competent ourselves to judge the nature of the illness; because the symptoms seem minor; because of time and cost; perhaps because of a lack of trust in physicians; because of the fear of the unknown; or because of previous experiences in the NHS. The broad point is that entrance into the professional referral system is variable because it is the layperson who largely determines when she has symptoms of illness which requires intervention. So, for instance, it may be that one layperson puts up with a chronic illness because it is manageable, while another will quite quickly seek the support of her GP.

From Freidson's model we can see the central role of the layperson in the identification and rectification of 'the problem'. But Freidson's model can also tell us something about practitioners themselves. Their position in the process of referrals matters. Freidson posits two kinds of practice. First, the independent practice, which attracts its own clientele but must work with and to some extent appeal to lay expectations; and second, dependent practice, which does not attract its own clientele, but serves the needs of others – usually an organisation – and so are more able to resist control of individual clients.

More broadly, Freidson's model of lay and professional networks can be understood as a general model of how laypeople seek out and make use of expertise, and as a reflection on the nature of expertise. Becker, for instance, has extrapolated on Freidson's model, giving the example of computer users and 'computer gurus'.[23] Most computer users have in practice limited computer literacy, only using a fraction of their computers' functions. When faced with a problem, they may reach out to gurus, 'who tell you what you need to know when you need to know it'.[24] In some cases, computer gurus have become regularised, in the form of the 'genius bar' at Apple stores, or the IT department in a university. But on an everyday basis, gurus are often people who just know more than you: colleagues or family friends have learned to resolve problems, not through school and qualifications, but by helping others. Thus, Becker suggests, it might be better to understand knowledge and expertise not as a quantity of which experts have more and laypeople less, but rather describes a 'social relationship between a more knowledgeable person and one who knows less'.[25]

For our purposes Freidson's model of lay and professional referral networks is suggestive; we need not adopt it rigidly. What it illustrates is the importance of the client in shaping the work of those with legal expertise, and the kinds of factors that the client considers in seeking and making use of expertise.

## 7.3 PARLIAMENT AS 'CLIENT'

How well does Freidson's model of lay and professional referral networks apply to Westminster? Given Freidson's emphasis on the client or 'consumer' of professional services, this first requires a discussion of what Parliament – 'the client' – is, how it is organised and what it does. But this is no simple matter: 'Parliament' is constitutional shorthand for a complex entity. As Paul Seaward has recently put it, 'parliament is not one thing, but many; not a simple organisation, but a highly complex one, if, indeed, it can be called an organisation at all; not a single mind, but very many minds concerned with very many different objectives'.[26] To explain: the Westminster Parliament

23 Howard Becker, *What about Mozart? What about Murder? Reasoning from Cases* (Chicago: University of Chicago Press, 2014), chapter 3.

24 Ibid., at 57.

25 Ibid., at 58.

26 Paul Seaward, 'Why the History of Parliament Has Not Been Written' (2021) 40(1) *Parliamentary History* 5, at 22.

consists of two houses, the House of Commons and the House of Lords. The Commons consists of 650 MPs, all elected and organised by political party. It is the most 'political' of the two Houses, and most matters are determined on a partisan basis – that is, by whatever party or parties have a majority in the House. The Lords consists of approximately 800 peers, the majority being appointed as life peers; ninety-nine hereditary peers; and twenty-six bishops. Approximately two-thirds of the appointed life peers belong to a political party; one-quarter of all peers belong to the non-partisan crossbenchers (often members of great professional expertise); the remainder to an amorphous 'other' group.[27] Since the reform of the House of Lords in 1999 and the removal of most hereditary peers, no political party has had a majority in the House: this means the executive must act more cautiously in the Lords. The two Houses are therefore quite different, in appointment, composition and culture: the Commons being a House of 'passion' and politics; the Lords being a House of relative expertise and deliberation.

Each House also consists of nominally equal members, which makes it difficult to impose any kind of hierarchy.[28] Indeed, the House of Commons is often likened to a group of 650 small businesses. Each parliamentarian may prioritise their roles and functions differently. Furthermore, like all legislatures, the Houses represent and contain disagreement.[29] These pressures towards disorganisation are offset to some extent by the self-organisation of members – in particular, political parties, but also in select committees and all-party parliamentary groups, amongst other arrangements.

Finally, leadership in Parliament is not clear. Each House has a governing body: a commission, which consists primarily of a cross-section of parliamentarians, and chaired by the relevant House's Presiding Officer. Each commission manages an administration of non-partisan officials which supports parliamentarians in their work – in particular, on the scrutiny of legislation and executive action. However, these commissions have had a history of weak governance, unable or unwilling to set explicit goals.[30] Thus, Lord Norton has argued: 'there is no one individual who can claim to speak for Parliament. There is no equivalent of a company chair, someone who can speak for the

27 House of Lords Library, 'House of Lords: Statistics on Size and Composition' (2019).

28 Gerhard Loewenberg, *On Legislatures: The Puzzle of Representation* (Boulder: Paradigm Publishers, 2011), p. 49; Gary Cox, 'The Organization of Democratic Legislatures' in Barry Weingast and Donald A. Wittman (eds.), *The Oxford Handbook of Political Economy* (Oxford: Oxford University Press, 2009), p. 141.

29 See generally Jeremy Waldron, *The Dignity of Legislation* (Oxford: Oxford University Press, 1999).

30 See Ben Yong, 'The Governance of Parliament' in Alexander Horne and Gavin Drewry (eds.), *Parliament and the Law* (2nd ed., Oxford: Hart Publishing, 2018), p. 75.

institution ... When there is a scandal, who can answer on behalf of the institution?'[31]

Moreover, as Seaward suggests, the many clients of Parliament have multiple objectives; and there are multiple arenas in which they can act and may require legal support. A report done by the Parliamentary Office of Science and Technology (POST) on the role of research in the UK Parliament noted that parliamentarians seek expertise in respect of their various roles – both as individuals (in committees, debates, constituency work) and in groups (committees, scrutiny of legislation and executive action, political parties, all party parliamentary groups). Moreover, they have a number of different aims in seeking expertise, some of which may conflict with the aims of other parliamentarians: amongst others, 'to support effective scrutiny and inform policy; to provide background knowledge; to substantiate pre-existing views; to provide balance; to provide credibility; and to score political points'.[32]

We have spent some time on the nature and (dis)organisation of Parliament for a reason. The literature on the sociology of the legal profession suggests that the use of legal expertise is profoundly influenced by the client. From the description above we can see 'Parliament' cannot be understood as a singular client; it is an arena, multicentred, comprised of multiple potential clients, and far less hierarchical than the executive branch of government. And therefore we should expect to see this reflected in the nature and use of legal expertise in Parliament. Indeed, we can see the influence in the sheer variety of legal support open to parliamentarians and the absence of a monopoly of legal support; the fluidity of what counts as legal support or expertise; and finally in the use and non-use of legal support by parliamentarians.

## 7.4 THE NON-HIERARCHICAL SOURCES OF LEGAL SUPPORT FOR PARLIAMENTARIANS

There are two matters which are striking about legal support for parliamentarians at Westminster. The first is the sheer variety; and the second is the absence of a clear monopoly over legal support. As one non-lawyer peer stated: 'Half the blighters are lawyers to begin with ... we're awash with QCs [Queen's Counsel] and lawyers'.[33]

31 Lord Norton, 'Speaking for Parliament' (2017) 70 *Parliamentary Affairs* 191, at 201.

32 Caroline Kenny, David Rose, Abbi Hobbs, Chris Tyler and Jason Blackstock, *The Role of Research in the UK Parliament* (London: Houses of Parliament, 2017), p. 11.

33 Interviewee 27, peer (13 September 2017).

### 7.4.1 *Internal Sources*

Parliamentarians from both Houses receive legal support from a range of sources. Kennon organises sources of legal support into two groups: those sources internal to Parliament and those external.[34] The internal sources include legally educated parliamentarians, library and research staff and parliamentary lawyers. External sources include academics, NGOs, think tanks, political parties, the judiciary and the executive. Below, we focus primarily on the internal sources of legal support.

#### 7.4.4.1 Lawyer-Politicians

There is a relatively high number of parliamentarians with legal education in the two Houses.[35] Over the past forty odd years, the number of lawyer-MPs has stayed relatively stable at approximately 15 per cent of the total number of MPs (approximately 100 MPs), although overall the proportion of lawyers in Parliament has been declining since the beginning of the twentieth century.[36] In the Lords, roughly 7 per cent are lawyers (perhaps fifty to sixty peers), but some of these are far more senior figures:[37] several retired Law Lords or UKSC justices (e.g. Lords Hope, Mance and Neuberger); former Lord Chancellors, ministers who dealt with the courts and justice system (e.g. Lords Falconer and MacKay); former Attorneys-General and Solicitor-Generals (e.g. Lords Goldsmith and Morris, Baroness Scotland); and prominent lawyers (e.g. Baroness Chakrabati and Lord Pannick). These lawyer-politicians may provide legal support in debate, select committees and privately with their colleagues – but it remains entirely informal.

#### 7.4.4.2 Parliamentary Staff

There are also staff who have legal training. There are five key sources here: members' staff; specialist advisers; committee staff; clerks in the House Libraries; and parliamentary lawyers. Members' staff are staff employed by

[34] Andrew Kennon, 'Legal Advice to Parliament' in Alexander Horne, Gavin Drewry and Dawn Oliver (eds.), *Parliament and the Law* (Oxford: Hart Publishing, 2013), p. 121.

[35] David Howarth, 'Lawyers in the House of Commons' in David Feldman (ed.), *Law in Politics, Politics in Law* (Oxford: Hart Publishing, 2013), p. 41; see also Ross Cranston, 'Lawyers, MPs and Judges' in David Feldman (ed.), *Law in Politics, Politics in Law* (Oxford: Hart Publishing, 2013), p. 17.

[36] House of Commons Library, 'Social background of MPs 1979–2019' (CBP 7483, 2020).

[37] Peter Dorey and Matthew Purvis, 'Representation in the House of Lords' in Cristina Leston-Bandeira and Louise Thompson (eds.), *Exploring Parliament* (Oxford: Oxford University Press, 2018), pp. 244 and 247.

parliamentarians themselves, and so may serve in a partisan capacity. Specialist advisers are experts appointed for a single inquiry held by a select committee: they are temporary, not permanent staff.

Committee staff, library clerks and parliamentary lawyers form a class of impartial 'permanent' officials who support the legislature in its various functions – permanent in the sense that they do not lose their job following a general election; and impartial in that they must support all parliamentarians, regardless of political disposition. Committee staff are usually experts in a particular area appointed to work with a particular committee on a permanent basis. Library staff belong to one of the libraries of the Houses of Parliament, and provide impartial analysis and briefings on core issues of the day. Finally, parliamentary lawyers are in-house lawyers employed by one of the Houses of Parliament to provide legal support to a number of different clients in Parliament.[38] Unfortunately, there is no official data on the numbers of legally trained members, committee staff or specialist advisers because statistics on these sources (where they exist at all) are not broken down by education. In terms of available data for library clerks, however, there are approximately sixty to seventy library clerks in the House of Commons Library, of whom approximately one-quarter have law degrees.[39] In the House of Lords Library there are approximately twenty-odd clerks.[40]

As of 2020, there are about twenty-three parliamentary lawyers in total, although some work part-time.[41] In the House of Commons, there are eighteen lawyers; in the House of Lords, five. Traditionally, parliamentary lawyers were organised functionally, attached to a particular committee, office or unit. This reflects the nature of Parliament: a body of semi-autonomous constituent parts – the Houses, select committees – each of whom act with limited thought to the needs of the body as a whole.[42] However, in recent years there has been a consolidation of legal services, particularly in the House of Commons. Now most Commons lawyers are organised under the Office of Speaker's Counsel, and work in one of three teams: general, domestic legislation and EU legislation. In the Lords, organisation remains looser.

38 The House of Lords Constitution Committee's two part-time legal advisers sit on the 'penumbra': they are appointed on a sessional basis, but remain with the Committee for much longer than a single inquiry: so we class them as parliamentary lawyers.

39 Private communication.

40 FOI request to House of Lords (30 August 2019).

41 These numbers are calculated from internal documents. We have not here included paralegal staff (two) or the one to two lawyers working for the Joint Procurement Service.

42 Ben Yong, 'The Governance of Parliament' in Alex Horne and Gavin Drewry (eds.), *Parliament and the Law* (2nd ed., Oxford: Hart Publishing, 2018), p. 75.

Parliamentary lawyers provide advice and legal support to various clients in Parliament: to one of the Houses in their corporate capacity on private law (e.g. employment law) or public law (e.g. parliamentary privilege); or to one of the Houses' many committees on a permanent basis (e.g. the Joint Committees on Human Rights and Statutory Instruments, the House of Commons EU Scrutiny Committee and until recently, the House of Lords EU Committee) or on an as-needed basis. They specifically do *not* support individual parliamentarians.

### 7.4.2 *External Sources*

External sources of legal support include academics, NGOs, think tanks, political parties' research units, the judiciary and the executive amongst others. Academics, NGOs, charities and think tanks will primarily provide legal support through private briefings and correspondence with parliamentarians, or in evidence sessions to select committees.[43] Political parties have their own partisan research staff: for example, the Conservatives have the Parliamentary Research Unit; and Labour has the Parliamentary Research Service.[44] Political parties may on occasion also seek formal legal advice from counsel.[45] As one peer noted, 'Opposition people will have [legal support] in their shadow teams, they're awash with lawyers, or they will have lawyers on their side whom they can approach.'[46]

Parliamentarians may also obtain legal support from the other two branches. As already noted, in the House of Lords, some retired Law Lords attend the chamber and will give their views on various issues. UK Supreme Court justices may give public speeches and give evidence before select committees. In terms of the executive, parliamentarians can obtain briefings and statements from ministers; from parliamentary counsel (government lawyers who draft primary legislation) on technical matters of legislation; and from the Law Officers (Ministers ultimately responsible for authoritative legal interpretation within the executive).[47]

43 For NGOs as providers of legal expertise, see Lee and Abbot, Chapter 12 and Korkea-aho, Chapter 11 in this volume.

44 Kenny, Rose, Hobbs, Tyler and Blackstock, *The Role of Research in the UK Parliament*, p. 18.

45 Denis Campbell, 'Hunt broke law by axing NHS 18-week treatment target, says Labour', *The Guardian* (27 April 2018), at www.theguardian.com/politics/2017/apr/27/labour-hunt-broke-law-over-nhs-axing-of-18-week-treatment-target.

46 Interviewee 27, peer (13 September 2017).

47 On the government legal service and the Law Officers, see Ben Yong, *Risk Management: Government Lawyers and the Provision of Legal Advice within Whitehall* (Constitution Unit and Constitution Society, London, 2013). See also House of Lords Library, 'Publishing

So already we can see from the description of sources available to parliamentarians and Parliament that Freidson's model of a lay and professional referral system has some analytical purchase. The external sources of legal support seem to equate to a lay referral system; the internal sources of legal support to a professional referral system. NGOs, think tanks and academics, the judiciary and the executive are all theoretically independent of their 'clients' – indeed, parliamentarians and Parliament are not their clients at all. By contrast internal sources of legal support are much more constrained in who they can support and when. Parliamentary staff are also more dependent: they are employed by one of the Houses, and they are constrained by impartiality, and in the case of parliamentary lawyers, by limiting their support to certain institutional units and functions and prohibiting their support to individuals.

Put differently, on many core functions no one source appears to have a monopoly on legal expertise: parliamentarians and Parliament can choose from whom to seek support. The key exception is parliamentary lawyers dealing with corporate matters (i.e. matters concerning the institution of Parliament as a corporate body – such as contract, procurement, privilege and freedom of information). We can contrast this with the way that legal support is arranged in the executive, where there is a hierarchy (with the Law Officers at the apex), and for the most part government lawyers have a monopoly over legal support.[48] The absence of a monopoly of legal support in Parliament ought not to surprise us. If the nature of Parliament is a set of complex relations and multiple actors with no one fully in charge, then it is hard to see how any one set of actors could assert a monopoly over legal support.

## 7.5 THE FLUID NATURE OF LEGAL EXPERTISE

It is worth clarifying at this point what constitutes legal support. Here are two different interviewees – first, a peer:

> [Law Lords] say what their point of view is about the law is, and that's one of the reasons that they're there really. They're not doing legal advice so much as expressing an opinion for the House to consider . . . it's not quite the same thing as the House are asking for legal advice. The House would normally ask for legal advice from the Attorney General.[49]

Government Legal Advice' (2018), at https://researchbriefings.files.parliament.uk/documents/LLN-2018-0115/LLN-2018-0115.pdf.

48 See generally Yong, *Risk Management: Government Lawyers and the Provision of Legal Advice within Whitehall.*

49 Interviewee 8, peer (22 June 2017).

Second, a parliamentary lawyer:

> If you compare to being in practice, you're asking an opinion on an issue. It's not like that, because [select committees] don't formulate issues for legal advice, questions for legal opinions. And of course, your role does include advising them in a way which means they're aware of stuff. So, it's kind of an informing role as well. So, the nature of things that go to them, you know, certain amounts of it is legal advice, in which you say, 'in my view the law is . . . ', but a certain amount of the rest of it is informing them, telling them about relevant legal things … So, it's much wider than just pure legal advice.[50]

From this we can suggest there are three 'ideal' kinds of legal support. There is *legal information*, which is a matter-of-fact statement about what the relevant law is and its immediate context, but no attempt is made to apply it to a particular set of facts. At its most extreme, this is the kind of support provided, for instance, by Library staff.[51] It adheres closely to 'the facts' to avoid claims that permanent staff are being partisan.

There is *legal advice*: a formal written opinion to a specific client, setting out the law, complete with legal references, and applying it to a particular fact situation. This is in practice much rarer, primarily given by parliamentary lawyers, although not always.[52] It is characterised by its reference to a formal client, a highly impartial tone, a cautiousness about predicted outcomes and an emphasis on what would happen were there litigation.

Finally, there is *legal opinion*, which will set out the relevant law and legal frameworks, and will apply the law (or prospective law) to particular situations. The line between legal opinion and legal advice can blur, but as suggested above, with legal opinion there is usually no clear client; with legal advice, there is. And because there is no specific client, legal opinion may be more speculative and less cautious; at the edges it may even move into the sphere of 'politics'.

Cutting across this taxonomy, however, are the means of delivery in practice. Legal support can be oral or written: written support is more likely to be formal; oral support perhaps less so and allowing for possible nuances. Moreover, legal support may be iterative. It may not be a simple response to

50 Interviewee 22, parliamentary lawyer (27 July 2017).

51 On legal information, see Jack Simson Caird, 'Public Legal Information and Law-making in Parliament' in Alex Horne and Gavin Drewry (eds.), *Parliament and the Law* (2nd ed., Oxford: Hart Publishing, 2018), p. 147.

52 For examples of this, see Yong, Davies and Leston-Bandeira, 'Tacticians, Stewards and Professionals: The Politics of Publishing Select Committee Legal Advice'.

a single question but rather a series of answers in response to a series of questions, so that legal information may come closer to legal opinion – or at least touch more upon application.

In any case, the key point is that legal support differs in shape, form and function depending both on the source of the support, and the client seeking that support. So, for instance, permanent officials provide impartial, apolitical forms of legal support: legal information and legal advice. Whereas the legal support that external organisations and persons offer will primarily be a mixture of legal information and legal opinion: in almost all cases there is no lawyer-client relationship between those providing legal support and the parliamentarian(s).

## 7.6 THE USE AND NON-USE OF LEGAL SUPPORT

Given the sheer variety of legal support available, how was it possible that Graham Allen and Margaret Hodge MP could complain of a lack of legal support? The answer is that how and when parliamentarians seek legal support is a separate matter. That is, an abundance of sources of legal support does not necessarily mean greater use. So, for instance, significant numbers of lawyer-politicians in both Houses does not necessarily translate into a greater understanding of legal issues, or a greater readiness to think about issues of legality. Cranston notes that many lawyer-politicians became involved in law because they thought it was an avenue to politics; nor is it clear that lawyer-politicians actually focus on legal issues or use their legal skills in Parliament.[53] In short, use depends on a number of factors: most relating to the client (demand factors), but some connected to those providing legal support (supply factors).

### 7.6.1 *Considerations of Demand and Supply*

We start with the demand factors. First, some parliamentarians may not even realise a particular issue has legal implications. Most parliamentarians are necessarily generalists at most things: no one can be expert at everything. As one peer with legal experience noted: 'the ordinary parliamentarian ... is not particularly acute to notice sensitive [legal issues]'.[54] One MP-turned-peer noted their experience: 'very often on bills, you don't know there's a problem until you get a letter from the square widgets organisation. So it could be pointed out, this

53 Cranston, 'Lawyers, MPs and Judges', p. 17.
54 Interviewee 8, peer (22 June 2017).

is flawed here and there'.[55] Moreover, many – perhaps most – parliamentarians have a limited attention span because of the many demands on their time.[56] As one interviewee told us: '[Parliamentarians] are not sufficiently well-resourced in terms of time. . . . there's just no time to scrutinise. What would [additional] lawyers be doing, writing things that these people never read?'[57]

Second, and coexisting with limited or no legal knowledge and time constraints, is information overload in a highly politicised environment. A POST report notes talks of parliamentarians being 'inundated' and 'overloaded' with information.[58] Parliamentarians may suffer from an information glut, and as noted above, may have little means to filter or evaluate the information coming in; as such, what legal information is received may be ignored or misunderstood.

Third, some members take the view that legal support is irrelevant to parliamentarians when they are legislating, because Parliament by virtue of the doctrine of parliamentary sovereignty cannot do anything illegal. Jacob Rees-Mogg MP (at the time of writing, the Leader of the House of Commons), stated in a debate about the human rights compatibility of a clause concerning the deportation of prisoners in an Immigration Bill:

> A principle that we should always state and restate in this House is that, by its very nature, Parliament cannot pass a law that is illegal. We can pass laws that contravene international obligations or that we may decide our diplomatic relations require us to remove or repeal, but Parliament cannot pass an illegal law. That point is important to remember, because there is a tyranny of lawyers. They give people advice stating that they think x or y, but until it has been judged by a court, that is no more than advice, which may be right or wrong.[59]

In short, some parliamentarians may not care about legal support or 'the law' at all. After all, part of the promise of politics is that the law can be changed.

Fourth, use can depend on client need. We have already seen that needs of the various clients in Parliament vary, depending on context and arena; this in turn affects parliamentarians' receptiveness to legal support. One interviewee gave the example of legislative amendments. At Westminster primary legislation is mostly initiated by the executive, and then drafted by parliamentary

55 Interviewee 27, peer (13 September 2017).

56 See generally Hansard Society, *A Year in the Life: from Member of Public to Member of Parliament* (London: Hansard Society, 2011).

57 Interviewee 24, third party (3 August 2017).

58 Kenny, Rose, Hobbs, Tyler and Blackstock, *The Role of Research in the UK Parliament*, p. 32.

59 HC Deb 30 Jan 2014 col 1084. I am grateful to Murray Hunt for this example.

counsel, who (despite the name) are lawyers employed by the executive. As part of the legislative scrutiny process, parliamentarians can suggest amendments to bills. At this point, it might be assumed that a lawyer could be useful in drafting amendments, but this ignores that parliamentarians do not necessarily want to correct or improve a government bill: they may want to signal to voters that there are problems with the bill, or even 'wreck' the bill.[60] The interviewee argued:

> I can remember explaining that to some spad[61] who was going, 'we're wondering if we need to get a lawyer to help us draft these amendments.' No of course you don't. . . . your amendments are not going to become law, even if you win a vote.[62] Technical perfection is not the issue. What you want is an amendment that gets to the point. And as long as you can get to the point, and put the minister on a pin, and attract the people you want to vote for you to vote for you, that's good enough . . . that's better than the technically perfect amendment that the minister can dodge because it's unclear . . . It's not about the best legal drafting . . . And also . . . It can be easier to get the MP's trust for something they see how it works. If you need a law degree to understand how the amendment does what you say . . . there's already a gap in trust. Whereas if it says, 'don't lock up babies', they know what they're putting down.[63]

The irony of this is that this example comes from a lawyer. They did not deny the importance of legal expertise, but their point was that the demand for legal support from parliamentarians might be less than might be presumed. Use and demand depends on the context, the client's understanding of the issue, and what they think will aid them in responding to the issue. In the case of legislative amendments, what often matters is the politics rather than 'the law'.

60 Louise Thompson, 'More of the Same or a Period of Change? Bill Committees in the Twenty-First Century House of Commons' (2013) 66(3) *Parliamentary Affairs* 459; and Meg Russell and Dan Gover, *Legislation at Westminster: Parliamentary Actors and Influencers in the Making of British Law* (Oxford: Oxford University Press, 2017), pp. 127–34.

61 A 'spad' is shorthand for 'special adviser'. In the UK, special advisers are partisan staff of the executive branch: they are civil servants but personally appointed by a minister and not subject to the requirement of political impartiality. See Ben Yong and Robert Hazell, *Special Advisers: Who they are, what they do and why they matter* (Oxford: Hart Publishing, 2014).

62 As a number of commentators have noted, non-government amendments are rarely incorporated. This is often because where a minister does accept the policy behind a proposed amendment, parliamentary counsel will then redraft the bill to ensure polish and cohesion: see Thompson, 'More of the same or a period of change? Bill committees in the twenty first century House of Commons'; Russell and Gover, *Legislation at Westminster: Parliamentary Actors and Influencers in the Making of British Law.*

63 Interviewee 24, third party (3 August 2017).

But there are also supply factors, which stem from the sources of legal support. The first factor is availability: not all sources are available all the time. Academics, for instance, may be highly expert, but are constrained by other commitments such as teaching and administration. The second is comprehensibility: the general ignorance of many outsiders about parliamentary processes and activities may mean whatever support they offer either does not reach parliamentarians or is unlikely to be taken up by them because of the form in which it is sent.[64] So, for instance, if the relevant legal support is too legalistic or too long, parliamentarians may simply ignore it.

The third factor is institutional constraints. These relate in particular to permanent parliamentary officials. Some of these we have already covered, but bear repeating. Parliamentary officials must be impartial; this constrains them in what they can provide to parliamentarians. That means the legal support they offer will be limited to legal information or legal advice: the support will be cautious and perhaps dry, rather than yielding to the fire of politics. But impartiality has other dimensions. One reason parliamentary lawyers in Westminster do not support individual parliamentarians is that the number of potential conflicts of interest would increase.

There are other institutional constraints. In the case of parliamentary lawyers, there was a strong awareness from permanent staff that the use of in-house lawyers was a limited and expensive resource, and that it needed to be used in a cost-effective manner.

Here is one parliamentary lawyer:

> what committees need varies. Sometimes, they need legal advice. On scrutiny … it's mostly focused on scrutiny of [e.g., EU, European Convention of Human Rights] issues. They clearly need legal advice … Other stuff that you're doing may be giving them legal information, or information about the legal system. But an awful lot of that can be done more cheaply than deploying … really expensive legal advisers if they use the library.[65]

Similarly, the number of in-house lawyers is small: the number of parliamentarians is high. To have individual parliamentarians as their clients would almost certainly make the workload of parliamentary lawyers impossible but also unpredictable. This concern with protecting resource could lead some staff to query parliamentarians' requests for legal support: 'there's much less

64 Marc Geddes, Katharine Dommett and Brenton Prosser, 'A Recipe for Impact? Exploring Knowledge Requirements in the UK Parliament and Beyond' (2018) 14(2) *Evidence & Policy* 259.

65 Interviewee 22, parliamentary lawyer (27 July 2017).

legal knowledge required in a Parliament than you might think. And that's really odd . . . most of the time, we're not giving anyone legal advice. . . . Quite often, people think they need legal advice. One of the first questions is, well, do you actually? What is your question here?'[66]

### 7.6.2 *The Use and Non-Use of Legal Support: The Filtering and Evaluation Process*

It should not surprise us then that a POST report found that the two most frequently selected sources of research for MPs were specific organisations and then House of Commons library staff.[67] For it follows from demand and supply factors that parliamentarians will not necessarily make use of the abundant sources of legal support available to them; and where they do, those sources chosen are not necessarily the most 'expert' or authoritative. That is, what we see is legal support chosen and determined by the client: the operation of a lay and professional referral network. One lawyer-MP, when asked who MPs were likely to approach if they suspected legal issues, said:

> It would depend a lot on the member, upon their background, there will be a raft of things as you can imagine . . . it would be perfectly reasonable to talk to Dominic Grieve[68] about something, for example, you know, [or] other lawyer politicians because many of us are friends . . . if you're not a lawyer . . . it is perfectly plausible that you'd ask friends. I've got a friend who is an employment lawyer and sometimes I'll say to him, 'What do you think about this job?' . . . Otherwise, informally, it's going to be the usual range of contacts, which I suppose is that how would they get their advice on industry or the economy or whatever. What you read, who you might know, that might be the solicitors in your constituency you might know, for example, or somebody [you] might've bumped into. What your own business background or sense tells you . . . I might know people, I could just say, 'just out of interest, off the record, what do you think about this?'[69]

Another MP was more blunt: 'Connections. I mean, it's terrible isn't it?'[70] But if there is an information glut and/or lack of knowledge about the law (indeed, both are simultaneously possible in Parliament) then using networks or

66 Interviewee 4, clerk (25 May 2017).
67 Kenny, Rose, Hobbs, Tyler and Blackstock, *The Role of Research in the UK Parliament*, p. 27.
68 At the time of the interview, Dominic Grieve had been a longstanding Conservative lawyer-MP (1997–2019) who had served as Attorney-General (2010–14).
69 Interviewee 20, peer (26 July 2017).
70 Interviewee 54, MP (16 January 2018).

focusing on trusted sources (connections) seems quite rational.[71] Parliamentarians – particularly non-lawyer parliamentarians – must seek some means by which to filter and evaluate the information they are being bombarded with. Moreover, parliamentarians operate in a highly politicised environment: the politics always matter, and so, trust and credibility of the sources are vital. Here is a one third party lawyer who dealt with parliamentarians regularly:

> what is extraordinary about politicians – they will say 'Oh I've got a problem, I don't know what to do', and they'll say, 'Go and see [X]'. … The fact is, politicians are … they're a pretty distrusting lot, but if you said 'Go and see [X], he's sorted this out. He's safe, don't worry, he's alright', then there is that element of them coming in here through the door with some confidence … One person told me years ago, he's now in the Lords, 'try to remember one thing: that politics is a sole trader business.' And it really is right, so people don't think of going off … it's about trust, you know, can you really trust people?[72]

Even where non-lawyer parliamentarians are confronted with legal expertise, though, they may dismiss it. They employ particular rules of thumb to help them evaluate the veracity and credibility of the support. Here is one interviewee on how peers evaluate what lawyer parliamentarians say in the House of Lords – which, as we have noted, has some very senior British lawyers:

> Lord Judge [former Lord Chief Justice of England and Wales] … speaks less frequently, and is listened to more carefully … Lord Pannick [well-known public law Queen's Counsel] speaks on too many things … When Lord Mackay of Clashfern [former Conservative Lord Chancellor and Law Lord] supports an amendment against the government …, one …, he's legally spot on, and two, everyone's going to pile behind him, and you will be defeated. So he carries an awful lot of gravitas if he backs an amendment contrary to the government … the House knows who to listen to.[73]

We can see expertise obviously matters: parliamentarians pay attention to those with legal knowledge. But there are also other criteria of credibility here. First, those offering legal support to the chamber have a kind of credibility capital, which they must dole out carefully, lest they lose persuasiveness with their colleagues generally. Second, politics can matter. Lord Mackay may have been particularly persuasive in his criticism of the Conservative Government because Mackay himself is a very senior Conservative peer.

71 See, e.g., Le Conte, *Haven't You Heard?: Gossip, Politics and Power.*
72 Interviewee 57, third party (2 May 2018).
73 Interviewee 27, peer (13 September 2017).

The combination of demand and supply considerations, then, means that parliamentarians are likely to seek legal support from some sources over others. Demand-based factors operate to ensure that parliamentarians generally work first through their 'lay' networks – a mixture of internal (colleagues, the library) and external sources (third parties etc.). These sources may provide all three kinds of legal support – legal advice, opinion and information, although primarily the latter two, because legal advice requires a formal relationship between lawyer and client. Supply-based factors ensure that the 'professional' referral network (all internal sources such as specialist advisers, committee staff, parliamentary lawyers), which tends to provide legal advice, is engaged only under specific and controlled circumstances – for instance, in select committees. The result is that many parliamentarians understandably know little of parliamentary lawyers.

## 7.7 CONCLUSION

The comments of Graham Allen and Margaret Hodge MP at the beginning of this chapter can be reconciled with the 'reality' of Parliament. Parliamentarians have access to a wide array of legal support. But most of them suffer from an information glut and lack the time and expertise to make effective use of the support they have. In seeking legal support, parliamentarians are more likely to make use of their own networks first – a mixture of sources internal and external to Parliament which provide mostly legal information and legal opinion. There is a cadre of permanent officials – parliamentary lawyers – who can provide more *formal* legal support in the form of 'legal advice' when necessary, but only under specific circumstances and in specific arenas (such as the House of Commons EU Scrutiny Committee) because of impartiality and resource constraints. That is, what we see at Westminster is the presence of a lay referral network and a professional one.

In a sense, we should not be surprised by this conclusion at all. Why should Westminster differ from wider society? After all, it is supposed to be a microcosm of society, representing its diverse interests. It is unsurprising that there should be a lay referral network (or networks), and that much of the professional referral network of parliamentary officials – particularly parliamentary lawyers – is relatively unknown by most parliamentarians.

This chapter has only focused on some empirical evidence of how parliamentarians make use of legal support and what legal support means to them. It does not address the normative question of whether parliamentarians *should* be making more use of legal support – and behind that, the question of whether more internal legal support should be provided for parliamentarians. This may be an issue following Brexit, and now that the House of Lords EU Committee (with its attached legal advisers) has been abolished. But it does suggest some tentative answers. There is a great deal of legal support to parliamentarians, albeit uneven and much of it unorganised. The 'problem', if there is one at all, is primarily with the clients (the demand side), not those providing support (the supply side).

# 8

# International Bureaucracies: Extraterritorial Reach of the European Commission's Legal Expertise

Anu Bradford

## 8.1 INTRODUCTION

European institutions – and the European Commission in particular – leverage their expertise outside the European Union in a myriad of ways.[1] While the Commission's ability to shape the European market with regulations is well-known, the extent to which those regulations are transmitted abroad to shape foreign markets and legal institutions is less well understood. At times, the Commission's expertise travels to foreign jurisdictions via market mechanisms – a process known as the 'Brussels Effect'.[2] Other times EU norms get entrenched globally through political channels, including via bilateral treaties, international organisations or transgovernmental networks. While the Brussels Effect reflects the EU's unilateral regulatory power and multilateral corporations' incentives to globalise EU regulations, various political channels rely on regulatory cooperation among governments. Both market-driven and politically driven mechanisms have contributed to a significant diffusion of EU regulations around the world. They have also bestowed upon the EU the role of a global regulatory hegemon, with significant influence over data privacy, market competition, environmental protection and consumer health and safety, among other policy domains. This global regulatory power has also elevated the role that experts residing within the European institutions play in global governance.

Thanks to Sami Marouf Cleland, HyunKyn Kim, and Lingeng Zhuang for excellent research assistance, and to the participants of the Workshop on Legal Expertise in Transnational Policymaking, at the University of Helsinki in 2018, for helpful comments. This Chapter was written in 2018 and the final version was submitted in August 2020.

[1] This contribution is, in part, adapted from Anu Bradford, *The Brussels Effect: How the European Union Rules the World* (New York: Oxford University Press, 2020).

[2] Bradford, *The Brussels Effect: How the European Union Rules the World.*

This contribution proceeds as follows. Section 8.2 introduces the Commission officials as key experts in the EU's regulatory system, and situates their legal expertise within the broader context within which that expertise operates. Section 8.3 discusses the unilateral, bilateral and multilateral channels through which the EU's legal expertise diffuses to foreign markets. Section 8.4 explores the political economy behind the supply and the demand of this diffusion. The final section concludes with a brief discussion of the economic, political and legal implications of the extraterritorial reach of the Commission's legal expertise.

## 8.2 LEGAL EXPERTISE IN CONTEXT

The legal, economic and scientific expertise within the EU institutions form the foundation of the regulatory state in Europe. While the Council and the European Parliament remain central actors in the EU's legislative process, this contribution focuses on the role of the Commission. In many policy areas, the Commission is a semi-autonomous actor with extensive powers to engage in legislative process and independent regulatory action.[3] It has significant agenda-setting power through its right to propose legislation and the authority to negotiate treaties on behalf of the EU. The Commission remains influential throughout the legislative process, acting in close cooperation with the Council and the Parliament. The Commission is further in charge of the implementation and enforcement of much of the EU legislation. It also enjoys, in several policy areas, the degree of delegation that allows it to pursue a regulatory agenda largely unconstrained by other institutions.

The history of the EU has been marked by a constantly expanding regulatory agenda.[4] The Commission has gained new competences and significant influence in this process. It is often portrayed as a 'competence-maximiser', always looking to expand its influence over policy-making. And when the Commission seeks to expand its competences, it has the tendency to do so via regulation.[5] This is largely a result of the EU's small budget, which restricts the Commission's ability to pursue direct-expenditure initiatives, such as large-scale industrial policies or job creation programs. In contrast, there is no 'regulatory budget' to limit the amount of policy-making done through

[3] European Commission, https://ec.europa.eu/commission/index_en.

[4] Lorna Woods and Philippa Watson, *Steiner & Woods EU Law* (12th ed. Oxford: Oxford University Press, 2014), p. 51.

[5] Giandomenico Majone, 'The European Commission as Regulator' in Giandomenico Majone (ed.), *Regulating Europe* (London: Routledge, 1996), p. 64.

regulation.[6] Regulatory policies are often near costless for the Commission to pursue because the actual costs of regulations fall on the firms and individuals targeted by the regulations. Alternatively, costs are borne by member state governments whose task is to implement the regulations.[7]

The expansion of the regulatory state in Europe has been facilitated by a steadily growing bureaucracy. In 1959 – the early years of the European Economic Community – the Commission had 1,930 staff members. This number had climbed to 24,044 by 2016, reflecting a 5 per cent average annual growth rate. The Commission bureaucracy is also distinctly skilled and mission-driven. Its staff consists of highly educated bureaucrats that share a commitment to the European integration. No fewer than 70 per cent of the Commission officials hold a postgraduate degree, and 58 per cent have studied in more than one country, reinforcing the impression of the Commission as a cosmopolitan, educated elite. The Commission officials possess significant technical expertise, which gives their rule-making an additional layer of legitimacy, contributing to the aura of objectivity and neutrality that enhances their authority.

The Commission's expertise is wide-ranging, blending legal expertise with scientific and economic expertise in particular.[8] Almost 70 per cent of the Commission staff have completed a degree in law or social sciences, such as economics or political science, while a quarter have a degree in science. Arts and humanities account for a small minority – only 5 per cent of the Commission staff have a degree in these fields. Lawyers represent nearly 25 per cent of the Commission officials, closely trailing the 29 per cent of officials who have studied economics or business, and the 26 per cent who have studied math, computing, engineering and science. Predictably, lawyers dominate the Commission Legal Service, where 92 per cent of the officials have a law degree.[9] Lawyers are also strongly represented in Directorate Generals (DGs) that deal with justice, freedom and security (46 per cent), competition (44 per cent), internal market (44 per cent) and trade

6 Giandomenico Majone, 'From the Positive to the Regulatory State: Causes and Consequences of Changes in the Mode of Governance' (1997) 17 *Journal of Public Policy* 139–67 at 150–1.

7 Majone, 'The European Commission as Regulator', pp. 63–4.

8 Hussein Kassim et al., *The European Commission of the Twenty-First Century* (Oxford: Oxford University Press, 2013), pp. 31–70. The names of DGs and numbers cited in this paragraph reflect the structure of the Commission in 2013. There has been some internal reorganisation but the basic argument is expected to have remained valid. Indeed, Kassim discusses the educational qualifications of Commission officials and notes how 'examination of recruitment over time shows little change in these proportions' (p. 40).

9 See Päivi Leino-Sandberg, *The Politics of Legal Expertise in EU Policy Making* (Cambridge: Cambridge University Press, 2021).

(43 per cent). Yet in several DGs, lawyers are outnumbered by economists or scientists. Thus, the Legal Service aside, the legal expertise at the Commission is typically channelled alongside with other types of expertise.

In this setting, legal expertise rarely operates in isolation but is blended with other types of expertise. For instance, at DG Competition, legal expertise (45 per cent of the staff) operates alongside with economic expertise (36 per cent of the staff). Any given case team examining a proposed merger or evaluating the conduct of a dominant company comprises of both lawyers and economists. Both groups of experts are committed to the goal of EU competition law – advancing consumer welfare by keeping markets competitive – while being guided by the strong background norm that reminds them how competitive markets serve the goal of European integration. Similarly, in DG Environment and DG Sante (which is responsible for health and food safety), legal expertise guides regulatory agenda alongside with scientific and other types of expertise. Legal expertise may, of course, retain its distinct character as 'legal' whenever lawyers contribute their legal analysis to the regulatory process, and deploy legal reasoning to justify certain policy choices. This is true in particular for the experts at the Commission Legal Service as their main responsibility is to ensure that any legislation complies with EU law.[10] Their expertise is therefore typically confined to questions of law and legal process. However, in other parts of the Commission, legal expertise is likely to become more generalised regulatory expertise over time, as legal questions intersect with questions of scientific or economic nature.

While the expertise within the Commission is wide-ranging, all experts share a commitment to the European integration. This shared mission of the staff enhances the Commission's rule-making capacity, and provides a crucial context within which the officials deploy their expertise. A recent survey of Commission officials carried out by Liesbet Hooghe reported that about 79 per cent of the respondents claimed 'commitment to Europe' as a motivation for joining the Commission.[11] An earlier survey found that 'top Commission officials appear[ed] significantly more pro-European than either national elites or public opinion'.[12] Rather strikingly, this survey also revealed

10 Jean Paul Jacqué, 'The Role of Legal Services in the Elaboration of European Legislation', in Antoine Vauchez and Bruno de Witte (eds.), *Lawyering Europe: European Law as a Transnational Social Field* (Oxford: Hart Publishing, 2013), pp. 43–54.

11 Liesbet Hooghe, 'Images of Europe: How Commission Officials Conceive Their Institution's Role' (2011) 50 *Journal of Common Market Studies* 87–111 at 105.

12 Liesbet Hooghe, 'Several Roads Lead to International Norms, but Few via International Socialization: A Case Study of the European Commission' (2005) 59 *International Organization* 861–98 at 874.

that while over 40 per cent of Europeans viewed themselves as maintaining national identity only, no member of the Commission staff surveyed shared this view, with over 80% identifying themselves as European to some degree.[13] The Commission culture also 'revolve[s] around a teleological vision of the EU, one that sees deeper integration as the means of achieving broader political goals'.[14] This distinct homogeneity in the experts' mission allows the Commission to substitute political infighting with a relatively clear vision of how to deploy its competences and channel its expertise, paving the way for more extensive and coherent rule-making.

Finally, legal expertise is not only intertwined with other types of technocratic expertise residing within the Commission. It is also often entangled with the executive power that the Commission deploys towards political goals. This 'co-production' of expert and executive power reflects how expertise is rarely apolitical but closely connected to the political authority.[15] Experts are involved in resolving pressing policy issues dominating the Commission's political agenda, and the Commission frequently and deliberately invokes expertise as a justification to legitimate many of its key policy decisions. Expert-led views on societal risks have been deployed to extend the regulatory state in Europe and expand the mandate of the Commission and EU regulatory agencies. It is therefore rarely feasible to separate legal expertise from non-legal expertise, and the expertise agenda from the political agenda. Thus, the word 'legal expertise' used in this contribution refers to policy-relevant or regulatory expertise[16] that often serves the Commission's executive power and political ends.

## 8.3 CHANNELS FOR EXTERNALISING THE COMMISSION'S LEGAL EXPERTISE

This section discusses different mechanisms through which the Commission's legal expertise migrates to foreign markets, establishing the Commission as

13 Ibid.

14 Antonis Ellinas and Ezra S. Suleiman, 'Supranationalism in a Transnational Bureaucracy: The Case of the European Commission' (2011) 4 *Journal of Common Market Studies* 923–47 at 941; Jeremy Richardson, 'The Onward March of Europeanization: Tectonic Movement and Seismic Events', in Jeremy Richardson (ed.), *Constructing a Policy-Making State?: Policy Dynamics in the EU* (Oxford: Oxford University Press, 2012), p. 340.

15 See Sheila Jasanoff, *States of Knowledge: The Co-production of Science and Social Order* (London: Routledge, 2004); see also Maria Weimer and Anniek de Ruijter (eds.), *Regulating Risks in the European Union: The Co-production of Expert and Executive Power* (Oxford: Hart Publishing, 2017).

16 Weimer and de Ruijter (eds.), *Regulating Risks in the European Union*, p. 5.

a global regulatory expert. It illustrates both the market-driven and the politically driven channels through which EU rules are externalised. First, the EU wields significant unilateral power to regulate global markets, allowing the EU to export its rules to third countries – passively but effectively – via markets. Second, the EU's legal expertise is externalised via governmental cooperation that takes place in the form of bilateral treaties, multilateral institutions and transgovernmental networks. These mechanisms offer complementary and, taken together, often powerful avenues for the EU's norms, values and expertise to shape the global regulatory environment.

### 8.3.1 *Market-Driven Externalisation*

The EU's unilateral power to regulate global markets occurs through a process I have described as the 'Brussels Effect'.[17] Most multinational companies want to access the EU's large and wealthy consumer market, which requires compliance with the EU's regulatory standards. While these companies could, of course, adopt one set of standards for the European market and multiple other standards for the rest of the world, scale economies and other benefits of uniform production make this strategy unlikely. Instead, companies typically choose the most stringent standard – which is often the EU standard – as their global standard to ensure access to all markets. In this way, companies' business interests are often sufficient to convert the EU standard into the global standard, without any need for the EU to negotiate common rules or impose its standards on anyone.

The EU's global influence is rooted in its large consumer market consisting of nearly 450 million consumers.[18] But the market size alone does not guarantee global regulatory influence. The jurisdiction must also have the regulatory capacity to leverage its market size into tangible regulatory influence.[19] Without regulatory expertise and resources to enforce its rules or impose sanctions in case of non-compliance, a regulator cannot exert effective authority over market participants – within or outside of its jurisdiction. The EU is

[17] See Bradford, *The Brussels Effect: How the European Union Rules the World*; Anu Bradford , 'The Brussels Effect' (2012) 107 *Northwestern University Law Review* 1–68 (where the term was originally coined).

[18] Bradford, *The Brussels Effect: How the European Union Rules the World*, pp. 26–30; Chad Damro, 'Market Power Europe' (2012) 19 *Journal of European Public Policy* 682–99 at 689.

[19] Bradford, *The Brussels Effect: How the European Union Rules the World*, pp. 30–7; David Bach & Abraham L. Newman, 'The European Regulatory State and Global Public Policy: Micro-Institutions, Macro-Influence' (2007) 14 *Journal of European Public Policy* 827–46 at 831.

known for its affinity for regulations as well as its skilled bureaucrats based in Brussels, who are ready and able to generate those regulations. Delegating to the Commission the extensive powers to guard the common market has been integral to the entire European project.

The Commission, meanwhile, have not let those regulatory powers rest idle. Instead, it has actively deployed those powers to promulgate stringent regulatory standards across numerous areas, ranging from competition to privacy, and from food safety to environmental protection.[20] EU policy-makers' preference for stringent regulations reflects their commitment to various public policies that are viewed as central elements of a social market economy.[21] European consumers have broadly supported these regulations, providing the critical democratic backing for high levels of consumer and environmental protection.[22] European political elites have also been ideologically less divided than their US counterparts in their willingness to respond to the public demand for higher regulatory protections.[23] Further, contrary to the US, the European precautionary approach to regulation allows government intervention even in instances where the risks targeted by the regulations are uncertain to materialise.[24] Thus, the various experts in the Commission operate in a political environment that is more favourable to regulation, giving them a broad mandate to enact and enforce regulations.

However, even the Commission cannot externalise all of its rules. The Brussels Effect only occurs when the EU regulates inelastic targets such as consumer markets, as opposed to more elastic targets such as capital.[25] While capital can flee a constraining regulatory environment, firms cannot

[20] Bradford, *The Brussels Effect: How the European Union Rules the World*, pp. 37–48.

[21] See Art. 1(4) of the Treaty of Lisbon Amending the Treaty on European Union and the Treaty Establishing the European Community, O.J. 2007 C 306/1 [hereinafter Treaty of Lisbon] (mentioning explicitly the EU's commitment to social market economy in '[The Union] shall work for the sustainable development of Europe based on balanced economic growth and price stability, a highly competitive social market economy, . . . and a high level of protection and improvement of the quality of the environment').

[22] See Zaki Laïdi, 'The Unintended Consequences of European Power' (2007) *Les Cahiers Européens de Sciences* Po. No. 5 at 8, www.sciencespo.fr/centre-etudes-europeennes/sites/sciencespo.fr.centre-etudes-europeennes/files/n5_2007_final.pdf [https://perma.cc/V5MK-SFNW]; see also European Commission, Special Eurobarometer 217: The Attitudes of European Citizens Towards Environment, April 2005, at 31–2, http://ec.europa.eu/public_opinion/archives/ebs/ebs_217_en.pdf (noting that close to 90 per cent of Europeans believe environmental policies are just as important as social or economic ones).

[23] David Vogel, *The Politics of Precaution: Regulating Health, Safety and Environmental Risks in Europe and the United States* (Princeton: Princeton University Press, 2012), pp. 31–2.

[24] Communication from the Commission on the Precautionary Principle, 2 February 2000, COM (2000) 1 final, at 1; in contrast, see Executive Order 13563, 3 C.F.R. 215, 215 (2011).

[25] Bradford, *The Brussels Effect: How the European Union Rules the World*, pp. 48–53.

circumvent the EU's protective regulations as long as they offer goods and services to European consumers. Further, EU standards become global standards only when multinational companies' production or conduct is non-divisible – in other words, when the benefits of adhering to a single standard exceed the benefits of taking advantage of more lenient standards in other markets.[26]

These conditions – market size, regulatory capacity, regulatory stringency, inelasticity and non-divisibility – explain why the Commission experts today are able to wield unilateral regulatory influence across global markets. For example, the US unwillingness to adopt stringent regulatory standards explains why there is no 'Washington Effect'. Similarly, the 'Beijing Effect' will not materialise until China has built more regulatory capacity and embraced more stringent regulations – conditions that are still largely missing. The EU, therefore, is in the unique position today to regulate global markets, be it through its ability to set the global standards in food safety, chemicals, competition, environmental protection or the protection of privacy among others.

The EU's recently adopted privacy regulation – the General Data Protection Regulation (GDPR)[27] – is a timely and significant illustration of the Brussels Effect. Many US technology companies apply the European privacy rules across their global operations. For example, in preparation for the GDPR's entry into force, Facebook COO Sheryl Sandberg announced that the company was going to '[roll] out a new privacy center globally that will put the core privacy settings for Facebook in one place and make it much easier for people to manage their data'.[28] This means that European privacy protections will be extended to the company's 2.2 billion users worldwide. Google similarly updated its privacy policy in anticipation of the GDPR, sending its users a notice saying that '[w]e're making these updates as new data protection regulations come into effect in the European Union, and we're taking the opportunity to make improvements for Google users around the world'.[29] Apple also subscribes to a single global privacy policy that adheres to

[26] Ibid., pp. 53–63.

[27] Regulation (EU) 2016/679 of the European Parliament and of the Council of 27 April 2016 on the protection of natural persons with regard to the processing of personal data and on the free movement of such data, and repealing Directive 95/46/EC, O.J. 2016 L 119/1 (hereinafter 'GDPR').

[28] Julia Fioretti, 'Facebook to Hand Privacy Controls to Users Ahead of EU Law', *Reuters*, 23 January 2018, https://de.reuters.com/article/us-facebook-sandberg-privacy-idUSKBN1FC1Q6.

[29] See email communication from Google.com to its users entitled 'Improvements to our Privacy Policy and Privacy Controls', 12 May 2018.

the GDPR.[30] Importantly, it implements GDPR's Article 25 principle of 'privacy by design', which entails that the company designs its products and services to comply with GDPR-consistent privacy rules by default, minimising data collection through the choice of privacy-conscious design at the outset.[31] Microsoft similarly follows the GDPR globally and develops its products with built-in features that help their clients maintain GDPR compliance.[32]

These examples from digital economy show how market forces are often effective in transmitting the EU's legal norms across jurisdictions: instead of having the often unparalleled technical expertise residing in powerful tech-companies such as Apple, Google, Facebook or Microsoft alone dictate the fundamental features of their products, it is the legal and other policy experts in the EU that also have a say on the products these companies produce, whether for their consumers in Europe, US the US or elsewhere in the world. The Brussels Effect therefore offers a powerful even if passive way for the EU's bureaucratic expertise to shape regulatory outcomes worldwide. All the Commission has to do is to regulate the EU's own internal market – the size and attractiveness of its market, together with the business incentives of multinational companies, do the rest.

### 8.3.2 *Politics-Driven Externalisation*

The Commission's experts wield significant influence also through bilateral and multilateral channels. Bilateral channels include various economic and political agreements, including accession and partnership treaties,[33] and preferential trade agreements (PTAs), which the Commission negotiates on

30 Apple, 'Apple Customer Privacy Policy', www.apple.com/legal/privacy/ (demonstrating the global, unitary nature of Apple's privacy policy as there is only En-WW option, instead of differentiating different English such as En-US or En-UK).

31 Apple, 'Privacy Governance', www.apple.com/legal/privacy/en-ww/governance.

32 See Rich Sauer, 'Earning Your Trust with Contractual Commitments to the General Data Protection Regulation', *Microsoft: Microsoft On the Issues*, 17 April 2017, https://blogs.microsoft.com/on-the-issues/2017/04/17/earning-trust-contractual-commitments-general-data-protection-regulation/#sm.00100s6561a1ud6wrgc2m3gwwlkuz; Brendon Lynch, 'Get GDPR Complaint with Microsoft Cloud', *Microsoft: Microsoft On the Issues*, 15 February 2017, https://blogs.microsoft.com/on-the-issues/2017/02/15/get-gdpr-compliant-with-the-microsoft-cloud/#sm.00100s6561a1ud6wrgc2m3gwwlkuz; Microsoft 365, 'Preparing for a New Era in Privacy Regulation', *Microsoft*, 16 April 2018, www.microsoft.com/en-us/microsoft-365/blog/2018/04/16/preparing-for-a-new-era-in-privacy-regulation-with-the-microsoft-cloud.

33 See Communication from the Commission to the Council and the European Parliament: Wider Europe – Neighbourhood: A New Framework for Relations with Our Eastern and Southern Neighbours, 11 March 2003, COM(2003) 104 final, 5.

behalf of the EU.[34] Through these instruments, the EU trades market access in return for foreign governments' commitment to certain European values or specific standards that govern the internal market.[35] The EU also promotes its regulatory standards in various international institutions and standard-setting organisations and through various issue-specific transgovernmental networks.[36]

The EU's bargaining power through conditional market access is most evident with respect to countries seeking accession to the EU.[37] As a condition for joining the EU, new member states need to demonstrate that they are complying with all EU standards and rules, effectively implementing the *acquis communitaire* in its entirety. In these negotiations, the Commission holds the bargaining power: it is able to extract almost any condition it wishes from the accession countries because of the lure of the ultimate prize of EU membership. The EU exerts similarly extensive influence over its neighbouring countries through the European Neighbourhood Policy (ENP).[38] While the ENP does not provide a path to EU membership, it offers these countries a closer economic and political relationship in return for 'concrete progress demonstrating shared values and effective implementation of political, economic and institutional reforms, including aligning legislation with the EU's *acquis*'.[39]

The EU's regulatory and policy influence extends beyond its immediate region and is often consolidated through bilateral trade agreements. The Commission has negotiated an extensive array of PTAs that influence the type of regulations that the EU's trade partners must have in place in order to secure access to the single market. Through this method, the EU uses its vast market size as a bargaining chip that allows it to demand changes in treaty partners' domestic legal regimes – whether on environmental policy, competition laws, development goals or human rights.[40] The EU's treaty

34 See also Kimura and Nicola, Chapter 9 in this volume.

35 Sophie Meuniere and Kalypso Nicolaïdis, 'The European Union as a Trade Power', in Christopher Hill and Michael Smith (eds.), *International Relations and the European Union*, 2nd ed. (Oxford: Oxford University Press, 2011), p. 279.

36 See Anne-Marie Slaughter, *A New World Order* (Princeton: Princeton University Press, 2004).

37 See European Commission, 'EU Enlargement Factsheet', https://ec.europa.eu/neighbourhood-enlargement/sites/near/files/pdf/publication/factsheet_en.pdf.

38 See European Union External Action, 'European Neighbourhood Policy (ENP)', https://eeas.europa.eu/diplomatic-network/european-neighbourhood-policy-enp_en.

39 Communication from the Commission to the Council and the European Parliament: Wider Europe – Neighbourhood: A New Framework for Relations with our Eastern and Southern Neighbours, 11 March 2003, COM(2003) 104 final, 10.

40 Emilie M. Hafner-Burton, 'Trading Human Rights: How Preferential Trade Agreements Influence Government Repression' (2005) 59 *International Organization*, 593–629; Meuniere & Nicolaïdis, 'The European Union as a Trade Power'.

partners comprise both large and small economies, ranging from economic powerhouses such as Japan and Canada to smaller economies such as Lesotho and the Faroe Islands; from other European countries such as Albania and Macedonia to countries halfway around the globe, such as Chile and Madagascar.[41]

The Commission is also actively shaping the global regulatory environment through multilateral channels. It exerts influence in various international institutions that focus on standard-setting in different areas of market regulation, including the Codex Alimentarius Commission that was set up to implement global food standards.[42] The Commission has had extensive influence at Codex, which can, at least, partially be attributed to the EU's long history of regulating food safety across the single market and the valuable expertise it gained in this process.[43] The EU was also able to export its motor vehicle emission control standards via UNECE – the UN's Economic Commission for Europe.[44] The relevant 'Euro' standards were widely adopted over the equivalent US 'Tiers' standards, even though many viewed the US standards to be more effective. The EU's success was explained by its more universally appealing policy design in contrast to the US standards, which were designed with US market idiosyncrasies in mind. This example highlights the benefit that the EU derives from its regulatory process that is designed to accommodate the diversity of legal traditions and political institutions. The experts in the Commission know that all regulations need to achieve uniformity while respecting some degree of member state sovereignty. This quality makes them more amendable for export as well.

Transgovernmental networks provide less formal but at times influential settings for the Commission to transfer its regulatory expertise abroad. In these settings, the EU rules diffuse through sector-specific technocratic outreach rather than traditional diplomacy.[45] This type of influence often takes place in the context of the Commission's (and European regulatory agencies') active engagement in technical assistance and capacity-building activities.

41 See European Commission, 'Negotiation and Agreements', https://ec.europa.eu/trade/policy/countries-and-regions/negotiations-and-agreements.

42 Food and Agriculture Organization of the United Nation, *Understanding Codex*, 5th ed. (2018), p. 16, www.fao.org/3/CA1176EN/ca1176en.pdf.

43 In-person Interview with Sabine Juelicher, Director of Directorate-General for Health and Food Safety, European Commission, 18 July 2018 (on file with author).

44 Bill Canis and Richard K. Lattanzio, 'US and EU Motor Vehicle Standards: Issues for Transatlantic Trade Negotiations', Congressional Research Service, 18 February 2014, www.hsdl.org/?view&did=751039.

45 Sandra Lavenex, 'The Power of Functionalist Extension: How EU Rules Travel' (2014) 21 *Journal of European Public Policy* 885–903.

EU representatives not only lend their expertise but also often promote, intentionally or unintentionally, the EU's regulatory approaches as 'best practice' in the process.[46] Often these dialogues complement the Brussels Effect or the EU's formal political agreements. For example, EU competition laws have diffused not only via the Brussels Effect or PTAs, but also through the Commission's active role in the International Competition Network (ICN) and in the context of bilateral cooperative agreements between the Commission's DG Competition and its foreign counterparts.[47] Similarly, the strong Brussels Effect associated with the EU chemical regulation REACH has been amplified by the EU's chemical agency ECHA's scientific and technical cooperation with its foreign counterparts.[48] The EU has also used other formal international organisations to promote its regulatory approach, including the Organisation for Economic Co-operation and Development (OECD), the UN's environmental program UNEP, the World Health Organization (WHO) and the Food and Agriculture Organization (FAO), in addition to informal networks such as the International Uniform Chemical Information database and the Global Portal to Information on Chemical Substances.[49]

While the above discussion has focused on market-based and treaty-based mechanisms, these are not the only channels through which the Commission's expertise travels abroad. Many foreign governments and regional organisations also engage in legislative borrowing, replicate EU institutions, cite legal concepts and principles developed by European courts or engage in copycat litigation in cases where the EU has acted first. In addition, many foreign companies strategically resort to the Commission or EU courts as their preferred forum for litigation, relying on the legal expertise residing in Europe to resolve disputes originating far outside the borders of the EU. These various channels further entrench the EU's role as the global regulatory hegemon, and illustrate how the Commission experts often wield significant influence across the world, whether they actively embrace this broader mandate or view it as an incidental side-effect of their work for the EU and European citizens.

46 David Bach and Abraham L. Newman, 'Governing Lipitor and Lipstick: Capacity, Sequencing, and Power in International Pharmaceutical and Cosmetics Regulation' (2010) 17 *Review of International Political Economy* 665–95 at 672.

47 See Anu Bradford, 'Antitrust Law in Global Markets', in Einer R. Elhauge (ed.), *Research Handbook on the Economics of Antitrust Law* (Cheltenham: Edward Elgar Publishing, 2012), pp. 314–16.

48 Lavenex, 'The Power of Functionalist Extension: How EU Rules Travel', 894. See generally also Herwig C. H. Hofmann, Ellen Vos and Merijn Chamon (eds.), *The External Dimension of EU Agencies and Bodies: Law and Policy* (Cheltenham: Edward Elgar, 2019).

49 Lavenex, ibid.

## 8.4 THE POLITICAL ECONOMY BEHIND THE EXTERNALISATION OF THE COMMISSION'S LEGAL EXPERTISE

This section discusses the political and economic forces behind the externalisation of the Commission's legal expertise. It first explores the reasons that vest the Commission with both the ability and the incentive to supply its regulations – and the expertise behind those regulations – to third countries. It argues that the EU's global regulatory influence has its origins in a purely inward-looking goal – to build and strengthen the single market. However, over time, a more conscious external regulatory agenda has emerged to complement the internal one. Next, it explores the reasons that explain the demand for EU regulations in third countries. It emphasises the role of foreign corporations and advocacy groups in globalising EU rules while discussing various economic and pragmatic reasons that have led many foreign governments to emulate the EU's regulatory regime. Whether the Commission's legal expertise gets entrenched in foreign markets because of the forces of supply or demand depends on the context but often contains elements of both.

### 8.4.1 *Supply of the Commission's Expertise Abroad*

The European regulatory state was not created to promulgate global standards but to establish and oversee an integrated, liberalised and competitive market in Europe. It was therefore a response to a political agenda that was largely inward looking. In its early decades – beginning in the 1960s but continuing often well into the 2000s – the EU's external influence can thus best be viewed as an incidental by-product of its internal motivations. Only more recently has the Commission come to realise how much its legal expertise is being channelled across the global marketplace.

Developing harmonised EU regulations is critical for the operation of the single market, since inconsistent product standards can hinder cross-border trade. For this reason, common standards became a key goal for the project of European integration early on. Thus, every directive and regulation – be it on chemical safety, environmental protection or data privacy – typically has a dual purpose: it serves to advance consumer or environmental protection, and at the same time creates a single market where divergent national regulations are aligned so as to ensure free movement of goods and services across the EU.[50]

50 Damro, 'Market Power Europe', 687.

The EU's regulation of data protection illustrates how its origins can be traced to the need to establish a single market for the transfer of data. Earlier statements by the Commission made no references to the external aspects of data protection but rather cited disparate national measures as negatively impacting the single market.[51] The 1994 Commission White Paper on 'Europe and the Global Information Society' emphasised the risks associated with '[d]isparities in the level of protection of such privacy rules [which] create the risk that national authorities might restrict free circulation of a wide range of new services between Member States in order to protect personal data'.[52] The 2010 Commission Communication on personal data protection similarly warned of the 'divergences between the national laws implementing the [Data Protection] Directive, which run counter to one of its main objectives, i.e. ensuring the free flow of personal data within the internal market', emphasising how private stakeholders had complained about administrative burden and costs stemming from the lack of harmonisation.[53] The legislative history of the 2016 GDPR continued to emphasise the need to remove 'the uncertainty and uneven protection for individuals' associated with the 'fragmented legal environment' in the EU's single market.[54]

These statements suggest that the experts drafting the EU's regulatory acts were not motivated by global ambitions but remained focused on the ways various regulations advance the economic and social goals underlying the single market. They provide an alternative narrative to the ones emphasising the EU's strong 'external agenda' or even portraying EU's bureaucrats as being motivated by 'regulatory imperialism' with a conscious effort to impose

[51] Gloria González Fuster, *The Emergence of Personal Date Protection as a Fundamental Right of the EU* (Vienna: Springer Publishing International, 2014), p. 126. See also Recital 3 of the Commission Recommendation of 29 July 1981 relating to the Council of Europe convention for the protection of individuals with regard to automatic processing of personal data, O. J. 1981 L 246/31; Communication from the Commission to the European Parliament and the Council: A European Data Protection Framework for the 21st Century, 25 January 2012, COM (2012) 9 final, 8.

[52] Report on Europe and the Global Information Society: Recommendations of the High-level Group on the Information Society to the Corfu European Council, Bulletin of the European Union, Supplement No. 2/94, 24 June 1994, 22, http://aei.pitt.edu/1199/1/info_society_bangeman_report.pdf.

[53] Communication from the Commission to the European Parliament, the Council, the Economic and Social Committee and the Committee of the Regions: A comprehensive approach on personal data protection in the EU, 4 November 2010, COM (2010) 609 final, 3–4, https://eur-lex.europa.eu/legal-content/EN/TXT/PDF/?uri=CELEX:52010DC0609&from=GA.

[54] Commission Staff Working Paper and Executive Summary of the Impact Assessment on the General Data Protection Regulation, 25 January 2012, SEC (2012) 73 final, 2.

EU's regulatory state on other jurisdictions.[55] This type of more passive externalisation of EU rules has been particularly effective in that the EU institutions have only had to generate the consensus to pursue a goal that lies at the heart of the EU project: European integration and the establishment of the single market.

However, more recently, a conscious external agenda has emerged to complement this internal regulatory agenda. The Commission has gradually realised that the regulations governing the EU's internal market have an unintended external effect, partly because the EU's trading partners have expressed concern that the single market imposes costs on them.[56] For example, in its 2007 Working Paper 'The External Dimension of the Single Market Review', the Commission acknowledged that 'the EU is emerging as a global rule maker, with the single market framework and the wider EU economic and social model increasingly serving as a reference point in third countries as well as in global and regional fora'.[57] The Commission also recognised that '[t]here is a window of opportunity to push global solutions forward. The EU is in a good position to take a lead, promoting its modern regulatory framework internationally'.[58] In another Communication, the Commission emphasised how the 'EU [is] being looked upon as the global standard-setter in many areas such as product safety, food safety, environmental protection, public procurement, financial regulation and accounting'.[59] All these statements point to a growing awareness of the ability of the EU to shape the global regulatory environment beyond the single market.

Whether the Commission exports its regulations deliberately or unintentionally, the EU benefits from the global adoption of its standards in several ways. Most concretely, the exportation of the EU's regulatory regime protects the competitiveness of European industries.[60] Europe is committed to high regulatory standards. The failure to export its standards to other markets,

55 Jan Zielonka, 'Europe as a Global Actor: SET mufoField:'N.N103' * MERGEFORMAT Empire by Example?' (2008) 84 *International Affairs* 471–84 at 475; Laïdi, 'The Unintended Consequences of European Power', 9–10.

56 See Sieglinde Gstöhl, 'Political Dimensions of an Externalization of the EU's Internal Market' (2007) *College of Europe Diplomacy Paper* 3/2007 at 4–5, http://aei.pitt.edu/9593.

57 Commission Staff Working Document on The External Dimension of the Single Market Review, 20 November 2007, SEC (2007) 1519, 5–6.

58 Ibid., 8.

59 Communication from the Commission to the European Parliament, the Council, the Economic and Social Committee and the Committee of the Regions: Services of general interest, including social services of general interest: a new European commitment, 20 November 2007, COM (2007) 725 final, 7.

60 See Communication from the Commission to the European Parliament, the Council and the European Economic and Social Committee: A strategic vision for European standards:

therefore, would often put European firms at a competitive disadvantage there.[61] If foreign companies adhere to EU norms in the European market, the import-competing industries are assured a level playing field. But if the EU's norms further spread to third countries, the EU can also ensure that its export-oriented firms are not disadvantaged in those markets. In a 2013 Speech, Viviane Reding, the EU's Justice Commissioner at the time, emphasised the need to protect European firms' competitiveness, noting that '[f]or a strong European digital industry to compete globally, we need a level-playing field. This is at the heart of the proposed EU data protection Regulation'. The same themes were echoed in her 2014 speech where she emphasised that '[t]he level playing field allowing European digital industry to compete globally is secured ... This is about ... fair competition in a globalised world'.[62]

But the Commission may have additional reasons to leverage its expertise and project its regulatory power abroad. For example, the EU has started to emphasise the importance of promoting EU privacy laws as a 'benchmark for global standards'. In its 2009 Communication, the Commission noted how the 'Union must be a driving force behind the development and promotion of international standards for personal data protection and in the conclusion of appropriate bilateral or multilateral instruments'.[63] In a 2010 Communication, the Commission defended stringent EU standards, noting that '[a] high and uniform level of data protection within the EU will be the best way of endorsing and promoting EU data protection standards globally'[64] and calling for universal principles based on EU norms.[65]

It is not always evident why the Commission cares about the EU being the global standard setter – beyond the tangible need to protect its firms' competitiveness. For one, the Commission may be motivated by a desire to replicate the EU's governance model and regulatory experience abroad. The EU's own successful experience in creating a common market has encouraged it to pursue a global order based on those same rules. More regulation in the EU

Moving forward to enhance and accelerate the sustainable growth of the European economy by 2020, 1 June 2011, COM (2011) 311 final, 2–3.

61 See, e.g., Emma Tucker, 'Plastic Toy Quandary that EU Cannot Duck', *Financial Times*, 9 December 1998, 3.

62 Viviane Reding, EU Justice Commissioner, 'Making the EU Data Protection Irreversible', 11 May 2004, https://ec.europa.eu/commission/presscorner/detail/en/SPEECH_14_208.

63 Communication from the Commission to the European Parliament and the Council: An area of freedom, security and justice serving the citizen, 10 June 2009, COM (2009) 262 final, 9.

64 Communication from the Commission to the European Parliament, the Council, the Economic and Social Committee, and the Committee of Regions: A comprehensive approach on personal data protection in the EU, 4 November 2010, COM (2010) 609 final, 19.

65 Ibid., 16 (original emphasis removed).

has meant more predictability and stability in Europe. This has fostered a belief that an extensive regulatory system is similarly needed to preserve global public goods. The EU subscribes to a view that trade liberalisation fails to achieve economic goals without a simultaneous harmonisation of policies. For the EU, this offers the most efficient and universally valid model of economic and political integration,[66] and potentially a compelling reason to replicate its experience abroad.

The Commission may also be motivated by its desire to obtain greater legitimacy for its rules through globalising them. If foreign companies and governments endorse and emulate EU regulations, those regulations are seen as carrying greater legitimacy.[67] One concrete benefit from this is that the EU's trade partners are less likely to challenge the legality of EU regulations before forums like the WTO if those rules are already replicated globally. Less tangibly, being the global standard-setter has the benefit of expanding the EU's soft power and validating its regulatory agenda, both at home and abroad.

In recent years, the broader geopolitical context may have provided an additional incentive for the Commission to assume the role of a global regulatory expert. The WTO has become increasingly dysfunctional since the closing of the Uruguay Round in 1995. Its inability to effectively address regulatory barriers to trade or settle trade disputes has left a vacuum that the EU has been uniquely positioned to fill. Also, the US government has increasingly retreated from domestic regulation and international institutions. The absence of US leadership in global regulation gives the Commission a further impetus to act. Finally, the awareness that the EU's role in the world economy is declining while Asia's is rising may have similarly contributed to the Commission's desire to cement its rules globally at the time when the EU still has the power to do so.

Finally, being able to set norms globally allows the Commission to prove to the EU's critics that the EU remains relevant as a global economic power. Embracing the role of a regulatory hegemon enhances the EU's global standing even at the times of crises where its effectiveness and relevance are constantly being questioned. If the EU wants to exert global influence, it must do so with the means available to it. In the absence of military power or unconstrained economic power, the EU can exercise genuine unilateral

66 See Zielonka, 'Europe as a Global Actor: Empire by Example?', 475.

67 Vogel, *The Politics of Precaution: Regulating Health, Safety and Environmental Risks in Europe and the United States*, p. 13.

power most effectively through its skilful bureaucracy that is able to leverage its expertise to fix standards of behaviour for the rest of the world.[68]

### 8.4.2 *Demand for the Commission's Expertise Abroad*

Many foreign companies, consumers and governments benefit from EU regulations, with multinational companies adopting those regulations globally, consumer groups or corporations advocating their emulation by the home governments and foreign governments imitating them – at times eagerly while other times more reluctantly. These foreign stakeholders therefore often actively seek the Commission expertise or passively incorporate this expertise into their domestic regulatory regimes.

Some hard-fought lobbying campaigns suggest that foreign companies can be, at least initially, staunch opponents of EU regulations. Foreign firms lobbied vehemently against the EU's chemical regulation, REACH.[69] Foreign corporate lobbying against the adoption of the GDPR was equally fierce, with companies citing high costs and 'unreasonable restraints' on their business practices.[70] Google, for example, stated that it had spent 'hundreds of years of human time' to achieve GDPR compliance.[71] At the same time, uniformity is a tremendous benefit to global businesses. Producing under a single standard allows firms to benefit from scale economies and pursue uniform branding and marketing. This same search for uniformity explains why multinational corporations often adopt EU rules to govern their global operations. Compliance with the most stringent standard – which typically is the EU standard – grants these firms access to markets across the world.

Companies recognise various additional advantages that come with regulation. They want customers to feel comfortable buying their products, and

68 See Laïdi, 'The Unintended Consequences of European Power', 5.

69 Lyndsey Layton, 'Chemical Law Has Global Impact', *Washington Post* (12 June 2008), www.washingtonpost.com/wp-dyn/content/article/2008/06/11/AR2008061103569.html; see also Emilia Korkea-aho, 'Mr Smith Goes to Brussels. Third Country Lobbying and the Making of European Law and Policy' [2016] *Cambridge Yearbook of European Legal Studies* 45–68.

70 Gregory Shaffer, 'Globalization and Social Protection: The Impact of EU and International Rules in the Ratcheting Up of U.S. Privacy Standards' (2000) 25 *Yale Journal of International Law* 1–88 at 75; cf. Arts. 17–20 of Parliament and Council Directive 95/46/EC of 24 October 1995 on the protection of individuals with regard to the processing of personal data and on the free movement of such data, O. J. 1995 L281/31.

71 Ashley Rodriguez, 'Google Says It Spent "Hundreds of Years of Human Time" Complying with Europe's Privacy Rules', *Quartz*, 26 September 2018, https://qz.com/1403080/google-spent-hundreds-of-years-of-human-time-complying-with-gdpr/ [https://perma.cc/SP4H-BKTK].

clear regulations can help accomplish that.[72] For example, Brad Smith, the President of Microsoft, recently called for the regulation of facial recognition technology, which, if left unregulated, can unsettle customers and be used 'for ill as well as good'.[73] Adherence to high regulatory standards also allows firms to enhance their legitimacy and obtain reputational gains. For example, observance of EU food standards engenders customer confidence in many parts of the world. Several Chinese dairy companies proclaim that their products comply with EU standards in an effort to send markets a signal of the safety of their products. A Chinese milk producer Jun Le Bao announced that it was using equipment imported from European countries, and that every technical aspect of the production line complied with EU standards.[74] Similarly, Shengmu Group produces organic infant milk powder that complies with EU standards, emphasising how EU-compliant milk powder will be available in China and worldwide.[75] The Chinese dairy industry has also actively advocated for the elevation of national standards to meet the EU standard in an effort to further enhance consumer confidence in the domestic dairy industry.[76]

Not only do multinational firms deploy EU standards as global standards in their own business processes; they often become advocates of EU regulations in their home markets. Emulation of EU regulations by their home governments levels the playing field with respect to these firms' domestic competitors who would otherwise remain unaffected by EU regulations. The US market illustrates this dynamic. In October 2018, Apple's CEO Tim Cook urged the

72 See, e.g., Daniel Carpenter et al., 'Approval Regulation and Endogenous Consumer Confidence: Theory and Analogies to Licensing, Safety and Financial Regulation' (2010) 4 *Regulation & Governance* 383–407.

73 Brad Smith, 'Facial Recognition Technology: The Need for Public Regulation and Corporate Responsibility', *Microsoft: Microsoft On the Issues*, 13 July 2018, https://blogs.microsoft.com/on-the-issues/2018/07/13/facial-recognition-technology-the-need-for-public-regulation-and-corporate-responsibility/ [https://perma.cc/8DV4-6WZ5].

74 See 'Jun Le Bao Zai We Xian Zeng She Xue Sheng Nai Sheng Chan Xian, Zhi Li Yu Wei Geng Duo Hai Zi Ti Gong Xin Xian You Zhi De Hao Niu Nai' (君乐宝在威县增设学生奶生产线 致力于为更多孩子提供新鲜优质的好牛奶) [Junlebao Recently Sets Production Line of Student Milk in Wei Xian, and Aims to Produce Fresh and High-quality Milk for More Children], Junlebao Dairy, January 2018, https://perma.cc/9EV8-FNG9.

75 See Post Hearing Information Pack of China Shengmu Organic Milk Limited, HKEXnews, 27 June 2014, 147–51, www3.hkexnews.hk/listedco/listconews/sehk/2014/0715/ltn20140715042.pdf [https://perma.cc/67EY-AW2A].

76 See Sun Jie (孙杰), '2016 Ru Ye Wan Li Xing Shang Ban Cheng Shou Guan, Wo Guo Sheng Ru Zhi Liang Wen Ding Ke Kao' (2016乳业万里行上半程收官 我国生乳质量稳定可靠) [First Half of the 2016 Interview Program on Dairy Quality has Completed, and the Quality of Raw Milk in China is Stable and Reliable], People.cn, 28 November 2016, http://yuqing.people.com.cn/n1/2016/1128/c210117-28904115.html.

US government to adopt a comprehensive EU-style privacy law at the federal level, noting how it was 'time for the rest of the world' to follow the EU's lead and adopt strict legal framework to protect users' personal data.[77] Six months later, Mark Zuckerberg, Facebook's founder and chief executive, similarly called for the adoption of GDPR-style laws in the US and worldwide.[78] These statements reflect the new political reality that the technology companies are facing, leading them to embrace, rather than disparage, the GDPR. When lobbying for a federal law, the GDPR presents an attractive template given that it already governs much of the corporate conduct by US-based global companies like Apple and Facebook.

Corporations are not alone in urging their home governments to welcome the Commission's legal expertise. Often, foreign advocacy groups deploy EU regulations to raise awareness of a policy problem at home.[79] For example, US consumers often seize on EU policies as benchmarks in their attempts to demand change in the United States.[80] In 2008, a US-based advocacy organisation, 'MomsRising', joined various experts and other activists in calling on the Obama Administration to address 'the urgent chemical exposure crises in the US'. The co-founder of MomsRising contrasted the US standards with those prevailing in Europe, noting – with outrage – that parents today need to look for labels that say the product meets European regulatory standards because they cannot trust the American standards.[81]

A different yet equally powerful reason to adopt EU-style rules can be foreign governments' desire to offset their own limited regulatory capacity

77 'Tim Cook Calls for US Federal Privacy Law to Tackle "Weaponized" Personal Data', *The Guardian*, 24 October 2018, www.theguardian.com/technology/2018/oct/24/tim-cook-us-federal-privacy-law-weaponized-personal-data [https://perma.cc/TG55-FTMB].

78 Mark Zuckerberg, 'The Internet Needs New Rules. Let's Start in These Four Areas', *Washington Post*, 30 March 2019, www.washingtonpost.com/opinions/mark-zuckerberg-the-internet-needs-new-rules-lets-start-in-these-four-areas/2019/03/29/9e6f0504-521a-11e9-a3f7-78b7525a8d5f_story.html?fbclid=IwAR2dyE8yvRAI2SIUUsAJEj6nwcZatkpOWaSok_cxHWsRkrpJI_qUZDpiDLw&utm_term=.bdb2c94b7c87 [https://perma.cc/QYS2-33T9].

79 Joanne Scott, 'From Brussels with Love: The Transatlantic Travels of European Law and the Chemistry of Regulatory Attraction' (2009) 57 *The American Journal of Comparative Law* 897–942 at 920–8; see generally Katerina Linos, *The Democratic Foundations of Policy Diffusion: How Health, Family and Employment Laws Spread Across Countries* (Oxford: Oxford University Press, 2013).

80 See Alasdair R. Young, 'Political Transfer and "Trading Up"?: Transatlantic Trade in Genetically Modified Food and U.S. Politics' (2003) 55 *World Politics* 457–84 at 474.

81 Coming Clean Workgroup for Public Policy Reform, 'Scientists, Physicians, Health Advocates, Parents to Obama: Chemical Exposure is an Urgent Crisis in the United States', Federal Chemical Policy Reform – Public Policy Reform, 20 November 2008, https://smartpolicyreform.org/for-the-media/news-releases/news-release-view?newsid=407&backid=37 [https://perma.cc/Y35E-6MCZ].

and free ride on the EU's legal expertise that informs its regulatory rule-making. For example, emulating EU competition law allows these jurisdictions to follow the EU's lead in evaluating anticompetitive practices in individual cases. This way, they are able to leverage fines or impose other remedies domestically without the need to develop their own theories of harm, market definition and competitive assessment. All of this takes time, legal and economic expertise, as well as substantial resources. This strategy – known as 'copycat litigation' – is particularly appealing for less experienced agencies, which lack the resources and the expertise to build the case on their own.[82] Replicating the Commission's reasoning and remedies will allow them to capture regulatory gains and pursue enforcement, their limited regulatory capacity notwithstanding.

At times, this foreign demand for the Commission's expertise also reflects the normative appeal of EU regulatory regime.[83] For example, foreign governments often turn to the GDPR as a legislative template because of its reputation as the 'gold standard' worldwide. Recent data breach scandals – such as the incident involving Cambridge Analytica and the misappropriation of Facebook users' data to influence elections – have also fuelled demand for tougher data protection laws abroad, exposing the limits of the US's techno-libertarianism. China's practice of deploying data as a tool for government surveillance and social control also concerns many, further contributing to the growing recognition that the EU's regulatory model best enhances public interest, checks corporate power and preserves the democratic structures of the society. Thus, the Commission's expertise is often associated with values that foreign governments are comfortable endorsing before their constituencies at home.

Pragmatic reasons, such as the ease of copying EU regulations, further increase the appeal of the Commission's expertise abroad. Trained largely in the civil law tradition, EU experts are accustomed to drafting precise and detailed rules that often stand in contrast with the US legal system where the legal regime evolves through case law. Competition law is a good example. Europeans are generally less comfortable with the US-style statutory drafting where more vague and open-ended rules are clarified over time by courts.[84] The EU's detailed competition provisions make them easier to copy and

82 Bradford, *The Brussels Effect: How the European Union Rules the World*, pp. 122–8.

83 Ian Manners, 'Normative Power Europe: A Contradiction in Terms?' (2002) 40 *JCMS: Journal of Common Market Studies* 235–58.

84 See, e.g., Roger Van den Bergh, 'The Difficult Reception of Economic Analysis in European Competition Law', in Antonio Cucinotta et al. (eds.), *Post-Chicago Developments in Antitrust Law* (Cheltenham: Edward Elgar Publishing, 2002), pp. 46–50; compare US Department of

hence more prone to diffusion among jurisdictions which share the EU's preference for legal certainly and detailed rule-making.[85] EU law is also more feasible to emulate by developing countries characterised by less skilled administrative agencies and judiciary. In these low-income countries, detailed, codified legal norms can act as substitutes for human capital, leading them to prefer precise rules over flexible standards.[86] Of course, EU regulations also have the additional advantage of being promulgated in several languages, including French, Portuguese and Spanish. This facilitates the copying of EU laws in particular in Latin America and Francophone Africa, especially as the Commission can always supplement any such copying with technical assistance and advice delivered by experts who are native speakers of those languages.

Finally, the Commission experts combine statutory precision with flexible drafting. They are mindful that the EU regulations must work across many different legal systems. Representing all twenty-seven member states, the Commission is well positioned to do this, knowing first-hand the diverse legal traditions and political institutions.[87] This balancing requires legislative techniques that achieve uniformity while preserving some degree of sovereignty. For example, many EU regulations are drafted as directives, which lay out clear objectives but allow for variation in implementation nationally. This flexibility embedded in EU regulation makes for better templates for export to foreign jurisdictions with characteristics different from those found in the EU.

These pragmatic reasons and the ease of copying may lead to greater emulation – at least when it comes to enacting laws on the books. However, whether this emulation is ultimately effective and leads to an actual change in

Justice and Federal Trade Commission, 1995 Antitrust Guidelines for the Licensing of Intellectual Property (6 April 1995), Trade Reg. Rep. 13132, with and Commission Regulation (EC) No. 772/ 2004 of 27 April 2004 on the application of Article 81(3) of the Treaty to categories of technology transfer agreements, O. J. 2004 L 123/11.

85 Anu Bradford et al., 'The Global Dominance of European Competition Law Over American Antitrust Law' (2019) 16 *Journal of Empirical Legal Studies* 731–66 at 759.

86 Hans-Bernand Schäfer, 'Rules versus Standards in Rich and Poor Countries: Precise Legal Norms as Substitutes for Human Capital in Low-Income Countries' (2006) 14 *The Supreme Court Economic Review* 113–34.

87 The Commission is committed to 'geographical balance' within the administration, making nationality a key criterion in personnel decisions and thus ensuring that all member states have a 'fair share' of their nationals at all levels of the Commission. See Kassim et al., *The European Commission in the Twenty-First Century*, p. 36; see also Art. 1(14) of Regulation (EU, Euratom) No. 1023/2013 of the European Parliament and of the Council of 22 October 2013 amending the Staff Regulations of Officials of the European Union and the Conditions of Employment of Other Servants of the European Union, O.J. 2013 L 287/15; Edward C. Page, *People Who Run Europe* (Oxford: Clarendon Press, 1997), p. 41.

the conduct of market actors is a different question. If a foreign country adopts EU-style rules because they are drafted in an accessible language, it is not certain that the country has fully committed to the actual implementation of such rules. The emulation of EU norms and expertise following a deep domestic debate or a change of actual preferences, in contrast, indicates a more genuine motivation to adopt similar rules. For example, a change in the preferences of domestic business interests due to the Brussels Effect may give a more lasting foundation for a regulatory reform.

## 8.5 CONCLUSION

Expertise – whether legal, economic or scientific – provides a foundation for the European regulatory state. This contribution has highlighted the extent to which the legal expertise vested with the Commission diffuses around the world. Commission civil servants are often viewed as technocrats deploying their expertise to serve the European integration through their work in their assigned regulatory domain, be it environmental protection, food safety or competition. But by way of market forces, and through the various concerted efforts to export the European regulatory state, these experts have over time also become architects of global regulation.

This contribution has focused on the EU's global regulatory influence without advancing a normative argument on whether this influence is desirable or not. Yet those normative questions are important. For example, critics cite high costs associated with extensive regulation, worrying how the Brussels Effect only reproduces those costs abroad.[88] Yet an alternative view emphasises the benefits of uniform regulations and takes comfort in consumers around the world having access to safer, more reliable and sustainable products and services because of the global reach of the European regulatory state.

Another common criticism relates to the very nature of governance by experts. The EU is often portrayed as being technocratic and undemocratic.[89] These concerns are magnified if we acknowledge that the Commission

88 Frédéric Simon, 'Reach "Monster" will Devour EU Innovation, Chemical Industry Warns', *EURACTIVE*, 29 April 2016, www.euractiv.com/section/science-policymaking/news/reach-monster-will-devour-eu-innovation-chemical-industry-warns [https://perma.cc/EHZ8-H83L] ; Oversight on EPA Toxic Chemical Policies: Hearing Before the S. Comm. on Env't & Pub. Works, 110th Cong. 122–23 (2008) (statement of Jim DeLisi, President, Fanwood Chemical, Inc.); United States International Trade Commission, 'Trade Barriers that U.S. Small and Medium-Sized Enterprises Perceive as Affecting Exports to the European Union', March 2014, Inv. No. 332-541, USITC Pub. 4455, 3–5.

89 See, e.g., Claudio M. Radaelli, *Technocracy in the European Union* (London: Routledge, 1999); Andreas Follesdal and Simon Hix, 'Why There is a Democratic Deficit in the EU:

bureaucrats are writing rules for the world, further extending the gap between the rulemaking and the democratic institutions abroad. The most critical voices accuse the EU of regulatory imperialism, noting how the EU compromises the democratic prerogatives of foreign sovereigns and the political autonomy of their citizens.[90] For example, many foreign consumers likely view the trade-off between product safety and cost differently than Europeans, but are denied these preferences when the Brussels Effect steers companies towards more stringent regulation also in those markets.[91] Yet the proponents of the EU's global regulatory power can point to its ability to offset shortfalls in democratic governance elsewhere. For example, while the EU's regulatory process is neither flawless nor perfectly democratic, it is arguably less susceptible to corporate influence compared to the United States.[92] The Brussels Effect may thus have the effect of balancing the alleged overrepresentation of business interests in American public life by empowering consumers.[93] These are but few examples to illustrate how the normative debate surrounding the EU's global regulatory power is more nuanced than what any unqualified criticism or similarly unqualified endorsement of the EU's global regulatory power would suggest.

Acknowledgement of the role of EU experts as global experts raises other important questions for future research. For example, is the expertise vested within the EU institutions universally valid? Is it objective and culturally neutral to the extent that it can be deployed to design the details of various regulatory policies abroad? Also, should various EU experts more systematically examine the foreign effects of their regulations as part of the legislative process?[94] Foreign stakeholders are often consulted as part of the impact

A Response to Majone and Moravcsik' (2006) 44 *JCMS: Journal of Common Market Studies* 533–62; Petr Kratochvíl and Zdenek Sychra, 'The End of Democracy in the EU? The Eurozone Crisis and the EU's Democratic Deficit' (2019) 41 *Journal of European Integration* 169–85.

90 See Zielonka, 'Europe as a Global Actor: Empire by Example?', 475; Laïdi, 'The Unintended Consequences of European Power', 9–10.

91 See, e.g., 'US Airline EU ETS Case Against the UK to Be Referred to European Court as NGO Coalition Joins Actions', *GreenAir Online*, 28 May 2010, www.greenaironline.com/news.php?viewStory=1129 [https://perma.cc/2RK2-TXJK].

92 Joseph H. H. Weiler et al., European Democracy and its Critique: Five Uneasy Pieces' (1995) EUR-RSCAS Working Paper No. 1995/11, http://cadmus.eui.eu/handle/1814/1386 [https://perma.cc/ZW4U-WV3Q].

93 See Robert O. Keohane et al., 'Democracy-Enhancing Multilateralism' (2009) 63 *International Organization* 1–31 at 14.

94 See a collection of papers edited by Päivi Leino-Sandberg and Marise Cremona, 'Special Section – The New Frontiers of EU Administrative Law: Is There an Accountability Gap in EU External Relations?' (2017) *European Papers: A Journal on Law and Integration*; Vol. 2, No. 2. European Forum, www.europeanpapers.eu/en/content/e-journal/EP_eJ_2017_2.

assessment or consultation procedures that precede new regulations, but that process alone may not satisfy all critics.[95] Finally, should we be concerned if the EU's global regulatory power pushes all market participants and governments towards certain regulatory regime? By removing experimentation, corporations and governments may risk all converging to a wrong or inefficient standard. The stakes for European experts are therefore high: if the Commission gets its policies right, it has the potential to get them globally right; but if the Commission gets them wrong, it may get them globally wrong.

In closing, two questions seem timely and hence worth asking today – one relating to geopolitics and the other to crises. International relations have taken a strong geopolitical turn as trade and technology wars have undermined global cooperation and elevated tensions among powerful states. This raises the question of whether the EU could or should leverage its global regulatory power towards broader geopolitical goals. The Commission itself has declared its intention to become a 'geopolitical Commission'.[96] Given the EU's limited military powers and its inability to weaponise the global financial system the way the US does, the EU's regulatory power may appear to be the EU's most potent candidate for advancing foreign policy goals. Yet it is unclear that this would be feasible or wise. The EU's global regulatory power has been effective in part because it has rested on depoliticised, expert-driven technocratic power that the Commission exercises quietly under the political radar. This technocratic agenda rarely elevates issues to the political agenda where more controversial battles are fought. Seeking to geo-politicise the EU's regulatory power would thus strip it of this important quality that has allowed it to thrive to date. It is also unclear that the Commission experts would be comfortable or effective if thrown into the middle of geopolitical conflicts and asked to deploy their expertise towards foreign policy aims, which lies far outside the expertise of many.

Finally, it is unclear if the Covid-19 pandemic will undermine or enhance the Commission experts' global regulatory power. The health and economic crises triggered by the pandemic come on the heels of multiple other crises that the EU has endured in the past decade, including the financial crises, migration crises and Brexit. While these crises have shaken the core of the European project, the European regulatory state has remained largely intact.

95 See, e.g., Emilia Korkea-aho, 'Evolution of the Role of Third Countries in EU Law: Towards Full Legal Subjectivity?' in Samo Bardutzky and Elaine Fahey (eds.), *Framing the Subjects and Objects of EU Law: Exploring a Research Platform* (Cheltenham: Edward Elgar, 2017).

96 See, e.g., Étienne Bassot, 'The von der Leyen Commission's Priorities for 2019–2024', European Parliamentary Research Service PE 646.148, January 2020, www.europarl.europa.eu/RegData/etudes/BRIE/2020/646148/EPRS_BRI(2020)646148_EN.pdf.

One reason for the EU's resilience lies in its experts. The EU's technocratic governance shields the EU's regulatory state to some extent from crises. The Commission bureaucrats remain focused on their assigned regulatory domains without being distracted by the broader crises. For example, neither the refugee crises nor the Brexit referendum derailed the adoption of the GDPR. The Commission similarly went ahead and unveiled its planned Digital Services Act. The pandemic may, of course, lead the EU to rethink how to balance the individual right to privacy with the need to harness technology to trace public health emergencies. But the Commission experts are unlikely to scale back their regulatory ambitions because of the pandemic. After all, they are not in charge of the public health crisis or the political and economic fallout caused by pandemics; instead, they are in charge of the regulation of digital technology. The narrow, technocratic focus of the European experts may thus be the EU's greatest saviour, allowing the EU's regulatory agenda to flourish even when a major political or economic shock hits its core.

# 9

# The Negotiating Capital of Trade Experts: Transparency in EU-Asian Free Trade Agreements

Chris Kimura[1] and Fernanda G. Nicola

## 9.1 INTRODUCTION

The EU has engaged in bilateral trade negotiations in Asia following the stagnation of the World Trade Organization (WTO) multilateral approach and in response to the Trans-Pacific Partnership (TPP) negotiations.[2] It has recently concluded four Free Trade Agreements (FTAs) that are examined in this chapter: the EU-South Korea Free Trade Agreement, the EU-Vietnam FTA and Investment Protection Agreement (IPA), the EU-Singapore FTA and IPA and the EU-Japan Economic Partnership Agreement (EPA).[3] These EU trade agreements each include varying levels of regulatory transparency. The terms 'transparency provisions' and 'commitments' refer to FTA provisions whose purpose is related to the regulation of transparency, such as notification to the other party of possibly trade-harming administrative actions before their actual implementation. An analysis of these transparency commitments offers insights into how national transparency mandates,[4] together with geopolitical realities of international trade regimes, constitute the bargaining power of trade negotiators. Trade negotiations are a team effort that is not strictly limited to lawyers, as trade specialists and economists also contribute their own particularised expertise to accompany that of trade negotiators.

1 The following viewpoints are my own and do not reflect those of the Department of Commerce or the United States Government.

2 Under President Trump, the United States withdrew from the TPP in 2017; the remaining states revised the agreement into the Comprehensive and Progressive Agreement for Trans-Pacific Partnership (CPTPP). See James McBride and Andrew Chatzky, 'What is the Trans-Pacific Partnership?' *Council on Foreign Relations*, 4 January 2019.

3 EU-Vietnam Free Trade Agreement & Investment Protection Agreement, signed 30 June 2019; EU-Singapore Free Trade Agreement & Investment Protection Agreement, signed 19 October 2018; EU-Japan Economic Partnership Agreement, signed 20 December 2018 and entered into force 1 February 2019.

4 The term 'mandate' is referred to loosely and is not in reference to Article 218(3)–(4) TFEU.

This chapter explores how the negotiating capital of these trade experts creates a set of constraints and agency that allows for wiggle room and strategic choices in articulating, bargaining and drafting what appears as neutral transparency provisions in FTAs.

FTA transparency provisions represent an important dimension of legal expertise and are not merely neutral practices in negotiations. Instead, transparency provisions align with Duncan Kennedy's analysis on what some consider to be 'merely technical' issues.[5] Kennedy defines 'merely technical' issues as those that '[do] not involve any of the dimensions of the institution that have been politically controversial'.[6] The same theory applies to transparency provisions in trade negotiations as they are not merely technical issues but they influence international public law standards on good regulatory practices, as well as reflecting the negotiators' bargaining strategy. The EU, per Anu Bradford's 'The Brussels Effect', often sees its high regulatory standards adopted overseas through trade agreements or unilateral adoption by way of market leverage.[7] The strategic implication for trade agreements such as the Trans-Atlantic Trade and Investment Partnership (TTIP) was its use as a 'policy initiative to help open global markets' as well as its potential to 'define new structures and modalities for all sorts of non-tariff barriers to trade'.[8] According to Dan Hamilton and Jacques Pelkmans, if TTIP was successful, the EU and the US would remain 'rule makers', rather than 'rule takers'.[9] The intertwining nature of the theories of Kennedy, Bradford and Hamilton and Pelkmans indicate the importance of 'merely technical' issues, such as transparency provisions in FTAs, in relation to crafting international public and private law as regulatory standards based on geopolitical realities. Thus, it is important to consider these transparency provisions when analysing states' and negotiators' strategies in crafting a desirable set of FTA commitments, especially in light of global regulatory standard setting and their spill-over effects on domestic governance.

By focusing on the negotiating capital of trade negotiators, this chapter explores the variables determining the differences in regulatory transparency provisions found in four EU-Asian FTAs. Such capital is based on both institutionalised transparency and geopolitical realities which constitute the

[5] Duncan Kennedy, 'The Stakes of Law, or Hale and Foucault!' (1991) XV:4 *Legal Studies Forum* 327–66.

[6] Ibid., 24–8.

[7] Anu Bradford, 'The Brussels Effect' (2012) 107 *Northwestern University Law Review* 1–67 and Chapter 8 in this volume.

[8] Dan Hamilton and Jacques Pelkmans, 'Rule-Makers or Rule-Takers?' *Center for European Policy Studies*, 2015, p. 3.

[9] Ibid.

trade expertise of negotiators who are empowered by their respective executives to articulate and draft trade agreements.[10] Trade negotiators' objectives are thus not results purely of their own expertise or individual choices but instead results from the state interests, constitutional and administrative processes and collective deliberations. We define institutionalised transparency as the domestic approach to openness in legislative or regulatory processes. This includes both access to information and public participation by industry and civil society in regulatory lawmaking.[11] We address geopolitical realities such as economic strength, military alliances, political agreements, investment ties and kinship bonds. From the EU's perspective, these play out in terms of whether states possess a strategic relationship to the Union that structures the bargaining power of the actors in trade negotiations.

The different articulations of transparency provisions in the toolkit of EU trade negotiators range from diffused to shared-integrative, adverse-integrative and shared approaches that represent four different degrees of integration and inclusiveness.[12] The current variation in the transparency provisions that negotiators have included in each Asian FTA is based on two different variables. The first variable focuses on whether the negotiating partners share the same transparency values in their domestic legal regimes and the second one if the EU views such trade partnership as a strategic one for a multiplicity of geopolitical reasons.

This chapter first offers a foundational understanding of institutionalised transparency in the EU, Singapore, Vietnam, South Korea and Japan. The different transparency mandates among these countries partially resonate and are highly relevant to grasp the diverse political economies and legal cultures that define the negotiators' trade expertise. Rather than investigating the negotiating process and concrete mandates in trade agreements, we focus on the domestic principles that represent the state's level of institutionalised

10 David Kennedy, *A World of Struggle: How Power, Law and Expertise Shape Global Political Economy* (Oxford: Oxford University Press, 2018), p. 135 defining expertise as a rule by articulation that in the case of trade negotiators happens in the drafting of trade agreements.

11 For a detailed definition of institutional transparency, see Carla C. J. M. Millar et al., 'Corporate Governance and Institutional Transparency in Emerging Markets' (2005) 59 *Journal of Business Ethics* 163–74. See also Jens Forssbaeck and Lars Oxelheim, *The Oxford Handbook of Economic and Institutional Transparency* (Oxford University Press, 2015), chapter 1, Section 1.2: The Meaning of Transparency, pp. 6–11; Sarah Moore, 'Towards a Sociology of Institutional Transparency: Openness, Deception and the Problem of Public Trust' (2018) 52(2) *Sociology* 416–30. For the purposes of this chapter, institutional transparency will be a measure of the openness, accountability and role of public participation in the respective state's legislative bodies.

12 See Figure 9.1.

transparency. These domestic principles further influence which approach negotiators take, the trade-offs, and bargaining strategies in attaining broader or narrower commitments with respect to different transparency provisions in FTAs.

In the second part, the chapter compares the different transparency provisions found in two mega-regional FTAs, one signed by the EU with Canada[13] and the other the unfinished TTIP between the EU and the US.[14] The transparency provisions in these FTAs serve as control variables to which we compare institutionalised transparency and geopolitical realities emerging in EU-Asian FTAs.

As these provisions manifest different degrees of diffusion or integration, such variation reflects the strategic use of transparency provisions by trade negotiators. Rather than neutral best practices stemming from regulatory cooperation, trade negotiators deploy diffused, shared-integrative, adverse-integrative or shared approaches to transparency provisions as a bargaining toolkit that is part of their negotiating capital.[15]

## 9.2 INSTITUTIONALISED TRANSPARENCY IN TRADE AGREEMENTS

### 9.2.1 *Transparency As a Measure of Legitimacy in the EU*

Transparency as a principle is enshrined in the EU treaties.[16] During recent years, the EU has sought greater transparency in its trade negotiations.[17] The Court of Justice of the European Union (CJEU) has also acted as a major

[13] The Comprehensive Economic and Trade Agreement (CETA), provisionally entered into force on 21 September 2017.

[14] The Transatlantic Trade and Investment Partnership was negotiated but never concluded under the Obama administration in 2013.

[15] Fernanda G. Nicola, 'The Politicization of Legal Expertise in the TTIP Negotiation' (2015) 78 *Law and Contemporary Problems* 175–204. For a similar perspective on the underlying influence of otherwise technical matters of law, see Duncan Kennedy, 'The Political Stakes in "Merely Technical" Issues of Contract Law' (2001) 1 *European Review of Private Law* 7–28.

[16] Article 1 of the Treaty on the European Union (TEU) states that decisions made in the European Union institutions will be taken 'as openly as possible and as closely as possible to the citizen'. Article 10(3) TEU, titled 'Declaration on the Right to Access to Information', re-emphasises the transparency principle that 'decisions shall be taken as openly and as closely as possible to the citizen'. Similarly, Article 15 on the Treaty on the Functioning of the European Union (TFEU) states that 'in order to promote good governance and ensure participation of civil society, the Union institutions, bodies, offices and agencies shall conduct their work as openly as possible'. Article 15 also requires that Member States maintain the right of access to documents by the public.

[17] See Päivi Leino, 'The Principle of Transparency in EU External Relations Law: Does Diplomatic Secrecy Stand a Chance of Surviving the Age of Twitter?' in Marise Cremona (ed.), *Structural Principles in EU External Relations Law* (Oxford: Hart Publishing, 2018).

balance on international negotiations transparency, particularly in the *In't Veld* case law relating to the Union's SWIFT and ACTA negotiations.[18] The CJEU's decision ultimately raises the standard by which Union institutions may apply for Regulation 1049/2001 public disclosure exceptions by requiring the institution to explain how disclosure would '"specifically and actually" undermine the interest protected' by such exceptions.[19] Also the EU Ombudsman took action during the negotiations by demanding the Union institutions provide increased levels of TTIP transparency in 2014.[20] The Ombudsman specifically requested that the institutions 'publish documents, establish a public register of TTIP documents, and publish an online list of the stakeholders the Commission meets with regard to TTIP'.[21] Despite a large public consultation by the Commission on the highly contested Investor-States Dispute Settlement (ISDS), civil unrest and complaints continued into late 2016 as CETA came to a close and the TTIP negotiations stalled.[22]

In 2015, the EU Trade Commissioner Cecilia Malmström proposed the 'Trade For All' strategy, focusing on 'three key principles – effectiveness, transparency, and values – it ensures trade policy benefits as many people as possible'.[23] As part of the overall Brussels Effect,[24] the EU further emphasises transparency as a measure of the Union's legitimacy in its global trade ambitions.[25] Malmström promised 'Trade For All' would make trade policy more responsible, effective and transparent, while continuing to project European interests and values.[26] Among numerous commitments, the strategy

[18] Case C-350/12 P, *Council* v. *Sophie In't Veld*, EU:C:2014:2039. See also Leino, 'The Principle of Transparency in EU External Relations Law'.

[19] Leino, ibid., 4.

[20] James Crisp, 'EU Ombudsman Demands More TTIP Transparency', *EURACTIV* (31 July 2014), www.euractiv.com/section/public-affairs/news/eu-ombudsman-demands-more-ttip-transparency/. See also European Ombudsman, 16 May 2018. Special Report of the European Ombudsman in strategic inquiry OI/2/2017 TE on the transparency of the Council legislative process, www.ombudsman.europa.eu/en/special-report/en/94921.

[21] Ibid.

[22] Michael Nienaber, 'Tens of Thousands Protest in Europe against Atlantic Free Trade Deals' *Reuters*, 17 September 2016, www.reuters.com/article/us-eu-usa-ttip-idUSKCN11N0H6.

[23] European Commission, 'Trade For All: European Commission presents new trade and investment strategy', 14 October 2015, https://trade.ec.europa.eu/doclib/press/index.cfm?id=1381.

[24] The Brussels Effect is the European Union's 'unilateral power to regulate global markets' by way of its market power and regulatory expertise and resources. See Bradford, 'The Brussels Effect'.

[25] Ibid., 19 explaining how lack of transparency undermines the legitimacy of EU trade policy and public trust.

[26] European Commission, 'Trade For All – towards a more responsible trade and investment policy' October 2015, https://trade.ec.europa.eu/doclib/docs/2015/october/tradoc_153846.pdf.

requires the Union institutions to disclose all FTA negotiating directives after adoption, publish all Union trade and investment negotiations online, to 'make clear to all new partners that negotiations will have to follow a transparent approach', and immediately publicly publish the agreement text 'as it stands'.[27] This trade-transparency prerogative gained traction during the EU trade negotiations with Canada and the US as civil society and NGOs voiced complaints over the negotiations being opaque and non-democratic.

Checks and balances within the Union system also exist to ensure that international agreements concluded by the EU do not violate EU legislation. In 2009, the Treaty of Lisbon granted the European Parliament increased authority over agreements and negotiations with third countries by granting a veto ability.[28] In 2010, Parliament used this newfound veto in the EU-US SWIFT Interim Agreement; the agreement's purpose was to increase cooperation in investigating terrorist financing between the EU and the US by sharing bank and financial transfer data.[29] Parliament's veto rested on the Council's decision to not consider the minimum conditions Parliament believed satisfied 'EU data protection standards, procedural rights of EU citizens, proportionality, and reciprocity'.[30] Thanks to the veto, the Council later considered Parliament's conditions, leading to the approval and adoption of SWIFT.[31] In 2012, Parliament again utilised its veto authority against the Anti-Counterfeiting Trade Agreement (ACTA).[32] Parliament, as evidenced by SWIFT and ACTA, is not afraid to squash legislation it believes are detrimental to the European citizens' rights. These agreements also led to transparency litigation before the CJEU, which has also acted as a major balance on international negotiations transparency.[33] The CJEU's decision ultimately raises the standard by which Union institutions may apply for Regulation 1049/2001 public

27 Ibid.

28 Article 218 TFEU.

29 Jörg Monar, 'The Rejection of the EU-US SWIFT Interim Agreement by the European Parliament: A Historic Vote and its Implications' (2010) 15 *European Foreign Affairs Review* 143–51.

30 Ibid., 144.

31 Toby Vogel, 'EU, US Sign SWIFT Agreement', *Politico*, 28 July 2010.

32 European Parliament, 'European Parliament Rejects ACTA', 4 July 2012, www.europarl.europa.eu/news/en/press-room/20120703IPR48247/european-parliament-rejects-acta.

33 European Parliament, Committee on International Trade 'EU Rapporteur's Draft Recommendation; Draft European Parliament Legislative Resolution'. 12 April 2012, www.europarl.europa.eu/sides/getDoc.do?pubRef=-//EP//NONSGML%2BCOMPARL%2BPE-486.174%2B02%2BDOC%2BPDF%2BV0//EN.

disclosure exceptions.[34] By establishing this line of case law, the CJEU has balanced transparency and secrecy in Union negotiations with third parties.

These developments provide incentives for the EU institutions to try to balance transparency, public access and secrecy. When EU institutions fail to adhere to standards under Regulation 1049/2001, various parts of the Union mobilise to check the transgression. It is clear EU legitimacy is 'inextricably linked'[35] to transparency in trade negotiations, and transparency provisions in EU FTAs sought to be highly integrated, given that the Commission negotiators are afforded the opportunity to include them. EU negotiators bargain for provisions that establish sufficient levels of legitimacy that enable the final approval of the agreement in the EU institutions.

### 9.2.2 *The Disregard for Transparency in Japan*

For instance, the EU and Japan share the strongest strategic relationship of the four FTAs discussed here, evidenced by treaties and mutual recognition in data privacy.[36] However, Japan's institutionalised transparency norms do not overlap with the EU values, thus placing the EU-Japan EPA negotiating strategy into the diffused, rather than shared, approach articulated above.

Japan's dismissive perspective on institutionalised transparency finds its roots in the post–World War II era. The political incentives for structural transparency faded once the US occupation came to an end in 1952. Trade tensions in the 1980s and 90s exposed the deeply engrained opaqueness of the Japanese governing systems. The panels and appellate bodies of Japan's WTO cases affirmed Japanese administrative guidance was a 'traditional tool of Japanese government policy based on consensus and peer pressure'.[37] By

34 See Leino, 'The Principle of Transparency in EU External Relations Law'. See also Päivi Leino, 'Secrecy, Efficiency, Transparency in EU Negotiations: Conflicting Paradigms?' (2017) 5(3) *Politics and Governance* 6–15, arguing that the 'categorical solutions relating to transparency or secrecy, or dichotomies based on a strict division between "internal" and "external", are fundamentally outdated'.

35 See Sophie Meunier, 'Trade Policy and Political Legitimacy in the European Union' (2003) 1 (1) *Comparative European Politics* 67–90. Meunier analyses the democratic deficit in the 'processes' and 'outcomes' of EU trade policy and, most importantly for our purposes, reaffirms that trade and legitimacy are 'inextricably linked', 86.

36 EU decision on data protection adequacy of Japan, C/2019/304/OJ L 76, 19.3.2019, https://eeas.europa.eu/sites/eeas/files/eu-japan_factsheet_may-2020_1.pdf.

37 WTO Dispute Settlement Body. *Japan-Restrictions on Imports of Certain Agricultural Products*. 18 November 1987. *WTO.org*, 61–2, WTO Dispute Settlement Body. *Japan-Semiconductors*. 24 March 1988. *WTO.org*, 348, WTO Dispute Settlement Body. *Japan-Photographic Film & Paper*. 31 March 1998. *WTO.org*, 29.

the 1990s, the US and Japanese administrations entered into bilateral negotiations to reduce their respective non-tariff barriers and to open the protectionist Japanese market to American industries. By way of the Structural Impediments Initiative (SII), the US recommended Japan make its government processes more transparent.[38] The 1991 asset bubble burst and subsequent economic crisis in Japan incentivised Japanese businesses to call for heightened standards of accountability and transparency commitments from the government. Annelise Riles notes that 'One of the key intellectual imports of the Japanese Big Bang financial reforms . . . was a new critique of bureaucratic corruption and associated progressive calls for "transparency, democracy and political accountability".'[39]

A series of political scandals in the 1990s, most notably the 'Douglas-Grumman' bribery, and mounting international criticisms further pressured the Japanese government to pass reforms, eventually leading to the 'Administrative Procedure Act' (APA) of 1993.[40] Reforms continued into the latter half of the 1990s under Hashimoto Ryutaro and the Administrative Reform Council.[41] However, the transparency trend of the 1990s declined over time.[42] Many have offered harsh criticism in Japan over the 2013 State Secrets Protection Bill, claiming 'administrative agencies would have sweeping discretionary authority', particularly because of a lack of a review mechanism.[43] Four years later, an Anti-Conspiracy Bill drew numerous criticisms, including from the UN

38 SII Report, TAC Program – Making Trade Agreements Work for You! Available at tcc.export.gov/Trade_Agreements/All_Trade_Agreements/exp_005583.asp. Found under 'Exclusionary Business Practices', Section I: Basic Recognition. See also David Vogel, 'Consumer Protection and Protectionism in Japan' (1992) 18(1) *The Journal of Japanese Studies* 119–22, finding that the Japanese system 'provides fewer opportunities for public and non-industry participation than does American'.

39 Annelise Riles, *Collateral Knowledge: Legal Reasoning in the Global Financial Markets* (Chicago: University of Chicago Press, 2011), p. 115 (quoting Azfar, Lee, and Swamy 2001).

40 Katsuya Uga, 'Development of the Concepts of Transparency and Accountability in Japanese Administrative Law', in Daniel H Foote (ed.), *Law in Japan: A Turning Point* (Washington: University of Washington Press, 2007), pp. 276–303. The Administrative Procedure Act, according to Uga, 'was expected that it would bring about a gradual change in the bureaucrats' perception of the government-citizen relationship'. Uga further describes Japanese bureaucrats as having a 'culture of secrecy'. Administrative Procedure Act (APA), Act No. 88 of 1993, www.cas.go.jp/jp/seisaku/hourei/data/APA_2.pdf.

41 Kazuyuki Takahashi, 'Ongoing Changes in the Infrastructure of a Constitutional System' in Daniel H. Foote (ed.), *Law in Japan: A Turning Point* (University of Washington Press, 2007) pp. 237–56.

42 See Simon Denyer and Akiko Kashiwagi, 'The Strange Tale of Japan's Prime Minister, Official Documents and a Very Large Shredder', *The Washington Post*, 27 November 2019.

43 Jeff Kingston, 'Abe Promotes Secrecy, Sidelining Transparency and Open Government', *The Japan Times*, 5 October 2013.

Special Rapporteur on the right to privacy.[44] Despite the passing of a Freedom of Information Act in Japan in 2001,[45] the Japanese government has become subject to a handful of scandals in which sensitive documents were destroyed.[46] These trends represent former Prime Minister Abe Shinzo and his administration's general lack of interest in maintaining institutionalised transparency. Alongside restrictive transparency measures, restrictive freedom of speech measures in Japan are also harshly criticised by foreign observers, including the EU,[47] and the UN Special Rapporteur in 2017 wrote a damning report of the diminishing freedom of opinion and expression in Japan, especially on media reporting.[48] The Japanese government rebuked the rapporteur, claiming the report was merely hearsay.[49]

Despite these tensions, the EU and Japan share a strong strategic relationship. In 2019, the EU-Japan Strategic Partnership Agreement came into force and commits both parties to, in a nutshell, 'strengthen the rules-based global order and enhance global governance'.[50] The agreement values 'democracy, human rights, good governance, and a market-based economy'. In addition, the EU added Japan to its list of countries having adequate data protection, meaning that personal data may be transferred between the EU and Japan

44 Mandate of the Special Rapporteur on the right to privacy, www.ohchr.org/Documents/Issues/Privacy/OL_JPN.pdf.

45 Officially titled 'Law Concerning Access to Information Held by Administrative Organs'. The law's origin comes from independent prefecture's own passing of freedom of information laws, convincing the resistant government to pass their own. Interview with Hiroshi Miyake, Partner at Hara-Sogo Law Firm in Yotsuya, Tokyo.

46 From 2016 to 2018, Prime Minister Abe was involved in a separate scandal regarding a land deal with the Moritomo Gakuen elementary school, notable for having a 'nationalistic moral education program'. See 'Abe's School Scandal Gains Steam on High-Profile Resignation', *Nikkei Asian Review*, 10 March 2018; Justin McCurry, 'Shinzo Abe and Wife under Pressure over Ties to Ultra-Nationalist School', *The Guardian*, 24 February 2017; Reiji Yoshida, 'Abe Stands His Ground As Moritomo Gakuen Scandal Drags on', *The Japan Times*, 13 March 2017.

47 'Our quarrel is with the way this system of kisha clubs is used to exclude foreign correspondents from access to news and from access to press conferences and press briefings'. European Commission, 'Statement by the Delegation of the European Commission in Japan in response to the Opinion of the Japanese Newspaper Publishers and Editors Association', *EU News* 39/03, 16 December 2003, https://web.archive.org/web/20081207060556/http://www.deljpn.ec.europa.eu/home/news_en_newsobj22.php.

48 Human Rights Council-Thirty-Fifth Session, 'Report of the Special Rapporteur on the promotion and protection of the right to freedom of opinion and expression in his mission to Japan' 29 May 2017, http://hrn.or.jp/wpHN/wp-content/uploads/2017/05/A_HRC_35_22_Add.1_AUV.pdf.

49 'Japan Gives Short Shrift to a UN Rapporteur Looking into Press Freedom', *The Economist*, 8 June 2017.

50 EU-Japan Strategic Partnership Agreement factsheet, https://eeas.europa.eu/sites/eeas/files/factsheet_eu-japan_strategic_partnership_agreement_japan.pdf.

while at the same time bypassing encumber-some mechanisms.[51] The EU and Japan also maintain an EU-Japan Centre for Industrial Cooperation.[52] These ties represent the strategic relationship shared between the EU and Japan, one of the two important factors considered in the approach trade negotiators ultimately choose when constructing a transparency chapter.

Transparency trends in Japan leave much to be desired as the government has not embraced this principle as part of its legitimacy or authority like the EU but chooses to diminish its importance through government actions and policies. The implication for trade transparency initiatives is that Japanese negotiators favour textual language either ignoring or limiting transparency commitments.

### 9.2.3 *Transparency As Good Governance in South Korea*

The purpose of transparency norms in South Korea is to institutionalise principles important to good governance.[53] Democracy in South Korea remains young, only beginning after the 1987 'June Struggle' and the end of the Fifth Republic.[54] According to Paik Nak-Chung, the government structure following the June Struggle, the 'regime of 1987', broadly agreed that it 'constitutes an order much superior to what preceded it, but that it was from the beginning an unstable structure based on a number of make-shift compromises'.[55]

Seok-Jin Eom's research on South Korean governmental transparency highlights major developments since the June Struggle. The military dictatorship preceding the Sixth Republic maintained a strong culture of secrecy parallel with government monopolisation on public information.[56] Soon

51 Tim Hickman and Shino Asayama, 'EU-Japan Adequacy Decision Now in Force' *White & Case*, 30 January 2019.

52 The EU-Japan Centre for Industrial Cooperation's mission is to develop 'all forms of industrial, trade and investment cooperation between the EU and Japan'. The Centre provides numerous services to businesses, including a helpdesk, training, technological support, logistical support and tax and public procurement, www.eu-japan.eu/.

53 Seok-Jin Eom, 'Improving Governmental Transparency in Korea: Toward Institutionalized and ICT-Enabled Transparency' (2014) 29(1) *The Korean Journal of Policy Studies* 70, explaining how respect to transparency developments, 'Korea can be considered as a good benchmark in examining how governmental transparency has rapidly improved . . . since the transition in 1987'.

54 Nak-Chung Paik, 'Democracy and Peace in South Korea Twenty Years After June 1987: Where Are We Now, and Where Do We Go From Here?' (2007) 5(6) *The Asia-Pacific Journal* 1–9.

55 Ibid.

56 Ibid., 78–9.

after the democratic transition, delegation of power shifted from the executive to the National Assembly.[57] Eom further notes the passing of pivotal transparency laws such as the 1996 Official Information Disclosure Act, the 1993 Property Registration System for Public Officials and the 1996 Administrative Procedures Act.[58] The Administrative Procedures Act's purpose is to 'attain fairness, transparency, and confidence in administration, and to protect the rights and interests of citizens'.[59] Such civil interests dedicated to transparency manifested in the massive 2017–18 protests against then-president Park Geun-hye.[60]

South Korea has taken major steps in negotiating free trade agreements. It has signed FTAs with Australia, Canada, China, the EU, Peru and the US. According to a WTO trade policy summary, South Korea's rebound from the 2008 financial crisis is primarily afforded to the 'opening of its market further to international trade through major bilateral free-trade agreements'.[61] There is not much on South Korea's trade transparency initiatives, but its free trade agreement with the US provides some examples of transparency commitments.[62] The South Korea-Canada and South Korea-Peru FTAs, however, do not include anti-corruption and instead resort to broad transparency commitments.[63] A standard set of transparency provisions is found in the EU FTA. However, due to the shared values between the negotiators, an additional provision on anti-discrimination has also been incorporated. This

57 Ibid., 82.

58 Ibid., 86.

59 South Korea Administrative Procedures Act, Chapter 1, Article 1. 1996, https://elaw.klri.re.kr/eng_service/lawView.do?hseq=335&lang=ENG. In 'Improving Governmental Transparency in Korea' Eom further notes increasing active civic engagement, as 'major civic groups have served as central advocates and building support coalitions for the movement to improve transparency', 92.

60 For a summary of the scandal, see 'South Korea's presidential scandal', *BBC News*, 6 April 2018.

61 Trade Policy Review: Republic of Korea – Summary, 19–21 September 2012.

62 Chapter 21 of the agreement, titled Transparency, contains standard commitments on publication, information, administrative proceedings, and review and appeals. However, the chapter places notable focus on anti-corruption commitments, requiring the parties to maintain legislation or similar measures to make it a criminal offense for public officials or persons to 'intentionally solicit or accept . . . any article of monetary value or other benefit . . . in exchange for any act or omission in the performance of his public functions'. United States-South Korea Free Trade Agreement, Article 21.6, https://ustr.gov/sites/default/files/uploads/agreements/fta/korus/asset_upload_file503_12720.pdf.

63 South Korea-Canada Free Trade Agreement, Chapter 19, www.international.gc.ca/trade-commerce/assets/pdfs/agreements-accords/korea-coree/19_CKFTA_EN.pdf.

South Korea-Peru Free Trade Agreement, Chapter 21, available at www.sice.oas.org/TPD/PER_KOR/PER_KOR_Texts_e/21_KPFTA_Transparency.pdf.

extra provision reflects the concurrence and potential agreeableness between negotiators with shared values.

### 9.2.4 *Transparency As a Means to an End in Singapore and Vietnam*

Like South Korea, Singapore has experienced major economic success and it is now a major financial centre in Asia. However, according to Garry Rodan, Singapore's economic success 'has gone hand in hand with low levels of commercial and political transparency as well as tight medial control'.[64] In contrast to the South Korean experience, Singapore's 'rapidly increasingly sophisticated market development has actually coincided with more effective control of the media'.[65] Government programmes to integrate information technology into daily life in Singapore were introduced in tandem with plans to further tighten restrictions on the media and internet freedoms.[66]

Political transparency in Singapore is highly opaque.[67] Like Japan, the Singaporean government's internal culture is generally uninterested in citizen's transparency claims pursuant to freedom of information and accountability.[68] Instead, the government permits transparency primarily when the information concerns the financial and business interests of international companies present in Singapore. In recent news, the Singaporean leadership passed a bill penalising the publication 'fake news', requiring internet media to 'correct or remove content the government considers false'.[69] The new law is expected to have a chilling effect in freedom of speech and information extending across South-East Asia, especially due to the law's harsh penalties.[70] Reporters Without Borders is especially critical of Singapore's restrictions, pointing to abuses against journalists, strict censorship and judicial and financial pressures.[71] As such, a handful of news and advocacy groups rank Singapore quite low on their transparency indexes.[72]

64 Garry Rodan, 'Asian Crisis, Transparency and the International Media in Singapore' (2000) 13 (2) *The Pacific Review* 218.

65 Ibid., 219.

66 Ibid., 221.

67 Ibid., 222.

68 Ibid.

69 'Singapore Fake News Law a "Disaster" for Freedom of Speech, Says Rights Group', *The Guardian*, 9 May 2019, www.theguardian.com/world/2019/may/09/singapore-fake-news-law-a-disaster-for-freedom-of-speech-says-rights-group.

70 Ibid.

71 Singapore page, *Reporters Without Borders*, https://rsf.org/en/singapore.

72 Reporters Without Borders ranks Singapore at 151 in its 2019 World Press Freedom Index.

However, regardless of these issues, some outlets rate Singapore highly, noting the previously mentioned financial reforms.[73]

Vietnam's transparency initiatives appear to take a similar shape as Singapore's, developing after the Asian financial crisis that compelled the Vietnamese government to implement a second wave of economic reforms.[74] In administrative law, the Vietnamese government initiated in 1999 a 'Public Administration Reform', which sought to 'renovate the development, issuance, and quality improvement of legal normative documents … roles, functions, organizational structures of the agencies in the administrative system … [and] modernization of the administrative system'.[75] Vietnam has also been promoting e-government and information and communication technologies to 'improve efficiency and effectiveness of its public administration', fostering increased transparency over time.[76] However, scholars have shed light on how transparency in Vietnam is a 'two-faced policy', as 'Vietnam has tried to send a signal to the world that it has changed to openness … but on the other hand, detrimental culture and information to national interest shall be prohibited'.[77] The communist regime in Vietnam has created some challenges for EU negotiators who are pushing for higher degrees of transparency and democratic participation in the EU-Vietnam FTA.

Transparency principles in Singapore and Vietnam are a means to support financial and economic development and growth. Institutionalised transparency in both is purposely pushed aside, evidenced by tight government restrictions on freedom of information and speech and, in Vietnam, harsh

73 Transparency International takes an alternative perspective and ranked Singapore at spot number four in its 2019 Corruption Perception Index. See Transparency International, *Corruption Perception Index 2019*, www.transparency.org/cpi2019. US News, who also maintains an annual country-ranking system, places Singapore at number seventeen on its transparency list. See 'Most Transparent Countries', *US News*, www.usnews.com/news/best-countries/best-transparency. According to the publication '[t]he most transparent countries, those with open business and government practices, well-distributed political power, high levels of trustworthiness and low levels of perceived corruption, tend to be among the world's strongest democracies and affluent nations'.

74 Thi Bich Tran, R. Quentin Grafton and Tom Kompas, 'Institutions Matter: The Case of Vietnam' (2008) *Crawford School of Economics and Government: The Australian National University*, January 4.

75 Martin Painter, 'Public Administration Reform in Vietnam: Problems and Prospects' (2003) 23 *Public Administration and Development*, 260 https://onlinelibrary.wiley.com/doi/pdf/10.1002/pad.249?casa_token=mARCU7RalT4AAAAA:Na6yEs6OJLAsf-6URMZAvK3323RSnwzCapPsvWO1EfgyI5FI4trXSgTuIrAY53863NTCXlXIL-W8pTs

76 Tran Van Long, Nyugen Trieu Hoa and Nyugen Thi Anh, 'E-government without E-democracy in the Case of Vietnam: Transparency Has Been a Sham?' (2017) 8 *Tidsskriftet Arkiv* 1.

77 Ibid., 2.

punishments for dissidents. With respect to the negotiating process, Singaporean and Vietnamese negotiator's focused on negotiating on goods and investment while forgoing political resources on fighting for favourable terms elsewhere. In contrast, EU negotiator's concern was incorporating broad transparency commitments that act to support the FTA's legitimacy while encouraging investments by EU businesses, especially SMEs.

## 9.3 INSTITUTIONALISED TRANSPARENCY AND GEOPOLITICAL REALITIES IN MEGA-REGIONAL FTAs

By considering the EU's trade agreements and negotiations with two strategic partners, Canada and the US, we assess the spectrum of trade-offs across different transparency and political economy visions. While the transparency values and the regulatory mandate between the EU and Canada appear to be one-and-the-same, the Union negotiations with the US shows how not having overlapping transparency values can ultimately affect the outcome of the trade negotiation. We define strategic partners states with an extensive and multifaceted relationship that takes into account factors such as strong economic ties, numerous and substantial foreign direct investments and similar political and security interests.[78]

The 2016 Comprehensive Economic and Trade Agreement (CETA) is a trade agreement negotiated by two long-time strategic partners that maintain transparency as a measure of political legitimacy.[79] As for CETA's transparency commitments, they are notably very basic and incorporate standard provisions on publication, providing information, maintaining administrative

78 See Sunghoon Park, 'EU's Strategic Partnership with Asian Countries: An Introductory Article for the Special Issue' (2019) 17 *Asia Europe Journal* 257–63, https://doi.org/10.1007/s10308-019-00552-4; See also Andriy Tyushka and Lucyna Czechowska, 'Strategic Partnerships, International Politics and IR Theory' in Lucyna Czechowska et al (eds.), *States, International Organizations and Strategic Partnerships* (Cheltenham: Edward Elgar Publishing, 2019).

79 The EU and Canada have a well-established information-sharing relationship. For instance, the first EEC agreement signed with a third country was the 1976 'Framework Agreement for Commercial and Economic Cooperation' with Canada. Further, the EU has recognised Canada's legal of data protection as 'adequate' per the GDPR's standards. Lastly, in 2017, the EU and Canada signed an agreement on security procedures for exchanging and protecting classified information. See Framework Agreement for Commercial and Economic Cooperation between the European Communities and Canada, https://ec.europa.eu/world/agreements/prepareCreateTreatiesWorkspace/treatiesGeneralData.do?step=0&redirect=true&treatyId=267; Adequacy Decisions, European Commission, https://ec.europa.eu/info/law/law-topic/data-protection/international-dimension-data-protection/adequacy-decisions_en; Council of the European Union, Decision 7984/17, http://data.consilium.europa.eu/doc/document/ST-7984-2017-INIT/en/pdf.

proceedings, review and appeal and regulatory cooperation on promoting increased transparency.[80] Given the already strong strategic partnership and similar regulatory approaches between the two states, it appears that the trade negotiators have adopted common frames and general clauses rather than incorporating either redundant or excessive transparency commitments.

Although the TTIP has no published transparency chapter, transparency provisions in the regulatory cooperation chapter offer unique insights into the negotiating process. The EU and the US are no doubt strategic partners.[81] However, both states heavily diverge on their transparency policies as seen in their respective regulatory agendas.[82] The EU negotiator's textual proposal includes commitments reflecting the Union's transparency and public participation values, and a greater focus on small and medium sized enterprises.[83] The existence of a strategic partnership mixed with divergent values proves a challenging landscape for trade negotiators as provisions must balance the interests of both states.

In conclusion, the texts of CETA and TTIP display a range of legal solutions when trade negotiators strategically adopt transparency provisions in regulatory cooperation that draw from their domestic framework to negotiate and reach compromises on how to draft specific treaty provisions. In CETA, both parties, the EU and Canada, were strategic partners and shared similar transparency policies, resulting in a standard set of agreeable transparency provisions included in the FTA. This approach similar to a good faith clause in private law or general principles in international law aims to use broad transparency provisions without wasting political resources or specificities on unnecessary negotiations. In contrast, the clashing political economy interests

80 Consolidated CETA Text. See annex for the associated articles, http://trade.ec.europa.eu/doclib/docs/2014/september/tradoc_152806.pdf.

81 Cooperation in NATO, the Transatlantic Economic Council, the EU-US Energy Council, and trade relations are strong indicators that the EU and US are strategic partners.

82 The TTIP negotiations was a way for the Obama administration to push the EU to reform its regulatory approaches under the Better Regulation agenda. See Fernanda Nicola, 'The Politicization of Legal Expertise in the TTIP Negotiation'; Sacha Garben, 'A Taste of Its Own Medicine: Assessing the Impact of the EU Better Regulation Agenda' (2020) 2 *European Law Journal* 83–103. See also Leino, 'The Principle of Transparency in EU External Relations Law'.

83 TTIP – EU Proposal for Chapter: Regulatory Cooperation, http://trade.ec.europa.eu/doclib/docs/2016/march/tradoc_154377.pdf. Commitments include the publication of all activities of the EU-US Annual Regulation Cooperation Program, as well as requiring the Program to consult with an Advisory Group composed by SMEs, trade unions, and public interest groups. The annex on transparency prioritises stakeholder involvement in regulatory cooperation activities and the need for appropriate modalities allowing for transparent dialogue with interested and legal persons.

present in TTIP between the EU and the US showed how trade negotiators struggled on transparency commitments in light of preserving a transatlantic trade relationship yet with increasing conflicting values and economic policies. The clash between EU and US trade negotiators resulted in divergences over the protection of the interests of small and medium enterprises (SME) in the EU versus multinational enterprises (MNE) in the US, among other issues.

## 9.4 NEGOTIATING CAPITAL

### 9.4.1 *Trade Expertise As Negotiating Capital*

In this section we describe how the trade expert's negation capital is a combination of their institutionalised transparency mandate, the geopolitical realities of trade regimes and the bargaining power they can exercise as trade experts. Trade negotiators must utilise their legal expertise to obtain negotiating capital, determine objectives and maximise results.[84] Further, trade negotiators work as a team on behalf of the state they represent. How trade negotiators maximise minimal resources, or how much flexibility they have in terms of exercising their legal expertise to achieve favourable results, is the key to understanding their role as legal expert.

Trade negotiators use their legal expertise to maximise results despite working within narrow confines. Negotiating capital is a difficult resource to acquire, especially for EU negotiators who have little bargaining room under the pressure of the Commission, Council and Parliament.[85] Negotiating capital represents the degrees of flexibility or wiggle-room within various constraining factors such as the government, businesses and civil society. The degrees of flexibility highly depend on the administrative procedures in which negotiators work. The Commission, for example, has developed a bottom-up procedure by which their negotiators receive their mandate. The Commission begins trade negotiations by developing an impact assessment where pros and cons, priorities and Member State and stakeholder interest and concerns are considered.[86] The Trade Policy Committee in the Council and the European Parliament continually receives input from

[84] For more on expertise in the context of the exchange of knowledge, information, and expertise, see Diane Stone, 'Introduction: Global Knowledge and Advocacy Networks' (2002) 2(1) *Global Networks* 1–12. See also chapters 4 and 5 in Kennedy, *A World of Struggle*.

[85] Virtual interview with representative of the Commission's Directorate-General for Trade on 16 October 2020 (on file with the authors).

[86] Ibid.

Member States and stakeholders. Through further consultations with the Member States a negotiating mandate is shaped, and approved by the Council, and EU trade negotiators in the Commission must negotiate within these confines.[87] There runs a risk where overcrowding the trade agenda may occur, and some principles that are important to the EU, such as sustainability and human rights, are essential to the agreement, lest the EP refuses ratification.[88] Considering the multiple factors and necessary components is a major challenge for EU negotiators, and from this they develop what we consider their legal expertise.

On the other hand, Japanese trade negotiators operate within a top-down system. While Japanese negotiators do not need to navigate multiple Member States, stakeholders and civil society, they must acquire negotiating capital from powerful ministries.[89] The Prime Minister's office can either tighten or expand the trade negotiator's mandate on short notice, say, in response to international developments.[90] Further, private interests in Japan are limited to a few powerful entities such as the Keidanren[91] representing major Japanese businesses and the Diet representing civil society. Further, the bureaucratic nature of law-making in Japan has impacts on negotiating strategy, as Japanese negotiators are highly risk avoidant and disfavour constructive ambiguity.[92] Negotiating capital represents the Japanese government and businesses flexibility to concede certain grounds, but the differing administrative procedures redefines the trade negotiators' legal expertise.

This brief cross-comparison shows that the trade negotiators' legal expertise is shaped by domestic administrative systems through which the negotiators operate. Trade negotiators work as a team to utilise the limited negotiating capital and the flexibility they enjoy to maximise results for their governments. Through the variation of transparency provisions in FTAs we analyse the flexibility and bargaining power of trade negotiators as part of their negotiating capital.

87 Ibid.

88 Ibid. See Article 218 TFEU.

89 Ibid, interviews in Tokyo, Japan with former and current civil service representatives during summer 2019 (on file with the authors).

90 Ibid.

91 The Japan Business Federation 'Keidanren' is a 'comprehensive economic organization with a membership comprised of 1,412 representative companies in Japan, 109 nationwide industrial associations and 47 regional economic organizations'. See: 'About Keidanren', Keidanren website, www.keidanren.or.jp/en/profile/pro001.html

92 Ibid.

### 9.4.2 *Transparency Commitments in EU-Singapore, Vietnam, South Korea and Japan*

Both Singapore and Vietnam have a history of viewing institutionalised transparency as merely a means to an end, a mandate that clashes with the EU's transparency interests. The Singapore FTA negotiations began in 2010, was signed in 2018, and approved by the Council with the consent of the European Parliament in 2019. The Vietnam FTA came at roughly the same time as negotiations concluded at the end of 2015, was signed in 2019 and approved by the European Parliament in 2020. Both agreements require the parties to publish measures and proposed changes to measures of general application and to 'provide reasonable opportunities for interested persons' to comment on those proposed measures or changes.[93] One notable difference is that the Singapore publication text requires publication of 'an explanation of the objective of, and rationale for, such measures'[94] while the Vietnam FTA only requires similar publications for proposals to adopt or amend.[95] The parties must also take into account/consider those comments received from interested persons in deciding the proposal.[96] In establishing 'enquiries and contact points', the parties must establish and maintain appropriate mechanisms to address enquiries from interested persons regarding measures of general application.[97]

Another notable difference in the 'enquiries' articles emerges from the Singapore agreement, requiring the parties to establish or maintain an appropriate mechanism to effectively solve problems of interested persons arising under measures of general application, and the mechanism must be 'easily accessible, time-bound, result-oriented, and transparent'.[98] The equivalent Vietnamese text merely requires a similar mechanism to be established.[99] Administrative proceedings must inform and provide affected persons reasonable opportunity to present facts and arguments prior to a final administrative decision.[100] Lastly, both agreements have provisions committing the parties to

[93] Annex A. See also the European Union – Singapore Free Trade Agreement, https://eur-lex.europa.eu/legal-content/EN/TXT/PDF/?uri=CELEX:22019A1114(01)&from=EN#page=104 and the European Union – Vietnam Free Trade Agreement: https://trade.ec.europa.eu/doclib/docs/2018/september/tradoc_157374.pdf. Articles 13.3 and 14.3, respectively.

[94] Ibid. Article 13.3.

[95] Ibid. Article 14.3.

[96] Ibid.

[97] Ibid. Articles 13.4 and 14.4.

[98] Ibid. Article 14.4, sub-provision 7.

[99] Ibid. Article 13.4, sub-provision 4.

[100] Ibid. Articles 13.5 and 14.5.

cooperate in regulatory quality and good administrative behaviour through the exchange of information and best practices.[101] These two provisions are quite different, as the Vietnam text implies an open list of ways both parties may improve respective regulatory policies by using the word 'including' and also by specifically mentioning 'regulatory reform processes and regulatory impact assessments'.[102] The Singapore and Vietnam provisions appear to be broad and reminiscent of CETA's transparency provisions.

In the EU-South Korea FTA, the negotiators have agreed to similar provisions to the Singapore and Vietnam agreements that were provisionally applied since 2011, although formally ratified only at the end of 2015. The publication and contact point provisions are the same as the Singapore FTA, including the requirement for publication of explanations and rationales for already implemented measures of general application, as well as the mechanisms established for problem solving must be 'easily accessible, time-bound, result-oriented, and transparent'.[103] Provisions for administrative proceedings and review and appeal were also similar to those found in the Singapore and Vietnam texts.[104]

However, the regulatory quality and good administrative behaviour commitments in the South Korea FTA aligns more with the Vietnamese agreement rather than the Singapore agreement. The last provision is unique to the South Korea agreement and covers non-discrimination, requiring parties 'provide interested persons of the other party transparency standards no less favourable than those accorded to its own interested persons'.[105] This agreement contains an extra provision on anti-discrimination, a commitment unique to this text not found in any of the other EU-Asia FTAs. The anti-discrimination provision commits both parties to afford the other party transparency standards no less favourable than those accorded to its own interested persons. The South Korea transparency chapter adds another layer of complexity to understanding the negotiator's intent as some provisions mirror the Singapore and Vietnam texts while others impose greater commitments to non-discrimination.

Finally, the EU-Japan EPA mentions very little on interested persons, the public or public interest groups, a major indication of Japan's domestic perception of institutionalised transparency. A major and notable difference

101 Ibid. Articles 13.7 and 14.7.

102 Ibid.

103 Ibid. See also the European Union – South Korea Free Trade Agreement, https://english.motie.go.kr/en/if/ftanetwork/ftanetwork.jsp. Articles 12.3 and 12.4.

104 Ibid. Articles 12.5 and 12.6.

105 Ibid. Article 12.8.

from the previous agreements is that the article on publication does not commit the parties to consider comments from interested persons.[106] A provision unique to the Japanese text is article 17.7 on cooperation on the promotion of increased transparency.[107] However, this commitment is very limited, only requiring both parties to cooperate on ways to promote transparency where it is deemed appropriate, and only in international trade and investment.[108] These provisions require parties to publish measures of general application and when administering them, to provide affected persons a 'reasonable opportunity to present facts and arguments in support of their positions prior to any final administrative decision'.[109] The EU-Japan EPA commitments are the least integrative compared to the Singaporean, Vietnamese and South Korean FTAs. This trend is highly reflective of Japan's domestic perceptions of transparency, and it is no surprise that Japanese negotiators, by adopting these domestic perception, strategically bargain for text that blunts the broad and inclusive commitments desired by European negotiators.

### 9.4.3 *Transparency Variations As Negotiating Capital*

As we showed in our cross-comparison, each trade agreement maintains varying levels of transparency commitments that correlate to each party's politicisation of domestic transparency principles. These varying levels result in either an integrated or diffused approach to transparency commitments in trade agreements. This variation is further correlated to the institutionalised transparency and the geopolitical relevance of the negotiator as having a pre-existing strategic relationship with each trading partner. As a consequence of the EU's sizable domestic market, sharing similar transparency values will lead to more integrative provisions in FTAs. Figure 9.1 is a diagram indicating the four types of observed transparency approaches by the EU in the Asian FTAs.

EU negotiators in the Singapore and Vietnam FTAs utilised an adverse-integrative approach to transparency provisions by requiring stronger universal commitments. This approach ensured a standard level of transparency is attained, thus promoting the democratic legitimacy mandate of the EU's negotiations. The EU's transparency relationship with Singapore and Vietnam is comparatively not as tried-and-true as it is with Canada, yet this

[106] European Union – Japan Economic Partnership Agreement, http://trade.ec.europa.eu/doclib/docs/2018/august/tradoc_157228.pdf#page=469. Article 17.3.

[107] Ibid. Article 17.7.

[108] Many similar, broad provisions carry over from the previous FTAs into the South Korean FTA such as Articles 17.2, 17.4 sub-provision 3, and 17.5 sub-provision 2.

[109] Ibid. Article 17.5–2-a.

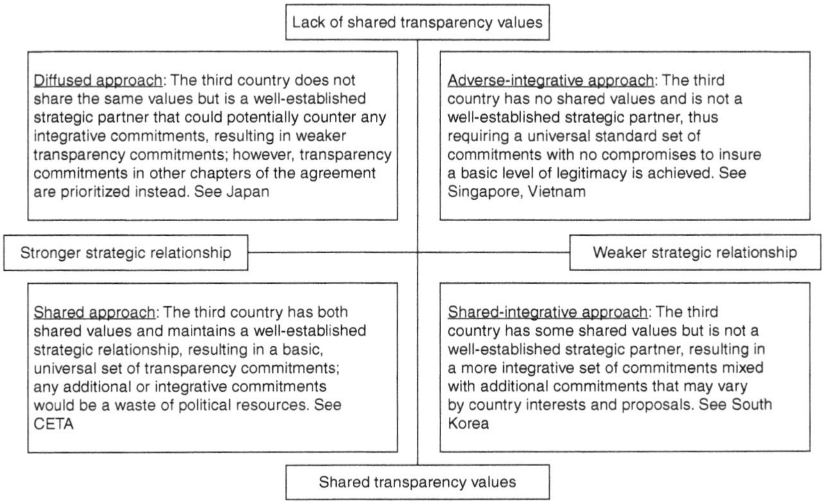


FIGURE 9.1 Negotiating transparency between values and strategies

relationship warrants the same integrative commitments to transparency principles given the shared transparency values and strategic relationship. When compared to CETA, it becomes clear that because the Singapore and Vietnam maintain low domestic transparency standards and possess markets that are smaller and less impactful on the EU, the transparency trade-offs were in favour of the EU's mandate, thus permitting its negotiators to impose stronger transparency chapters on the smaller Asian trade partners.

The EU-South Korea FTA is as equally integrative as Singapore and Vietnam, but it includes a higher commitment on non-discrimination vis à vis transparency standards. These characteristics represent a shared approach of transparency values yet the lack of a tried-and-true strategic relationship. The EU negotiating capital stems from the fact that EU and South Korean negotiators shared views on the importance of institutionalised transparency. However, South Korean negotiators have been willing to incorporate the higher standard provisions in non-discrimination in exchange for increased market access to European consumers.

The EU-Japan FTA is the least integrative of these agreements, representing a diffused approach to transparency provisions. Given the increased leverage derived from the pre-existing strategic relationship,[110] the size of the Japanese

110 The EU and Japan also signed a Strategic Partnership Agreement; see summary Andrei Lungu, 'Japan and Europe's Triple Partnership' *The Diplomat*, 14 February, 2019, https://th

market in international trade, and the nature of Japanese institutionalised transparency, it is no wonder the EU's transparency mandate was blunted. Instead, EU negotiators relied on incorporating basic transparency provisions in other chapters rather than looking only to bolstering the transparency chapter.[111] European negotiators could not risk pushing Japanese negotiators under an adverse-integrative approach given their hopes of including provisions on the multilateral investment court (MIC), a pillar of the Juncker Commission's trade and investment initiative.[112] The MIC was resolutely pursued and incorporated into the Singapore and Vietnam investment agreements, and re-opening of investment talks with South Korea are on the horizon.[113] Further, European negotiators may have acquiesced to a lower transparency standard in favour of obtaining important geographical indicators and access to Japan's protectionist agricultural sector.[114] Nevertheless, Japanese trade negotiators successfully incorporated, in their perspective, a less integrative yet more diffused set of transparency commitments.

## 9.5 CONCLUSION

This chapter mapped the varying approaches chosen by European trade negotiators in the four EU-Asian FTAs. These seemingly neutral transparency provisions are in reality the result of the bargaining powers that negotiators exercise as legal experts. Their negotiating capital is the wiggle room that they have in pushing for more integrative or diffused provisions correlating with domestic transparency preferences and the geopolitical realities that shape each negotiator's framework. While Singapore and Vietnam have strict rules and regulations limiting institutionalised transparency at home, EU

ediplomat.com/2019/02/japan-and-europes-triple-partnership/. The EU has also added Japan to its Data Protection Adequacy whitepaper bypassing additional safeguards on data flows.

111 Japan-EU EPA, sub-provisions on transparency commitments appear in Chapter 4 on Customs Matters and Trade Facilitation, Chapter 5 on Trade Remedies, Chapter 6 on Sanitary and Phytosanitary Measures, Chapter 7 on Technical Barriers to Trade, Chapter 8 on Trade in Services, Investment Liberalization, and Electronic Commerce, Chapter 11 on Competition Policy, Chapter 14 on Intellectual Property, and lastly Chapter 16 on Trade and Sustainable Development.

112 European Commission, State of the Union 2017, 'A Multilateral Investment Court', https://trade.ec.europa.eu/doclib/docs/2017/september/tradoc_156042.pdf.

113 Since no consensus was reached, the Japan FTA has no system on investor dispute settlement and instead resorts to the traditional state-to-state mechanism.

114 'Copa and Cogeca, CELCAA and FoodDrinkEurope Welcome Political Agreement on EU-Japan Trade Deal', *EUBusiness*, 6 July 2017, www.eubusiness.com/focus/17-07-063/. 'The EU Wine Industry Welcomes the Trade Agreement with Japan', *Comité Européen des Entreprises Vins* (CEEV), 2018.

negotiators prevailed on their smaller trading partners by including integrative transparency commitments in these FTAs. South Korea's views on institutionalised transparency align more closely to that of the EU and desired access to the EU market, resulted in mutually satisfactory integrative transparency commitments, including a non-discrimination provision. Japanese negotiators, the most influential strategic trading partner among the Asian countries,[115] resisted the EU's integrative approach thus reducing the negotiating capital of EU trade negotiators. Given Japan's influential role in the region, its longstanding protectionist policies, and prior agreements and relationship with the EU, this FTA included diffused transparency commitments. This analysis shows that transparency provisions are not merely neutral practices in trade negotiations, but are an important dimension of a trade negotiator's legal expertise. EU negotiators deploy their negotiating capital to achieve more favourable regulatory outcomes that are similar to European institutionalised transparency principles. In the EU-Asian FTAs, European negotiators, by using market leverage alongside their ability to find regulatory commonalities, integrated a different range of transparency commitments that shaped trade policies in a way that were acceptable to their Asian counterparts.

115 The below footnote provides European Commission web addresses for data on trade flows of Japan, South Korea, Singapore and Vietnam with the European Union in Euros, available at webgate.ec.europa.eu/isdb_results/factsheets/country/details_japan_en.pdf. webgate.ec.europa.eu/isdb_results/factsheets/country/details_south-korea_en.pdf. webgate.ec.europa.eu/isdb_results/factsheets/country/details_vietnam_en.pdf.

# PART III

# EXTERNAL LEGAL EXPERTISE

# 10

# The Rise of Transnational Legal Experts: Two Lessons from Research on Private Practitioners As Euro-Lawyers

Lola Avril

## 10.1 INTRODUCTION

'The Common Market has *nothing* to do with lawyers'.[1] This was the answer of an official from the European Commission after the signing of the Treaty of Rome to Marcel Raymond, president of the *Association Nationale des Avocats*. The lawyer expressed his concerns about the absence of legal professionals in the European Economic and Social Committee. More than sixty years later, European integration seems to have *everything* to do with lawyers. How did that happen?

From the 'integration through law'[2] approaches to the studies on the role of lawyers' networks[3], academic literature has highlighted the many ways in which law and lawyers have become such central actors in shaping and disseminating European law and policies. However, private practitioners still remain outside the scope of most of these studies. Discussing the impact of European integration on the legal profession, scholars argue that private practitioners in Brussels managed to get on good terms with the officials of the EU Commission, developing 'familiarity with the functionaries of the DG Competition'. They were 'progressively confirmed as the ideal intermediaries' for companies.[4] Studies have focused

1 July/August 1958, quoted in Serge-Pierre Laguette and Patrick Latham, *Lawyers in the European Community*, Commission européenne, The European Perspectives Series (1987) (emphasis added).

2 See the Introduction, Chapter 1 in this volume.

3 Antoine Vauchez, *Brokering Europe* (Cambridge: Cambridge University Press, 2015); Antonin Cohen and Antoine Vauchez (eds.), 'Symposium: Law, Lawyers, and Transnational Politics in the Production of Europe', *Law and Social Inquiry* (2007), 75–199; Harm Schepel and Rein Wesseling, 'The Legal Community: Judges, Lawyers, Officials and Clerks in the Writing of Europe' (1997) 3(2) *European Law Journal* 165–88; Julie Bailleux, *Penser l'Europe par le droit* (Paris: Dalloz, 2014); Rebekka Byberg, 'A Miscellaneous Network: The History of FIDE 1961–94' (2017) 57(2) *American Journal of Legal History* 142–65.

4 Yves Dezalay, 'Technological Warfare: The Battle to Control the Mergers and Acquisitions Market in Europe' in Yves Dezalay and David Sugarman (eds.), *Professional Competition and*

mainly on the theoretical level, and empirical field studies on the process through which lawyers have become such 'ideal intermediaries' for European public policies are mostly missing.

Scholars studying legal professions seem to think that the very existence of a body of European rules and its quantitative and qualitative development in the 1980s has produced, almost mechanically, a body of specialised professionals.[5] They argue that this has generated a higher demand for new legal services. The economic and political context of the 1980s and 1990s was favourable to the development of legal services on European policies. The Single Act in 1987 and the adoption of the Merger Regulation in 1989 prompted a wave of foreign law firms opening offices in Brussels at the end of the 1980s. The 1989 Merger Regulation introduced ex ante checks of concentrations between companies at the European level. This opened a new market for legal services that was 'attractive for American law firms'.[6] The changes in European economies also fostered an increased demand for legal services. In the 1980s–90s, two successive waves of company mergers, both on the national level and across borders, significantly changed the European economies.[7] Faced with this concentration of economic power, companies were in need of coordinated legal advice on national legislation and European public affairs in general. No longer subject to only one jurisdiction, they looked for law firms capable of assisting them with their transformations. Brussels, the capital of the European Economic Community, was therefore becoming 'the place to be for continental economic operators'.[8] As a result, the supply of legal services expanded rapidly in Brussels: at the beginning of 1988, eleven Anglo-Saxon law firms had offices in Brussels, expanding to more than a hundred firms by 1993.[9]

*Professional Power: Lawyers, Accountants and the Social Construction of Markets* (London and New York: Routledge, 1995), p. 65.

5 See for example Karen Alter, *Establishing the Supremacy of European Law. The Making of an International Rule of Law in Europe* (New York: Oxford University Press, 2009), Anne-Marie Slaughter, Alec Stone Sweet and J. H. H. Weiler, *The Europe Court and National Courts – Doctrine and Jurisprudence. Legal Change in Its Social Context* (Oxford: Hart Publishing, 1998) ('lawyers specialising in EC law got more business through the growth and expansion of EC law'); Yves Dezalay, 'Global Restructuring and the Law: Studies of the Internationalization of Legal Fields and the Creation of Transnational Arenas' (1994) 44(2) *Case Western Reserve Law Review* 407.

6 David Trubek and Yves Dezalay, 'Global Restructuring and the Law: Studies of the Internationalization of Legal Fields and the Creation of Transnational Arenas' (1994) 44(2) *Case Western Reserve Law Review* 407.

7 Sylvain Laurens, *Les Courtiers du capitalisme. Milieux d'affaires et bureaucrates à Bruxelles* (Marseille: Agone, 2015).

8 Ibid.

9 Robert Budden, 'Making a Brussels Office Pay' (1993) 12 *International Financial Law Review* 8–11.

However, this development alone cannot explain why lawyers, and not other consultants, became such powerful intermediaries between companies and European institutions, and why they took an interest in offering services exceeding their traditional legal activities. Drawing on my doctoral research,[10] this chapter aims to give some insights into how a group of transnational experts, Euro-lawyers,[11] was formed and how they consolidated their position. I implement a mixed methodology. My fieldwork consisted of a combination of archival work, interviews, analysis of professional journals and the building of a database.

To move away from the narrative of an almost mechanical response by lawyers and law firms to external incentives described above, I draw here on the political sociology of transnational professions. This literature builds on Pierre Bourdieu's work on the legal field,[12] and to other scholars drawing upon Bourdieusian concepts and methodology to understand legal professions and the European integration process.[13] Understanding social areas as fields enables an analysis of their structure, values on which fields build, as well as formal and informal rules that are used to organise them. Yet, the notion of fields also allows to go beyond the discourse of homogeneity and unity of professions. The term of 'lawyer' covers various activities, backgrounds and specialities in each Member State. This heterogeneity 'often generate[s] principles of structural opposition'[14] and 'underlie[s] power relations that structure fields and the internal conflicts that are at the origin of their transformations'.[15] Therefore, I paid particular attention to the internal conflicts within each national legal profession, especially between the 'traditional bar' and the rising business bar.

Euro-lawyers are part of a transnational field, partly independent of national legal fields and yet rooted in national politics of the legal profession. The historical formation of this community of lawyers involved in EU law and policy-making has

10 Lola Avril, *Le costume sous la robe. Les avocats en professionnels multi-cartes de l'Etat régulateur européen: Genèse, consolidation, contestations* (1957–2019) (2019) PhD dissertation, Université Paris-I Panthéon Sorbonne, Paris.

11 Antoine Vauchez, *Brokering Europe* (Cambridge: Cambridge University Press, 2015).

12 Pierre Bourdieu, 'The Force of Law: Toward a Sociology of the Juridical Field' (1987) 38(5) *Hastings Law Journal* 805–13.

13 Yves Dezalay and Mikael Rask Madsen, 'The Force of Law and Lawyers: Pierre Bourdieu and the Reflexive Sociology of Law' (2012) 8 *Annual Review of Law and Social Science* 433–52; Antone Vauchez, 'The Force of a Weak Field: Law and Lawyers in the Government of the European Union (For a Renewed Research Agenda)' (2008) 2(2) *International Political Sociology* 128–44; Niilo Kauppi, 'Bourdieu's Political Sociology and the Politics of European Integration' (2003) 32(5–6) *Theory and Society* 775–89; Didier Georgakakis and Jay Rowell, *The Field of Eurocracy: Mapping the EU Staff and Professionals* (Basingstoke: Palgrave, 2013).

14 Gisele Sapiro, 'Field Theory from a Transnational Perspective', in Thomas Medvetz and Jeffrey Sallaz (eds.), *Oxford Handbook of Pierre Bourdieu* (Oxford: Oxford University Press, 2018).

15 Ibid.

been studied from an institutional point of view, for instance the Legal Service of the European Commission[16] or the legal academia.[17] Vauchez has also shown how lawyers have played many roles in the European integration process, acting alternately as 'jurisconsults-diplomats, corporate lawyers, EU institutions' legal advisers, "politicians of the law", institution-builders, academics, etc'.[18] While my research is based on this body of work, I will focus here on private practitioners, trying to better understand how business lawyers have been able to take on the role of European transnational legal experts.

I analyse how the legal profession has used European law to offer new services and in doing so has reached out to new jurisdictions. The notion of jurisdiction, as used in this chapter, was developed by Andrew Abbott.[19] For Abbott, each profession is a system, whose activities are delimited by boundaries, which form a jurisdiction. The notion of jurisdiction makes it possible to draw a (sometimes blurred, sometimes disputed) boundary between those who are members of the profession and those who are not. Secondly, the concept of jurisdiction captures how the profession is in perpetual evolution, subject to struggle and in competition with other professions. The interest of lawyers in the European affairs legal services' market is therefore seen here as an extension of the jurisdiction of the legal profession. The evolutionary dimension of the concept makes it possible to focus on those professionals outside of the legal field – such as European affairs consultants and lobbyists – who have been able to make similar claims on new jurisdictions.[20]

Finally, this chapter sheds further light on the relationship between the legal profession and the state. The works of historian Maria Malatesta,[21] sociologist Lucien Karpik,[22] but also of Terry Halliday[23] and Richard

[16] Julie Bailleux, 'L'Europe et ses légistes. Le Service juridique des Exécutifs européens et la promotion d'un droit communautaire autonome (1957–1964)' (2013) 3(41) *Politique européenne* 84–113.

[17] Harm Schepel and Rein Wesseling, 'The Legal Community: Judges, Lawyers, Officials and Clerks in the Writing of Europe' (1997) 3(2) *European Law Journal* 165–88.

[18] Antoine Vauchez, *Brokering Europe* (Cambridge: Cambridge University Press, 2015).

[19] Andrew Abbott, *The System of Profession: An Essay on the Division of Expert Labor* (Chicago: University of Chicago Press, 1998).

[20] For an in-depth empirical study of a similar process of professional 'turf-wars', see Yves Dezalay and Bryant Garth, *The Internationalization of Palace Wars: Lawyers, Economists, and the Contest to Transform Latin American States* (Chicago: University of Chicago Press, 2002).

[21] Maria Malatesta, *Professionisti e gentiluomini Storia delle professioni nell'Europa contemporanea* (Turin: Biblioteca, 2006).

[22] Lucien Karpik, *Les avocats. Entre l'État, le public et le marché, XIIIe-XXe* (Paris: Gallimard, 1995).

[23] Terrence Halliday and Lucien Karpik, *Lawyers and the Rise of Western Political Liberalism: Europe and North America from the Eighteenth to Twentieth Centuries* (Oxford: Oxford University Press, 1997).

Abel,[24] have shown the extent to which the emergence of the modern state as a 'rule of law' has been linked to the institutionalisation of national bars. Just as the national legal professions were built as part of the modern state, I show how a group of Euro-lawyers emerged and 'co-constituted' itself together with the European institutions. To provide empirical insights into this process, this chapter will focus on competition policies as a representative sector of market re-regulation.[25] Competition policies provided the context in which the first Euro-lawyers established themselves in the European legal field.[26]

Throughout this chapter and over the course of six decades of European integration, we follow the emergence and development of this group of European legal experts. My findings are twofold: first, transnational legal experts did not emerge out of a vacuum. To understand why they took an interest in European integration, we must understand their position in their national professional environments. Second, they actively participated in the building of the demand for their services. Some members of the legal profession and especially those of business bars, which developed in Member States and internationally, actively engaged in the drafting and implementation of European public policies. Lawyers created a new role in the market of EU legal services for themselves, extending their jurisdiction[27] to new activities, especially as mediators between companies and the European institutions. Dissociating themselves from the traditional lawyer figure pleading in courts, they now represent their clients' interests at every stage of the European public policymaking process.

## 10.2 LESSON 1: TRANSNATIONAL LEGAL EXPERTS DO NOT COME OUT OF A VACUUM

To understand how a group of transnational legal experts appeared at the European level, we must first study the Euro-lawyers in their *national* professional field. The European integration process did not erase national legal fields.[28]

[24] Richard Abel and Philip S. C. Lewis (eds.), *Lawyers and Society* (Berkeley: University of California Press, 1989); Mark Osiel, 'Lawyers As Monopolists, Aristocrats, and Entrepreneurs' (1990) 8(103) *Harvard Law Review* 2009–66.

[25] Giandomenico Majone, *Regulating Europe* (New York: Routledge, 1996); Jacint Jordana and David Levi-Faur (eds.), *The Politics of Regulation. Institutions and Regulatory Reforms for The Age of Governance* (Cheltenham: Edward Elgar, 2005).

[26] Antonin Cohen, 'Bourdieu Hits Brussels: The Genesis and Structure of the European Field of Power' (2011) 5(3) *International Political Sociology* 335–9.

[27] Andrew Abbot, *The System of Profession* (Chicago: University of Chicago Press, 1988).

[28] Gisele Sapiro, 'Field Theory from a Transnational Perspective', in Thomas Medvetz and Jeffrey Sallaz (eds.), *Oxford Handbook of Pierre Bourdieu* (Oxford: Oxford University Press, 2018).

Therefore, it is only by understanding the position of the first Euro-lawyers within their national bar associations, their social predispositions towards the international scene and the evolving power struggles within national bars that we can grasp the reasons for their engagement with European affairs.

### 10.2.1 *Transnational Experts in Their National Professional Field*

Where do Euro-lawyers come from? A small group of lawyers became interested and involved in Community law, especially competition law, as early as the end of the 1950s and early 1960s. They were from Belgium, France and Germany. Their training, practices and professional ethics varied in many ways: the titles of *Rechtsanwalt*, lawyer, or *avocat* signal different national trainings methods and professional boundaries that differed from one European country to another.

In this chapter I have reconstructed the trajectories of this first group of Euro-lawyers and then attempted to understand these paths in light of the transformations of their national professional field. In the 1960s–70s, the first specialists in European competition law, mostly in Germany, France or Belgium, were considered 'outsiders' within their bar for two reasons. First, the legal profession in the 1960s–70s was still very much oriented toward litigation activities. Second, neither European law nor competition policies were perceived as high-ranking practices amongst the legal profession in France or Belgium.

French competition policies were largely overshadowed by the existence of price control, 'the backbone of French competition law'.[29] The latter was based on a powerful administration inside the Ministry of Economy and Finance (*the Direction des prix*) and relied on a wide range of administrative tools (blocking, fixing, taxation or scales) that had been in place since the 1930s.[30] The shift from a fixed price policy to competition policy took place only during the 1970s, with a gradual return to price freedom, the refocusing of the *Direction des prix* to consumer interests,[31] and the creation of a Competition Commission in 1977. Given these modest beginnings of French competition policy, it is hardly surprising that European law was not of interest to the leading members of the bar.

29 Dominique Brault, *L'État et l'esprit de la concurrence en France* (Paris: Economica, 1987).

30 Michel-Pierre Chélini, *Inflation, État et opinion en France de 1944 à 1952* (Vincennes: Institut de la gestion publique et du développement économique' 1988).

31 Sebastian Billows, 'À qui profite la "concurrence"? Modèles de concurrence et régulation de la grande distribution française (1949–1986)' (2016) 5(4) *Gouvernement et action publique* 69–91.

In France, the first generation of lawyers discovered European law 'by chance', following their clients' legal cases. This was the case of Jacques Lassier and Robert Collin, two lawyers at the Paris bar, who headed small generalist law firms. Both were involved, albeit on opposite sides, in the famous *Grundig/Consten* case[32] leading to the annulment of a Commission decision on Article 85 TEC.[33] In the 1970s, the two lawyers became the most important French specialists in European competition policies. However, Lassier and Collin could not be considered influential personalities in the French legal profession: they invested little in representing their profession and did not occupy significant positions within the Bar. Moreover, in France, profession at that time was dominated by litigation lawyers,[34] even though an increasing number of young lawyers within the Paris bar tried to create new opportunities by specialising in commercial clientele's needs and legal advice.[35] Lassier, who had started his career as a corporate lawyer, and Collin, who had gradually specialised in intellectual property matters, were not involved in what were considered at the time to be the highest-profile areas of law.

In Germany, the competition law terminology had been used since the 1930s: the ordoliberal school made the state (and its laws) the protector of a competitive economy.[36] Moreover, after the Second World War, the Allied powers regarded the high level of economic concentration as one of the causes of German militarism.[37] Anti-trust legislation was therefore under constant negotiation.[38] In 1957, the Bundeskartellamt (BKA), an independent administrative authority, was established. The first German lawyers in European law were trained in the practice of decartelisation policies. Alfred Gleiss, who

[32] Judgment of the Court of 13 July 1966, *Établissements Consten S.à.R.L. and Grundig-Verkaufs-GmbH* v. *Commission of the European Economic Community*, Joined cases 56 and 58–64.

[33] Judgment of the Court of 13 July 1966 in Joined cases 56 and 58–64, *Établissements Consten S. à.R.L. and Grundig-Verkaufs-GmbH* v. *Commission of the European Economic Community*.

[34] Lucien Karpik, 'Les Avocats Entre Le Renouveau et Le Déclin' (2003) 35(1) *Hermès, La Revue* 203–11.

[35] Anne Boigeol and Yves Dezalay, 'De l'agent d'affaires au barreau : les conseils juridiques et la construction d'un espace professionnel' (1997) 1(27) *Genèses* 49–68.

[36] Patricia Commun (ed.), *L'ordo liberalisme allemand. Aux sources de l'économie sociale de marché* (2003), CIRAC/CICC.

[37] David Gerber, *Global Competition. Law, Markets and Globalization* (Oxford: Oxford University Press, 2010).

[38] Sigrid Quack and Marie-Laure Djelic, 'Adaptation, Recombination and Reinforcement: The Story of Antitrust and Competition Law in Germany and Europe' in Wolfgang Streeck and Kathleen Thelen (eds.), *Beyond Continuity Institutional Change in Advanced Political Economies* (Oxford: Oxford University Press, 2005).

opened a firm specialising in antitrust law in 1949 in Stuttgart, recruited Arved Deringer in the early 1950s. He would become the most renowned German specialist in competition law, as well as a leading figure in the European Parliament.[39] Here again, German Euro-lawyers were not considered leading figures within the German legal profession. Their role as advisors to business circles distanced them from the mainstream German profession that was characterised by 'quasi-judicial attitudes' and was 'embedded in the wider categories of the legal profession as a whole and of university-educated people'.[40]

Finally, like in France, Belgian competition policies were oriented towards price control until the adoption of a law on the protection of competition in 1991. However, the proximity with the European institutions, particularly DG Competition which was in charge of the application of the cartel regulation, prompted some practitioners to offer services on the regulatory activities of the European administration. Lawyers such as Ivo Van Bael, Michel Waelbroeck and Jean-François Bellis were working for Belgian law firms but also for US law firms (Baker & McKenzie opened an office in 1957, Cleary Gottlieb in 1960). The profiles of the lawyers who were employed by the latter did not fit the traditional legal career trajectory. For example, at Baker & McKenzie, lawyers recruited in the 1960s to support the firm's international expansion were described as the 'boys of the 60s', young lawyers in their early thirties with little experience in the work of local professional bodies. They were chosen precisely because they had 'no connection with the establishment that controls the legal profession' and had 'a fighting spirit' because American firms had to 'fight in every country against the rules of the bar'.[41]

The specialisation in corporate law or the occupation of a position as a legal adviser within a company before joining other firms, places the first Euro-lawyers at the periphery of their national legal career trajectories. They did not share the characteristics of traditional legal elites because they were more market-oriented, their clientele was mainly companies, and their services were more oriented towards legal advice than litigation in court.

Overall, the primary motivation of a handful of lawyers for engaging in European legal affairs seems to stem from their marginalised position within

39 Guillaume Sacriste, 'L'Europe est-elle un État comme les autres ? Retour sur la distinction public/privé au sein de la commission juridique du Parlement européen des années 1960' (2012) 1(85–6) *Cultures & Conflits* 35–60; Mélanie Vay, 'L'impossible doctrine européenne du service public. Aux origines du service d'intérêt économique général (1958–1968)' (2019) 69(1) *Revue française de science politique* 75–94.

40 Dietrich Rueschemeyer, *Lawyers and Their Society* (Cambridge: Harvard University Press, 1973).

41 John Bauman, *Pioneering a Global Vision. The Story of Baker & McKenzie* (Chicago: Harcourt Professional Education Group, 1999).

the national professional space. Thus, for these first Euro-lawyers developing European legal expertise was an opportunity to climb the professional ladder outside the national system.

### 10.2.2 *The Social Predispositions of Legal Experts to Go International*

If the first Euro-lawyers had a marginal position within their national bar, which pushed them to look for opportunities elsewhere, they also had common social predispositions towards the international scene.

Euro-lawyers are 'international' lawyers, accumulating resources to evolve in a cosmopolitan environment.[42] The first lawyers in European law possessed this form of social resource described as international capital, 'inseparably cultural, linguistic, and social, largely inherited, reinforced by international school curricula and professional experience in several countries'.[43] This capital takes many forms. First, resources are inherited through the generations of family. Second, they are built up through academic and professional career trajectories. Several of the lawyers in this professional group acquired international – social or familial – cosmopolitan capital at an early stage.[44] This enables them to master not only foreign languages, but also the rules of an international institution such as the European Commission. In addition, they have common social properties (family background, educational pedigree, social circles, leisure activities) with the Commission officials, with whom they are in regular contact in the application of European competition law.

Of the abovementioned lawyers, Michel Waelbroeck was born in Geneva, then moved to Montreal. His father was a civil servant at the International Labour Office, whose headquarters were transferred there in 1940. He returned to Belgium after the war, obtaining his doctorate in law from the Université Libre de Bruxelles in 1956. The ancestors of the German lawyer Arved Deringer immigrated to the Ukrainian territories of the Russian Empire at the beginning of the nineteenth century. Following the 1917 revolution, his family returned to settle in Berlin. He studied theology and law in Tübingen, Kiel, Berlin and

42 Carole Silver, 'Internationalizing U.S. Legal Education: A Report on the Education of Transnational Lawyers' (2006) *Cardozo Journal of International and Comparative Law* 143–77; David Trubek and Yves Dezalay, 'Global Restructuring and the Law: Studies of the Internationalization of Legal Fields and the Creation of Transnational Arenas' (1994) 2(44) *Case Western Reserve Law Review* 407–98.

43 Anne-Catherine Wagner, 'Les classes dominantes à l'épreuve de la mondialisation' (2011) 190 (5) *Actes de la recherche en sciences sociales* 4–9.

44 Yves Dezalay, 'Les courtiers de l'international. Héritiers cosmopolites, mercenaires de l'impérialisme et missionnaires de l'universel' (2004) 151–2(1) *Actes de la recherche en sciences sociales* 4–35.

Geneva. As for the French lawyer Jacques Lassier, he entered an English grammar school at the age of fourteen, and later studied law in London.

The paths of the 'boys of 60s' in the Brussels office of Baker & McKenzie were also shaped by the displacements caused by the war. The Brussels office was opened by Thomas Coleman, a Polish immigrant to the United States, who studied at Georgetown. He served in the US Army during the Second World War, where he met his future Belgian wife. After the war, he worked for the US government under the Marshall Plan in Belgium and graduated from the University of Brussels in 1962 before opening his office there. He was joined by Klaus Newes, an Austrian Jew who had fled Europe for the United States, and then Otto Grolig, born in the German-speaking region of Czechoslovakia and whose father had been taken prisoner by the Americans.

This early international socialisation is complemented by a professional career marked by transatlantic travel. Some discovered European law and competition law during their studies at American universities, while others worked for East Coast law firms. They represented a new generation of business lawyers emerging in Europe after the Second World War,[45] at a time when student and professional mobility was still in its infancy. Michel Waelbroeck was awarded a Fulbright scholarship to attend an LLM in Comparative Law at New York University. In particular, Michigan Law School emerged as the place to go for the essential training in European law: Ivo Van Bael graduated from Michigan in 1963, as did Jean-François Bellis, ten years later. In the German group, Otfried Lieberknecht studied law at Harvard (1953) and Cornelis Canenbley went to Georgetown in the early 1970s. Most of them also worked for the first American law firms that arrived in Brussels: Ivo Van Bael for White & Case (from 1963 to 1967 in New York, then from 1967 to 1969 in Brussels), Michel Waelbroeck for Dewey Ballantine (1967–72). These transatlantic links could also be found in Germany: at Bruckhaus, Hanns Winkhaus worked for American law firms in Washington and New York.

The transatlantic interaction/connections that marked the path of the first Euro-lawyers in the 1960s and 1970s had a twofold consequence: first, a knowledge of antitrust law and, second, familiarity with American law firms' legal practices. These lawyers' antitrust training was an asset that enabled them to become influential in shaping European policies. Similar antitrust trainings were taught only in few universities.

45 Glenn Morgan and Sigrid Quack, 'Institutional Legacies and Firm Dynamics: The Growth and Internationalization of UK and German Law Firms' (2005) 12 *Organization Studies* 1765–85.

### 10.2.3 *The Influence of Professional National Policies on the Development of Transnational Legal Expertise*

How did we move from a group of twenty lawyers interested in Europe to several hundred lawyers in Brussels alone today? A lot of foreign law firms opened their offices in Brussels in the end of the 1980s. At the beginning of 1988, there were only five UK law firm offices in the European capital and six from the United States. By 1989–90, on average one new foreign law firm per month set up branches in Brussels; between 1989 and 1993, more than a hundred foreign law firms were active in what was then known as the 'European capital'. By the end of the 1990s, Brussels had become the first city across the channel where British law firms opened offices.[46]

Here again, we have to take into account the changes in the national bar associations' policies, which facilitated the international expansion of law firms. European bars experienced a change in the balance of power between the reformist fringe (business law, oriented towards legal advice) and the more traditional side focusing on litigation. In the 1960s–70s, relations between the Brussels Bar and foreign law firms were tense. yet, the former adopted a much more welcoming attitude from the mid-1980s onwards. In 1984, the Brussels Bar allowed Belgian lawyers to associate with foreign lawyers on a specific list (B list) on the condition that they had been established in Belgium for three years, agreed to abide by the ethics and disciplinary rules of the host Bar and abstained from practising Belgian law.[47] In the first year, only Cleary Gottlieb's and Baker & McKenzie's Brussels-based lawyers qualified for inclusion on the B list, which enabled them to recruit Belgian lawyers. By the end of 1992, 120 lawyers were on this list. Other American firms chose to develop informal associations with Belgian firms, such as Gibson Dunn with van Bael & Bellis and Akin Gump with De Smedt Dassesse. Some law firms did not register. They could therefore advise their clients on Belgian law but could not plead before courts or enter into associations with Belgian lawyers.

The attitudes of other European bars towards the international expansion of their law firms were also changing. For example, the German Bar Association authorised its member firms to open an office abroad in 1987.[48] This generated a wave of new offices in Brussels: in 1988, there were two openings (Bruckaus

46 James V. Beaverstock, P. J. Taylor and R. G. Smith, 'The Long Arm of the Law: London's Law Firms in a Globalising World Economy' (1999) 10(31) *Environment and Planning* 1857–76.

47 Richard L. Abel, 'Transnational Law Practice' (1994) 44(2) *Case Western Law Review* 737–870.

48 Ulrike Schultz, 'Germany in Regulated Deregulation: The Case of the German Legal Profession' in William Felstiner (ed.), *Reorganisation and Resistance: Legal Professions Confront a Changing World* (Portland: Hart Publishing, 2005), pp. 93–133.

Westrick Stegemann and Winkhaus & Lieberknecht); three in 1989 (Deringer Tessin Herrmann & Sedemund, Boden Oppenhoff Rasor Schneider & Schiedermair and Mueller Weitzel Weisner), then one in 1990 (Noorr, Stiefenhofer & Lutz) and another the following year (Droste Killius & Tiebel).

The history of the expansion of the Deringer law firm links these two developments taking place in the Brussels and the German bars. Arved Deringer's law firm is one of the first to specialise in European law, in particular competition law. Recruited in 1951 by Alfred Gleiss, he founded his own law firm in 1962. Parallel to his career as a lawyer, he pursued a political career, becoming a member of the Bundestag in 1957 and a member of the European Parliamentary Assembly (1958–70). In the 1980s, his firm expanded considerably and broadened its activities following the wave of privatisation of German companies. In 1990, the firm had nine partners (in a country where in 8100 registered law firms only 90 had more than 10 partners).[49] After German law firms were authorised to expand abroad, Deringer opened an office in Brussels in 1989.

As this example also shows, the changing policies of European bars towards the expansion abroad and the welcoming of foreign law firms contributed to the development of a transnational legal field of expertise on European policies. Whereas the group of Euro-lawyers was made of individuals with few connections with the legal establishments, offering European expertise became part of the strategy of law firms expanding in Europe by the 1990s.

Euro-lawyers do not emerge out of a vacuum. They come from legal professions historically built in a national context. To understand their move towards Europe, and more broadly to grasp the interests of legal experts to go transnational, we must look closer at their social background and their position within their national fields. These lawyers took an interest in European policies because of their marginalisation in their national contexts and unique backgrounds which allowed them to thrive in an international environment.

## 10.3 LESSON 2: TRANSNATIONAL LEGAL EXPERTS CREATED THE NEED FOR THEIR EXPERTISE

European legal expertise is not the mechanical product of the deepening of European integration. On the contrary, if we look at the mobilisations of Euro-lawyers, their claims and the evolution of their practice, we can see that they have contributed to creating a demand for their new services as intermediaries in the European policy-making process.

[49] Charles H. Beck, *A History of Thinking Ahead. 175 Years of Bruckhaus Deringer in Germany* (Freshfields Bruckhaus Deringer LLP, 2015).

### 10.3.1 *Imposing Lawyers' Presence in the Interactions between EU Institutions and Companies*

Regulation 17/62 on agreements and concerted practices in the area of competition law was the first European legislation organising the implementation of competition principles set out in the Treaty establishing the European Economic Community (EEC).[50] In this regulation, the lack of references to lawyers is striking: there is no mention of them in the text. This can be explained to some extent by the lack of representation of the legal profession within the EC at the time of the regulation's drafting. In addition, European Commission officials arguably aimed to avoid intermediaries in their working processes.[51] To this end, the procedure set up by Regulation 99/63[52] favoured written exchanges between the Commission's DG Competition and companies. There were no provisions on lawyers or informal settlements of competition cases. However, from the beginning of the 1970s, a group of company representatives, lawyers and Members of the European Parliament lobbied/pressured the Commission to reform the procedure.

Legal professionals, supported by business interests, expressed concerns about the legal certainty and predictability of the outcome of competition cases. Legal professionals hence advocated for the codification and formalisation of the competition procedure, and for a judicialisation of competition procedures. Throughout the 1970s, some of the most important organisations representing lawyers' interests (International Bar Association (IBA); The Council of Bars and Law Societies of Europe (CCBE)), supported by business actors (Conference of British Industries (CBI), UNICE/Business Europe), attempted to reform the competition case procedure before the Commission. They supported a shift from a mostly written procedure to an oral one, with rules derived from the proceedings of trials. Criticising the legitimacy of the administrative aspects of the procedure, they believed that decisions were under the existing circumstances political rather than legal.

At the IBA, it was the Antitrust Committee, set up in 1970, which took up issues of competition procedure. This committee was composed of business

[50] EEC Council: Regulation No 17: First Regulation implementing Articles 85 and 86 of the Treaty.

[51] This paragraphs and the followings are based on my study of the Commission's archives, see Avril, *Le costume sous la robe*. See in particular these following files: BAC 104/1993 287; BAC 104/1993 288; BAC 104/1993 288 and BAC 73/1995 29. For an example of a note written by an official from DG Competition about the role of lawyers in the procedure, see BAC 104/1993 378, DG Competition, 'Note péparant l'intervention devant la House of Lords', June 1981.

[52] Regulation 99/63 of 25 July 1963 on the hearings provided for in article 19 (1) and (2) of Council regulation 17, Official Journal 127, 20 August 1963: 2268–70.

lawyers and was headed by leading figures from Europe's competition bar, such as Arved Deringer, Jochim Sedemund and Ivo Van Bael. Their demands were all in favour of a 'more formal and judicial procedure'. They met with DG Competition three times between 1979 and 1981. For its part, the CCBE, which consists of representatives of Member States' bars and law societies, published a proposal to 'improve the Commission's procedure in competition investigations' and a report on the rights of defence in Community sanction proceedings. The Law Society and the Inns of Bar, representing British solicitors and barristers, also joined the debate and set up a Joint Working Party (JWP) on the issue in the early 1970s. The JWP also included two British CCBE members, David Vaughan and Graham Child. It published a memorandum on the European Commission's investigation procedures as well as commentaries on the European annual reports on competition policy.[53]

One of the claims made by the above-mentioned groups was respect for the principle of legal professional privilege. This meant that the correspondence between lawyers and their clients could not be used by DG Competition in their investigations. Underlying these claims was the groups' wish to advance the judicialisation of Commission procedures, because – so they reasoned – it would give them an opportunity to redefine and control the interactions between the private sector and the European politico-administrative actors. Competition lawyers used the cases they had to defend in the ECJ to promote a judicialisation of competition law procedures. They demanded a more prominent role for hearings, which would increase lawyers' participation in those proceedings. At the same time, such hearings were expected to secure a new market of 'European law' in the context of competition with accountants, lobbyists and other counselling professions. The first Euro-lawyers engaged in a long-running legal battle that led the CJEU to rule 26 times on procedural law aspects of competition issues between 1959 and 1984. The development of case law on fundamental rights provided a powerful argument for the annulment of decisions taken by the European Commission. In all major competition law cases the applicants raised a violation of the rights of the defence. The grounds raised are very diverse (the company's right of reply, right to be heard, publication of the dossier), but all refer to the lack of guarantees within the DG Competition's decision-making procedures.

53 Joint Working Party, 'Memorandum of comments on the European Commission's Eleventh Report on Competition policy', Archives of the European Commission, DG Competition, BAC 104/1993 288, August 1982.

The results of this mobilisation gave the profession a privileged position in the mediation of interactions between businesses and the European administration. One of the great successes in this area for lawyers is the *AM&S* ruling,[54] which enshrines the respect of legal privilege in competition proceedings, including during the administrative phase. Supported by the European Parliament and the business community, lawyers also obtained a revision of the competition procedure and the creation of a hearing officer position, confirming the formalisation of hearings of DG Competition.

With regard to European competition policies, it can be seen that lawyers have been intervening in proceedings by resorting to two types of actions: during legal proceedings, in the name of their clients' interests; and collectively on behalf of the profession, defending corporatist interests through their representative organisations. Euro-lawyers therefore emerged as active players in European integration processes. Far from having only benefited from the extension and autonomisation of European law, they joined forces to become the essential intermediaries between companies and the European institutions. Much of this mobilisation has been brought about through a range of actions relating to the rights of the defence, and in a bid to bring about the judicialisation of procedures.

### 10.3.2 *Extension of the Jurisdiction As a Consequence of the Hybridisation of the European Legal Field of Expertise*

In the early 1980s, Euro-lawyers were able to secure a prominent place in the implementation process of European competition policies. However, they were not yet cross-sectoral legal experts on European policies. Only during the 1990s Euro-lawyers extended their professional expertise to a wider range of European policies, offering services that reached far beyond assisting companies with the application procedures of competition policies.

The above-mentioned developments within legal services in Brussels are relevant for this expansion. As we have seen above, the Brussels Bar opened its doors to foreign law firms in the 1980s. Combined with the adoption of the Single Act in 1986, the Merger Regulation in 1989, the prospect of the Common Market in 1992 and the development of a transnational legal field, Brussels experienced an unprecedented wave of foreign law firms setting up offices at the turn of the 1980s and 1990s. In many respects, in Brussels at that

54 Judgment of the Court of 18 May 1982. *AM & S Europe Limited* v. *Commission of the European Communities*, Case 155/79.

time the demand for and role of a European public affairs lawyer was created. This figure was born of the unprecedented meeting between American law firms, which exported the lobbying techniques perfected in Washington, and a transnational European legal field. The hybridisation of these models resulted in the rise of a new European legal expert.

Kelemen argues that 'American law firms active in Europe have played an important role as transmission belts, accelerating the spread of American models of legal practice'.[55] The American legal style also serves as a repellent, affirming a 'European-style lobbying'.[56] The arrival of Washington law firms, which had been specialising for decades in lobbying political institutions in the US, prompted the development of lobbying and intermediation activities in the legal profession based in Brussels. Washington law firms started to show an interest in Brussels towards the end of the 1980s. In 1989, Akin Gump, one of the leading Washington law firms, signed a partnership with a Belgian law firm 'after realising that 1992 [would] demand radical restructuring in the international legal profession and that there [were] clear gains to be made by exploiting the Washington-Brussels nexus'.[57] In 1990, another Washington law firm, Wilmer Cutler & Pickering, settled in Brussels planning 'to capitalize on the similarities between legal practice in Washington and Brussels'.[58] The New York law firm Winthrop Stimson also sent a partner who had built up their lobbying practice in the Washington office 'to try the same formula in Brussels'.[59]

The arrival of American law firms contributed to normalising legal lobbying activities at a time when they were still marginal in European national bars. The American model of lobbying was not transposed as such to the Brussels' policy processes, but required adaptation to the new environment.[60] The European bar had already developed its own ethics and rules, and some American practices fitted poorly within the European context. Some attempts to transpose US techniques to Brussels led to failures and tensions within the

55 Daniel R. Kelemen, *Eurolegalism: The Transformation of Law and Regulation in the European Union* (Cambridge: Harvard University Press, 2011).

56 Samantha Bolton, 'Euro Lobbying on the Defensive' (1992) 11 *International Financial Law Review* 11–14.

57 'Brussels Breakthrough' (1989) 8(2) *International Financial Law Review* 2–3.

58 'Brussels Still Filling Up' (1989) 8(2) *International Financial Law Review* 3.

59 Robert Budden, 'Making a Brussels Office Pay' (1993) 12(8) *International Financial Law Review* 8–11.

60 As Cornelia Woll shows, lobbying styles, rather than being merely 'culture traits', are shaped by institutions constraints and linked with the structure of political systems as well as their legitimisation processes. See Cornelia Woll, 'The Brash and the Soft-Spoken: Lobbying Styles in a Transatlantic Comparison' (2012) 2(1) *Interest Groups & Advocacy* 193–214.

local legal community and sometimes with European officials: lobbying 'à l'européenne' was said to be more informal than its American counterpart and would rely more on tacit interpersonal relationships than formal 'business' meetings.

Thus, in addition to mainstreaming legal lobbying activities in Europe, the arrival of American law firms at the beginning of the 1990s reinforced the detachment of Euro-lawyers from the litigation-oriented practice of law, consolidating their role as experts of European policies.

### 10.3.3 *Extension of the Jurisdiction or De-Professionalisation? Euro-Lawyers As Public Affairs Professionals*

The diversification of Euro-lawyers' activities has led to an increasing division of tasks within law firms, separating legal argumentation from more political/media-related actions. New services, called 'European regulatory affairs' or 'public affairs', emerged within law firms at the end of the 1990s. These innovations reflect a transformation of law firms, analysed by Felstiner as a 'corporatisation', that is, a shift in the organisation of law firms towards a more corporate structure.[61]

In Brussels, the American law firm White & Case opened its public affairs department in 1994. The British law firms followed quickly: in 1997, it was the turn of Freshfields and two years later, Allen & Overy. These new departments offered a variety of services, ranging from legislative monitoring to the development of lobbying strategies. In the same way that the offered services were diversified, the staff portfolios became also more diverse. Non-lawyers within these departments were given positions as 'consultant', 'counsel' or 'policy advisor'. These titles cover two types of careers. On the one hand, there is a set of politico-administrative profiles like the 'EU Public Policy and Government' team at Covington & Burling. In 2020, the team was led by a lawyer, but the rest was composed solely of senior advisors and policy advisors with a background in the politico-administrative field in the Member States or within the European institutions. The members of the team have thus held positions as Director General or Deputy Director General at the European Commission, Prime Minister, Permanent Representative to the European Union or Member of the European Parliament.[62] These departments also include profiles from the private

[61] William Felstiner, *Reorganisation and Resistance: Legal Profession Confront a Changing World* (Portland: Hart Publishing, 2005).

[62] See www.cov.com/en/offices/brussels.

sector coming from consultancy firms or interest groups. For example, Freshfields recruited Christiaan Smith,[63] who has spent more than ten years in the private sector, notably in the institutional relations department of InsuranceEurope.

These consultancy firms moved to Brussels at the same time as law firms started to organise their lobbying activities, heavily recruiting from the latter. Looking again at the case of European competition policies, large consultancy firms created competition departments from the 2000s onwards. One of the best-known cases of transitioning from a law to a consultancy firm is Elisabeth Crossick. A former competition lawyer and founder of the public affairs department of Freshfields (1997–2007), she became director of institutional relations in an American company before being recruited by APCO (a firm specialising in public affairs) and then Reed Elsevier (which became the RELX group in 2015). Other lawyers left their law firm to open their own consulting firms, such as Sarah Biontino in 2005, a former competition lawyer who created the public affairs department at Allen & Overy.

These movements, combined with the extension (to the point of breaking up?) of the expertise of Euro-lawyers, ultimately challenge the specific nature of the legal profession within European public affairs. As early as the 1970s, the first Euro-lawyers questioned the profession's relationship with the market and contributed to the development of legal activities outside the courts. Today, the considerable development of European legal services and the emergence of competitors is questioning the place of Euro-lawyers in a wider community of transnational legal experts.[64] This evolution can generate certain tensions that are visible in attempts to regulate lobbying activities. On the one hand, the extension of lawyers' expertise is leading to an increasing visibility of lobbying activities within law firms. On the other hand, legal professionals refuse to be fully assimilated to other consultants and claim their special status within the public affairs service market. Further, they benefit from regulatory exemptions on the grounds of professional secrecy within the European Transparency Register for lobbyists.[65]

63 See www.freshfields.com/en-gb/what-we-do/services/regulatory/regulatory-and-public-affairs.

64 Sebastian M. Büttner, Lucia Leopold, Steffen Mau and Matthias Posvic, 'Professionalization in EU Policy-Making? The Topology of the Transnational Field of EU Affairs' (2015) 4(17) *European Societies* 569–92; Christian Lahusen, 'Law and Lawyers in Brussels' World of Commercial Consultants', *EUI Working Papers*, vol. 36, 2008.

65 Emilia Korkea-aho, 'Legal Lobbying: The Evolving (But Hidden) Role of Lawyers and Law Firms in the EU Public Affairs Market' (2021) 22 *German Law Journal* 65–84.

## 10.4 CONCLUSION

Overall, the case of the rise and consolidation of a group of Euro-lawyers is an example of how transnational legal expertise can be built. Euro-lawyers emerged in the first decades of the European integration process as a small group of individuals at the fringes of their national profession. They are now well established in the European polity. As the group has grown, it has penetrated the institutions, expanding its role as an intermediate between business and the European administration. While in the early days of European integration Euro-lawyers were mainly competition lawyers, they can now provide legal advice on the whole range of European policies. The scope of services offered now encompasses a wider range, from legal representation to lobbying.

This chapter has examined the agency of Euro-lawyers in the process of European integration. It has been shown that, far from having only benefited mechanically from the extension and development of European law, Euro-lawyers have played their part in order to become the essential intermediaries between companies and the European administration.

Euro-lawyers have not only contributed to the development of European policies, but they have also questioned the foundations of the legal profession. By redefining their role within the European institutions, they have considerably extended the profession's jurisdiction, to the point of questioning the specificity of lawyers in respect of other intermediaries, such as lobbyists and consultants.

# 11

# Rock 'n' Roll Stars or Guitar Technicians? Legal Advisors As Legal Experts in NGO Lobbying

Emilia Korkea-aho

## 11.1 INTRODUCTION

When advocating for various social justice causes, from the environment to human rights in local and global arenas, non-governmental organisations (NGOs) deploy law as a means to those ends. Some NGOs build their entire strategic position on the utilisation of tools offered by the legal system. For instance, ClientEarth, an NGO established in 2006 and operating in Europe both nationally and at the EU level, is a charity that uses 'the power of the law to change the system'.[1] It translates the sense of urgency we feel about climate change and the loss of biodiversity into litigation, and in fact many high-profile climate change and environmental cases in recent years have been initiated by civil society actors.[2] But the system is also being changed and challenged outside court rooms, with many NGOs using legal expertise to reach out to policy-makers and publicly demand a change. The role of legal expertise in NGO political advocacy is barely acknowledged by studies of NGO legal mobilisation. This chapter provides one of the first analyses of how NGOs use legal expertise to lobby.[3]

The first draft was presented at the Socio-Legal Studies Annual Conference at Leeds University in 2019. I thank the participants of the Legal Professions stream, and especially John Flood for valuable comments. This chapter would not have been possible without the generosity of legal advisors who agreed to be interviewed. These discussions brought this chapter alive. Anni Watson provided excellent research assistance.

1 www.clientearth.org.

2 The Urgenda Climate Case against the Dutch government was the first in the world in which citizens established that their government has a legal duty to prevent climate change. On 20 December 2019, the Dutch Supreme Court found the Dutch government has obligations to urgently and significantly reduce emissions in line with its human rights obligations, http://climatecasechart.com/non-us-case/urgenda-foundation-v-kingdom-of-the-netherlands/.

3 See also Lee and Abbot, Chapter 12 in this volume.

Drawing on expert interviews conducted among legal advisors at environmental and human rights NGOs based in Brussels and Helsinki, this chapter shows how, over time, NGOs' ways of working have evolved and how today many NGOs have added legal advisors to their ranks, playing an integral role in a broad spectrum of NGO activities. This chapter is interested in how the increased in-house legal expertise manifests itself in the political advocacy work that NGOs do and how legal advisors see their own professional lawyer role. Does the involvement of NGO lawyers assist NGOs in getting their message across to policy-makers? What are the consequences of engaging legal experts with respect to the identity and self-perception of NGOs and the groups they serve? Does the lawyer have to be an 'activist' in order to work successfully in an NGO? Is law a trump card in winning over policy-makers? It is these sorts of questions that serve as the foundation upon which this contribution is built.

The contribution is divided into four substantive parts. Section 11.2 defines NGOs as an object of research and explains the chapter's methodological choices. Section 11.3 explains key developments in the NGO political advocacy literature. Section 11.4 looks at what literature exists regarding NGOs and law, discussing briefly in turn (1) strategic litigation, (2) social movements and (3) cause lawyering. After synthesising a provisional conceptual framework from these three sections, I proceed, in Section 11.5, to reflect on the framework in the light of empirical evidence, that is, expert interviews. In the conclusions, I will reflect on whether the framework is plausible and whether adjustments are needed to understand the distinct role of NGO lawyers.

## 11.2 DEFINING AND CHOOSING NGOS

### 11.2.1 *NGOs As an Object of Study*

By some accounts, NGOs 'may constitute as significant a social and political development of the latter twentieth century as the rise of the nation state was of the nineteenth century'.[4] Although there are in all likelihood more NGOs now than ever in history, precise numbers are difficult to provide.[5] This is partly because of definitional difficulties (more on this in the rest of this section), but

[4] Michael Edwards and David Hulme, 'Introduction: NGO Performance and Accountability' in Edwards and Hulme (eds.), *Beyond the Magic Bullet: NGO Performance and Accountability in the Post-Cold War World* (West Hartford, CT: Kumarian Press, 1996), p. 2.

[5] According to the European Transparency Register, there are 3295 NGOs in January 2021, available at http://ec.europa.eu/transparencyregister/public/homePage.do?redir=false&locale=en.

also due to the wide variety of activities in which NGOs engage these days. It has been estimated that 'by the turn of the twenty-first century, NGOs were carrying out most of the tasks of governing complex societies – delivering development assistance, mediating social conflicts, setting standards for business, developing expert knowledge . . . '.[6] In short, NGOs have become instrumental in upholding fundamental values in the face of increasing crises as well as participating in the governance of various aspects of society.

Salamon and Anheier define an NGO as an organisation that is private, self-governing, membership-based, non-profit distributing and which has a formalised structure.[7] An NGO does not constitute part of the state administration, nor is it formally or discreetly managed by government officials. It carries out programmes according to its own standards and often, but not always, raises its own funds for its own purposes. As a term, NGO is one of many used to describe voluntary organisations, others being 'civil society organisation', 'non-profit organisation', 'charity', 'interest group', 'public interest organisation' or 'social movement'. While some of the terms overlap with others or are synonymous, all terms are not on the same conceptual level. For instance, to the extent that NGOs influence public policy, they can also be characterised as interest groups – just as companies and professional associations can be.[8] Some terms come with administrative consequences, and an NGO may be legally organised as a charity for tax or social insurance purposes. Sometimes the differences between the terms indicate different disciplinary traditions. For example, scholars of NGOs emphasise a distance from the government (*non-governmental* organisation), whereas for those who research 'non-profit organisations', the question of autonomy and some sort of distance from the profit-making world of the private sector are of central importance to an understanding of voluntary societal action.[9] Only rarely have any of these scholarly traditions paid attention to the role of law and legal expertise in NGO work.[10] The exception to which I return below is the US

[6] Christopher Todd Beer, Tim Bartley and Wade T. Roberts, 'NGOs: Between Advocacy, Service Provision, and Regulation' in David Levi-Faur (ed.), *The Oxford Handbook of Governance* (Oxford: Oxford University Press, 2012), p. 325.

[7] Lester M. Salamon and Helmut K. Anheier, 'In Search of the Non-Profit Sector. I: The Question of Definitions' (1992) 3(2) *Voluntas: International Journal of Voluntary and Nonprofit Organizations* 125–51.

[8] Nicole Bolleyer, *The State and Civil Society. Regulating Interest Groups, Parties, and Public Benefit Organizations in Contemporary Democracies* (Oxford: Oxford University Press, 2018), p. 42.

[9] Ibid., 4 and 43.

[10] There is some literature on NGOs as actors in the context of international law, see Math Noortmann, 'NGOs in International Law: Reconsidering Personality and Participation (Again)' in Thomas Davies (ed.), *Routledge Handbook of NGOs and International Relations* (Abingdon and New York: Routledge, 2019).

'cause lawyering' literature, a term that conceptualises a socially and morally conscious form of lawyering. Thus defined, cause lawyers can exist in many settings, including in NGOs.

In the literature, NGOs are typically categorised into three main roles: advocates, service providers, and regulators. As advocates, NGOs engage in political activities, shape and support policy agendas and exercise influence on public policy choices. In the second category, NGOs, often funded by international donors, deliver development aid and services, in particular in low-income countries. Finally, as regulators, NGOs direct attention to misbehaving companies and governments, holding them accountable for various forms of human rights and labour abuse. Together with states and international organisations, NGOs also develop and maintain standards and code of conduct certifications and then monitor company compliance against them. These different actor roles are not clear-cut in the everyday activities of NGOs, and for instance activities associated with the advocate and regulator role often blur and converge into one unified role.[11] Even though the term 'NGO' implies financial and organisational independence from governments, some NGOs rely heavily on governments or international organisations such as the UN, WTO or World Bank for their grants. But some, such as Amnesty International, work only on membership donations. Funding is a key consideration in understanding of NGOs, as the nature and source of their funding directly affect the levels of NGO political advocacy. Schmid et al. have shown for service-focused NGOs that if an NGO is government-funded, it is unlikely to engage in intense advocacy.[12]

In this chapter, I use the term NGO to refer to actors that influence public policy as advocates but do not distribute profits. This definition is aligned with the EU's Interinstitutional Agreement underpinning the Transparency Register that defines NGOs as 'not-for-profit organisations (with or without legal status), which are independent from public authorities or commercial organisations. Includes foundations, charities, etc.'.[13] NGO political advocacy (and, interchangeably with it, lobbying) refers to attempts to change policies or to influence the decisions of government and the state with the aim of promoting a collective goal or interest.

11 Beer, Bartley and Roberts, 'NGOs: Between Advocacy, Service Provision, and Regulation'.

12 Hillel Schmid, Michal Bar and Ronit Nirel, 'Advocacy Activities in Nonprofit Human Service Organizations: Implications for Policy' (2008) 37 *Nonprofit & Voluntary Sector Quarterly* 581–602. Tax legislation may also prevent service focused NGOs from engaging in political advocacy.

13 Agreement between the European Parliament and the European Commission on the transparency register for organisations and self-employed individuals engaged in EU policy-making and policy implementation. *Official Journal* L 277, 19.9.2014, pp. 11–24, Annex I. This agreement is replaced with a new IIA, see Agreement of 20 May 2021 on a mandatory transparency register. *Official Journal* L 207, 11.6.2021, p. 1–17.

### 11.2.2 *Choosing NGOs: The Methodological Framework*

This chapter is sociolegal in its theoretical and methodological orientation, with qualitative expert interviews conducted among legal advisors working in environmental and human rights organisations. The precise methodological framework is discussed later in this section.

NGOs working in the fields of the environment and human rights were chosen on the basis of the existing literature which has demonstrated the importance that law has for them in particular. Environmental NGOs have long resorted to seeking relief from courts. Whilst litigation has been a key tool for advancing environmental issues, its attractiveness has only increased in recent years as a means to address the adverse consequences of climate change.[14] But human rights NGOs have also used legal arguments and tools, and today many offer expert legal assistance to disadvantaged groups to help them fight for their rights. Human rights organisations have not been as keen to engage in litigation – at least if compared to their environmental counterparts – but they have used it successfully to, for instance, defend and advance Roma rights before courts.[15] It should, however, be noted that the two policy fields are different in terms of the intensity and the nature of political advocacy.

Judged by spending alone, the environment is one of the core fields for political advocacy. According to recent estimates, the five biggest companies (BP, Chevron, ExxonMobil, Shell and Total) spent at least €251 million on lobbying EU decision-makers between 2010 and 2019.[16] This means that in order to get their message across and be taken into account by policymakers, environmental groups must also spend resources on lobbying. The picture is more complex for human rights organisations that have not traditionally been 'aware of the importance of political activity, its contribution to strengthening civil society, and its role in ensuring more resources'.[17] Besides political appetite, they may also lack the skills to

[14] http://climatecasechart.com. The US Climate Change Litigation database tracks developments (both US and non-US) in litigation and administrative proceedings related to climate change.

[15] Mark Bell, *Racism and Equality in the European Union* (Oxford: Oxford University Press, 2008), p. 82.

[16] https://corporateeurope.org/en/2019/10/big-oil-and-gas-buying-influence-brussels. More than $2 billion was spent on lobbying climate change legislation in the US from 2000 to 2016, with the industry outspending environmental groups 10 to 1. See Robert J. Brulle, 'The Climate Lobby: A Sectoral Analysis of Lobbying Spending on Climate Change in the USA, 2000 to 2016' (2018) 149 *Climatic Change* 289–303.

[17] See Schmid, Bar and Nirel, 'Advocacy Activities in Nonprofit Human Service Organizations: Implications for Policy', 597. See also Debra C. Minkoff, 'The Emergence of Hybrid

influence the political agenda.[18] This is especially so if the core activities of human rights NGOs consist of providing services, such as running legal clinics or help centres. The broader policy dynamics of the field also matter; there is less ideological rivalry in the human rights sector, unlike in the environmental policy, where industry and NGOs, both clamouring to get the attention of the decision-maker, often have opposing and radically different views on what should be done. The absence of clear battle lines likely reduces the keenness of human rights organisations to engage in political advocacy.

The interview data collected for this contribution covers environmental and human rights NGOs in Brussels, as the EU's capital, and Finland. Although political systems and decision-making processes are different in Finland and Brussels/EU, the interviews reveal that NGO lawyers describe their functions and activities in similar terms. Two things possibly explain these similarities despite the differences in the political context. First, Brussels-based NGOs are advocacy organisations in the sense that they are rarely engaged in service provision. They are based in Brussels in order to be as close as possible to EU decision-makers. The selected Finnish NGOs are also advocacy organisations. In Finland, as in the Nordic countries more generally, social services are delivered by the state, and NGOs have been traditionally free to engage in public advocacy. Second, both Brussels/EU and Finland regulate NGOs with a light touch, which may explain why the work in a Finnish NGO does not fundamentally differ from the work in a Belgian/EU organisation.[19] But it is not only the regulation of NGOs that matters, as the activities of lawyers are also subject to statutory rules and professional discipline. Yet in Finland and Brussels/EU, no particular rules or specific ethical considerations are in place with regard to lawyers working in NGOs.

Most NGOs employ paid full-time staff, consisting of 'expert' employees, such as biologists and chemists in the environmental sector, or human trafficking or Roma rights experts in human rights organisations. They are 'substance experts' in the sense that they have policy level or technical/scientific information on the issues for which the NGO is advocating. But an NGOs' workforce also includes research staff such as project managers and IT specialists to coordinate and run surveys and to analyse data, as well as administrative personnel whose tasks range from fundraising to staff recruitment and general human resource management. Especially smaller NGOs also recruit

Organizational Forms: Combining Identity-Based Service Provision and Political Action' (2002) 31 *Nonprofit & Voluntary Sector Quarterly* 377–401.

18 Ibid. (Schmid, Bar and Nirel).

19 Bolleyer, *The State and Civil Society*, p. 20.

volunteers whose efforts with respect to fundraising are often crucial to NGO longevity. Lawyers – defined as individuals with a law degree – may be employed by NGOs in a variety of capacities and job titles. For present purposes, I am, however, interested in what I call *NGO legal advisors*, that is, lawyers who work in NGOs and whose tasks include planning and executing advocacy strategies (writing and compiling documents, organising and meeting with policy-makers, participating in working groups) or providing information and advice on the ramifications of actions being considered by an NGO. These types of legal advisors can also engage in other activities, such as assisting individuals through an NGO's legal clinic or legal aid service. Some may occasionally engage in litigation, but usually the NGOs that are regular litigators have lawyers whose sole task is to go to court. A couple of the interviewed legal advisors also took care of standard legal tasks, such as checking contracts or ensuring data protection compliance.[20]

There is no statistical data on how many NGOs have 'legal advisors' in their ranks and under what exact job title. No directories of NGO lawyers or legal advisors exist. The preliminary research, conducted prior to the commencement of the empirical work, suggested that the numbers of NGO legal advisors are on the rise. The interviews seemed to confirm this trend, as many of the respondents reported that they either had no predecessor in the office or only had one, so organisationally they were first- and second-generation legal advisors.

The lack of directories and the fact that the term 'legal advisor' is not universally used by NGOs meant that NGO lawyers were not easy to reach. Besides legal advisors, the interviewed lawyers are employed under titles such as 'legal (policy) officer', 'lawyer', 'public affairs officer' or 'law and policy advisor'. Most NGOs have information on staff members on their websites, but they do not necessarily disclose their occupational status, educational background or their current job description. The interviewees were located on the basis of a two-stage systematic search and snow-balling. First, relevant NGOs were identified using information in the EU Transparency Register as well as personal contacts. The second step of the search covered the NGOs' social media presences (website, Facebook, Twitter), identifying those employees whose occupational title included 'law', 'legal', 'lawyer' or 'regulatory'. 'Legal advisors' whose main function is to litigate or assist in litigation were excluded

20 The breadth of NGO legal advisors' tasks justifies a comparison to in-house lawyers. See Richard Moorhead, Steven Vaughan and Cristina Godinho, *In-House Lawyers' Ethics. Institutional Logics, Legal Risk and the Tournament of Influence* (Oxford: Hart Publishing, 2018).

from the sample.[21] The interviewees were also asked to nominate legal advisors they considered relevant for the project. I conducted fifteen semi-structured interviews with NGO lawyers in Brussels and Helsinki, most face to face, some via Skype.[22] The interviews, conducted between March 2019 and May 2020, lasted between one and two hours and were all taped and transcribed.[23]

## 11.3 PUBLIC INTEREST ADVOCATES? NGO AS LOBBYISTS

The literature on NGO political advocacy comprises two different – methodological and ideological – traditions. The first draws on social movement theory, analysing how NGOs offer 'key organizational infrastructure for broader social movements'[24] to call out and put pressure on states, international organisations and corporations. Under social movement theory, an NGO is a regulator and service provider in the context of social causes, such as indigenous rights, gender equality, the abolition of child labour and environmental protection.[25] Lawyers and legal expertise have, as of yet, not been the focus of any social movement literature.

Another tradition is interested in NGOs as interest groups and policy advocates. As public interest advocates, NGO activities range from attempting to influence legislation and engage in decision-making processes to raising awareness and sharing expertise and advice, as well as providing innovation in addressing social needs. The activities can be divided into insider and outsider tactics.[26] The former are aimed at gaining access to directly influence policy-makers, so that they would support – and if possible adopt – the policy preferred by the interest group. This requires professional expertise not necessarily available to small and medium-sized NGOs with few paid staff. The latter type of activities typically involve mobilising citizens through, for instance, grassroots campaigning, demonstrations and social media influencing. Although NGOs routinely use a combination of both, they may spontaneously be drawn into outsider tactics, because 'it is easier to

[21] In some cases, to confirm both the educational background and the main function required email correspondence.

[22] The interviews have been reported anonymously using a number and R (referring to Respondent). The interviewees or their organisation are not identifiable by name. Neither is the country in which the respondent works mentioned. Below I mention the type of NGO if required by the analysis. The respondents have been offered an opportunity to verify the final draft.

[23] Anni Watson translated into English relevant parts of the interviews conducted in Finnish.

[24] Beer, Bartley and Roberts, 'NGOs: Between Advocacy, Service Provision, and Regulation', p. 327.

[25] Rhonda Evans and Tamara Kay, 'How Environmentalists Greened Trade Policy: Strategic Action and the Architecture of Field Overlap' (2008) 73 *American Sociological Review* 970–91.

[26] Andreas Dür and Gemma Mateo, *Insiders versus Outsiders: Interest Group Politics in Multilevel Europe* (Oxford: Oxford University Press, 2016).

mobilize support to defend a threatened right, such as environmental security, than support for innovations, such as new laws or government programs'.[27] The standard NGO membership may be attracted to 'louder' and more social media fit causes than to funding an NGO lawyer involved in minutiae expert negotiations over the details of a new piece of legislation.

NGO activities promote the public interest, which is defined as the collective or indivisible interests of the general public as opposed to the interests of special interest groups – a view firmly shared by both the social movement and interest group traditions. The key issues raised by the debate about the public interest and NGOs as the concept's representatives are reflected in the discussion on the professionalisation of NGO advocacy. At the root of the discourse is the idea of NGOs as advocates for particular modes of organisation and organisational virtues: 'The NGO signifies a world of voluntarism, rationalization and scientific knowledge.'[28] Over time, NGOs have increasingly come to rely on full-time professional staff and centralised administration. There is no single overarching reason for the professionalisation of NGO advocacy, but it seems that the overall increased complexity of contemporary societies has pushed NGOs to increase their informational capacities. Research has confirmed that the most effective type of advocacy builds on expertise and emphasises research and insider information, avoids burning bridges and creates information dependencies.[29] The logic is that decision-makers grant access to groups who, in return, provide them with expert knowledge and information, in Bouwen's words, 'access goods'.[30] Two takeaways from the research on the uses of expertise in advocacy are particularly relevant for assessing NGO advocacy activities. First, the turn to expertise in advocacy activities is good for industry organisations that are well-positioned to accumulate relevant knowledge and have money to buy expertise on an as-needed basis. Second, expertise-based advocacy has traditionally been successful with

27 J. Craig Jenkins, 'Nonprofit Organizations and Political Advocacy' in Walter W. Powell and Richard Steinberg (eds.), *The Nonprofit Sector: A Research Handbook* (2nd ed., New Haven: Yale University Press, 2006), p. 319.

28 Beer, Bartley and Roberts, 'NGOs: Between Advocacy, Service Provision, and Regulation', p. 328. See also John Boli and George M. Thomas, *Constructing World Culture: International Nongovernmental Organizations Since 1875* (Stanford University Press, 1999).

29 Jo de Berry, 'Exploring the Concept of Community: Implications for NGO management' (1997) CVO International Working Paper Number 8, available at http://eprints.lse.ac.uk/29100/1/IWP8de-berry.pdf; John P. Heinz, Edward O. Laumann, Robert L. Nelson and Robert H. Salisbury, *The Hollow Core* (Cambridge: Harvard University Press, 1993).

30 Pieter Bouwen, 'Exchanging Access Goods for Access: A Comparative Study of Business Lobbying in the European Union Institutions' (2004) 43 *European Journal of Political Research* 337–69.

the European Commission, but it its relevance with respect to the European Parliament has also increased.[31]

It is important to note that decision-makers not only seek out expertise, but are also involved in nurturing the expertise that they then rely on when making decisions. In 2011, the Commission established a financial programme to support the creation and running of two NGOs in the area of EU financial policy-making. In a press release, the Commission announced its support for 'the development of a *European centre of financial expertise* that would stimulate the involvement of consumers and non-industry stakeholders'.[32] In essence, the Commission assisted NGOs in becoming experts. To the extent that public funding may, as noted above, disincentivise NGO advocacy, government funding may also be used to kick-start NGO advocacy. Apart from providing financial support for stakeholder representation in return, the Commission's programme also shows how the relationship between governments and NGOs is increasingly defined by expertise and professionalisation.

Has this turn towards more expertise-oriented professional political advocacy overtaken more traditional NGO activities, such as grassroots mobilisation, elite pressure and maintaining a clear moral stance? A related question concerns the implications of the professionalisation of NGO activities for lawyers and legal expertise. While professionalisation and formalisation reduce internal factions and enhance coordination, contributing to the overall effectiveness of the organisation, they may weaken a kind of voluntarism on which NGOs depend.[33] The literature acknowledges 'the NGO-isation dilemma',[34] a concept whereby NGOs 'undergo a professionalization process, that is usually associated with organizational centralization, which leads to "mission drift" and a growing distance from those social actors that organizations were initially formed to represent'.[35] It is

31 David Coen, Alexander Katsaitis, *Institutional and Constitutional Aspects of Special Interest Representation*. Study for the Committee on Constitutional Affairs, European Parliament. Directorate General for Internal Policies, Policy Department C: Citizens' Rights and Constitutional Affairs, 2015.

32 EU Commission, Press Release: 'EU Commission adopts proposal to help fund financial services NGOs', 15 June 2016, emphasis added. These financial programmes exist across policy sectors, see for instance in relation to development NGOs, available at www.welcomeurope.com/european-subsidies-beneficiary-Development+NGOs.html.

33 William Gamson, *The Strategy of Social Protest* (2nd ed., Homewood, Ill: Dorsey Press, 1990).

34 Lina Buchely, 'The NGO-isation Dilemma: International Cooperation, Grassroots Relations, and Government Action from an Accountability Perspective: A Case Study of Colombian Migration NGOs and the National System of Migration' (2012) 31 *Buffalo Environmental Law Journal* 63–116.

35 Bolleyer, *The State and Civil Society*, p. 12. See also Sabine Lang, *NGOs, Civil Society and the Public Sphere* (Cambridge: Cambridge University Press, 2012). The professionalisation of NGO advocacy is linked to how NGOs are regulated. For a comprehensive view of the

also suggested that the professionalisation of NGOs tends to 'domesticate' movements, and the original radical goals are diluted to more moderate ones.[36] Interestingly, it is in the context of voluntarism versus professionalisation where references are repeatedly made to law and lawyers. Jenkins writes that those organisations that primarily rely on legal means and rights advocacy tend to be successful at accomplishing their tasks and that by having lawyers in the organisations' ranks, NGOs 'have clear technical and legitimacy advantages in conducting rights advocacy before governmental bodies'.[37] In other words, the professionalisation of NGO advocacy implies increasing legal NGO legal capacity.

## 11.4 NGO ADVOCACY AND LAW

This subsection discusses the literature on NGO advocacy and law, starting with strategic litigation and the courts as a means of political change and moving then on to social movements and cause lawyering. From the point of view of strategic litigation, law is an inherently liberating force with lawyers acting as the drivers of change; for social movements theorists on the hand, lawyers are viewed with scepticism. Scholars of cause lawyering recognise lawyers' contributions to political advocacy, but whether it is good or bad depends on the scholar's view regarding the nature of NGO activities.

### 11.4.1 *Strategic Litigation*

Strategic litigation means the use of courts to advance political and social causes, a well-used strategy for environmental NGOs and the animal rights movement in particular.[38] The US research on environmental advocacy

regulatory framework, see the Council of Europe, *Regulating Political Activities of Non-Governmental Organisations* (December 2013).

36 J. Craig Jenkins and Craig M. Eckert, 'Channeling Black Insurgency: Elite Patronage and Professional Social Movement Organizations in the Development of the Black Movement' (1986) 51(6) *American Sociological Review* 812–29; Frances Piven and Richard Cloward, *Poor People's Movement* (New York: Pantheon, 1977).

37 Jenkins, 'Nonprofit Organizations and Political Advocacy', p. 317. See also Christopher J. Bosso, 'The Color of Money: Environmental Groups and the Pathologies of Fund Raising' in Allan J. Cigler and Burdett A. Loomis (eds.), *Interest Group Politics* (4th ed.,Washington, DC: CQ Press, 1995).

38 Ulrich Beyerlin, 'The Role of NGOs in International Environmental Litigation' (2001) 61 *ZaöRV* 357–78; Loveday Hodson, *NGOs and the Struggle for Human Rights in Europe* (Oxford: Hart Publishing, 2011); Lisa Vanhala, 'Legal Opportunity Structures and the Paradox of Legal Mobilization by the Environmental Movement in the UK' (2012) *Law & Society Review* 523–56; Andrea C. Loux, 'Losing the Battle, Winning the War: Litigation

suggests that litigation can be an effective tool, especially if pursued together with other strategies.[39] Silverstein, for instance, shows how the animal rights movement in the US combined protest with high-profile litigation and media events, thereby creating a 'double-barrelled' threat.[40] In Europe, environmental and human rights/equality NGOs especially have resorted to litigation. Not only do they initiate and lead cases themselves, but they also train others to do so. ClientEarth lawyers have recently launched a guide Access to Justice in European Union Law, containing information on the EU-level legal framework, to assist legal professionals and organisations in Europe with taking legal action to protect the environment.[41]

Lawyers are of course central to conducting litigation, but they also have a fundamental role with respect to framing the strategic narratives around litigation.[42] Litigation, like any organised social action, is preceded by frame construction. According to social construction theory, the formation of a new advocacy organisation requires the development of a charter for the organisation, a conception of the social problem that it addresses and a convincing method for bringing about change.[43] Jenkins points out that the 'importance of frame construction to organizational foundings is also illustrated by the environmental movement, which has long depended on the constructive efforts of lawyers, policy experts, and scientists'.[44] From the perspective of frame construction, law is an instrument to counter the 'iron law of decadence',[45] in which

Strategy and Pressure Group Organisation in the Era of Incorporation' (2000) 11 *King's Law Journal* 90–104.

39 Michael W. McCann, *Taking Reform Seriously: Perspectives on Public Interest Liberalism* (Ithaca: Cornell University Press, 1986).

40 Helena Silverstein, *Unleashing Rights: Law, Meaning, and the Animal Rights Movement* (Michigan: University of Michigan Press 1996).

41 ClientEarth's guide is part of the ATOJ-EARL (Access to Justice – Education and Awareness raising of Legal professionals) project, which is led by ClientEarth and Justice and Environment with the support of the European Commission LIFE programme, www.documents.clientearth.org/wp-content/uploads/library/2019-02-26-access-to-justice-in-european-union-law-a-legal-guide-on-access-to-justice-in-environmental-matters-ce-en.pdf.

42 For framing see Windsor, Chapter 3 in this volume.

43 Robert D. Benford and David A. Snow, 'Framing Processes and Social Movements: An Overview and Assessment' (2000) 26 *Annual Sociological Review* 611–39.

44 Jenkins, 'Nonprofit Organizations and Political Advocacy', p. 313. See also Paul McLaughlin and Marwan Khawaja, 'The Organizational Dynamics of the U.S. Environmental Movement: Legitimation, Resource Mobilization, and Political Opportunity' (2000) 65 *Rural Sociology* 422–39; Elizabeth Boris and Rachel Mosher-Williams, 'Nonprofit Advocacy Organizations: Assessing the Definitions, Classifications, and Data' (1998) 27 *Nonprofit & Voluntary Sector Quarterly* 488–506.

45 Theodore J. Lowi, *The Politics of Disorder* (New York: Basic Books, 1971).

narrow organised groups gain control over governmental institutions claiming to serve the public interest.

But the instrumental use of law can turn the law into a force equal to the 'iron law' against which it was used, with the critics of strategic litigation focusing on two issues in particular. First, they contend that strategic litigation overemphasises the role of lawyers – a major bone of contention for the social movement literature (of which more below). Second, critics argue that litigation limits NGOs' horizons and prevents them from mobilising non-litigation strategies:

> litigation alone is often limited in that courts are better at blocking actions than at creating positive changes. The environmental movement has found that litigation can block construction projects and penalize polluters but is limited as a tool for bringing about positive compliance with environmental laws. Nonetheless *the law has a moral force that, when reinforced by other pressures, often brings about change*.[46]

The social movement literature is nevertheless more sceptical about the 'moral force' of law and its usefulness for social movements in particular.

### 11.4.2 *Social Movements*

For social movements literature, lawyers are dubious characters. The unease about lawyers is expressed in relation to professional expertise: lawyers are 'technical experts who contribute to movements in their professional capacity, usually defined as "outsiders" or lumped into a category of professionals'.[47] By bringing their professional skills and ideologies to movements, lawyers are thought to 'risk the disruptive power of grassroots movements by narrowly channelling the cause into often costly legal strategies, that is, costly in terms of time and money, or costly in that disruptive potential'.[48] It is difficult, if not impossible, for social movements literature

46 Jenkins, 'Nonprofit Organizations and Political Advocacy', p. 323 (emphasis added).

47 Lynn C. Jones, 'Exploring the Sources of Cause and Career Correspondence among Cause Lawyers' in Austin Sarat and Stuart A. Scheingold (eds.), *The Worlds Cause Lawyers Make: Structure and Agency in Legal Practice* (Stanford: Stanford University Press, 2005), p. 203.

48 Ibid, p. 203 and pp. 205–6. See also Donatella della Porta, 'Social Movements and the State: Thoughts on the Policing of Protest', in Doug McAdam, John D. McCarthy, and Mayer N. Zald (eds.), *Comparative Perspectives on Social Movements. Political Opportunities, Mobilizing Structures, and Cultural Framing* (Cambridge and New York: Cambridge University Press, 1996), pp. 62–92; Charles Tilly, *Durable Inequality* (Berkeley: California University Press, 1998).

to view lawyers as insiders, as actors integral to, and a natural part of, these types of movements.

This unease stems from the assumption that lawyers automatically prefer litigation and divert attention away from alternative, potentially more effective, ways of seeking change, such as grass-roots mobilisation and public protests. Lawyers' tendency to frame conflicts as concrete issues between two parties undermines the potential for broader alliances. However, after enumerating the reasons for lawyers' poor reputation among social movements scholars, McCann and Silverstein debunk them as being mere myths. Lawyers do not always emphasise legalistic activities, nor do they 'overwhelm movements with this single-minded commitment to litigation as a tool for social change'.[49] Negative perspectives on lawyers in social movements are based on the idea that movements 'fall under the spell of legal professionals and their legalistic biases' as a result of 'widespread acceptance of the "myth of rights" and *deference to professional expertise* in our society'.[50]

Therefore, it is professional expertise (and our deference to it) through which lawyers are thought to control social movements. Shdaimah explains that the lawyer's professional role as an expert may come to loggerheads with progressive lawyering that emphasises 'autonomy or client decision-making, collaboration, and the more amorphous elements of respect and dignity'[51] – core values to social movements. Jones also – implicitly at least – turns on the expertise aspect when she accuses (sociolegal) legal profession research of viewing cause lawyers as 'a subset of the legal profession' who are armed with specialised knowledge, rather than seeing them – like everyone else in the movement – as just ordinary activists.[52]

### 11.4.3 *Cause Lawyering*

Cause lawyering is a practice of using the law to do 'good'. Sarat and Scheingold, key intellectual figures behind cause lawyering research, describe a cause lawyer as a 'morally activist lawyer', someone who does not simply sell

49 Michael McCann and Helena Silverstein, 'Rethinking Law's "Allurements": A Relational Analysis of Social Movement Lawyers in the United States' in Austin Sarat and Stuart Scheingold (eds.), *Cause Lawyering: Political Commitments and Professional Responsibilities* (Oxford: Oxford University Press, 1998), p. 263. See to this effect Robert L. Kidder and Setsuo Miyazawa, 'Long-Term Strategies in Japanese Environmental Litigation' (1993) 18 *Law & Social Inquiry* 605–28.

50 Ibid. (McCann and Silverstein, emphasis added).

51 Corey S. Shdaimah, 'Dilemmas of "Progressive" Lawyering: Empowerment and Hierarchy' in Sarat and Scheingold (eds.), *The Worlds Cause Lawyers Make*, cited by Sarat and Scheingold in 'Introduction' in the same book, p. 24.

52 Jones, 'Exploring the Sources of Cause and Career Correspondence among Cause Lawyers', p. 204.

services 'as a set of technical skills available to the highest bidder'.[53] Cause lawyering distances itself from, and positions itself as an alternative to, the classic conception of lawyering. Lawyering in this classic conception is 'neither a domain for moral or political activity nor a place to express a lawyer's beliefs about the way society should be organized, disputes resolved, and values expressed'.[54] Classic lawyering is client-centred,[55] and emphasises moral neutrality and technical competence. As a result, the legal profession is not equipped to adequately address the tension between the public interest and the interests of individual clients.

For cause lawyers, however, lawyering is a moral and political commitment. Cause lawyering is an inherently radical activity, aimed at 'altering some aspect of the social, economic and political status quo'.[56] These types of lawyers are, therefore, not partisan and non-accountable client-oriented technicians who use their skills to further whatever cause they are paid to represent. Sarat and Scheingold write that cause lawyering is 'attractive precisely because it is a deeply moral or political activity, a kind of work that encourages pursuit of the right, the good, or the just. Cause lawyers have something to believe in and bring their beliefs to bear in their work lives'.[57] Cause lawyers emphasise the public interest nature of the legal profession, 'one whose contribution to society goes beyond the aggregation, assembling and deployment of technical skills' on behalf of a client.[58]

53 Sarat and Scheingold, 'The Dynamics of Cause Lawyering. Constraints and Opportunities', p. 1. Their first edited collection focused on exploring how conventional forms of lawyering feel threatened by the emergence by cause lawyering, yet also in need of it, because cause lawyering provides a more human and positive narrative of lawyering, see Sarat and Scheingold, *Cause Lawyering: Political Commitments and Professional Responsibilities*. In the second book *Cause Lawyering and the State in a Global Era* (Oxford: Oxford University Press, 2001) Sarat and Scheingold asked how cause lawyering is shaped by globalisation and state formation. For the third book *The Worlds Cause Lawyers Make* (2005), their attention turned to a microanalysis of social settings in which cause lawyers operate, investigating 'the ways in they marshal social capital and make strategic decisions', p. 4.

54 Ibid. (Sarat and Scheingold (eds.), *The Worlds Cause Lawyers Make*).

55 William Simon, 'The Ideology of Advocacy' (1978) 29 *Wisconsin Law Review* 30–144.

56 Sarat and Scheingold, 'Cause Lawyering and the Reproduction of Professional Authority: An Introduction' in *Cause Lawyering*, p. 4.

57 Ibid., 3. Political views associated with cause lawyering are often from the left, although conservative politics of cause lawyering is not out of question. See Jones, 'Exploring the Sources of Cause and Career Correspondence among Cause Lawyers', p. 205. Cause lawyering emerged within the Law and Society movement in the US. Reflecting its US intellectual origins, as a legal practice it is also shaped by ideas about rights and the structures and practices of power in the US legal system.

58 Sarat and Scheingold, 'An Introduction' in *Cause Lawyering*, p. 3.

Because cause lawyering is a general way of conceiving working as a lawyer, cause lawyers are found to work in many different settings, such as law firms, legal clinics at universities, public administration or NGOs. Irrespective of the setting, cause lawyers face a major strategic decision between what the literature calls *legal* and *political advocacy*. The former, also called 'legal engagement'/'rule of law cause lawyering', means prioritising the courts and litigation through class actions and amicus briefs, or by raising legal and constitutional issues in connection with the representation of a particular client. The latter, political lawyering, encompasses activities ranging from lobbying and political mobilisation to street demonstrations and civil disobedience.[59] These forms of political mobilisation are emphasised in critical lawyering research, a subfield of cause lawyering. Closely related to feminist and critical race jurisprudence, critical lawyering emphasises the level playing field in the lawyer-client collaboration and looks for new ways to respect the dignity and autonomy of a client. One such way involves 'lobbying in legislative forums on issues related to their clients'.[60] Theorists of cause lawyering see engaging in lobbying and other forms of political advocacy, however, as an activity that '*tests and probably violates the nethermost boundaries of mainstream professionalism*, and this ordinarily means running into substantial structural obstacles'.[61]

For some cause lawyers, the practice of cause lawyering prompts a conflict in terms of law versus politics. Sarat and Scheingold themselves acknowledge that for cause lawyering to be successful (however this is measured), law must trump politics.[62] Another more interesting theme raised by critical lawyering – a theme that has been overshadowed by the law versus politics debate – relates to the boundary between the *political* and the *professional* in cause lawyering.

Law is one of the classical professions where authority over the respective field is granted by the state through a process of licensing designed to ensure both competency and a commitment to act responsibly in the interests of those served.[63] On the one hand, professions promise to engage in the competent exercise of skills based on complex, systematic knowledge obtained through formal training. This is expert professionalism. On the other, professionalism

59 Ibid., pp. 13–14.

60 Louise Trubek and M. Elizabeth Kransberg, 'Critical Lawyers: Social Justice and the Structures of Private Practice' in *Cause Lawyering*, p. 210.

61 Sarat and Scheingold, 'An Introduction', p. 14 (emphasis added).

62 Ibid., p. 8. For how cause lawyering is based on a strong dichotomy between law and politics and how it impedes analysis, see also Christos Boukalas, 'Politics as Legal Action/Lawyers as Political Actors: Towards a Reconceptualisation of Cause Lawyering' (2013) 22(3) *Social and Legal Studies* 395–420.

63 Eliot Freidson, *Professional Powers. A Study of the Institutionalization of Formal Knowledge* (Chicago: University of Chicago Press, 1986).

involves an agreement to be morally guided by an understanding of and commitment to socially accepted goals and the values on which they rest. This is social trustee professionalism.[64] The arguments made for expert and social trustee professionalism resemble those made in cause lawyering literature. For those ascribing to the social trustee professionalism view (or cause lawyering), the (expert) professionals are 'in danger of losing their soul' in what one writer has described as a 'race to the bottom'.[65] To reverse the trend, a return to social responsibility and public commitment is needed. The development where doctors and lawyers (classic examples of representatives of expert professions) began to work for organisations seemed to then bridge the rift that had emerged between the two types of professionalism. These new professions such as NGO lawyers are typically concerned with particular policy areas such as health, education and social work. They combine professional knowledge with an understanding of the organisational work of their employers, such as an NGO, for example. In time, the management of organisations, both public and private, has in itself come to be considered a professional activity.[66]

This discussion is interesting since it directly taps into the above tension in cause lawyering between political/ethical commitment on the one hand and technical professionalism and formal knowledge on the other.[67] Two sets of questions arise from the tension.[68] The first concerns the relationship between the NGO lawyer and the NGO. Can a professional be an expert and a political

64 Frank Fischer, *Citizens, Experts, and the Environment: The Politics of Local Knowledge* (Durham: Duke University Press, 2000), p. 4. See also Albert W. Dzur, *Democratic Professionalism: Citizen Participation and the Reconstruction of Professional Ethics, Identity, and Practice* (Pennsylvania: Penn State University Press, 2008) (proposing an approach he calls 'democratic professionalism' to build bridges between specialists in domains like law and the lay public in such a way as to enable broader public deliberation about major social issues).

65 Lincoln C. Caplan, 'The Lawyers Race to the Bottom' *New York Times*, 6 August 1993, A29. The debate culminated around the same time that the legal profession experienced a commercial turn. For instance, Hilary Sommerlad has demonstrated that the paradigm of legal services offered by large law firms to their clients has changed over time from lawyers as professionals and advisers to their clients towards service-providers engaging with customers, see Hilary Sommerlad, 'The Commercialisation of Law and the Enterprising Legal Practitioner: Continuity and Change' (2011) 18 *The International Journal of the Legal Profession* 73–108.

66 Fischer, *Citizens, Experts and the Environment*, p. 26.

67 Jones, 'Exploring the Sources of Cause and Career Correspondence among Cause Lawyers', p. 205.

68 Both sets resonate with Koskenniemi's notion of the professional identity of the international lawyer, see Martti Koskenniemi, *From Apology to Utopia: The Structure of International Legal Argument*. Reissue with a new epilogue (Cambridge: Cambridge University Press, 2005).

actor? What if there is a conflict between a cause lawyer's professional and ideological commitments? Are NGO lawyers legal inventors or, as feared in social movement literature, a stifling force on NGO innovation? The second set of questions concerns the relationship between the NGO lawyer and the outside world. How does the NGO lawyer choose between different advocacy strategies? Does the demand from the government affect the choice of advocacy strategies? Do NGO lawyers have greater room to manoeuvre than 'classic' lawyers because they occupy a somewhat marginalised position in the legal profession?

Having reflected on the literature and identified a conceptual template from which to view the empirical material, I now turn to my interview data. In so doing, I am able to explore the ways in which those I have spoken to conceived of their professional role both in relation to the NGO they work for and for the world they speak to.

## 11.5 LEGAL ADVISORS IN NGOS: EMPIRICAL DATA

The interview data consists of fifteen interviews with NGO legal advisors. Six were conducted with Helsinki-based legal advisors, and nine with Brussels-based legal advisors. Eight interviews were with lawyers working for human rights organisations, and seven with environmental organisations. Below I mention the type of NGO where it is relevant to the analysis. Roughly half of the interviewees had worked less than two years in their role, and the other half more than two years.[69] Five had previous NGO experience,[70] and three had a background in private practice.[71] Six were the only lawyers in the organisation, and eight worked as part of a team of lawyers or had lawyer colleagues.[72]

There is no ready-made template dictating what a lawyer working in an NGO does, and especially those legal advisors who are the 'first-generation' lawyers in their organisations emphasise how they have been free to create their own vision rather than having a top-down vision imposed on them.[73] Many, however, invariably described their work days consisting of 'writing responses to consultation, or assisting in writing responses to consultation,

69 Less than two years: R1, R2, R5, R4, R9, R13, R14, R15, more than two years: R3, R6, R8, R7, R10, R11, R12.

70 R5, R4, R8, R13, R14.

71 R2, R6, R10.

72 Legal advisors with lawyers as colleagues were: R5, R6, R7, R8, R9, R10, and those who had no lawyer colleagues were: R1, R2, R3, R4, R11, R12, R14, R15. One did not know (R13).

73 Four respondents were 'first generation' lawyers: R2, R3, R7, R12.

writing or following the procedures for access to documents, analysing legislative proposals or suggesting ... amendments, analysing the compatibility of proposals ... writing court pleadings'.[74] In human rights NGOs, some legal advisors assisted clients, but it did not constitute the main part of the job.[75] Only three respondents had management or 'in-house lawyer' duties.[76]

### 11.5.1 *An NGO Lawyer: Of Me and Others*

Although the respondents described their daily tasks in similar terms, there were more diverse descriptions when asked about their own role in the organisation and their relationship with other NGO staff. Three broader observations cut across the interview data. First, the respondents emphasised their role in ensuring that the NGO comes across as an expert organisation with a clear and accurate message:

> I want the messages that come out of this office to be 100% legally accurate so that we don't make unrealistic or baseless claims even in the way the policy should evolve but we make sure that we ask something that is consistent with the legal system, we exploit all the possibilities that are already there in the legal system.[77]
>
> We cannot be an organisation that just comes up with things off the top of our heads, for our supporters' sake too.[78]
>
> We cannot be caught stating half-truths or caught for not having things properly prepared.[79]

This sense of being responsible for legally accurate statements, however, affects the relationship of legal advisors with their non-lawyer colleagues. One respondent sums up the sentiment echoed in many interviews:

> Perhaps it is my role to be the nasty nit-picker here. I often get this feeling.[80]
>
> I feel that my role is kind of a 'reality checker'.[81]

Second, one of the questions raised by the social movements and cause lawyering research is whether NGO lawyers legalise movements or if they take into their own work the more political orientation of the movements they

74 R7. Litigation was part of four legal advisors' work portfolio: R5, R6, R7, R8.
75 R4, R9, R15.
76 R8, R10, R15.
77 R7.
78 R1.
79 R2.
80 R1.
81 R15.

serve. Legal advisors seem well aware of the risks of legalising or hijacking the NGO message, or depriving the people the NGO is representing of their voice; both human rights and environmental lawyers articulate the risk. NGO lawyers say that they are playing in the background, making sure that their colleagues have all the instruments that they need to pursue their policy and campaign work effectively.

> I once described my job as one of those guitar technicians in rock 'n' roll concerts, you know you have the musicians on the stage and they play and there is always somebody in the background that is making sure the instruments are well tuned and they play right and that's what I do.[82]

Research on cause lawyers has suggested that the desire to stay in the background is not false modesty but a strategic choice. In the US, researchers have argued that 'even the most radical of the activist lawyers understood the importance of professionalism, and this would only enhance the success for clients and for movements'.[83] This is what Jones calls being 'an activist behaviorally',[84] knowing which strategies work in which contexts. One respondent gives an example of targeting a message to different audiences. Whilst it is 'definitely good to have a lawyer-like approach when approaching politicians', things look different when

> we are talking about campaigning, in which we are perhaps trying to influence normal people's opinions and to gain support for their issues, this approach might hinder me from putting forward the issue. For example, I often notice that the way I write or edit the written work of our media team might get feedback saying that "This is without a doubt correct but we cannot publish it in this form in our release or on our blog." A more personal approach, such as providing an anonymous case may be more effective than neutral lawyer talk, because even in politics where some may be very aware of how things actually are, people might take a different stand. Influencing on a more personal level and appealing to emotions may in some situations forward the issue better. It is a bit of a balancing-act.[85]

Making a choice between accuracy and accessibility, and the risk of 'legal nitpicking' comes across with respect to social media presence. Legal advisors reported that they are often asked to comment on the NGO's social media activities from a legal point of view. Whilst they want to ensure legally accurate

82 R7.
83 Jones, 'Exploring the Sources of Cause and Career Correspondence among Cause Lawyers', p. 229.
84 Ibid., 230.
85 R1.

content, they are keen to avoid a policing role for fear of stifling the NGO activity but also because 'you're not going to mobilise anyone by sending out boring stuff about the law'.[86]

High expectations or fear of disappointing is the third theme. Many feel that they – or they as a medium of law – disappoint their colleagues, as they cannot meet their colleagues' expectations of 'Finally we have a lawyer, finally you can solve this problem!'[87] Many see the root of the problem hiding in the nature of legal expertise.

> Maybe it is the fact that there is too much faith in a lawyer finding an article or clause that can be slammed on a table and that would change everything. Perhaps there are unrealistic expectations like that which may then cause disappointment.[88]
>
> There is perhaps some disappointment in the means of the law, the difficulty of the processes. Not so much in the person, the interpreter.[89]
>
> ... often the answers that you give are not always sort of the ones that people want to hear ... legal processes can take a lot of time and aren't necessarily clear cut and it's not always a silver bullet ... people can sometimes be a little bit disappointed.[90]

The research has suggested that during the early stages of organisational and agenda formation, lawyers help define the realm of the possible, 'offering advice about the relative efficacy of legal versus political strategies'.[91] Disappointing is an unavoidable component of defining the realms of the possible. The interview data supports this, because the fear of disappointing was visible in the interviews of the first-generation legal advisors but less so of second-generation lawyers whose predecessors had already offered salutary reminders of the limits of law in the NGO.

When asked what they had found challenging in their job, many NGO lawyers admitted that they sometimes felt that 'it is never enough, more can always be done':

> Here the work is largely related to what the world should become so there is no clear objective as to where we are going. It is more about ambition and we try to get as good results as possible. This is sometimes challenging for me. I would rather get things done and finished but the work in organisations such

86 R8. See also R9 and R10.
87 R4. See also R15.
88 R11.
89 R2.
90 R12.
91 Sarat and Scheingold, 'The Dynamics of Cause Lawyering', p. 10.

> as this is not like that. It is in people's very core to always strive for more here, it is never enough, more can always be done.[92]
>
> For me it has been a bit of an internal conflict realising that my approach is maybe a bit more cooperation oriented.[93]
>
> . . . it's not that I necessarily believe that that compromise is justice, it's just that that is our best option.[94]

For many legal advisors, NGOs are not supposed to be terriers but experts, taking baby steps in the right direction, and having a lawyer within a NGO has a calming effect and can help steer the course of the NGO and strengthen the message:

> I do believe that most people who work for a cause believe in the cause. And sometimes you're blinded by that cause. And it's difficult to look at a situation objectively. So as soon as you see something that's slightly wrong, you kind of jump ahead and it's, you see things as if they're terrible and catastrophic and you want to denounce and you want to scream and shout but then that reaction could then backfire . . . And in that sense I think a lawyer within an NGO is also helpful, it's important that you have a kind of, you sit down and you have to look at everything in the opposite way, what would it look like if I were on the other side, what would I attack. If you act reactively, you don't think that way.[95]
>
> I collect comments from our experts and dress them in a legal robe, considering what is feasible and what is not and putting the feasible suggestions on top.[96]

NGO lawyers seem to professionalise the organisation's approach to advocacy, but how then does working in an NGO shape a lawyer's self-understanding? The cause lawyering research rejects classic lawyering's client-centrism, moral neutrality and technical competence that can be sold to the highest bidder. Is an NGO lawyer a different kind of lawyer?

For the majority, being a lawyer in an NGO poses no particular issues or concerns:

> there is no contradiction because as a lawyer, of course if you are working for a client, you have certain obligations and so on. That's clear and that's very good it's like this. But basically, when you are employed by an organisation, the only thing you do is you work on the objective of the organisation . . . but

92 R2.
93 R1.
94 R4.
95 R4.
96 R15.

> I don't see any contradiction in working for a cause. I think it is exactly the same if you work for a client that wants you to make a merger and, of course, you're representing the interests of your client within the bounds of the law and you try to get the best contract. There's no, I think there's no difference in what we are trying to do.[97]

The organisation they work for becomes, in a way, a client whom they assist with the best legal competence they have. When describing their lawyer role in an NGO, many explicitly rejected the notion of neutrality and the idea that their expertise is to be hailed like a taxi:

> Because we're not neutral. I mean we're here to favour a movement. So in that sense, trying to be a legal arm of a movement . . . this kind of taxi stand rule is the ideal image of the lawyer and I'm pretty far from that.[98]

The cause definitely seems to matter. While some had drifted to the NGO sector, for others it was a planned career. Working in an NGO provides lawyers with a way to express their beliefs about the way society should be organised:

> Here I can do my job with a clear conscience.[99]
>
> I felt that I wanted to apply my legal skills for a good cause that would really motivate me and feel that the work is less dry.[100]
>
> I definitely wanted to do something good with my degree.[101]

But working as an NGO lawyer is also an opportunity to make a difference. Commenting on their previous job in government one noted that

> I didn't feel like there was really much of a difference that you could make. Unless of course you're a commissioner maybe . . . you have a voice that maybe is not the official voice that is followed but you have a lot more freedom to really fight for what you believe in and I just thought that that was kind of more in line with why I started to study law in the first place. I'm actually very happy in the NGO sector. Of course, sometimes you have to do things that you don't think are particularly useful but overall I feel like there's a real cause behind it.[102]

When asked whether they identified themselves as activists, lawyers or some combination, there were no clear response patterns based on the work setting

97 R5.
98 R8. See also R5 and R15.
99 R1.
100 R8.
101 R13.
102 R4.

or country. Half of the respondents said that they were definitely activists,[103] while the other half opposed on equally definite terms.[104]

For those who described themselves as an activist, activism was associated with passion:

> I feel it is the fire, the passion and the fire, and the way of working. That it comes from the heart and it really is a sort of activism ... it is good to have such a fire which I would call activism.[105]
>
> ... maybe the better question would actually be do I see myself as a lawyer, because what I do is so strange.[106]

On the other hand, those who rejected the activist label emphasised expertise and felt expertise was incompatible with activism:

> ... we really kind of pride ourselves on being a science-based organisation so yes, what we do, we always make sure our positions are strongly backed up by scientific evidence so yeah, I feel like the kind of the activism doesn't really fit it with that.[107]

Even the lawyers who were self-professed activists distanced themselves from what they described as demonstrative activism (occupying public buildings and so on). Their version of activism is one of an internal fire, conviction and expertise. Rather than downplaying expertise and technical competence, the NGO lawyers see technical skills as a radical force, something with which they can make a difference.

### 11.5.2 *The Government: Is There Anyone Out There Who Knows the Law?*

For a lawyer, an NGO career is not the most obvious choice. Lawyers have traditionally sat on management boards, had administrative roles or served as a chairperson, but as employees at an NGO, their role has not perhaps been so powerful or distinctive.[108] Nearly all interviewed legal advisors recognised the trend of NGOs hiring legal advisors, and generally agreed on the usefulness of a law degree for advocacy work and legal advice as a way to promote legislative change.[109]

103 R5, R8, R10, R11, R13, R14.

104 R2, R3, R6, R7, R9, R12, R15.

105 R11.

106 R8.

107 R12.

108 R11.

109 R11, R5, R7. They also pointed out that lawyers are good at keeping an eye on legislative implementation.

Hiring a lawyer seems to be a rising trend, but many lawyers are still seen as a high cost for an NGO. NGO legal advisor positions are often tied up with particular projects or campaigns, which makes hiring permanent lawyers a financial risk for NGOs.[110] In the end, it is funding that dictates what can be done. Some legal advisors point out that it is not always easy for them to explain the impact of what they do, especially given that things take a long time, even sometimes ending up back at square one with no identifiable progress.[111]

The importance of having legal advisors in NGOs is more pronounced in the environmental sector where, as one respondent put it, 'as companies have lawyers, we need to have them too'.[112] Many respondents pointed out the (increasing) demand from policy-makers for NGOs to have more legal capacity. One legal advisor pointed out that even donors have started to pay attention to legal competences. In their view, the lawyer was hired as the organisation had received criticism concerning

> legislative proposals that although they are very nice, they have been written in a way that is not beneficial for the lawmaker . . . there was pressure to have a person who knows these things.[113]

The same sentiment, if not the same pressure, was reported across NGOs, emphasising the usefulness of having a lawyer in the house to propose legislative amendments:

> I could really draft the amendment to the text, and I think I was kind of able to say this "when we write this and this, this will have an effect and this won't have an effect". And also speaking to the people from the Parliament and so on, we actually received very good feedback . . . that [our contribution] was actually quite successful, almost surprisingly successful.[114]

Sometimes NGOs and especially their legal advisors are sought after for their ability to come up with ideas outside the box:

> It is quite interesting also to work with governments or government representatives because sometimes you have a deadlock in the Council and they come to us not just because we are NGOs but maybe because we are resourceful and we can help them think outside the box and try and write a diplomatic solution.[115]

110 R5, R4.

111 R8, R6, R10.

112 R10. Referring to the legal armies of the industry, some felt that NGOs are not moving fast enough and that there is a lot of ground to cover, see R7.

113 R2. For NGOs as external sources of legal expertise see also Yong, Chapter 7 in this volume.

114 R5.

115 R7.

NGO lawyers feel they have greater room to manoeuvre and find legal arguments than their peers working in corporations or administration, because as NGO lawyers they exist in a marginalised position in regard to the professional project of organised legal professions.

> I find it quite liberating actually to be somewhere else where the law isn't what comes first and foremost, the law is at the service of something. So if I'm making a strained legal argument, no one's going to call me up on it and say "oh that's not really like that" you know, because there's a bigger purpose here. And I quite like that.[116]

Legal advisors seem to be involved in legal drafting to the extent that one said that what they do is not lobbying, but 'it is a legal drafting exercise'.[117] However, for NGOs themselves, lawyers are not simply technocrats that they second to governments to help in drafting legislation, they exude authority:

> I have been used in email correspondence before when they actually don't need me at all but then they put me in copy and then they say 'I'm putting our legal officer in copy', as kind of a threatening card and I think that's actually helped.[118]
>
> there is a lot of need for lawyers and I think there is some truth in the fact that, I mean when you have the title of legal officer, or legal advisor, and you meet people externally, the attitude changes somehow. And even though substance, nothing might change actually, it's just the tone and the atmosphere changes.[119]

Not everyone agrees. Especially those who work in human rights organisations are wary of their lawyer role – even in relation to decision-makers. One of them curtly notes that: 'I never present myself as a lawyer. Like ever.'[120]

In their view, lawyers may tend to lack a certain amount of emotional intelligence and emphasising the legal content may stand in the way of getting the message across:

> I think that some lawyers can be very . . . they don't understand the emotional context of things. I think advocacy is, you need to know obviously the law, you need to be able to advocate for things and you need to have like the emotional narrative also to convince people and I think some lawyers who get into

116 R8.
117 R5.
118 R4.
119 R4.
120 R13. But see also R5: 'I will still go and say "I am working for an environmental organisation", I won't say "I'm a lawyer"'.

> advocacy, don't really understand that you know, they talk in very stark, public terms but don't communicate things to the average person. And that is something that you need to learn.[121]

NGO lawyers recognise that what is expected of them (by governments and their employers) is expertise, but many wonder whether

> . . . we are as a profession creating . . . that illusion too by saying that 'look, we are the ones that know, we are the only ones.[122]
>
> . . . let's . . . come out of this kind of esoteric role that lawyers sometimes see for themselves that they think that they live in a sealed room where there is all the knowledge and sometimes they offer this knowledge to the poor guys, like the common folks.[123]
>
> So I think that, if we have this elitist idea that only people who have a legal background can contribute to the definition and the adoption of laws, then we won't reach the people who are furthest behind and that's not an inclusive way of making law.[124]

## 11.6 CONCLUSION

The NGO is an inherently conflicting actor, simultaneously a product of voluntarism on the one hand and rationalisation and expertise on the other. It would seem only natural that these conflicting roles are also reflected in NGO lawyers. The interview data suggests that the NGO lawyer is a conceptually conflicting actor, but perhaps in a different way than might have been assumed on the basis of the literature.

ClientEarth describes its own mission as wanting to use the 'power of law' to defend the environment. Richard Abel, a grand old man of the legal professions research, once described how lawyers 'speak law to power'.[125] These two statements perfectly encapsulate the role expectations thrust upon NGO lawyers. On the one hand, NGOs hire lawyers not only to increase their legal capacity but also to 'change the tone and the atmosphere' (the rock 'n' roll effect). NGO lawyers are supposed to 'exploit all the possibilities that are already there in the legal system': to exploit the power of law. On the other hand, NGO lawyers report how policy-makers and employers expect them to

[121] R13.

[122] R5.

[123] R7. See also R15 who speaks of the 'glorified role' of lawyers and how much of what they say is taken seriously because it comes from the position of a lawyer.

[124] R13.

[125] Richard L. Abel, 'Lawyers and the Power to Change' (1985) 7 *Law and Policy* 5–18.

speak law to them, not perhaps in the high moral sense meant by Abel, but to speak law in the sense of a technocratic contribution, or a factually correct and formally accurate legal draft (guitar technician contribution). The lawyers' choice, as interpreted through the interviews, is the role of a guitar technician. The NGO lawyers find themselves more comfortable in this latter role, preferring to stay in the background and provide their expertise allowing the institutional organisation to take centre stage.

The conceptual framework developed for this chapter built on the tension that exists in cause lawyering between political commitment and technical professionalism, and identified two contexts – between the NGO lawyer and the NGO, and between the NGO lawyer and the political community – for settling the tension between the political and professional. The cause lawyering research has emphasised the former context, enlightening us on how NGOs and their lawyers mutually shape each other, and how cause lawyers actively produce and shape the message of their organisations. The interview data analysed in this chapter suggests that we should perhaps not only focus on the relationship between the NGO and their lawyers, or how the NGO lawyers 'speak law to power'. Namely, policy-makers do not simply passively receive the message but they also actively reach out to NGOs with their concerns and hopes, inevitably shaping the NGO activities and the expert role of lawyers working in them. Future research would be well-advised to not look at policy-makers only as funders or regulators and NGOs as fund recipients or regulatees, but also as partners in expertise.

12

# Legal Expertise, Environmental Groups and Brexit: Beyond the Limits

Maria Lee and Carolyn Abbot

> Law is a critical discipline. . . . it's whole economy, it's enduring, it's adaptable. It holds the consensus, it reflects the consensus, it drives the consensus, it mobilises every part of the state, every part of society. It is a mirror back to society. It's just, it's endemic.
>
> (Interviewee 1)

## 12.1 INTRODUCTION

In the referendum of June 2016, 52 per cent of the UK population voted to leave the EU. The fact of leaving the EU is an enormous wrench, for us and for many in the environmental community. But aside from the fact of being outside the EU, the political process by which the UK left the EU was fraught and dysfunctional. Between the referendum in June 2016 and February 2021, the UK has had three prime ministers, two general elections and five Secretaries of State for the Environment.

The tumultuous journey to exiting the EU, and the slow progress of the Environment Bill between 2019 and 2021, provided the setting for intensive civil society work to try to prevent the weakening of pre-Brexit levels of environmental protection. We have carried out research exploring the role of legal expertise in environmental group work between the referendum and the middle of 2020, with some observations going beyond that time. 'Remain' versus 'leave' became a key political division, within political parties, government and parliament,[1] and also the public. This created significant challenges for environmental NGOs, since 'almost certainly half of the environment groups' membership voted leave. Because it's broadly representative of

[1] See, e.g., Lewis Lloyd, *The Brexit Effect: How Government Has Changed Since the EU Referendum* (London: Institute for Government, 2019).

where the public's at' (Interviewee 11). The community largely avoided campaigning for leave/remain,[2] both before and after the referendum. Instead, environmental groups both shaped and participated in the long and often tortuous process leading to the prospect of an Environment Act 2021, a law-heavy process that shines a bright light on the use of legal expertise by environmental groups, beyond litigation.

There is a considerable literature on NGO use of litigation, defined broadly to include not just cases in court but 'the presentation of claims to be decided by courts (or court-like agencies) and the whole penumbra of threats, feints, and so forth, surrounding such presentation'.[3] 'Studies of legal mobilization in social reform struggles almost always involve litigation campaigns',[4] and the literature on the role of legal expertise in lobbying and advocacy is limited.[5] Our work contributes to filling that gap.

In this chapter, we argue that notwithstanding some clear weaknesses in the general place of legal expertise in UK environmental groups, environmental NGOs impressively brought their legal expertise to play in advocacy around Brexit-environment. 'Advocacy' or 'lobbying' (terms we use interchangeably to mean direct interactions with decision-makers) is the preferred approach of *insider* groups, who enjoy privileged access and status and adopt insider strategies.[6] We refer to 'environmental NGOs' and 'environmental groups' synonymously to describe not-for-profit public interest organisations

[2] There were some interventions, see Louisa Parks, 'All Quiet on the Brexit Front? UK Civil Society Before and After the UK's Referendum on Membership of the EU' in L. Antoniolli, L. Bonatti and C. Ruzza (eds.), *Highs and Lows of European Integration: Sixty Years After the Treaty of Rome* (Berlin: Springer, 2020).

[3] Marc Galanter, 'Why the "Haves" Come Out Ahead: Speculations on the Limits of Legal Change' (1974) 9 *Law and Society Review* 165–230, p.165.

[4] Michael McCann, 'Litigation and Legal Mobilization' in Keith E. Whittington, R. Daniel Kelemen and Gregory A. Caldeira (eds.), *The Oxford Handbook of Law and Politics* (Oxford: Oxford University Press, 2008), p. 532.

[5] Katie Ghose, *Beyond the Courtroom: A Lawyer's Guide to Campaigning* (London: Legal Action Group, 2005) offers a practical guide, and Martin Goodman and James Thornton, *Client Earth* (London: Scribe, 2017) discuss a range of activities. E.g. Christos Boukalas, 'Politics As Legal Action/Lawyers As Political Actors: Towards a Reconceptualisation of Cause Lawyering' (2013) 22 *Social & Legal Studies* 395–420; Chris Hilson, 'Framing the Local and the Global in the Anti-Nuclear Movement: Law and the Politics of Place' (2009) 36 *Journal of Law and Society* 94–109, also touch on non-litigious activity. See also Korkea-aho, Chapter 11 in this volume.

[6] See, e.g., Wyn Grant, *Insider Groups, Outsider Groups and Interest Groups Strategies in Britain* (University of Warwick, Department of Politics, 1978) and William A. Maloney, Grant Jordan and Andrew M. McLaughlin, 'Interest Groups and Public Policy: The Insider/Outsider Model Revisited' (1994) *Journal of Public Policy* 17–38; outsider groups are those for whom access to the corridors of power is limited and outsider strategies such as protest are preferred. For NGOs as providers of external legal expertise, see Yong, Chapter 7 in this volume.

(including think tanks) that operate independently of government to address, in our case, environmental issues and challenges.

We begin this chapter with the political journey from referendum, beyond the UK's exit from the EU in January 2020, through the shock of Covid-19 ('we are in extraordinary, new extraordinary times' (Interviewee 2)), to the current (February 2021) position of the Environment Bill.[7] The following section outlines our methodology. We then turn to the general weaknesses of environmental NGO use of legal expertise in advocacy. We have found these weaknesses to revolve especially around a lack of adequate legal expertise, a failure properly to appreciate the complexity and significance of legal expertise and a relative absence of legal expertise in the leadership of environmental groups. Our discussion of these issues with our interviewees was not Brexit specific. In the following section we turn to our conversations about Brexit, where we found, perhaps paradoxically, a much more intense and sophisticated use of legal expertise, notwithstanding the underlying challenges. We attribute this, not only to some very skilled individuals, but also to some things that were 'special' about Brexit. Brexit allowed particular openings for the use of legal expertise in advocacy, which were shaped and grasped by NGOs. Further, intense and extensive collaboration on Brexit enhanced and facilitated the use of legal expertise.

## 12.2 THE BREXIT–ENVIRONMENT DEBATE

EU membership dominated the UK environmental arena for over forty years. The EU (Withdrawal) Act 2018 provided for the survival of law (including environmental law) with EU origins as 'retained law', which can now be amended or repealed domestically. Retained law does not, however, include what became known as the 'governance gap'. The governance gap captures the loss of the accountability- and transparency-enhancing institutional architecture that sits over individual environmental rules and standards in the EU. The most obvious loss is the Commission-plus-Court enforcement regime. The public routines of planning and reporting contained in most EU environmental legislation were also not 'retained', nor were the environmental principles that have formed part of EU environmental law for many years.[8] Further, as members of the EU, UK environmental law and standards had

[7] For a more detailed story from an environmental perspective, see Carolyn Abbot and Maria Lee, *Environmental Groups and Legal Expertise: Shaping the Brexit Process* (London: UCL Press, 2021), https://www.uclpress.co.uk/collections/all/by-author-carolyn-abbot-and-maria-lee chapter 3.

[8] To simplify, EU interpretations of law (including those that used the principles) are retained under the EU (Withdrawal) Act 2018 but will be subject to reinterpretation by domestic courts.

evolved collaboratively, through the pooling of expertise and of participatory and democratic mechanisms; filling that gap domestically is no easy task.

Between the referendum and the 2017 general election, government insisted that there was no governance gap, and that existing UK mechanisms for political and legal accountability (parliamentary scrutiny and judicial review) would be perfectly adequate.[9] The Conservative Party performed unexpectedly poorly in the 2017 election, and formed a minority government. The governing party generally enjoys a clear majority in the UK parliament, and this unfamiliar situation gave parliament unusual power. As well as adding to the sense of drama around Brexit, this provided, as we discuss further below, space for environmental groups to exercise influence, which they grasped. The perception that environmental measures would help appeal to the younger voters, who had turned out in large numbers for the Labour Party, also increased the focus on the environment.[10]

After the 2017 general election, government turned increasingly to a rhetoric of 'green Brexit', framed in part around 'equivalence'. Equivalence involved constant government reassurance that environmental measures would be at least as strong after Brexit as before: 'Brexit will not mean a lowering of environmental standards.'[11] This commitment was taken seriously by the environmental community, and much effort and expertise was devoted to identifying whether proposed new measures (or their absence) would be as stringent as those in place before Brexit. Government accepted the need, broadly speaking, to fill the governance gap.

After many preliminary promises in the press and parliament, in early 2018 the UK Department for Environment Food & Rural Affairs (DEFRA) launched its *Consultation on Environmental Principles and Governance After EU Exit*, which received a stunning (given the dry title) 176,000 consultation responses.[12] A draft Environment (Principles and Governance) Bill was

[9] See the comments of the Secretary of State and the Minister in House of Lords European Union Select Committee, *Brexit: Environment and Climate Change, 12th Report of Session 2016–17 HL Paper 109*. (London: House of Lords, 2017), para. 80.

[10] Chris Curtis. 'How Britain Voted at the 2017 General Election' (YouGov, 2017), available at https://yougov.co.uk/topics/politics/articles-reports/2017/06/13/how-britain-voted-2017-general-election; Bright Blue, 'Tories Must Be Greener to Win Younger Voters, Says Bright Blue', available at https://brightblue.org.uk/tories-must-be-greener-to-win-younger-voters-says-bright-blue; Politico, 'The Greenwashing of Theresa May', available at www.politico.eu/article/the-greenwashing-of-theresa-may.

[11] Theresa May, *Major Speech on the Environment* (London: HM Government, 2018).

[12] Department for Environment, Food and Rural Affairs, *Consultation on Environmental Principles and Governance After EU Exit*. (London: HM Government, 2018), consultation outcome, www.gov.uk/government/consultations/environment-developing-environmental-principles-and-accountability.

published in December 2018, building on the proposals in the consultation, and indeed improving on them. The draft Bill was subject to pre-legislative scrutiny by two House of Commons committees. The draft Bill purported to address the governance gap. It contained provisions on the environmental principles[13] and provided for the creation of a new environmental body, the Office for Environmental Protection (OEP),[14] to fill the scrutiny and enforcement functions of the European Commission. It also provided for a novel framework for UK environmental policy, in the form of Environmental Improvement Plans, to replace EU policy-making frameworks such as Environmental Action Programmes.

Theresa May resigned as Prime Minister in summer 2019, after three failed attempts to get her Withdrawal Agreement with the EU through parliament, as well as a more general loss of authority.[15] Boris Johnson was chosen by party members to lead the Conservative Party, and hence became Prime Minister in July 2019. The full Environment Bill was put before Parliament for the first time in October 2019. It contained modest improvements on the provisions of the draft Bill. It was also much extended. Part One, 'Environmental Governance' is of greatest interest for current purposes. It contained the three elements of the draft Bill as above, slightly amended, and added a legislative framework for setting and monitoring environmental targets in the future. The other Parts of the Bill contained many Brexit-independent provisions on different environmental issues, from waste to tree felling. This version of the Environment Bill swiftly fell away when the Prime Minister, with the support of opposition parties in parliament, called the 2019 general election. The Conservative Party won that election with a working majority of over 80 MPs in Parliament. This government majority changed the mood and role of parliament. Further, government rejected the rhetoric of 'green Brexit' and 'equivalence', having campaigned on a slogan of 'get Brexit done' and having easily and rapidly passed a Withdrawal Agreement with the EU through Parliament.[16] From its perspective, Brexit was 'done'.

A new, almost identical, Environment Bill was put before parliament in January 2020. In March, the Bill was suspended due to the Covid-19 pandemic, and was slow to return to parliament. When it did return, in

13 Maria Lee and Eloise Scotford, *Environmental Principles After Brexit: The Draft Environment (Principles and Governance) Bill* (2019), https://ssrn.com/abstract=3322341.

14 Maria Lee, *The New Office for Environmental Protection: Scrutinising and Enforcing Environmental Law After Brexit* (2019), https://papers.ssrn.com/sol3/cf_dev/AbsByAuth.cfm?per_id=869755.

15 Lloyd, The Brexit Effect: How Government Has Changed Since the EU Referendum.

16 European Union (Withdrawal Agreement) Act 2020.

November 2020, the large government majority meant that only amendments put forward, or at least approved, by the government were likely to succeed. The Bill was paused again in January 2021, to be carried over into the new parliamentary session. The intention is for the Bill to have received Royal Assent (and become the Environment Act 2021) in the autumn.

It is not the purpose of this chapter to review the Bill, even the Brexit-specific provisions.[17] It is clear from the summary above that the development of the legislation has been iterative, and the environmental community had many opportunities to explore its detail and lobby on progress. In broad terms, the simple fact of an Act will be a big achievement for the environmental NGO community. The existence of the new features of UK environmental governance are positive and important: the OEP; a target setting framework; some planning, monitoring and reporting structures; environmental principles within policy. However, these provisions are flawed, and fail to provide equivalence with EU membership. The Bill will provide framework legislation, constituting significant executive power with limited oversight.[18] The OEP's enforcement powers are limited, the environmental principles lose the legal and overarching status that they enjoy in the EU,[19] and the targets framework is far from guaranteeing that environmental standards and environmental protection will not regress.

## 12.3 METHODOLOGY

This chapter is part of a broader project on the role of legal expertise in environmental group advocacy. Our case study, as introduced above, is the mobilisation of environmental groups around Brexit, and then around various iterations of the Environment Bill. In 2019–20, we interviewed seventeen people, most of whom were deeply involved in the activity around Brexit, the rest were familiar with the debate to varying degrees. We drew on personal knowledge of the field and personal contacts, plus their recommendations, to identify potential interviewees.[20]

17 See, e.g., Maria Lee, 'The Next Generation of Environmental Law: Environmental Accountability and Beyond in the Draft Environment (Principles and Governance) Bill' UCL European Institute (March 2019), www.ucl.ac.uk/european-institute/sites/european-institute/files/next_generation_environmental_law_paper_final.pdf; Elizabeth Fisher, 'Executive Environmental Law' (2020) 83 *Modern Law Review* 163–189.

18 Fisher, 'Executive Environmental Law'.

19 Lee and Scotford, *Environmental Principles after Brexit*.

20 Note that one of the authors, Maria Lee, has been working on the environmental implications of Brexit since well before the referendum, including with NGOs. She has to some extent participated in, and contributed to shaping, the phenomena being investigated. This

Ten of our interviewees were employed by environmental NGOs (including think tanks). These included a variety of long-established, more recently formed, membership and non-membership, NGOs, all active nationally, and in some cases also with an explicit European or international remit. They have a broad range of environmental interests, including species and landscape protection, pollution and climate change. Because of our focus on Brexit and law, our NGOs might be described as sitting at the larger, more 'establishment' side of the NGO movement, and our conclusions will reflect that. Seven of our interviewees were not employed by environmental NGOs, but have worked with, and in some cases been employed by, such groups in the past: two worked in large philanthropic re-granting organisations with a good overview of the NGO community; two worked in private legal practice; two were senior actors in government or non-departmental public bodies; and one was an academic with strong links to legal practice.

Our participants had diverse professional backgrounds. Ten of our interviewees had a legal background (i.e. had studied law at undergraduate or postgraduate level), although not all of those had professional legal qualifications. At the time of the interviews, they had between one and over forty years of experience working in or with environmental NGOs. All worked primarily in England, although some have been and continue to be involved in Brussels, Wales and Scotland.

The interviews were semi-structured, around a common set of core questions, which were slightly different for those employed by NGOs and the others. All participants agreed to be recorded. Interviews were transcribed by a professional transcriber. We have lightly edited some of the quotations for ease of reading. To maintain anonymity in this small community, we are not identifying the characteristics of individual interviewees, or the organisations they represent; we have ascribed an anonymous identifier to our participants, although in some cases have not attributed quotations to avoid identification.

For external evidence of what environmental groups actually do with law, and to get some sense of a broader community's activity on Brexit, we also analysed NGO submissions to parliamentary Select Committee inquiries on Brexit and the environment. These provide an accessible and coherent body of material, and the punctuation of the slow journey from referendum to the Environment Act 2021 by Select Committee inquiries was an important focus of public NGO advocacy on Brexit. We did not systematically analyse 'behind closed doors', face to face or written interactions with government and

involvement enriches our data and understanding, but also requires us to be cautious about what we hear.

parliamentarians. We recognise that this is important, but the public-facing work is sufficient to place alongside what interviewees told us.

## 12.4 THE LIMITATIONS IN NGO LEGAL EXPERTISE FOR ADVOCACY

Our research revealed three key weaknesses in legal expertise for advocacy in environmental NGOs: first, legal expertise is a relatively scarce resource; second, an understanding of what legal expertise can do for a movement (at least beyond litigation) is patchy; and finally, legal expertise is not prominent in NGO leadership and strategic thinking. These weaknesses are tightly connected: limited experienced legal expertise in the sector is both a result of and a reason for an absence of legal expertise in leadership; limited resource and limited strategic thinking limits reflection on and understanding of legal expertise; and that limited reflection means the gaps go unnoticed.

We turn to each of these weaknesses in this section, but must make three provisos. First, notwithstanding these weaknesses, we wish to emphasise the existence of sophisticated and effective legal expertise across the sector. Second, our conclusions may not apply to ClientEarth, which is a specifically legal environmental NGO, using 'the power of the law to change the system'.[21] We did not explore ClientEarth, or its impact in the sector. It is however clearly well-resourced with legal expertise and takes a strategic approach to law (although of course there is space for disagreement about its approach). And third, there may be some indications that legal expertise is increasingly significant in environmental activism; although the focus remains on litigation, rather than lobbying.[22]

Expertise generally, and legal expertise specifically, are rich and complex phenomena.[23] Something recognisably composed of 'legal expertise' *is* sometimes called on by environmental groups (and others) when they advocate social, policy or legal change. Elizabeth Fisher's approach to expertise as a matter of 'knowledge, skills and experience'[24] is a useful analytical starting point, although by no means a decisive definition. We do not believe that legal

[21] www.clientearth.org.

[22] See Korkea-aho's Chapter 11 in which she notes how there is a heightened sense of importance of legal expertise in NGO lobbying work.

[23] See, e.g., Abbot and Lee, *Environmental Groups and Legal Expertise: Shaping the Brexit Process*, chapter 4.

[24] Elizabeth Fisher, 'The Rise of Transnational Environmental Law and the Expertise of Environmental Lawyers' (2012) 1 *Transnational Environmental Law* 43–53, p. 48.

expertise is found only in individuals with academic or professional qualifications in law; we came across a number of individuals with no such qualifications whom we considered, and who were clearly considered by their peers, to be legal experts.

### 12.4.1 *Scarcity of Legal Resource*

Although the environmental sector may be legally 'well tooled up' compared to other NGO sectors (Interviewee 5), 'the absence of lawyers' (Interviewee 1) and 'limited legal capacity' (Interviewee 3) came through strongly in our interviews; and 'if an organisation has a lawyer, generally they will only have one or two. No-one has a massive team of lawyers' (Interviewee 15). We cannot straightforwardly conclude that NGOs are legally poorly resourced, since we could equally focus on the strong strands of legal expertise. But legal expertise does seem to be spread too thinly across and within environmental NGOs to support sustained use of law in advocacy. Further, we shared the sense of a number of our interviewees that lawyers in the environmental sector are on the whole relatively inexperienced: 'Most people working in NGOs are very young' (Interviewee 1). A young workforce has benefits, including perhaps fewer people who are 'jaded and sort of you know, defensive about what's gone before' (Interviewee 9), but a lack of experience will weaken the legal expertise available, and its role, overall. In discussion with public bodies, 'if we had a lawyer, they had to be quite a high-calibre lawyer. It was no good having a junior' (Interviewee 3).

The resource, including money, needed to mobilise law is a familiar issue around access to justice.[25] Cost was a constant theme in our interviews, suggesting that cost is equally a factor in the use of legal expertise in advocacy: 'lawyers have been regarded as quite a rare and expensive commodity' (Interviewee 3); 'pesky lawyers asking for more cash' (Interviewee 14). NGOs also face competition on pay from other sectors: 'Lawyers have other career avenues and civil society doesn't pay that well' (Interviewee 1). Cost is a factor with respect to experience: 'yeah, [experienced lawyers] did look expensive'

[25] E.g. Galanter, 'Why the "Haves" Come Out Ahead: Speculations on the Limits of Legal Change'. Epp's work on the 'support structure' needed to use litigation (rights advocacy organisations, supportive lawyers and sources of financing) has been very influential, see Charles Epp, *The Rights Revolution: Lawyers, Activists, and Supreme Courts in Comparative Perspective* (Chicago: University of Chicago Press, 1998). See also e.g. Lisa Vanhala, 'Coproducing the Endangered Polar Bear: Science, Climate Change, and Legal Mobilization' (2020) 42 *Law and Policy* 105–24.

(Interviewee 3). And 'mind-boggling' charges (Interviewee 7) may be 'the biggest barrier to accessing external legal advice' (Interviewee 6).

In addition to cost, career opportunities for lawyers inside NGOs may also be somewhat limited: 'you can't within the organisation structure move to have more responsibility' (unattributed); and the sector is 'not bringing on new environmental lawyers' (Interviewee 14). There may also be questions about the quality of the legal work around NGO advocacy, 'the sort of day-to-day stuff: oh, you know, quick look at this directive ... it's just less exciting' (Interviewee 3). The relatively heavy use of law on Brexit may be different:

> And this is a bit more glamorous, and you're in with a lot of community of your peers, other lawyers ... you're visible in something which is clearly quite significant. And not only that, but other lawyers see as significant.' (Interviewee 3)

These questions around the quality of work, organisational investment in the development of individual expertise and career progression point towards the way in which the sector *understands* the role of law and values legal contributions. The strategies adopted by environmental NGOs are rarely neutral, but are expressive of their collective identity. The question of 'fit' with an organisation's understanding of itself and questions of identity, are crucial to the use of law.[26] Our participants say that law is 'not sort of in the DNA' of some organisations (Interviewee 16); whilst others are 'naturally going to feel very comfortable in that space ... It's hard-wired into them' (Interviewee 9). An organisation's understanding of itself, and of law, is likely to be reflected in investment (or not) in law; and in turn, expertise in law reverberates in the understanding of law, in a self-perpetuating cycle.

The culture of funding may also be significant, whether funding comes from philanthropy or membership. Philanthropy was described by one of our interviewees as 'a very fickle, almost capricious world. Where they want results now'; by contrast with 'policy investments', legal campaigns 'tend to be longer, harder battles. And philanthropy, it's hard to keep philanthropy engaged in those marches' (unattributed). And members equally, are perceived to think that 'Your focus should be on protecting habitats rather than suing the

[26] E.g. Lisa Vanhala, 'Anti-Discrimination Policy Actors and Their Use of Litigation Strategies: The Influence of Identity Politics' (2009) 16 *Journal of European Public Policy* 738–54; Lisa Vanhala, 'Is Legal Mobilization for the Birds? Legal Opportunity Structures and Environmental Nongovernmental Organizations in the United Kingdom, France, Finland, and Italy' (2018) 51 *Comparative Political Studies* 380–412; Chris Hilson, 'New Social Movements: The Role of Legal Opportunity' (2002) 9 *Journal of European Public Policy* 238–55.

government or writing legislation for the government and doing their job for them. Why are you talking to MPs all the time, when you should be shouting at them?' (unattributed).

### 12.4.2 *Appreciation of Legal Expertise*

The nature of the legal expertise called on by Brexit is large and diverse. Environmental law covers an enormous range of difficult topics. Jurisdictionally, EU and UK, devolved and international environmental law were all significant. And environmental law is only the beginning. The condition of the environment and the effectiveness of environmental measures are fundamentally linked to the institutions that surround environmental law, including the governance issues mentioned above. The intricacies of trade, constitutional and administrative law have been recurring issues. The preoccupation of civil servants and legislators during the Brexit process with successful working examples from other jurisdictions or areas of law ('discourses of diffusion')[27] further expands the scope of legal expertise. Whilst well-intended as 'evidence based' policy-making and a useful tool of persuasion,[28] this expansion is necessarily superficial.

Our interviewees on the whole did not engage with the diverse nature of legal expertise, although gaps in expertise, most often trade, were raised. Those few who did engage in a meaningful way with the complexity of legal expertise were experienced and sophisticated users of law. One of our interviewees was critical:

> NGOs tend to recruit in a much more willy-nilly way [than universities or businesses]. So a policy crisis or political crisis like Brexit will suddenly flare up, and they won't look around themselves and say, 'Hmm, we need to have particular people to help us to win this battle.' That is not how the sector organises. (unattributed)

We were particularly struck by how few NGO actors working on Brexit had prior expertise in EU law. One interviewee expressed mixed feelings about specialist legal knowledge or training: 'I think it's often an advantage [not to have] a traditional legal background ... sometimes I feel that lawyers have been trained in a certain way, think that things are immutable which I don't

[27] Natasha Affolder, 'Contagious Environmental Law Making' (2019) 31 *Journal of Environmental Law* 187–212.

[28] Sheila Jasanoff, 'NGOs and the Environment: From Knowledge to Action' (1997) 18 *Third World Quarterly* 579–94.

think are' (Interviewee 7). The same person however later acknowledged that 'I think sometimes for the team doing some of the more kind of nitty gritty work, actually, a deeper understanding of specifically EU law, would be valuable. But I mean you can't have everything'.

This is just the clearest example of a widespread ambivalence towards intense legal specialisation.[29] More generally, we sense a naivety or even dismissiveness about legal expertise. Just how complex and diverse legal expertise is seems to be underestimated, with possible complacency about how easy it is to pick up requisite specialist legal expertise. Contributions based on lengthy specialisation seem to be simply absorbed as a (sometimes simplified) 'common knowledge', rather than noted for what they are. Of course, different types of knowledge and expertise can enrich the debate, non-specialist perspectives are helpful, and expertise can be acquired by those not trained in an area. But this requires sufficient expertise for meaningful communication with experts in an area, for example trade or constitutional law experts.[30]

Above, we suggest that resources are a *practical* limit on what expertise is available. Resources also however spill into the very understanding of what *constitutes* expertise: the sort of expertise available shapes not only what NGOs do, but what they think they ought to do, and hence what resources they think they need.

Many of our NGO interviewees struggled to explain literally what they do with law, even if they said that they use law or legal expertise in their work, or we witnessed their high legal accomplishment. Policing precisely what is legal work and what is not would require some tricky boundary work,[31] and we do not want to be critical of busy and accomplished professionals' priorities. Our conversations may have given our participants a valuable space to reflect on the place of law within their organisation and their community. But the absence of reflection on what they do with law does reinforce a sense that law may not be well appreciated, and brings out that self-perpetuating nature of a lack of sufficient legal expertise informing the understanding of legal expertise.

29 Richard Moorhead, Steven Vaughan and Cristina Godinho, *In-House Lawyers' Ethics: Institutional Logics, Legal Risk and the Tournament of Influence* (Oxford: Hart Publishing, 2019), suggest that in-house work may more generally have the effect of 'blunting technical specialisation', p. 190.

30 Harry M. Collins and Robert Evans, *Rethinking Expertise* (Chicago: University of Chicago Press, 2009) call this interactional expertise.

31 Boukalas, 'Politics As Legal Action/Lawyers As Political Actors: Towards a Reconceptualisation of Cause Lawyering'.

### 12.4.3 *Leadership and Strategy*

Legal expertise makes at most limited contributions to leadership and strategy: 'Leaders of NGOs and culture-setters at NGOs in the UK . . . are not lawyers. They're more communicators, political animals, scientists, for the most part' (Interviewee 3). Given the importance of culture and 'fit', the absence of legal expertise in leadership is likely to affect an organisation's general understanding of itself. Richard Moorhead and colleagues describe the jockeying for position between lawyers and others in their organisation as 'a tournament of influence'.[32] Whilst they say that lawyers often expect to lose in that tournament of influence, legal experts within environmental NGO seem rarely even to participate.

Our interviewees see legal expertise as playing a supportive and instrumental role, helping to deliver objectives set elsewhere, rather than shaping those objectives or the route to change. This may be apparent in Interviewee 15's description of NGO lawyers' role in the passage of the Environment Bill:

> . . . actually having the legal mind look at it and translate it into what the actual impact will be, it's very useful for other teams across organisations . . . to understand what the implications are, and then they can say what the problems are.

We do not wish to suggest that this instrumental, supportive role is anything less than crucial. But from the perspective of our work, an absence of legal expertise in the leadership of environmental groups reinforces relatively shallow engagement with what legal expertise demands from and offers an organisation. Less legal expertise in leadership *both* contributes to *and* reflects a relative absence of individuals with long legal NGO experience, as well as a certain flatness in appreciating the complexity and diversity of legal expertise. The same non-linear relationship may apply to the availability of legal resources, where over-stretched legal capacity may both result from and contribute to a relatively weak engagement with the strategic need for or potential for legal expertise. By revealing contrast, we might note that there was more legal leadership around the collaborative activity on Brexit.[33]

32 Moorhead, Vaughan and Gordinho, *In-House Lawyers' Ethics: Institutional Logics, Legal Risk and the Tournament of Influence*, p. 243.

33 In particular, note the presence of legal expertise on the Board of Greener UK when it was first set up; see Greener UK, *A Manifesto for a Greener UK* (London: Greener UK, 2017).

### 12.4.4 *Limitations Concluded*

Although the situation is complex, our research suggests weaknesses in the potential for legal expertise to play a role in environmental NGO advocacy. Beyond our own participants, the Environmental Funders Network suggests that legal skills are low down on the list of skills that environmental groups are looking for. And yet, paradoxically perhaps, ClientEarth was seen as the 'most effective' group in the same review.[34]

## 12.5 LEGAL EXPERTISE IN BREXIT-ENVIRONMENT ADVOCACY

Given these weaknesses in legal expertise for advocacy, it is perhaps surprising that the sector leant heavily on the legal expertise it did have during the Brexit process, and with some success. With their allies (in academia, government, parliament, practice), they identified and convinced government of the existence of the governance gap, and the need to fill it. They then engaged energetically with the detail of all parts of the proposed response to the Brexit-environment dilemma. Legal expertise was central to this work: to the basic governance gap and equivalence framings, and to the analysis of the legislative proposals and absences. It was never inevitable that Brexit would be seen as a legal, let alone a governance, problem.

Quite what NGO lawyers 'do' is relatively underexplored, relative to lawyers in other organisations.[35] We certainly found that legal experts in large environmental organisations do a lot of varied legal work. We are concerned specifically with using legal expertise in advocacy. Legal expertise can play the instrumental role raised above. Further, the persuasiveness of law, its use as a 'powerful bargaining tool' (Interviewee 6) comes through many of our interviews and is apparent in our analysis of Select Committee submissions by environmental groups:[36] law has 'a certain authority' or 'mystique'

[34] Florence Miller, Jon Cracknell and Harriet Williams, *What the Green Groups Said: Insights from the UK Environment Sector* (Environmental Funders Network, 2017).

[35] The literature on 'cause lawyering', e.g. Andrew Boon, 'Cause Lawyers and the Alternative Ethical Paradigm: Ideology and Transgression' (2004) 7(2) *Legal Ethics* 250-268; Boukalas, 'Politics As Legal Action / Lawyers As Political Actors: Towards a Reconceptualisation of Cause Lawyering', provides some insights into NGO lawyers. Korkea-aho in this volume builds on the cause lawyering literature. Lawyers in the third sector are represented in the research by Moorhead, Vaughan and Gordinho, *In-House Lawyers' Ethics: Institutional Logics, Legal Risk and the Tournament of Influence*, along with other in-house lawyers, although the purpose of that research is not to explore the distinctiveness of NGO lawyering.

[36] Abbot and Lee, *Environmental Groups and Legal Expertise: Shaping the Brexit Process*, chapter 5.

(Interviewee 10), it can be used 'to lay into some fairly sort of soft political stuff' (Interviewee 3).

We also saw law's less instrumental, more substantive role in understanding and shaping the world in the Brexit–environment debate.[37] For example, before arguing about how clean the air and water should be (not unimportant), the debate focused on institutionally enhancing the meaningfulness of existing commitments, and creating a process for developing those commitments. The Brexit–environment 'problem' was not a simple fact waiting to be revealed, but emerged in an active and constructive process. The insights of those with skills and experience in (EU) law contributed to framing that process,[38] and legal experts then further developed the detail of that position.

Two closely related features of the Brexit context contribute to explaining the insider focus of environmental groups at this time, as well as the apparent paradox of a heavy use of legal expertise in Brexit. First, political opportunities, the external factors that shape NGO strategies,[39] during the Brexit process made particular demands on, and provided particular openings for, insider legally expert advocacy. This, we argue, created a very specific set of what we call hybrid political-legal opportunities. Second, the post-referendum landscape created an important space for intensive collaborative activity between environmental NGOs; the pooling of legal (and other) expertise through collaboration was a core theme of our interviews.

### 12.5.1 *Political-Legal Opportunity and the Brexit Process*

A number of issues can influence the strategies that interest groups pursue to achieve social change; we discussed the internal factors of resources and culture and 'fit' above. Political opportunities are external factors that 'enhance or inhibit prospects for mobilization, for particular strategies of influence to be exercised, and for movements to affect mainstream institutional politics and policy'.[40] A body of work on legal opportunities grew out of the literature on political opportunities. Scholars of legal opportunity[41] explore the factors that influence a turn to the courts by NGOs, with Vanhala

37 Especially in our review of Select Committee submissions, see Abbot and Lee, *Environmental Groups and Legal Expertise: Shaping the Brexit Process*, chapter 5.

38 For framing, see Windsor, Chapter 3 in this volume.

39 Hilson, 'New Social Movements: The Role of Legal Opportunity'; Vanhala, 'Is Legal Mobilization for the Birds? Legal Opportunity Structures and Environmental Nongovernmental Organizations in the United Kingdom, France, Finland, and Italy'.

40 David S. Meyer and Debra C. Minkoff, 'Conceptualizing Political Opportunity' (2004) 82 *Social Forces* 1457–492, p. 1457–8.

41 Hilson, 'New Social Movements: The Role of Legal Opportunity'.

identifying the three dominant issues of legal stock (i.e. the body of substantive law), rules of standing before the court and rules on the costs of litigation.[42]

When looking specifically at the role of legal expertise in NGO *advocacy* rather than *litigation*, we need to expand both political and legal opportunity to a new hybrid political-legal opportunity. Hybrid political-legal opportunities are phenomena that enhance the role of law in lobbying for social and legal change. They reflect the space for law *and* or *in* politics. The Brexit process did, however, provide additional political-legal opportunities for environmental groups. Our case study revealed the importance of the technical and legal difficulty of Brexit, for example most recently in the environmental provisions in the EU-UK Trade and Cooperation Agreement, which provide important context for domestic legislation.[43] Coupled with the sheer volume and intensity of legislative and administrative activity, this enhances the receptivity of parliament, government and other powerholders to NGO advocacy. Leaving the EU was (and remains) a difficult technical and legal process.

Between the referendum on Brexit and the 2019 General Election (and its return of a large government majority), 'parliament became the forum for increasingly bitter policy battles, leaving the executive and legislature divided in a way most uncharacteristic of parliamentary systems'.[44] We touched upon these unusual Parliamentary logics above. The governing party generally has an at least comfortable majority in the UK Parliament. Between the two 'Brexit' general elections in June 2017 and December 2019, however, Theresa May followed by Boris Johnson led minority Conservative Governments.[45] In this period, perhaps obviously, the influence of Parliament increased, and Government was not able to push through its legislative agenda: 'the politics were such and the parliamentary arithmetic was such that it was possible to win stuff in parliament' (Interviewee 16). This created an

42 Vanhala, 'Is Legal Mobilization for the Birds? Legal Opportunity Structures and Environmental Nongovernmental Organizations in the United Kingdom, France, Finland, and Italy'.

43 See, e.g., Greener UK, *Initial Environmental Analysis of the EU-UK Trade and Cooperation Agreement* (2020), https://greeneruk.org/sites/default/files/download/2020-12/GreenerUK_initial_analysis_of_the_EU-UK_deal.pdf; Emily Lydgate et al., *Taking Stock of the New UK-EU Trade and Cooperation Agreement: Governance, State Subsidies and the Level Playing Field*, https://blogs.sussex.ac.uk/uktpo/publications/taking-stock-of-the-uk-eu-trade-and-cooperation-agreement-governance-state-subsidies-and-the-level-playing-field/.

44 Meg Russell, 'Brexit and Parliament: The Anatomy of a Perfect Storm' (2020) 73 *Parliamentary Affairs* 1, p.1.

45 For context, see Christopher Prosser, 'The Strange Death of Multi-Party Britain: The UK General Election of 2017' (2018) 41 *West European Politics* 1226–36.

incentive for environmental groups to attempt to influence outcomes by engaging with and convincing parliamentarians. Given the enormous amount of parliamentary activity around Brexit, the receptiveness of some in parliament to learn from environmental (including legal) experts, should not be underestimated. Engagement occurred in briefings and meetings with individual parliamentarians and their staff, but also in multiple Select Committee inquiries. Heavy environmental community engagement was designed to advance positions on both governance/equivalence and substantive environmental protection, and frequently relied on legal expertise to craft arguments.[46]

As we note above, following the 2017 election, the government's 'green Brexit' narrative led to an increasing engagement with the environmental NGO community by DEFRA. This agenda was enormous, and came on top of the major impact of Brexit on even 'business as usual' for DEFRA.[47] There had been a large reduction in DEFRA staff numbers during the 'austerity' period between 2010 and 2016,[48] and an enormous recruitment exercise in DEFRA followed the resurgence of interest in the environment. Civil servants (including the many new recruits) were under considerable pressure. Turnover in the civil service remained high through our case-study period; expertise and experience, 'not to mention institutional memory' was lost.[49]

So, as well as the political perceived need for engagement with environmental groups to pursue the green Brexit agenda, there was a real thirst at a technical level for engagement with trusted and knowledgeable interlocutors. The 'unprecedented' nature of 'access' (Interviewee 6) to DEFRA was acknowledged by many of our interviewees, in part a recognition of the needs of DEFRA during this time: 'they genuinely need the help and know that they want and aspire towards that challenge as well' (Interviewee 6).[50]

46 See the detailed discussion in Abbot and Lee, *Environmental Groups and Legal Expertise: Shaping the Brexit Process*, chapter 5.

47 The National Audit Office 2017–19 singled out DEFRA's 'unprecedented management challenge' both in managing exit through legislation and negotiation, and also in the need to prepare to provide new services and functions after Brexit; 'approximately 80% of Defra's areas of responsibility are currently framed by EU legislation'. See The National Audit Office, 'Departmental Overview, February 2019. Department for Environment, Food & Rural Affairs', www.nao.org.uk/wp-content/uploads/2019/02/Department-for-Environment-Food-Rural-Affairs.pdf, p. 5.

48 Lloyd, *The Brexit Effect: How Government Has Changed Since the EU Referendum*, p. 13.

49 Institute for Government, *Whitehall Monitor 2020*, www.instituteforgovernment.org.uk/sites/default/files/publications/whitehall-monitor-2020_0.pdf, p. 44.

50 Not all government departments were receptive to the NGO community. See Abbot and Lee, *Environmental Groups and Legal Expertise: Shaping the Brexit Process*, p. 63.

Even after the 2019 General Election, the environmental community continued with its trusted insider approach, and seems to have retained good access to both DEFRA and parliament, even though 'the politics of it also have shifted, so obviously now we've a Government with an eighty majority, and so there is a realisation that, you know, getting the bill amended will be very difficult' (Interviewee 2). Insider work was no less significant, just different. Even a parliament in which government has a large majority may enjoy some influence at different policy stages, in behind the scenes discussions and in government efforts to anticipate parliamentary reactions.[51] A changing approach to Parliament is recognised by Interviewee 9:

> we shouldn't expect really any amendments to be made frankly. What we need to do is to create an environment where we can persuade the Government of our arguments, if possible, and that can be much more about making sure that the debate is the one that you want to have, rather than the actual accuracy of every specific amendment.

This suggests a continued role for strong and focused insider lobbying of both parliament and government. This is clearly happening, notwithstanding the challenges of working remotely during the Covid-19 pandemic.

Political and legal opportunities only, however, provide a partial account of interest group activity. We can see a range of other factors at play during the Brexit referendum process itself, when most environmental groups were rather muted in their public stance on Brexit.[52] Parks, for example, points to limits placed on the political campaigning of NGOs by the Charities Commission, and one of our interviewees did suggest (unprompted) that some groups may have seen 'the Charities Commission as a hostile force ... there to silence them' (Interviewee 1). Parks suggests that there may also have been challenges in adopting a 'remain' position that, on the face of it at least, was difficult to align with earlier criticism of the EU environmental project. We did not hear this in our interviews, although it is perhaps something that many of us have felt at a personal level.[53] Both of these factors may reinforce a tendency towards insider activity, and a reliance on quiet expertise.

[51] Meg Russell and Philip Cowley, 'The Policy Power of the Westminster Parliament: The "Parliamentary State" and the Empirical Evidence' (2016) 29 *Governance* 121–37. (Note that they are consciously recalibrating the scholarship.)

[52] Not all environmental organisations were quiet during the referendum. Parks notes, in particular, the active stance of Greenpeace and Friends of the Earth during this time, both of whom argued in favour of a remain vote. Parks, 'All Quiet on the Brexit Front? UK Civil Society Before and After the UK's Referendum on Membership of the EU', p. 111.

[53] Chantal Mouffe, discussing the dismantling of socio-democratic advances, speaks of 'the paradoxical situation of having to defend various welfare state institutions that we criticised

Some of our interviewees reflected upon the particular challenges faced by membership groups during (and indeed after) the referendum. NGO members were divided over Brexit, and those 'organisations with members don't really want to talk to their members about Brexit, because their memberships tend to be split or/and bored with it' (Interviewee 8). Focusing on big picture and then detailed legislative and policy responses to the environmental losses of Brexit, rather than campaigning to remain, avoided antagonising members, and pointed towards a more 'insider' advocacy campaign, providing expertise, including legal expertise, to those with power.

### 12.5.2 *NGO Collaboration on Brexit*

Brexit provided another, different kind of opportunity; an opportunity for environmental groups to collaborate in their Brexit advocacy and pool legal resource. There are multiple challenges and rewards ('swings and roundabouts' (Interviewee 14)) of working in coalition.[54] It requires significant commitments and resources if it is to work, and may challenge individual NGO organisational identity, which could be buried within the collaboration, or even contradicted by some collaborative activities. Compromises and concessions are inevitable in building shared goals. And yet working in coalition can strengthen the hand of NGO lobbying or advocacy in multiple ways.

A strong theme running through our interviews was that Brexit provided NGOs with a somewhat unique opportunity to work together, in coalition, moving beyond the adoption of a shared position, to a way of working that involves 'the conscious exchange of resources and information, some division of labor, or the coordination of advocacy efforts with the aim of influencing policy outcomes.'[55]

During our case-study period, collaborative work on Brexit-environment was largely undertaken through Greener UK, a formal coalition of thirteen major environmental groups with a combined membership of over eight million. Established in 2016, the Greener UK coalition is 'united in the belief that

earlier for not being radical enough'. Chantal Mouffe, *For a Left Populism* (London: Verso, 2018), p. 36.

54 See for example Marie Hojnacki, 'Interest Groups' Decisions to Join Alliances or Work Alone' (1997) 41 *American Journal of Political Science* 61–87; Laila Sorurbakhsh, 'Interest Group Coalitions and Lobbying Environments: Toward a New Theoretical Perspective' (2016) 5 *Interest Groups Advocacy* 200–23; Jan Beyers and Iskander De Bruycker, 'Lobbying Makes (Strange) Bedfellows: Explaining the Formation and Composition of Lobbying Coalitions in EU Legislative Politics' (2018) 66 *Political Studies* 959–84.

55 Beyers and De Bruycker, 'Lobbying Makes (Strange) Bedfellows: Explaining the Formation and Composition of Lobbying Coalitions in EU Legislative Politics', 961.

leaving the EU is a pivotal moment to restore and enhance the UK's environment'.[56] Hosted by Green Alliance, a think tank that adopts a predominantly insider approach to influence, Greener UK has mainly used insider strategies, focusing almost all of its energy on the lobbying and Westminster and Whitehall, and has been agile in responding to the shifting political, legal and political-legal opportunities discussed in the previous section.

Collaboration through Greener UK and its influence on the Brexit process and the Environment Bill was acknowledged by many of our interviewees as a key feature of NGO advocacy during this time; 'an absolute bright side of what's going on' (Interviewee 15).[57] Although the sector is not new to collaboration,[58] Greener UK has, in the words of one interviewee 'been on a different scale and the appetite for it has been different and that's because of Brexit I think' (Interviewee 6).

Collaboration is much more likely (and certainly more likely to have impact) if member groups are able to pursue shared goals. The UK environmental NGO sector is largely consensual in that it shares an overarching commitment to further environmental protection and nature conservation. But it has, in the words of one of our interviewees, been 'vexed over the years by, sort of, badge waving' (Interviewee 13), with groups seeking to protect their organisational identity within a sector that is competing for income and influence. Brexit, however, 'involved the realisation of core political goals to which most interest groups were opposed'.[59] In light of the threat posed by the UK's withdrawal from the EU, an 'exceptional willingness to bury individual organisation interests' (Interviewee 3) led groups to work in coalition: 'It's an emotional issue as well as an intellectual one for people. I think there is a sense that most NGO people, they're on the same side on this really . . . So whatever differences they have, it was just totally fundamental . . . ' (Interviewee 3).

There was certainly alignment over governance and principles post-Brexit. We (and some of our interviewees) anticipated some tensions around the non-governance aspects of the Environment Bill (water, waste, nature, etc.), which appeared later in the process. However, although our research into these parts of the Bill was limited, our interview data indicates that collaboration

56 www.green-alliance.org.uk/greener_uk_coalition_info.php.

57 Greener UK also collaborated with other coalitions, including Wildlife and Countryside Link in a 'grand coalition' (Interviewee 6), most notably perhaps on the non-governance aspects of the Environment Bill, and business coalitions such as the Broadway Initiative and the Aldersgate Group. Greener UK also worked closely with academics (from law and other disciplines) on aspects of the Bill.

58 See for example the Wildlife and Countryside Link, www.wcl.org.uk/about.asp.

59 LSE GV314 Group, 'Brexit, Interest Groups and Changes to "Logic of Negotiation": A Research Note' (2020) *Interest Groups and Advocacy* 541–551, p. 543.

remained largely consensual. Two particular elements of the Bill came up most frequently as potentially problematic. When prioritising and agreeing specific environmental targets, 'It's quite difficult to keep the whole coalition on the same page' (Interviewee 3).[60] And reaching consensus on trade was difficult for different reasons, where some groups 'have got a clear interest or position, a history of working in this area, and see trade as something impinging on their objectives', whilst others do not (Interviewee 3).

The sharing of resources can be a valuable feature of collaborative working. Our interviewees recognised the ability to extend political reach through the sharing of political (and procedural) intelligence, and expertise in issues such as parliamentary communications. Importantly for the purposes of this chapter, collaboration through Greener UK has also provided group members with an opportunity to pool their legal expertise. Although probably not anticipated when Greener UK was set up, 'being able to draw on the pockets of expertise across the sector was very important … ' (Interviewee 8). This extends to making particular specialisations available to the collective. One interviewee, using trade law expertise as an example, suggested that 'there needs to be more sort of pooling of resources. Because there's no sense in [XXX] hiring trade experts and keeping them to themselves. So it should be an organisation like Greener UK then gets in someone like that' (Interviewee 15). There would, of course, be challenges inherent in this approach. In their drive to remain competitive, specialised and autonomous, any individual group would likely want to 'own' any expertise that they funded.

Within coalitions, legal expertise can be seen as a service or resource made available to the sector. In reflecting upon ClientEarth's rather unique position within the sector, one interviewee noted that 'we try not to be a service provider in that sense, because we do have our own strategy and we're not sort of taking instructions from others. And we can't do that but we do, you know … the work does serve the wider coalition' (unattributed). But legal expertise is more than a service. Importantly, we concluded that working in coalition not only pools legal expertise, but also deepens that expertise. Bringing experts together in a deliberative, discursive forum creates more than the sum of its parts, is more powerful than individual lawyers working independently. It enhances the richness of debate and discussion, potentially improving the quality of legal argument in advocacy: 'in order to get your head around a lot of this stuff, you need to have a sensible conversation with someone who's actually thought about it a bit and you can talk about it' (unattributed).

60 See Abbot and Lee, *Environmental Groups and Legal Expertise: Shaping the Brexit Process*, chapter 6.

In addition to improving the *output* of the coalition, providing a space for debate and deliberation can also give groups the confidence to make the argument in the first place: 'I think I would have been nervous if it was just one person and that's an advantage of pooling' (Interviewee 8).

The pooling of legal expertise through coalition working can also have a more indirect effect, we argue, on the space for law and legal expertise in advocacy. As we highlight above, organisational culture and identity can play an important role in shaping the strategic choices made by NGOs.[61] In the longer term, the deepening and broadening of legal expertise through collaboration may strengthen the way in which that expertise is valued by the sector; it

> raises the profile [of law] within organisations . . . [For] one lawyer to raise an issue in an organisation like XXX, it's a bit of an uphill struggle, because you've got a team of ten people working on species, a team of ten people working on fresh water, and then one lawyer, it's very difficult to actually drive the direction and agenda of an organisation like that. (Interviewee 15)

This may, with time, influence the culture and identity of groups and place legal expertise more at the forefront of NGO activity.

## 12.6 CONCLUSIONS

Legal expertise was heavily, and we suggest effectively, used in NGO advocacy around the UK's response to Brexit. Legal expertise is not more important than other forms of expertise, and we have some sympathy for concerns that law can overwhelm other ways of thinking about the world; indeed expertise generally can close down political space.[62] But legal expertise is certainly an important part of the story. Understanding both the detailed implications of law, and the overarching frameworks and institutions that govern outcomes, can provide a different way of seeing the world, in which some of the structures underpinning and enabling behaviours and actions become visible. Law and legal experts play a significant role in shaping the rules of the social and economic game, in determining the way things get done. Those with environmental

[61] E.g. Brian Doherty and Graeme A Hayes, 'Tactics and Strategic Action', in David A. Snow, Sarah Anne Soule, Hanspeter Kriesi and Holly J. McCammon (eds.), *The Wiley Blackwell Companion to Social Movements* (West Sussex: Wiley-Blackwell, 2018), p. 276; also see Vanhala, 'Coproducing the Endangered Polar Bear: Science, Climate Change, and Legal Mobilization'.

[62] Abbot and Lee, *Environmental Groups and Legal Expertise: Shaping the Brexit Process*, especially chapter 4.

objectives need to be part of this shaping, alongside the legal expertise of, for example, finance and industry.

Some may infer from our paradoxical conclusion that environmental NGOs both suffer from weaknesses in their approach to legal expertise, and yet were able to muster legal expertise when it really mattered, that there is nothing to worry about. However, we have two concerns on that front. First, the very broad mobilisation of lawyers from academia and practice around Brexit, generally and environmentally, contributed to the framing of Brexit as a 'legal' problem, bringing it not only to the attention of those with power in government and parliament, but also to the attention of those with power in environmental groups. This broader mobilisation will not always happen; Brexit was special. Second, the significance of the structural, architectural legal issues may on other occasions be overlooked by a community that is not reflecting on the contributions of legal experts at the highest level, so that legal experts are never called upon and their absence never noted.

# 13

# Bureaucrats in the Classroom? Epistemic Governance and the Expert Legal Scholar

Jan Klabbers

## 13.1 INTRODUCTION

We live by and through the stories we tell ourselves and each other about the world around us, and many of the stories we trust the most are those that are told to us by experts: doctors, engineers and economists, as well as people who have lived through events, who have experienced things. But storytelling comes at a price: our stories are vehicles for the exercise of power, however mundane and unspectacular. Power, as Foucault taught us, does not only come out of the barrel of a gun, but inheres in the ways our relations are structured. In those structures, in the capillaries of power, the stories we tell about ourselves and the world assume prominence: 'governance works by way of influencing other actors' beliefs and views of the way in which the social world is organized, the role and subject positions of actors, and the nature of ethical or valued goals of social change'.[1] And oftentimes the stories we tell take on a life of their own and influence the way governance, including global governance, is exercised.[2]

Possibly the best example of such a story, taking on a life of its own, is the story we tell ourselves about politics. Politics, we suggest, is all about power: politics is about 'who gets what, when and how', as Harold Lasswell famously put it in 1936.[3] The mantra (for that is what it is) is repeated in introductory

[1] Pertti Alasuutari and Ali Qadir, 'Epistemic Governance: An Approach to the Politics of Policy-making' (2014) 1 *European Journal of Cultural and Political Sociology* 67–84.

[2] See generally also Maarten Hajer, *Authoritative Governance: Policy-Making in the Age of Mediatization* (Oxford: Oxford University Press, 2009); Deborah D. Avant, Martha Finnemore and Susan K. Sell (eds.), *Who Governs the Globe?* (Cambridge: Cambridge University Press, 2010).

[3] An abridged version of his well-known article is reproduced in Harold D. Lasswell, *On Political Sociology* (Chicago IL: University of Chicago Press, 1977, Dwaine Marvick ed.), pp. 108–113.

classes to political science all over the world, influencing many generations of policy-makers and policy-advisers. And those policy-advisers cannot help but look at the world around them from precisely that perspective: the perspective that politics is about 'who gets what, when and how'. The claim has become a truism of the highest order, a self-fulfilling prophecy: it has become something we take for granted as knowledge about the world, and as something we would be ill-advised to ignore. Indeed, the policy adviser neglecting this basic idea about politics would probably fear for her job: it is too risky not to assume that politics is about who gets what, when and how – it is too risky to assume that other political actors are not out to increase their piece of the pie, whether absolutely or relatively. As a result, the claim that politics is about who gets what, when and how is no longer seen as intelligent shorthand, voicing an assumption that ought to be interrogated and verified or falsified, but has become its own truth. Politics is about who gets what, when and how, precisely because this is the story we have been telling ourselves for a long time.[4]

The stories emanating from experts matter, and research into the role of expertise in governance has become an accepted way of studying governance. Political scientists,[5] anthropologists,[6] accountants,[7] economists[8] and even lawyers,[9] publish about expert governance in one way or another. Among those, the lawyers, perhaps somewhat curiously, tend to write mostly about expert governance by others; rarely do they examine their own role as expert. The study of expert governance is engaged in from various perspectives, and it seems fair to suggest that conceptualisation has not yet fully developed. Thus, it remains an open question what exactly the word 'expert' refers to: is an expert someone who knows a lot about a particular topic and if

4 For a critique, see Jan Klabbers, 'On Responsible Global Governance', in Jan Klabbers, Maria Varaki and Guilherme Vasconcelos Vilaça (eds.), *Towards Responsible Global Governance* (Helsinki: University of Helsinki, 2018), pp. 7–30.

5 Erin Hannah, James Scott and Silke Trommer (eds.), *Expert Knowledge in Global Trade* (London: Routledge, 2016).

6 Marilyn Strathern (ed.), *Audit Cultures: Anthropological Studies in Accountability, Ethics and the Academy* (London: Routledge, 2000); Galit A. Sarfaty, *Values in Translation: Human Rights and the Culture of the World Bank* (Stanford CA: Stanford University Press, 2012).

7 Michael Power, *The Audit Society: Rituals of Verification* (Oxford: Oxford University Press, 1997).

8 Roger Koppl, *Expert Failure* (Cambridge: Cambridge University Press, 2018).

9 David Kennedy, *A World of Struggle: How Power, Law and Expertise Shape Global Political Economy* (Princeton NJ: Princeton University Press, 2016); Monika Ambrus et al. (eds.), *The Role of 'Experts' in International and European Decision-Making Processes: Advisors, Decision Makers or Irrelevant Actors?* (Cambridge: Cambridge University Press, 2014).

so, is that enough to be considered an expert? Is an expert someone who *claims* to know a lot and charges for his opinion? Is an expert best regarded as someone working for a governance institution, or can there be freelance experts?[10]

Likewise, governance by experts is not fully conceptualised either just yet, with considerable uncertainty existing around questions such as whether the result of work by experts not doing their job properly can still qualify as expertise governance. Even if we think that an economist deciding on a development project normally qualifies as an expert, and her work as expert governance, does this still apply in case of bribery, if she decides not solely or mostly on the basis of her expertise but instead largely on the basis of an inappropriate monetary incentive? And is it expert governance if the experts implement flawed instructions? Such questions are not merely academic: they go to the heart of the very notion of expert governance, for often enough, expert governance intersects with 'politics as usual'. Experts act on instructions (even if they may have considerable discretion); are expected to help implement a particular mandate. But what if the mandate is controversial and the instructions are flawed? It is tempting to blame the experts here, but those experts may have felt curtailed by their political instructions. And those instructions, in turn, may have been based on (in whole or in part) on expert advice. Either way, the political role of experts ought not to be underestimated, and this role plays out not just in more or less formal decision-making processes, but also – and this is less often explored – through epistemic governance. In what follows I will focus on the role of academic lawyers as experts, exercising authority in academia by epistemic means: though their writings and the classroom, and while engaging in specific tasks, such as editing a journal.[11] Needless to say, being an academic lawyer myself, my own activities are implicated, and part of what follows rests on stylised personal experiences and observations as well as, hopefully, a healthy dose of self-reflection.

10 See also Jan Klabbers, 'Conceptualizing Expert Accountability: Toward Virtue', in Alessandra Arcuri and Florin Coman-Kund (eds.), *Technocracy and Multilevel Governance; What Role for Accountability?* (Abingdon: Routledge, 2021), pp. 27–43.

11 I have elsewhere discussed other manifestations of epistemic authority, in particular with respect to the work of international organizations. See, e.g., Jan Klabbers, 'Notes on the Ideology of International Organizations Law: The International Organization for Migration, State-making, and the Market for Migration' (2019) 32 *Leiden Journal of International Law* 383–400; Jan Klabbers, 'The Normative Gap in International Organizations Law: The Case of the World Health Organization' (2019) 16 *International Organizations Law Review* 272–98.

## 13.2 EPISTEMIC GOVERNANCE AND THE LEGAL ACADEMY

Expert governance is an academic growth industry, and it has become commonplace to address the work of economists, engineers and medical doctors in these terms. By contrast, lawyers usually escape scrutiny, possibly because law is mostly hermeneutics, self-referential, autopoietic, without a corresponding counterpart in the non-legal world.[12] The validity of a legal norm depends on what other legal norms say, but does not depend on social factors such as compliance or enforcement. Perhaps as a result, legal experts are generally considered less influential in governance, and thus, perhaps, less worthy of attention as experts.

There is, to be sure, a strong tradition of studying and discussing legal ethics. This puts lawyers in a central position as experts of some sort, but stays within the hermeneutics of the law, so to speak. It addresses questions not of how lawyers govern the world, but rather how they relate to their clients, what sort of action is acceptable in the courtroom in order to defend a client or in order to launch a successful prosecution, or what behaviour becomes a judge. What is relevant here is not the governance effects of legal expertise, but the legal effects of expertise. The expertise rarely looks outside the law, but tends to stay within, discussing how lawyers relate to other lawyers or those with whom they are in a direct relationship (as barrister, prosecutor, counsel or judge), and does so typically in the form of codes of conduct for defence attorneys or judges, listing 'best practices', elements of prosecutorial discretion and related phenomena.[13] This strand of the literature is relatively well-developed, and this is what is generally considered to constitute the field of 'legal ethics',[14] with separate branches devoted to the ethics of judging[15] and the extent to which law is ethical or should conform to ethics.[16]

12 Gunther Teubner, *Law As an Autopoietic System* (Oxford: Blackwell, 1993).

13 See, e.g., with respect to international legal practice, Arman Sarvarian, *Professional Ethics at the International Bar* (Oxford: Oxford University Press, 2013); Michael Reisman and Christina Skinner, *Fraudulent Evidence before Public International Tribunals* (Cambridge: Cambridge University Press, 2014).

14 Leading studies include David Luban, *Lawyers and Justice: An Ethical Study* (Princeton NJ: Princeton University Press, 1988); Arthur Isak Applbaum, *The Morality of Roles in Public and Professional Life* (Princeton NJ: Princeton University Press, 1999); Gerald J. Postema, 'Moral Responsibility in Professional Ethics' (1980) 55 *New York University Law Review* 63–89.

15 See, e.g., Colin Farrelly and Lawrence B. Solum (eds.), *Virtue Jurisprudence* (New York: Palgrave Macmillan, 2008); Jonathan Soeharno, *The Integrity of the Judge: A Philosophical Inquiry* (Farnham: Ashgate, 2009); Iris van Domselaar, *The Fragility of Rightness* (doctoral thesis, University of Amsterdam, 2014); Jan Klabbers, 'Judging Inter-legality', in Jan Klabbers and Gianluigi Palombella (eds.), *The Challenge of Inter-legality* (Cambridge: Cambridge University Press, 2019), pp. 339–62.

16 For a fine recent collection, see Amalia Amaya and Ho Hock Lai (eds.), *Law, Virtue and Justice* (Oxford: Hart, 2013).

In addition, there is a body of literature on political ethics, or the ethics of being involved in politics in one way or another (perhaps one might speak of governance ethics). Much work is dedicated to the question whether elected or appointed office-holders can, in exercising their office, engage in the sort of activities they cannot engage in as private persons. Relevant questions here include whether one can lie and cheat for one's country,[17] and how to choose from among several questionable policy options – the well-known dirty hands problem, which can come in various manifestations.[18]

I have thus far suggested that lawyers are often excluded from scrutiny on the ground that their work is mostly hermeneutic in nature, rather than having a direct social relevance – lawyers are mostly seen to affect the social world through advising their clients: governments, criminal suspects, corporations, rather than directly and immediately. But if it is true to say that we live by and through our stories, then stories about the law should also be considered, for on the borderline between law and society (however conceptualised), lawyers too tell stories about the law, more specifically about how the law relates to the social world.[19] Thus, lawyers, domestic and international alike, talk of consent as the social factor creating binding law, for instance in the form of a social contract of some kind. Likewise, lawyers tend to think that contracts and treaties are ultimately based on a meeting of the minds, *do ut des* or similar constructions in the social world.[20] Lawyers are often keen to stress that there can be no right without a remedy, thus attaching a social consequence – the remedy – to the existence (*vel non*) of legal rights. Lawyers tend to think that when something bad happens, someone ought to be held accountable.[21] Lawyers working in a rationalist tradition, merely by doing so, engage with society and leave the hermeneutics of the law behind, for instance when

[17] Of great significance is the work of Dennis F. Thompson, *Political Ethics and Public Office* (Cambridge MA: Harvard University Press, 1987) and his *Restoring Responsibility: Ethics in Government, Business, and Healthcare* (Cambridge: Cambridge University Press, 2005).

[18] Some relevant writings are reproduced in Stuart Hampshire (ed.), *Public and Private Morality* (Cambridge: Cambridge University Press, 1978).

[19] This is realised to some extent, but not further explored in terms of epistemic governance, in Anthony T. Kronman, *The Lost Lawyer: Failing Ideals of the Legal Profession* (Cambridge MA: Harvard University Press, 1993). Instead, Kronman laments the disappearance of the lawyer-statesmen, who seems largely to have been displaced by the emergence of the lawyer as profit-seeking actor.

[20] For a discussion of treaties and their connection to the social world, see Jan Klabbers, *The Concept of Treaty in International Law* (The Hague: Kluwer, 1996).

[21] See generally Jan Klabbers, 'From Sources Doctrine to Responsibility? Reflections on the Private Lives of States', in Pierre d'Argent, Béatrice Bonafé and Jean Combacau (eds.), *Les limites du droit international: Essais en l'honneur de Joe Verhoeven* (Brussels: Bruylant, 2015), pp. 69–85.

assuming that actors are rational and are out to maximise their gain – a state of mind not unlike the one according to which politics is about who gets what, when and how. And lawyers are keen to emphasise that interpretation of legal texts should follow particular rules: the interpretation of texts, a hermeneutic exercise, comes to be seen to be influenced by rules (another hermeneutic twist) in order to do justice to social concerns, whether the intentions of the drafters or the outcome deemed most desirable.

And that brings us to stories about academic lawyers: how then do we, academic lawyers, engage in epistemic expert governance (to give it a name)? For these *topoi*, as Kratochwil would call them,[22] often form the basis of the way we think about concrete phenomena and help to reproduce hierarchy, as Duncan Kennedy might put it.[23] And that, in turn, brings us to legal academic ethics: how do we come up with, and reproduce, our stories about the law – how do academic lawyers, or legal scholars, engage in epistemic governance and how do they portray themselves as experts?

If academic ethics are discussed at all, such discussions usually focus on a handful of distinct topics, some in research,[24] some in teaching. A popular one to discuss, in particular since the competitive turn[25] in scholarship of the last few decades, is plagiarism. Traditionally, imitation may have been considered the sincerest form of flattery, but in a world where scholars are to compete with one another, plagiarism has become anathema. After all, the plagiarising scholar will benefit from his behaviour, at the expense not only of the plagiarised scholar, but of all others working in the same field and competing for the same scarce resources, such as publication in top journals, or research grants. This has spread so as to even include what has come to be known as 'self-plagiarism' which, far from marking a contradiction in terms, is considered cheating: one should not score too many goals with the same ball – one should not repeat one's research results across various publications. Again, this is no longer considered to be the expression of mere vanity or laziness, because milking one's research may lead to unfair competitive advantages on

[22] See Friedrich V. Kratochwil, *Rules, Norms, and Decisions: On the Conditions of Practical and Legal Reasoning in International Relations and Domestic Affairs* (Cambridge: Cambridge University Press, 1989).

[23] See Duncan Kennedy, 'Legal Education and the Reproduction of Hierarchy' (1982) 32 *Journal of Legal Education* 591–615.

[24] See, e.g., the *Guidelines of the Finnish Advisory Board on Research Integrity* 2012 (Helsinki: TENK, 2013), focusing on a handful of irresponsible practices such as fabrication of data or plagiarism, and setting up a sophisticated accountability procedure.

[25] On scholarly competition with respect to academic international law, see Jan Klabbers, 'On Epistemic Universalism and the Melancholy of International Law' (2018) 29 *European Journal of International Law* 1057–69.

the market for recognition and grants.[26] Another staple of ethical concern is the massive fabrication and manipulation of data, something that seems to afflict in particular social psychologists. In the Netherlands, this has resulted in several highly publicised scandals, with one prominent professor being forced out of the academy[27], and another having lost much of her credibility for having displayed a certain carelessness with data.[28]

Alternatively academic ethics focuses on classroom behaviour: such things as equal marking of exams, without taking the person of the student into account. This often entails anonymous marking, which seems to defy much of the original idea behind exams: if the exam is supposed to give the teacher insight into the strengths and weaknesses of the student – a task closely associated with education – then anonymity ends up being counterproductive. As with plagiarism, anonymous marking makes sense in a competitive environment, but owes little to classic ideas about learning and *Bildung*.[29]

And another staple of academic ethical discourse relates to taking classroom relations to a personal level, in particular involving male teachers and supervisors and female students or subordinates.[30] The power difference is such as to make people frown about such relationships, although one might also wonder what would be a better place to find a spouse than the workplace. Be that as it may, in some jurisdictions extracurricular relationships are taken as raising very serious ethical questions.

These are all fairly obvious ethical issues, but they hardly exhaust the matter, and may even deflect attention from other, equally serious issues. Moreover, they are hardly specifically related to legal academics. A framework for a further conversation on the topic, with particular reference to the legal academic,[31] could consist of three steps: a first step investigating how, and in what sort of capacity or role, legal academics exercise epistemic power. Second, to tie these various roles to specific ethical demands, and third,

[26] There is also a certain paradox here, in that scholars are often asked to write about themes they have addressed before, which comes close to being invited to reproduce earlier insights.

[27] www.nytimes.com/2013/04/28/magazine/diederik-stapels-audacious-academic-fraud.html.

[28] www.ad.nl/nieuws/hoogleraar-roos-vonk-berispt-om-onderzoek-vleeseters~afd987b0/.

[29] On those, see, e.g., Michael Oakeshott's nostalgic writings (and then realise that his was very early onset nostalgia; the papers collected here were largely written in the 1940s and 1950s): Michael Oakeshott, *The Voice of Liberal Learning* (Indianapolis IN: Liberty Fund, 2001, Timothy Fuller ed.).

[30] But not exclusively: one curious instance surfacing in 2018 involved a gay female professor allegedly harassing a gay male graduate student: www.nytimes.com/2018/08/13/nyregion/sexual-harassment-nyu-female-professor.html.

[31] For present purposes, it does not seem particularly relevant in which precise domain the lawyer is an expert: the issues singled out will apply across the board, to corporate lawyers and criminal procedure lawyers as well as to international lawyers and EU lawyers.

to discuss some specific instances – this is best done through illustrative stories demonstrating what can happen and how possibly to approach it. The focus on the legal academic is no doubt justified by the circumstance that this has been neglected. As I will suggest, academic ethics is neglected to begin with, and when discussed at all, it focuses on different issues altogether. In addition, I am not familiar with many explorations of the ethics of the legal academic – and those that exist tend to focus nigh-on exclusively on ethical duties, employing deontological perspectives.[32] By contrast, I draw some of the inspiration for what follows from the virtue tradition.

## 13.3 THE CAPILLARIES OF ACADEMIC POWER: BEGINNINGS OF A TAXONOMY

The most obvious way for legal academics to exercise power is as teachers in the classroom. Teaching is not a mechanistic exercise – it is not merely about conveying information in such a way that the vehicle providing the information is irrelevant. Instead, teachers engage with the literature or materials, most obviously so in the humanities and social sciences. Russia's annexation of the Crimea in 2014 can be discussed in class, but hardly in neutral terms: calling it an 'invasion' evokes different sentiments than calling it an 'intervention' or 'liberation'; calling it 'annexation' engenders different emotions than speaking of 'occupation' and displays a different understanding of the event; but all will have some effect. Telling the story involves conveying a view on the world, whether the teacher wants to or not. Likewise, it is impossible to address the building of a wall by Israel without simultaneously offering an evaluation: whether it is called 'wall' or 'fence' will evoke different responses. The only way out is to use a term of such high abstraction that it loses its descriptive force: one can speak of a 'structure' or 'edifice' perhaps, or the 'thing' that Israel built, but this will leave students wondering what kind of structure or edifice the thing under discussion is.[33] Effective teaching in law cannot be done without taking a stand, without embedding things in a broader worldview, and it is no coincidence that the best teachers, the most inspirational teachers, are precisely those who manage to convey a love for their topic – and this cannot be done by first sterilising it. Much the same

[32] See, e.g., Deborah L. Rhode, 'The Professional Ethics of Professors' (2006) 56 *Journal of Legal Education* 70–85.

[33] See, generally, Friedrich V. Kratochwil, *Praxis: On Acting and Knowing* (Cambridge: Cambridge University Press, 2018).

applies to the writing of textbooks and, to a lesser extent perhaps, research papers and monographs. In particular the reach of textbooks is often underestimated: the writer of a popular textbook reaches thousands of students every year, far more than even the most widely publicised research paper or monograph, and imprints on impressionable readers a view of the world.[34]

A second cluster of roles relates to academic supervision. Students on many levels of education (bachelor, master, doctoral) are required to write essays and papers, sometimes amounting to book-length dissertations, and are supposed to do this under supervision of senior faculty. The underlying idea is sound enough: it is borrowed from traditional guild practices in which pupils would learn the craft from those who had already mastered it, partly by observing, partly by practicing, partly by being corrected. Oakeshott once put it brilliantly when suggesting that the type of practical knowledge, such as is typically involved in academic writing, 'can neither be taught nor learned, but only imparted and acquired. It exists only in practice, and the only way to acquire it is by apprenticeship to a master – not because the master can teach it (he cannot), but because it can be acquired only by continuous contact with one who is perpetually practicing it'.[35] In today's university, this is no longer feasible: your average law professor may have to supervise a dozen or more doctoral students at any given moment, plus the annual cohort of bachelor's and master's students as well as, quite possibly, visiting students and researchers. The dynamics of supervision have, in other words, changed dramatically: what was a plausible concept modelled on apprenticeship until perhaps even the 1970s, is no longer quite as plausible. Either way, many ethical questions may arise. How to divide time between students? Should one pursue students in order to make them perform, or trust them to be self-motivated enough? What to do if they refuse to take reasonable well-intentioned advice? Should they be steered towards a particular position or conclusion? And what to do if it transpires that they are punching above their weight, and their work fails to meet minimum standards? In addition, a sense of responsibility towards one's students will have to be balanced by a sense of responsibility towards one's institution (which may get funded per successful graduate but may also need to maintain a scholarly reputation) and one's

34 No lesser authority than Keynes realised as much, dedicating his dissection of the Versailles Treaty a century ago to the 'formation of the general opinion of the future' which, he realized, depended on 'instruction and imagination'. See John Maynard Keynes, *The Economic Consequences of the Peace* (London: Macmillan, 1920), at pp. 279 and 278, respectively.

35 Michael Oakeshott, 'Rationalism in Politics', reproduced in Michael Oakeshott, *Rationalism in Politics and Other Essays* (London: Methuen, 1962), pp. 1–36, at 11.

discipline, which probably does not benefit from being flooded by too many below-par graduates.[36]

Another way in which legal academics may exercise power is in the broad process of evaluation. This can take the form of peer review of manuscripts, but may also take on different forms. It is increasingly common for faculty appointments to be outsourced to outside experts: typically colleagues from other universities, endowed with the task of making a reasoned evaluation of the relative merits and de-merits of the work of several short-listed applicants. Obviously, in such cases the outside expert potentially[37] wields a huge amount of power: his or her evaluation may end up being probative, may extend the career of one applicant at the expense of the careers of others. And increasingly academic experts are used for purposes of tenure review, promotion review, or probation review, discussing whether a particular colleague should be granted tenure (where tenure still exists), merits promotion to a higher rank, or whether he or she merits a continuation of a particular line of funding. And much the same applies to positions such as director of prestigious institutes: here too, often experts are consulted to verify whether the individual that is finally selected is actually considered good enough by colleagues from the field.[38]

A surprisingly time-consuming variation on this is the more abstract recommendation. It used to be the case that students wishing to pursue an LLM degree or wishing to pursue doctoral studies immediately upon graduation would need to present one or two academic recommendations – this was bad enough but, considering that it concerned starting academics, understandable enough. The practice has, however, hugely developed, and at the moment often entails that even people applying for professorial positions need to present recommendations, or at least provide the names of several possible referees. This is curious: if the applicant is widely known within the discipline (as one might legitimately expect when it comes to high-level appointments at prestigious institutions), then recommendations strike as rather unnecessary.

36 And so as to illustrate the power of framing, I could have also put this final point as helping to create possibilities for choice: a large number of graduates at various skills levels provides potential employers with a wealthy reservoir to choose from.

37 I write 'potentially' because it is not uncommon that selection is 'pre-cooked': a putative law school may have an internal candidate that it wants to appoint regardless of the outsider evaluation. The trouble is that, as evaluator, one often only realises this *ex post facto*: the good advice is neglected because the internal candidate turns out to be appointed. A more subtle variation is to frame the position's qualifications in such a manner that only one candidate – the desired candidate – meets them.

38 What causes this widespread outsourcing of decision-making is a story for another day; I would imagine it has a lot to do with abdicating and shifting responsibility.

If the candidate is not widely known, by contrast, then it typically means that she has not been very visible. This in turn may reflect the quality of their scholarship, perhaps to such an extent that they should not be considered eligible for a position at a prestigious institution – if the idea is to appoint on the basis of academic merit, then this is scarcely reconcilable with the need to ask for recommendations. Be that as it may, the referee wields considerable power: a jubilant recommendation may secure a candidate with research funding or a place in a post-graduate program; a lukewarm or hastily written recommendation may prevent this from happening.[39]

A further cluster of roles relates to academic decision-making: as journal editors, editors of book series and members of advisory boards to journal and book series. While some wield more power than others (some journals are run by single prominent editors, others are a more collegiate exercise), in all circumstances power is involved: the power of deciding whether an article or book gets published, and the power to decide in which form. More broadly, moreover, members of advisory boards in particular, while usually not much engaged in the day-to-day running of the journal or book series, nonetheless are implicated. Usually it concerns prominent scholars, and usually their name is used to add credibility and legitimacy to a particular journal or book series. The hierarchical structure of the academy strongly manifests itself here, and this places members of advisory boards in some position of responsibility, even if their everyday influence on what gets published and what does not, is usually rather minimal.

A more obvious and related position of power is that of the peer reviewer: typically again a more or less prominent scholar who is asked to evaluate whether a submission is fit for publication, whether it needs revision, or whether it is unacceptable. This is a task riddled with difficulties and temptations, and in the humanities (including legal scholarship) it may be wondered what sort of role it can play to begin with. Naturally peer review may help to separate the bad from the excellent scholarship, but one would hardly need peers to do so. Beyond this rough distinction, the temptation often looms large of accepting submissions that agree with one's own view of the world, and reject those that do not. The rationalist scholar may often (and from her own perspective, justifiably so) criticise a non-rationalist piece for want of a rigorous methodology; the critical scholar in turn may often (and again, from her perspective justifiably so) lament that a submitted rationalist article

39 This also suggests serious inflationary potential: any suggestion that the candidate is less than exceptionally brilliant and working on a scientific breakthrough involving a handful of paradigm shifts might be considered insufficient.

may be robust, but lacks any possible connection to the real world, and both may (again, from their respective perspectives justifiably so) criticise legal doctrinal work as being 'unscientific'[40] or 'art for art's sake'. In addition to all the regular human temptations (the peer may recognise the submission as the work of a competitor) and the curious difficulty involved in finding peers to review the work of leading scholars (they are leading and thus, literally, have no peers, except in a formal sense), in the humanities and the legal disciplines the problem is often not so much related to the quality of a piece per se, but to the premises on which it is based – if these are deemed unacceptable by a reviewer, then the reviewer may be tempted to discard the contribution altogether, even if on its own premises the piece may be exemplary.

Hence, great ethical discipline is demanded from the peer reviewer, but even then it is doubtful what peer review adds to the overall quality of scholarship. In the natural and life sciences (and quantitative social sciences) peer review plays a relatively clear role; in the humanities, its possible contribution is far more elusive – and there is a suspicion that peer review is engaged in mostly because models from the natural and life sciences are thoughtlessly imposed on other academic fields.

A final group of tasks is embedded in various formal decision-making roles. Academics are called upon to function as deans, associate deans or assistant deans. They are called upon to chair committees and working groups, or at least to be members of committees and working groups. Learned societies, such as the European Society of International Law or the International Law Association, are typically run by academics, and offer a platform for the exercise of power. A public endorsement of some kinds of research by the President of a learned society may be hugely influential, as are decisions on where to hold the next annual conference. Academics can exercise considerable influence over others as members of faculty appointment committees. The decisions may not only affect the internal workings of the institution concerned, but also radiate outward: given Harvard's reputation, newly appointed faculty at Harvard may increasingly be asked for policy consultancy, for example, and some law schools traditionally have close ties to governments.[41]

This enumeration will hardly be exhaustive of the matter. Legal academics may exercise power when appearing on television to discuss the legality (*vel non*) of certain kinds of political action, or when discussing the same in blogs; they may exercise influence as expert consultants writing on behalf of clients;

40 Note that this presumes a certain concept of 'science', which may itself be questionable.

41 In the Netherlands, this applies to Leiden; in Austria it might apply to Vienna.

they actually aim to exercise such influence when writing *amicus curiae* briefs. In some fields of law, the boundary between academic work and practice is porous: the same individuals who apply investment arbitration law tend to write about that branch of law, and chances are that the demands of practice and scholarship come to be entangled.

## 13.4 ACADEMIC ROLE RESPONSIBILITY

Having established that academic power can flow through a number of distinct and not always immediately self-evident capillaries, the next step is to investigate which demands go with which role, and to notice that sometimes, a professional role can entail several distinct, and possibly competing or downright conflicting ethical demands. Role responsibility as such is a difficult topic to treat, and can only briefly be sketched here. The basic idea is something like this: different social or professional roles come with different responsibilities, and behaviour that might be perfectly acceptable or unremarkable in everyday life may be suspect when done in particular roles or, conversely, activities that are prohibited in everyday morality may be justified in particular roles. One standard example of the former situation relates to the responsibility of the captain of a ship: ordinary passengers may leave a sinking ship behind (although possibly not while trampling on others), but the captain is expected to stay behind to supervise the orderly departure of the shipwrecked.[42] The captain leaving too early will be chided for departing from his or her role as captain. An example of the latter is that of the member of a jury in a criminal trial: unlike their neighbours, jurors are not allowed freely to discuss the ongoing proceedings or voice an opinion on the defendant's guilt or innocence. Even if not sequestered, they should respect the secrecy of the jury deliberations.[43]

The idea behind role responsibility, it has sometimes been suggested, has a long pedigree, and harks back to pre-Enlightenment centuries, when individuals knew their place in the social hierarchy, and would act accordingly.[44] The landlord and the peasant, the priest and the magistrate, all knew what was expected, and much the same even applied to the trader. In the latter case

42 The example derives from H. L. A. Hart, *Punishment and Responsibility: Essays in the Philosophy of Law* (Oxford: Oxford University Press, 1968), pp. 212–13.

43 The example is liberally adapted from Meir Dan-Cohen, 'Interpreting Official Speech', reproduced in his *Harmful Thoughts: Essays on Law, Self, and Morality* (Princeton NJ: Princeton University Press, 2002), pp. 246–63.

44 For a discussion on the general relevance of role and status, see Nicholas G. Onuf, *The Republican Legacy in International Thought* (Cambridge: Cambridge University Press, 1998).

though, this became untenable with the spread of markets: commercial contacts proved so irregular and random, that the earlier connection between market and ethics dissipated, and could never properly be replaced other than by standard market ideas related to efficiency and profitability.[45]

Still, the basic idea remains: already the different roles identified above which the legal academic can take on, may come with different responsibilities.[46] Thus, when the academic serves as editor of a journal, her responsibilities differ from those that are at play when she writes a textbook or sits on a faculty hiring committee. While it has plausibly been suggested that she cannot de-activate herself,[47] nonetheless it seems obvious enough that different roles come with different demands. The underlying individual will shine through of course: it would be implausible to suggest that the academic as journal editor dons an entirely different persona than the same academic as teacher, textbook writer, or faculty appointment member, if only because the individual concerned is the same, and will take her values along whether editing, writing or appointing.[48]

What complicates matters further is that the same individual will work within different parameters in different situations, and will have to align her own ideas and values with those of other interested actors or communities. As a journal editor, she will naturally want to attain or retain a high level of scholarship under her stewardship. The publisher, however, may wish to see the journal produced in timely fashion: sometimes lesser articles may have to be included. More pointedly perhaps, as a PhD supervisor the academic may well wish to maintain a proper standard. This may derive both from her own ambition to uphold certain levels of scholarship, but also from a sense of responsibility towards her discipline: if scholarship is not of a certain level, it should not be allowed to pass. Or then it may stem from a desire to bring out the best in a student, or all of the above. This desire to uphold certain standards, however, may in turn conflict with her employer's desire to produce as many PhDs as possible, especially in systems where university funding depends on quantifiable output. And it may conflict with her student's wishes to spend a limited amount of time working on a doctorate – and practice

45 The argument derives from Emile Durkheim, *Professional Ethics and Civic Morals*, 2nd ed. (London: Routledge, 1992, Cornelia Brookfield trans.).

46 Justin Oakley and Dean Cocking, *Virtue Ethics and Professional Roles* (Cambridge: Cambridge University Press, 2001).

47 Gerald A. Cohen, 'Beliefs and Rôles' (1966–67) 67 *Proceedings of the Aristotelian Society*, 17–29; Robert S. Downie, *Roles and Values: An Introduction to Social Ethics* (London: Methuen, 1971).

48 See similarly Alasdair MacIntyre, 'Social Structures and Their Threats to Moral Agency' (1999) 74 *Philosophy* 311–29.

suggests that students can often set themselves deadlines or targets that are not entirely realistic.

When it comes to faculty appointments, personal sympathies and their opposite may also come to play a role. Those sympathies can relate to the candidate's approach to the discipline: it is tempting when one considers oneself a rationalist scholar to prefer other rationalists being appointed, to the detriment of legal scholars of a more doctrinal or a more critical provenance. And creative arguments can be found to support this: perhaps an existing 'brand' would be strengthened by the appointment of further rationalist scholars. Or perhaps there is a siege mentality: if rationalists are still a minority, appointing another rationalist is an act of 'positive discrimination', which helps to 'level the playing field', and helps to balance the field as a whole, dominated as it is by doctrinal scholars.

Deans and associate deans may face variations on this issue, for instance when they need to decide where to concentrate resources – whether to create a new chair in contract law or in environmental law or European law. It is tempting for a dean with a background in European law to think that European law is under-appreciated generally and ought to be stimulated by a new faculty hire; it is equally tempting for such a dean to suggest that contract law may already be well-served. Plus, her own deanship has left a gap in the European law section; the former colleagues lack her quality, and thus a new appointment serves also in qualitative terms. Indeed, she may well come to think she owes it to her former colleagues to find a high-class replacement now that they will have to do without her.

## 13.5 THREE SCENARIOS (STYLISED)

Moral wisdom, the wisdom to do the right thing in the right circumstances, cannot easily be transmitted in the form of rules. If codes and guidelines are unlikely to do the trick, perhaps a better approach is to focus on stories about people who have been in similar situations and have managed to find a reasonable way out or, perhaps, not found a decent way out. Such stories can be fictional,[49] or they can be more or less stylised versions derived from real life experiences – often referred to as studying (or positing) exemplars. The point of exemplars is not to follow the exemplar's or example's model in all cases.[50] After all, the context may be radically different, and what worked

49 An example is Martha C. Nussbaum, *Poetic Justice: The Literary Imagination and Public Life* (Boston: Beacon Press, 1995).

50 Amalia Amaya, 'Exemplarism and Judicial Virtue' (2013) 25 *Law & Literature* 428–45.

in one setting may not work nearly as well – or not at all – in another setting. The point of exemplars is not that they be slavishly followed, but to serve as sources of inspiration: the way the exemplar approached the matter may well prove instructive. While usually the notion of exemplars is construed as connected to good examples,[51] there seems to be no inherent or structural reason for doing so. Or rather, there is no reason to exclude less than felicitous behaviour from scrutiny, although the label 'exemplar' might not be the most appropriate.[52] In fact, it may be highly instructive to draw attention to wrongdoing, to situations where behaviour was irresponsible rather than responsible. In what follows I will discuss three scenarios, best seen as attempts to think through what the ethical characteristics of the situation are, and as attempts to explore possible ways of dealing with the issue. The first scenario involves a textbook writer, with the story being anonymised to protect the lead character's identity. The point is, after all, merely to flesh out the ethical side of textbook writing. The second scenario is a stylised rendition of a dilemma that may come to plague the members of the advisory board of a journal. And the third scenario relates to faculty administration, more in particular the hiring of a new colleague.

### 13.5.1 *Scenario 1: The Putative Textbook*

About a decade ago a leading publishing house asked me to evaluate a manuscript for an introductory textbook on public international law with a view to possible publication. The author had spent a number of years in practice and had some six years earlier decided to move to the academy, and it was clear from his descriptions of his former area of practice that he knew that part of the law really well, and could explain it lucidly. More problematic however were the general parts. These were, understandably perhaps, strongly influenced by his practical experience, and thus showed the limits thereof: someone with a background in, say, international environmental law will approach issues of state responsibility differently from someone with a background in trade law, or international criminal law. This affected the

[51] Zagzebski, in what is probably the leading monograph, identifies three kinds of exemplars: the saint, the hero and the sage. See Linda Zagzebski, *Exemplarist Moral Theory* (Oxford: Oxford University Press, 2017).

[52] Traditionally exemplars have been deemed worthy of admiration, as the oft-used synonym 'paragon' also suggests. See, e.g., Lawrence Blum, 'Moral Exemplars: Reflections on Schindler, the Trocmés, and Others', reproduced in his *Moral Perception and Particularity* (Cambridge: Cambridge University Press, 1994), pp. 65–97.

textbook in that the general parts of international law were often discussed through a particular sub-disciplinary prism, and that sometimes made for awkward reading.

Far more problematic still was the theoretical chapter. Like most introductory textbooks, this too started with a theoretical section, and as is often the case, the author mostly went through the motions. But even then, there are different ways of going through the motions. It quickly transpired that the author had not actually been reading the authors he discussed in any serious manner: he had perhaps looked at an article or two by his protagonists (note that 'theory' is inevitably be discussed through a focus on certain individuals: one does not discuss critical theory, but the writings of Koskenniemi or Kennedy; one does not discuss feminist theory, but the writings of Charlesworth and Chinkin), and had maybe read a few more pieces about his protagonists, but it was painfully obvious that he was really unfamiliar with some of the main theoretical works in the discipline, and this affected his chapter on theory. In particular since theory aims to make sense of the discipline at large (or large chunks thereof), the poverty of the theory chapter, in conjunction with the particular perspective colouring much of the general part of international law, rendered the manuscript unsuitable as a textbook. It is not so much that it was bad (although the theory chapter actually was not good), but mostly because the manuscript sent the wrong message to students. It sent the message that theory is a bit superfluous: at best the icing on the cake or an embellishment – an attitude which makes a mockery of academic work and does students a disservice, for how else will they come to understand the object of their study but through some theoretical orientation? The author displayed a somewhat cavalier attitude to scholarship, and that is not suitable in an academic work, especially not in an introductory textbook.

One peculiar circumstance I needed to come to terms with was that I was writing an introductory textbook at the same time and, as it happens, for the same publisher. So naturally I needed to look in the mirror: was my negative appraisal influenced by my desire to get rid of a competitor? Was I about to dismiss the manuscript on improper grounds? In the end, I doubt that this was the case. I like to think that I would have given a positive appraisal even if the manuscript would have endorsed a world view different from mine. It is not that the author had a different outlook; it is rather that I was unimpressed by his attitude and the resulting quality of some of the work, and thought that his relative lack of academic experience shone through. I was not particularly worried about the competition: few responsible teachers, I thought, would prescribe this book to their students.[53]

The point to remember is that the textbook writer carries great responsibility: his or her book is used to inculcate knowledge, but, more importantly, also installs frames of thinking and epistemic truisms in future policy-makers.[54] Thus regarded, the introductory textbook is the most important work of scholarship imaginable (short of the few works perhaps that are truly paradigm shifting), and an argument could be made that such textbooks ideally are written by scholars with considerable academic experience who have digested many different materials and have taken the time to develop their own views on the world and their discipline. It also helps if those scholars are themselves active researchers – textbooks written by individuals who do their research in different disciplines (or who refrain from doing original research at all) eventually can do little more than regurgitate standard wisdom and standard tropes. If it is true that we learn best through stories and narratives[55], then such textbooks, much like the manuscript I evaluated, tend to suffer from the absence of a convincing narrative, no matter how technically sound they are.

### 13.5.2 *Scenario 2: The Advisory Board Member*

Most of the non-student edited journals in the field of law have an advisory board, or a board of honorary editors. In theory, this serves to assist the editorial board, perhaps by proposing themes for special issues, perhaps to help in reviewing manuscripts, or perhaps to direct junior scholars to the journal.[56] And to be sure, this happens. Advisory board members are sometimes called upon to help review submissions; they are sometimes called upon to propose themes for a special issue, and they will sometimes direct junior scholars to the journal. An additional function however, and one not to be taken lightly, is

53 Update: the manuscript was eventually published by a different publisher, and does not seem to feature in many law schools as compulsory reading – although a quick google search suggests that it is sometimes mentioned as one of two handfuls of 'suggested readings' in public international law.

54 On the relevance of framing, see also Matthew Windsor's contribution elsewhere in this volume.

55 The point is emphatically made in Maggie Berg and Barbara K. Seeber, *The Slow Professor: Challenging the Culture of Speed in the Academy* (Toronto: University of Toronto Press, 2016).

56 There is, in a sense, a constant tension between the academic demands and those (real or imaginary) of a commercial publisher. This became painfully clear when the publisher of the venerable *European Law Journal*, in early 2020, decided to appoint new editors-in-chief without so much as consulting the editorial and advisory boards, which consequently resigned. The former editors-in-chief explain the reasons for resignation in an open letter, https://verfassungsblog.de/what-a-journal-makes-as-we-say-goodbye-to-the-european-law-journal/.

commercial: journals are commodities, published and marketed by publishing houses, and a journal is thought to gain in credibility if it can point out that the most prominent scholars in the discipline are members of its advisory board. The advisory board therewith becomes something of a blurb: buy this product, and quality is guaranteed. Except it is not – not always, at any rate.

In most cases, things just proceed. The average journal will publish some good pieces on occasion, some mediocre or indifferent ones, and some bad ones, regardless of the composition of its advisory board. But sometimes things do not just proceed. What to do, for instance, when a journal affiliated with a particular state becomes a vehicle for the politics espoused by that state? In a sense, there is nothing new or unexpected about this: the *American Journal of International Law* often ends up publishing pieces endorsing the position of the US government and has done so ever since it was first published in 1906. Indeed, in an important sense, it could hardly be otherwise: there is no such thing as the 'view from nowhere', as Anthea Roberts has so effectively suggested.[57]

But things become problematic when the journal in question endorses a country's foreign policies and in doing so shuns the regular academic standards, in various ways. It may systematically refuse pieces critical of said government; it may accept sloppy works (and do so systematically)[58] endorsing the government's point of view: pieces without proper referencing, or even containing downright lies and fabrications. If this happens, the prominent scholar serving on the advisory board faces a dilemma: realising that her name helps to give the journal academic credibility, she becomes complicit in endorsing that particular government's views on the world. So what to do?

What most often seems to happen is that the prominent scholar just lets things slip and cannot be bothered. Making a fuss is just too complicated; it would mean a few hours spent in awkward discussion or filled with awkward thoughts, and mark a distraction from scholarly pursuits. It is not so much that there are material interests at stake, as membership of advisory boards usually goes unremunerated. The most one gains is a free subscription to the journal concerned, in conjunction perhaps with some form of academic recognition: the more memberships of advisory boards our prominent scholar collects, the more prominent she is.

57 Anthea Roberts, *Is International Law International?* (Oxford: Oxford University Press, 2017).

58 In the industry that scholarship has become it can happen that sometimes a flawed product is produced without immediately being recognised. This is unfortunate, but not cause for much uproar. The systematic use of a journal as a vehicle for partisan views, not meeting basic standards of scholarship, is however a far greater concern.

Alternatively, our prominent scholar may take her advisory role seriously (bearing academic standards in mind), and propose that the journal publishes some articles critical of the position of the government concerned, for example in the form of a special section; she might even offer to work as guest editor for such a critical section, something which, given her prominence, ought to be very attractive to the journal. This may call the journal's bluff: if it is unwilling to go along, then this refusal suggests it is not overly interested in academic values. And if that is the case, if the prominent scholar proves unable to change the attitude of the journal from within, then she might consider terminating her affiliation with the journal, all the more so as the costs of doing so are negligible. Perhaps a young scholar would need the accolades (unlikely as it is that these will be bestowed on junior faculty), but the prominent scholar has nothing to lose, except her credibility when staying affiliated with a journal that so obviously serves as a vehicle for a particular government. And things are considerably worse if the government concerned is known for its disrespect of the rule of law, for its flagrant violation of human rights, its disrespect for democracy, and the violence with which it stifles the opposition.

### 13.5.3 *Scenario 3: The Faculty Appointment Committee*

When reviewing other people's work, it makes sense that there are some rules in existence relating to conflicts of interests, all the more so when these are predicated on actually existing or plausible conflicts of interests. Thus, for purposes of grant application reviews, one should usually indicate if one is a relative of an applicant, a close personal friend, or has closely worked with him or her in the recent past or is currently involved in some common project. All this makes sense against the background of the idea that most applicants will not be personal relatives of the reviewer, so that the ones who are, will not be unduly advantaged. And a second background factor to take into account is the availability of expertise: typically, with grant applications or even peer review, several reviewers with knowledge of the field will be involved, so as to evaluate the status of the proposed 'principal investigator' in case of a grant application, or the quality of the work in light of the state of the art within the discipline. All this is par for the course, and perfectly sensible. Thus, for purposes of peer review of manuscripts, or reviewing grant applications, the reviewer may have to recuse herself if the paper is written by a colleague from the same department, or if the grant is being applied by a former doctoral student.

The same logic cannot, however, immediately be applied to faculty appointments, largely because the setting is different. Chances are that for any advertised position, persons within the discipline will personally know many of the applicants, and may have supervised the doctoral works of several of them. In such circumstances, the logic is radically different. Where it may have made sense to exclude PhD supervisors at a time when a professor had no more than two or three supervisees during his entire career, these days the logic is different: it is difficult to play favourites if there are a large number of them. In addition, there is the problem of expertise: appoint a new colleague in European law presupposes sufficient expertise in the discipline to decide which of the candidates is a good European law academic, and distinguish these form candidates who may have a good-looking CV but are eventually mediocre scholars. In most law schools, it would be unthinkable to decide on the appointment of a new European law professor without involving the current teaching staff in European law; in most law schools it would be unthinkable to appoint a new professor in administrative law without involving the current teaching staff in administrative law, and for the good reason that one cannot evaluate expertise by merely looking at someone's curriculum vitae. This is an administrative conceit which has long been in the making (preceded by requests to evaluate teaching skills on the sole basis of documentation), but which is eventually disastrous: it will reward those who can produce a handsome portfolio over those who are actually good at research and teaching.

A more general point, moreover, to consider is that fairness or even-handedness should apply in different directions. Obviously (and this seems to be the basis for most exclusionary rules), fairness should be done to those who apply to the position: one should not treat some candidates more favourable than others. But there are other persons and groups with something at stake. Future colleagues need to be treated fairly as well: whoever will be hired should be acceptable to those with whom she will most closely need to work (both on a personal level and in terms of respect for their scholarship), and should not be forced on a team.[59] And then there are the students to consider: the brilliant scholar who has no time for her students may not represent the best possible appointment.

The thing for faculty appointment committees to consider then is not to insist on antiquated or inappropriately borrowed rules on conflicts of interests: these address real concerns in peer review and grant application, but not in faculty appointments. And such rules as are being applied should not serve as

[59] This can easily be abused, which may be why it is easily overlooked, especially by administrators who present themselves as 'neutral' and 'non-partisan'.

excuses for being partisan. If the rule says that one should not sit in committee when having co-edited a book with a candidate during the most recent five years, then having co-edited something with a candidate six years ago might still be a good reason to recuse oneself. Faculty appointments do not exist, after all, to help friends to positions: the least one should expect is that the committee and its members seriously investigate what the faculty's needs are in terms of substantive coverage, and which of the candidates has a strong academic record and would fit well into the currently existing team.

## 13.6 CONCLUDING REMARKS

Power, as they say, corrupts, and absolute power corrupts absolutely. So it is no surprise that wherever power is exercised, somehow questions will arise as to how this power should be exercised: what are proper, and what are not so proper, exercises of power. And for this power, it does not seem to matter much whether the power is exercised through regular decision-making channels by persons authorised to do so, or whether the power exercised is of the epistemic kind, emanating from for instance religious leaders, opinion makers or 'influencers', newspaper editors or academic experts, including legal academic experts. The point to note though is that power, even power in international affairs, can be exercised in all sorts of ways.

But there is more to politics than the exercise of power; there is more to politics than Lasswell's 'who gets what, when and how'. Hannah Arendt famously suggested politics entails an obligation to take care of our common world, and related notions have been suggested by thinkers such as Avishai Margalit, advocating a 'negative politics' in order to avoid humiliating people,[60] or Raimond Gaita, endorsing love and goodness and preciousness as central political concepts,[61] or Iris Marion Young, noting that all of us can do good in our everyday life, even as consumers.[62] This is also affecting academics in their capacity as academics: they are members of an academic community, and thus might be called upon to help take care of their community, no matter how competitive the academic environment has become.[63]

60 Avishai Margalit, *The Decent Society* (Cambridge MA: Harvard University Press, 1996, Naomi Goldblum trans.); Avishai Margalit, *The Ethics of Memory* (Cambridge MA: Harvard University Press, 2002).

61 Raimond Gaita, *A Common Humanity: Thinking about Love and Truth and Justice*, 2nd ed. (Abingdon: Routledge, 2000).

62 Iris Marion Young, *Responsibility for Justice* (Oxford: Oxford University Press, 2011).

63 Klabbers, 'On Epistemic Universalism'.

This entails responding to requests for peer review,[64] participating in seminars and discussion, commenting on drafts written by colleagues and a degree of solidarity with one's closest colleagues. Not all of this can be measured and find a place in the curriculum vitae, but that hardly means it is not important – quite the opposite perhaps.[65]

More generally, epistemic governance demands epistemic virtue.[66] To some extent this is obvious: scholarship produced by women is not to be downplayed as 'female intuition', as opposed to hard facts; scholarship produced by individuals from minorities should not be downplayed as ever so many exercises of identity politics. But it goes deeper than this and involves other virtues as well, specifically intellectual virtues but also such virtues as civil courage or humility. For otherwise, the academic risks becoming a bureaucrat in the classroom.

64 Reportedly, some universities prohibit their staff from engaging in peer review during their working hours, which is obnoxious on various levels: it prevents them from serving their academic community, and it suggests that academics keep official hours to begin with.

65 Commenting on the work of colleagues and younger scholars falls into this category: immensely important, but difficult to quantify. Then again, as the poet said, 'Nothing measurable matters'.

66 Very helpful on this point is Miranda Fricker, *Epistemic Injustice: Power and the Ethics of Knowing* (Oxford: Oxford University Press, 2007).

# 14

# *Verfassungsblog*, Legal Expertise and Why Europe's 'Computer Is Not Working As It Should'

Maximilian Steinbeis with the Editors

A large part of contemporary political debate takes place on social media. In these debates, legal expertise (or the lack of it) matters. Take for instance Twitter. Many authoritative legal experts have established a strong presence on Twitter. In the context of EU policy-making, in addition to academics, one example would be Jean-Claude Piris, the former Director General of the Council Legal Service.[1] By the end of January 2021, he had tweeted more than 8,400 times and was followed by more than 14,300 persons. Twitter is used by persons who have built a professional reputation, for example in the EU institutions to reach a broader audience, while given its unmediated and low key accessibility it also serves as a platform of access for less reputable persons with a lack of a comparable track record. At the same time, the joint editor-in-chief of *I.CON* Joseph Weiler has cautioned against blogs and Twitter, describing blogs – together with Martti Koskenniemi – as 'second-rate' and 'hamburger-size' scholarship.[2]

Our interest in the involvement of legal expertise in these debates and the way in which lawyers use various online platforms to appear as legal experts stems not only from the transnational context in which we work, but also from our national background. In Finland, constitutional law experts interpreting the broad principles and provisions of the Finnish Constitution have at times prevented comprehensive legislative reforms ranking high on the government's list of priorities. This power transfer to non-elected constitutional law experts has in recent years provoked a critical debate among politicians, academics and the general

[1] On his Twitter account, Piris describes himself as 'Citizen of the world. European. French. Consultant EU law/internat law. DG EU Council's Legal Service (1988–2010). Hon. Conseiller d'Etat, former diplomat at UN', https://twitter.com/piris_jc.

[2] Antoine Duval, 'Publish (Tweets and Blogs) or Perish? Legal Academia in Times of Social Media' (2018) 23 *Tilburg Law Review* 91 at fn. 99.

public.[3] Much of this constitutional debate has taken place on social media: on Twitter and on the blog of the Finnish constitutional law society, *Perustuslakiblogi*.[4] Another debate has identified constitutional law as a masculine field pointing out the strict control of access to expert positions and the emergence of female constitutional law experts as a very recent phenomenon.[5] What makes a (constitutional law) expert, and what effect do new platforms have on access to expert positions and expertise? Or what is the difference between edited blogs or such online platforms and Twitter, where anyone can define themselves as 'legal experts' and join the debate?

This chapter discusses the question of legal expertise behind blogs and other social media forums and their policy impact through the example of *Verfassungsblog*. Established in 2009, the platform provides a journalistic and academic forum of debate on topical events and developments in constitutional law and politics in Germany, the emerging European constitutional space and internationally. The blog was initially created as an intersection between academia and the political public community, to engage and encourage debates, not to present academic research results.

The demand for scientific expertise is high, particularly on topical judicial decisions or legislative proposals.[6] In less than ten years, *Verfassungsblog* has become a key platform with nearly 2,000 authors. Its weekly editorial now goes out to more than 9,000 subscribers worldwide. From September to December 2020, *Verfassungsblog* also hosted a podcast with the German Bar Association (Deutscher Anwaltsverein), 'We Need to Talk about the Rule of Law'.

In this chapter Maximilian Steinbeis, the founder and editor of *Verfassungsblog*, provides an account of how legal expertise is created and fed into the policy-making process through a legal blog platform and how this new form of legal expertise compares to more traditional forms of legal expertise already established in the policy-making process. Is legal expertise in social media merely an academic (ivory tower type) exercise or does it have a societal impact? Can (and should) it influence actual policy outcomes? The

3 Maija Dahlberg, 'Kohti kokonaisvaltaisempaa käsitystä perustuslain tulkinnasta – perustuslakikontrollin läpinäkyvyys ja legitiimiys Suomessa', *Perustuslakiblogi*, 21 December 2020, https://perustuslakiblogi.wordpress.com/2020/12/21/maija-dahlberg-kohti-kokonaisvaltaisempaa-kasitysta-perustuslain-tulkinnasta-perustuslakikontrollin-lapinakyvyys-ja-legitiimiys-suomessa/.

4 *Perustuslakiblogi*, https://perustuslakiblogi.wordpress.com.

5 Is constitutional law for men only? Interviewing docent, university lecturer Liisa Nieminen, 'Portraying the Invisible Professionals of Law' blog, 18 January 2021, https://blogs.helsinki.fi/portrayingtheinvisiblelawyers/.

6 Astrid Herbold, 'Bloggende Wissenschaftler- Kurz und persönlich', *Tagesspiegel*, 19 February 2015, www.tagesspiegel.de/wissen/bloggende-wissenschaftler-kurz-und-persoenlich/11396556-all.html.

chapter builds on a discussion with the editors that has been lightly edited afterwards.[7] In conclusion, the editors reflect on the importance of including in this collection a chapter on legal expertise in topical societal debates based on internet platforms and social media.

***

**Tell us about your professional background and education.**
I am a lawyer by training and a journalist by profession. I studied law in Munich in the early 1990s. After my Second State Exam, I went to Karlsruhe to start covering the Federal Court of Justice and the Federal Constitutional Court jurisdiction as a freelancer for a range of regional papers. This was the afterglow of the golden era of newspaper publishing, and I slipped into this career at the very last moment, as the doors were already closing. I was in Karlsruhe only a couple of months when a position opened for a legal editor at *Handelsblatt*, a large German daily newspaper focusing on economics and business. I applied for that position, got the job and stayed for ten years. There, I learned the trade and became a 'proper' journalist and experienced all the difficulties and successes of the journalistic profession – particularly the downs in terms of the decline of newspaper publishing. Half a year after I started at *Handelsblatt* the first wave of termination of employment went through the newsroom. I was luckily spared. After some years, I moved to Berlin to work as a political correspondent, and in 2009 I decided to quit. I was fed up with both the job itself and the depressive and cynical mood that was palpable in the newsroom all the time. I started working as a freelance writer and writing a book. As a side occupation I launched a blog about my favourite field of covering, which was constitutional law. This was at the time a rather obscure and nerdy beat for a journalist, very much a special interest. For the first couple of weeks I dabbled around and tried various ideas. Soon I noticed that there was a public demand for that kind of writing. This was the time when the conflict between the German Federal Constitutional Court and the European Court of Justice was at its first peak after the Lisbon Treaty in 2009. I started writing about that conflict on *Verfassungsblog*, trying to get European law academics to write blog posts as well. There was much reluctance within German academia to use blogs as a new publishing format. *Verfassungsblog* only started to turn into a platform for moderated academic discussion after

7 The discussion was conducted on Zoom on 1 December 2020, with transcriptions provided by Anna van der Velde.

I teamed up with Christoph Möllers and Alexandra Kemmerer at the *Wissenschaftskolleg* in 2011.

Alexandra Kemmerer got in touch with me because they had set up the research network called 'Law in Context', and were thinking of establishing a blog. They wanted to talk to me about how this could be done. I basically told them: 'Look, what you are trying to do is exactly what I am trying to do, so why don't you just use what I already have.' This is what we did and it turned out to be a rather successful move. After people saw a scholar as established as Christoph Möllers back this project, many lost their fear of compromising themselves if they make use of a blog platform for publishing. *Wissenschaftskolleg* is a very respected institution in Germany, and I guess all over the world, and this definitely helped a lot. This was the start of *Verfassungsblog* as a discourse platform. We also developed a new format, which we called online symposia, a series of blog posts revolving around a central thesis or a research question. The symposia format is a very efficient and fast way of having a scholarly debate about interesting questions. We collaborated with Armin von Bogdandy at the Max Planck Institute of International and Comparative Public Law in Heidelberg. At the time, he and his team had developed the idea of 'Reverse Solange', which had also to do with this conflict between Karlsruhe and Luxemburg. This idea of Reverse Solange was a very innovative way of conceptualising the tension between the two courts, and we launched a debate about this in a short time frame. Online symposia were a success too, and basically that is what I have been doing ever since.

**What is your relationship with legal scholarship? Do you see yourself as a legal scholar or a journalist?**

I am a journalist, but I always stayed in touch with legal academia. I am kind of like a runaway academic myself. Part of me always wanted to pursue an academic career, write a doctoral thesis and try becoming a law professor. In the early 1990s, the Ludwig-Maximilian University in Munich, where I studied, was a great place in many respects but also – a rigid, conservative place where authority played a huge role. What made matters worse was that I ended up with a doctoral thesis project on the history of German idealist legal philosophy, which was the wrong topic for me. After an unhappy year and a half, I dropped the whole project and ran away into what then appeared as the golden future of journalism. That was that. So, with half of my heart I am within legal scholarship and with the other half outside of academia. This is where I find myself and have always done.

**Is the blog more oriented towards academics or practitioners?**

We view ourselves as an interface between the academic and the political sphere. What we are trying to do is to provide access for the political public to the academic, scholarly expertise of legal scholars and vice versa. This works both ways, so we do not see ourselves as a purely expert discourse with academics talking to other academics. We always have in mind the impact that our activities have on the public discourse at large. Our authors have in most cases an academic background, as opposed to coming from legal practice. We have several lawyers and judges among our authors, but not that many, and it is certainly not the focus of what we are doing.

**How do you define your audience? Was the blog intended for a German audience or more broadly for an international audience?**

In a way both. At the time I perceived the German discourse particularly on these European issues as rather parochial and nation state-centred, closed in itself and disinterested in what was going on and how these matters were discussed beyond the German borders. I saw that there was so much going on beyond the specific German or domestic discourse that needed to be taken into account. From a journalistic point of view, it is also very attractive to discover interesting things that have not been reported on yet.

We reached out to law scholars all over Europe for the first time when we organised the online symposium with Armin von Bogdandy that I mentioned earlier, and we were lucky enough to ensure the participation of a number of great scholars in the debate. We took this as a token of how fruitful and productive having legal discussions online could be.

**What kind of instructions do you give to your authors? What role does editing play in the process?**

Making texts about difficult subjects as accessible as possible for as many people as possible is what journalists do. We put a lot of effort into editing texts. Being subject to editing can be unfamiliar and sometimes annoying to authors who think that we are meddling with their authorship, so it's important to emphasise that our editing is just providing suggestions about how we, from a professional point of view, think that the text could be improved. The German legal language is also rather particular in that respect. A large part of the German legal training when you go to university and start preparing for the dreaded First State Exam – really a deformative experience for most people who go through it – consists of picking up a certain style of phrasing, the so-called *Gutachtenstil*, which can be an impediment if your aim is to engage the attention of readers with a blog post. It is interesting to think about why particularly German lawyers write that way.

A specific characteristic of German legal language is that people use many nouns as opposed to verbs. I could go on about this for hours.

Many academic texts tend to rather beat about the bush and go like: 'I am going to make the argument in four parts, the first part is an introduction, the second part . . . ', and if the reader is lucky the scholar finally reveals on page four the reason why she should engage with the text in the first place. Much of our editorial work is dedicated to advising our authors to sharpen the focus of their texts. In a blog post, you have to tell the reader right away why they should take the time and effort to read the text, or else they just won't, and that would be a pity and waste of resources. So, this is a big part of the editing work that we are doing. I am a journalist, I am used to viewing texts as stories, and stories need to engage the attention of the reader. Academics often underestimate this emotional side of writing.

**What drives you? Is it journalistic curiosity or do you have a stance in the stories that you write and choose to publish on *Verfassungsblog*?**
Of course, it is a matter of professional discipline to not let your personal preferences and political standpoints take over your editorial work. As I said in the beginning, we always had a profile of pushing against what was at the time the conservative mainstream in constitutional law and a strive to open that up with respect to Europe and the global discourse. On the other hand, we are not the public relations platform of some political campaign. We are independent and we try to create a discourse. If we receive a submission with which I do not agree politically, this is of course not a reason to decline it as long as it is argued well in a substantive and productive way. We do have a distinct profile, however, when it comes to our focus on constitutionalism itself. In recent years, we have published a lot about Hungary, about Poland, about authoritarian populism and its corrosive effects on the rule of law and the European Union. This is where we are perceived as fighting a fight and this also reflects our self-perception.

**How much do you think about the impact of *Verfassungsblog* and the chance to influence ongoing discussions?**
It is always nice to see that an article goes viral, that our readership numbers spike or some article's argument is picked up in the political debate, in parliament or by the government. That is flattering, a reassurance that we matter, that we have an impact. This response serves as an indication that we succeed in what we do: to provide knowledge, insights and expertise, informed opinions about ongoing developments to the public to facilitate the formation of their informed opinions.

**Can you tell us more about your fight for constitutionalism?**
Our principal job is to provide scholarly comments and analysis about current affairs in constitutional law and policy. Yet, at a time when constitutional law has become a matter of political contestation itself to the extent as it is today, we cannot do this by limiting ourselves to the role of neutral observers. It is also questionable whether this can generally be achieved. We are actively taking part in the fight for constitutionalism itself. In 2011, I wrote my first text about Hungary. I remember how it completely blew my mind when I saw what was going on in Hungary because at the time most people believed that what was disquieting about Orbán was mostly his media policy. Few had realised that the assault was actually directed at the constitution. This was the first time that I noticed how much is at stake when politics is no longer just about settling conflicts going on within the framework of the constitution but about that very constitutional framework itself.

**Your website states that '[w]e are always interested in well-written and thoughtful comment and analysis on topical events or developments (e.g. court decisions, legislation etc.) of constitutional law and policy. If you observe any of that in your field of research, you are warmly encouraged to submit a blog post. Just shoot us an email or a message on Twitter/ Facebook, explaining briefly the relevance of the topic and your background as an expert.'**

**How do you select the people whose legal expertise gets to be published on Verfassungsblog and how many do you reject in proportion to those published?**
Approximately half of our content is unsolicited: people approach us and send in their article drafts. We also actively reach out to potential authors if something noteworthy is going on and we think that this needs to be explained or commented on. By now, we are privileged in being able to draw from our large network of authors to either provide an article themselves or point us to someone who could. We decline roughly a third of the submitted posts.

We do have an editorial board structure, which we call associate editors. They are legal scholars specialised in particular fields of constitutional law who provide us with their expertise both in terms of assessing submissions and pointing us to potential authors. In case of doubt, it is their advice which is decisive for making the decision whether a submission appears on *Verfassungsblog* or not. A full-blown peer-review process, where you have two reasoned opinions for every text, would be too cumbersome and time-consuming for the mostly topical content we have. I also do not believe that such a process is necessary for our kind of publication because we usually publish expert opinions, comments and analysis on topical discussions and put them up for a debate. We try to publish our posts within days, sometimes even hours after the event, when the demand for constitutional expertise is at its peak. The editing itself is mostly done by the staff.

**Can you tell us more about your authors?**
Our authors range from undergraduate students to law professors with a global reputation. We give scholars who have only recently started climbing the career ladder an opportunity to make themselves visible in a rather effective and accessible way. This cuts both ways, you always run the risk of making yourself unpopular with some people if you stick your neck out, but this is a risk that you have to take anyway if you are serious about your research. On the whole, I think that the fact that venues like ours exist makes the academic discourse more flexible and accessible and less rigid in terms of authoritative voices.

**Has there been a change in the quality of submissions in the last years?**
Certainly in quantity but not quality. The submissions represent different dimensions of text quality, of style or in terms of the profoundness of thought and the originality of research.

**Would you publish something on the blog if the quality of the argument is good, even though you disagree with the substance?**
Of course I would.

**Do you have staff and volunteers? How do you choose and finance them?**
This has been a difficult question in the last years. By now, we have a staff of four editors, including myself, plus some volunteers, student assistants and interns. We are independent and not affiliated with any academic institution, which is crucial for us if we want to remain an open platform with no obligations towards any institutional PR interests. A part of our funding comes from our readers through crowdfunding. There are also some institutions which support us, particularly Matthias Kumm at the Center for Global Constitutionalism at the WZB Berlin Social Science Center here in Berlin. Then there are advertisements in the weekly editorial which goes out to 9,000 subscribers and reaches a large part of the constitutionalist community worldwide, such as job openings, events, calls for papers and calls for applications. To make ends meet we also have to take on editing jobs for outside clients. The bad thing is that our funding does not grow in correspondence with the growth of the project itself. In 2020, we have seen a tremendous growth, both in terms of reach – the number of readers has doubled – but also in terms of blogposts. Now we sometimes publish the

same number of blogposts in a day that we used to publish in a week. This has become a really big project. We are and always have been an open access medium and we want to find out how to position ourselves with respect to the funding for open access media. This is a project that we will take on in 2021 – how we envision our future in a way that we get remunerated for what we are providing to the academic community.

**Is *Verfassungsblog* a social media outlet? How do you see your responsibility as editor-in-chief?**

We do not see ourselves as a social media outlet. We are in some sense an old-school, media enterprise, making editorial decisions and taking responsibility for those. Our idea of publishing is emphatically not that people can just upload unedited content on our platform, which I would say is a characteristic of social media. We take responsibility for the activities on *Verfassungsblog*. Yet, we make use of social media. We have a presence on Facebook, Twitter and LinkedIn, most actively on Twitter. This presence is secondary, though, a channel through which we reach part of our audience in addition to those whom we reach directly through our website.

**What experiences do you have from enabling a public debate on your website?**

We used to have an issue with comment trolls some years ago. Initially, the comment section was open for everyone and we did not have much of an issue in that respect, luckily. In 2016, we noticed a change in tone and substance in our comments section subsequent to the refugee crisis and the rise of the far-right AfD party in Germany. In response, we changed our policy and insisted that people provide a proper email address and accept some minimum accountability so that they cannot completely hide behind anonymity. That policy change was rather effective at the time, and trolling vanished overnight. Recently, we have also inserted a moderation loop before we publish comments. We just could not take the risk of harassment anymore.

**Are you afraid of the power that comes with the blog as you are clearly the face of the blog? Have you ever needed to take on editor-in-chief responsibility for published publication on the blog?**

Not in the sense that I have been taken to court – luckily. As I said earlier, of course we take responsibility for our editorial decisions. I am the chief editor and ultimately in charge, but I do not take the decisions alone. I have a dedicated and extremely smart team of co-editors and an experienced editorial board to make sure that we make the right decisions, and I am very grateful for that.

**Many academics are nowadays on Twitter. Does this online presence change legal expertise – does it become less neutral/more politicised? Does it make some academic celebrities?**
Some legal academics have successfully built a public presence for themselves on Twitter, with large numbers of followers and accordingly considerable influence on public opinion. I am not sure, though, if that is the cause for the politicisation which you mentioned or rather a side effect of a politicisation which has been there in the first place for political reasons. I observe that there is a huge public and political demand for constitutional expertise. This is, by the way, a sign that something is going profoundly wrong, in my view. Twenty years ago, constitutional law was considered mostly boring, nerdy stuff for people with weird intellectual predilections. People talked about their crashing computer programs all the time. Now it is the other way around. Our devices and apps run smoothly, and nobody needs to pick up expertise in how and why they work and what to do if they do not: they just do. This is how it should be with constitutional law. Yet it is not, Europe's computer is crashing, and this is, sadly in a way, why *Verfassungsblog* is flourishing. Constitutional law exists to enable politics, to provide a framework of procedures and institutions to come to collectively binding decisions and maintain diversity at the same time. If that works properly, you do not have to care much about how and why it works unless you are an expert. Yet it does not, which is good for us and bad for everyone else, I guess.

**Academics quote *Verfassungsblog* more frequently in the footnotes in the last years. Have you seen any judges or courts refer to *Verfassungsblog*?**
Yes, that is the case increasingly, particularly now in the Coronavirus crisis. When the pandemic broke out, there was a lack of legal expertise at a moment it was demanded the most, as cases were piling up in the courts. We were in a position to deliver some of that on short notice. Many courts used arguments published on *Verfassungsblog* and quoted them accordingly. Recently, even the German Federal Constitutional Court had quoted two *Verfassungsblog* articles in its decision about parity in parliament.[8] Generally, the wall between 'proper academic publishing' in journals and book chapters on the one hand and blog posts on the other hand seems to have been crumbling in recent

[8] German Federal Constitutional Court, Beschluss des Zweiten Senats vom 15. Dezember 2020, 2 BvC 46/19, Rn. 1–120, www.bundesverfassungsgericht.de/SharedDocs/Entscheidungen/DE/2020/12/cs20201215_2bvc004619.html, para. 94.

years. We have seen that elsewhere as well.[9] The UK Supreme Court in its seminal *Miller* decision quoted UK Constitutional Law blogposts because this was where the debate was mostly taking place, and this was where the core arguments had been published.[10]

**Have you by now convinced most academics that blogs are an important avenue to talk about important things?**

As I said, we see a lot less scepticism towards blogs than we saw a few years ago. I think that writing blogposts is seen as useful and legitimate academic work which is accepted for the most part by now. That does not mean that everyone will do it. Writing blogposts is not for everyone, I suppose, and I am totally fine with that. I know for a fact that many academics whom I greatly respect prefer classical formats for their writing, and who am I to argue with that. What I do observe, though, is a rising recognition of the fact that what we do has value too.

**Why have there not been any contenders to *Verfassungsblog*?**

I think there are. There are all sorts of successful and innovative projects, some of which already existed when *Verfassungsblog* was launched in 2009. There is the UK constitutional law blog, there is *EJIL Talk*, there is *Völkerrechtsblog*, there is Daniel Sarmiento's *EU Law Live*, there is Tom Daly's IACL blog, and there is of course *I-CONnect*, which is doing a Spanish version right now [December 2020] and I think that is a great idea, not to mention a great many other fantastic projects. I do not see them as opponents or competitors. I know many of the people behind these projects and consider us as working on the same project, which is organising a global constitutional discourse. I am really proud to be part of that sphere. I have no ambition to be the only game in town nor do I think it correctly describes our place to say that we are.

***

We are now seeing a change taking place in traditional academic publishing channels, with universities moving towards open science and scholars working

[9] For Germany, see Federal Supreme Court Judgement VI ZR 439/17, 18 December 2018, https://juris.bundesgerichtshof.de/cgi-bin/rechtsprechung/document.py?Gericht=bgh&Art=en&nr=94971&pos=0&anz=1, para. 21. See also the Polish Supreme Court Decision Ref. Act II PO 3/19, 15 July 2029, www.sn.pl/sites/orzecznictwo/OrzeczeniaHTML/ii%20po%203-19-5.docx.html, paras. 30 and 69.

[10] See UK Supreme Court Judgment R *(on the application of Miller and another)* v. *Secretary of State for Exiting the European Union*, [2017] UKSC 5, 24 January 2017, www.supremecourt.uk/cases/docs/uksc-2016–0196-judgment.pdf, para. 274: 'The very full debate in the courts has been supplemented by a vigorous and illuminating academic debate conducted on the web (particularly through the UK Constitutional Law Blog site).'

to remove paywalls, funders demanding open publishing and stronger interaction with non-scientific audiences. Blogs and other internet platforms have already changed the academic writing culture and influenced writing styles and the use of language. What else may be or has already changed in the expression and evaluation of legal expertise?

One important theme is how non-traditional channels of producing and disseminating legal expertise contribute to the diversification of voices especially in constitutional law scholarship. Legal expertise is more than knowledge of constitutional law issues, but as the chapters in this volume show, legal expertise is often understood as being more knowledgeable than others about constitutional law. Steinbeis described above his German university as a 'a rigid, conservative place where authority played a huge role'. While our sample (anecdotal and personal evidence from Finland and Germany) is limited, this could suggest that constitutional law has traditionally been a realm of (older, white) male voices. In a way, Maximilian Steinbeis comparing constitutional law to computer science is eerily apt – as computer science has also been a male dominated field. In an editorial of the *International Journal of Constitutional Law* (*I.CON*), Michaela Hailbronner, Marcela Prieto Rudolphy and Gráinne de Búrca ask where women are in academic publishing and note that

> Not only is the percentage of the overall number of papers submitted to the journal [*I.CON*] by female authors each year significantly lower than the percentage of submissions by male authors, but the percentage of submissions by women has been declining each year over the past three years. Thirty-four percent of submissions in 2016 were from female authors, but this percentage declined in 2017 to 32 percent and in 2018 it dropped to 30 percent. And while the journal's rate of acceptance of articles submitted by women during those years turns out to have been higher than the rate of acceptance of articles submitted by men, the end result is that just over one-third of the articles appearing in I.CON from 2016 to 2018 were authored by women.[11]

The authors do not comment on social media as a publishing avenue apart from noting that women tend to shy away from self-marketing their work.

We are certainly not suggesting that contributing to blogs solves the issue of underrepresentation of female voices, let alone those of other marginalised groups. As regards blogs as 'second-rate' and 'hamburger-size' scholarship,[12] we

[11] Michaela Hailbronner, Marcela Prieto Rudolphy and Gráinne de Búrca, 'ICON Editorial' (2020) 17 *Blog of the International Journal of Constitutional Law* 4, www.iconnectblog.com/2020/01/icon-volume-17-issue-4-editorial/.

[12] Duval, 'Publish (Tweets and Blogs) or Perish?' at fn. 99.

agree that blogs do not provide similar levels of 'quality control' as refereed journals, nor are they particularly concerned with methodological issues – nor should they be. Their function is different: to provide quick reactions to topical issues. Koskenniemi writes elsewhere in this volume that to appear as a competent 'lawyer' is the outcome of a performance. Quite irrespective of what we think of this element of performance in creating a lawyer and legal expert, blogs, Twitter and other social media forums provide a new platform to 'perform' law. As regards underrepresentation, we remain optimistic and believe that sites such as *Verfassungsblog* offer avenues for new voices to be heard. Given that blogs do have an impact outside academic circles, these voices matter to policy-making as well as more established forms of expertise.

# 15

# Afterword: The Four Questions and One Answer

Emilia Korkea-aho and Päivi Leino-Sandberg

When we were discussing the idea of an edited volume on legal experts and legal expertise for the first time, our aim was to a large extent descriptive, to lay before the reader many types of legal experts that have so far remained invisible. But our idea for the conclusion was slightly different. We hoped to be able to draw together multiple lines of investigation and to create a typology of legal experts. The envisioned typology would group legal experts working in the most varied kinds of regulatory, policy-making and operative tasks in the EU policy-making context on the basis of some recognisable and common traits that all legal experts share. For instance, we would depict a legal expert as someone who knows a lot about a particular topic or topics in law and someone who works for an institution that governs through law. Then we would proceed to categorise different expert types: an activist-expert, technocratic-expert, intellectual-expert, the 'money talks' business-oriented expert, and so on.

The world of EU legal experts surprised us. It is more diverse, complex, fast-moving and ambiguous than we ever anticipated. We found many of these expert roles in governance institutions. We also discovered that legal experts frequently rotate between these roles. In his chapter Koskenniemi writes that '[l]aw and lawyers are everywhere in transnational governance'. The chapters in this volume bear witness to his observation. Many recent law graduates who enter the job market still take on perhaps more 'classical' roles as judges, legal advisers, attorneys and academics; but an increasing number work as corporate lawyers and in-house lobbyists, managers and directors, and officials in international and domestic institutions. Legal expertise is found in an increasing number of occupations. Legal experts are trained as lawyers, which shapes their world view and method of approaching problems. Yet, they are engaged in the most varied kinds of tasks applying their legal tools. In these capacities, they frame the worlds of economic and technical development, political freedom, delivery of justice and sustainable uses of resources in particular language through which problems are delineated, agency is distributed and authority is called upon to adjudicate on specific claims. And this ubiquity in turn reflects just how pervasive and relevant legal constructions and legal structures are. Law is the foundation of society, and lawyers help to make society tick. Avril begins her chapter with a quote by Marcel Raymond, president of the *Association Nationale des Avocats*, on how 'the Common Market has *nothing* to do with lawyers'. Now, more than sixty years later, Avril points out how European integration seems to have *everything* to do with lawyers.

We see the descriptive mission of the collection accomplished. The typology of legal experts, instead, seems a futile exercise on the basis of what we have learned about legal experts in the EU context. Such typology would require boundary policing work (legal/non-legal, expert/layperson). This kind of boundary drawing was exactly what the descriptive chapters questioned, because these boundaries do not make sense of the real life, the richness of the world in which legal experts work.

Instead, in this conclusion we will illustrate what we have learned about legal experts in the EU policy-making context and revisit the research questions we posed to the authors of this volume, looking at them in a fresh light. The work towards this volume began with us editors identifying the following four questions: (1) Who is a legal expert?, (2) how does a legal expert frame and shape the issues she is dealing with?, (3) how does she interact with competing legal experts, that is, in situations of 'hybridisation' of legal expertise?, and (4) how is a legal expert different, if at all, from other professionals providing policy expertise?

So, who is the legal expert? In the introduction, we argue that a formal degree and work experience are significant criteria for a legal expert. However, the chapters in this collection demonstrate how being recognised as a legal expert requires so much more than legal studies at a university. We are accustomed to thinking that legal expertise is knowing the 'law' and how it is practised. This requires knowledge of the legal procedures and being experienced in pleading in courts or advising multinational companies on mergers and acquisitions. However, what comes across in many chapters is that an important aspect of legal expertise is knowledge of decision-making processes in multilevel governance environments and the mechanisms needed to navigate these processes competently. Much of what is required from legal experts in our context of the EU policy-making is learned by doing, through engaging in the world of legal expertise and policy-making.

However, law is often not enough, not even for legal experts whose job it is to provide expertise in law. Kimura and Nicola's chapter demonstrates, for example, that legal experts engaging in bilateral trade negotiations between the EU and third countries require not only knowledge of the law but also of trade. For legal experts in Bradford's chapter regulatory expertise and its use in various legal systems would seem to be needed. She writes that 'the Commission's expertise is wide-ranging, blending legal expertise with scientific and economic expertise in particular', hence deserving the label 'regulatory' expertise, not legal. Micklitz stresses that the EU, maybe much more than the nation state, also promotes the transformation of the legal profession through governance, through integration *without law*. In this context, it is not easy to find substantive criteria of what makes a legal expert.

One finding is that legal experts need to know more than law. Another finding is one can be a legal expert without formal qualifications in law. France and Vauchez remind us how the Paris bar has assimilated

> parliamentarians to so-called category A civil servants (top civil servants) and held that the exercise of a parliamentary mandate or ministerial functions counts as twelve years of 'juridical activity' on the ground that it entails 'participation in law-making'. Furthermore, the Bar has adopted a flexible definition of the type of 'law degree' required for simplified access to the Bar, thus opening it up to a broad range of candidates.

A similar relaxation is found elsewhere, too. When discussing the use of legal expertise in NGO advocacy around Brexit, Lee and Abbot write that they 'do not believe that legal expertise is found only in individuals with academic or professional qualifications in law; we came across a number of individuals with no such qualifications whom we considered, and who were clearly considered by their peers, to be legal experts'.

Expertise is also relational and inherently social. Yong cites Becker who suggests that it might be better to understand knowledge and expertise not as a quantity of which experts have more and laypeople less, but rather describes a 'social relationship between a more knowledgeable person and one who knows less'.[1]

Another challenge to the received narrow idea of what makes a legal expert comes in the form of (social) media where everyone can in principle claim to be a legal expert, irrespective of background or education. Social media may have become one such platform where such claims are made. As reflected on in the interview with Steinbeis – the founder of *Verfassungsblog* – blogs and other online platforms offer a level playing field for new voices. Yet, the legal profession is a professional project and legal expertise is not 'common

[1] Howard Becker, *What about Mozart? What about Murder? Reasoning from Cases* (Chicago: University of Chicago Press, 2014), p. 58.

knowledge', as Lee and Abbot note, but the result of lengthy specialisation. When political scientists, for example, express opinions about what the Treaties (should) allow, or whether a proposal is legally solid, many legal experts feel uncomfortable. Legal expertise is, as Koskenniemi writes in his chapter, 'a linguistic competence, the possession of a specific lexicon and a set of idioms plus a grammar that allows the making of distinctions that frame the world in a specific way'. It hurts our professional pride when someone uses the terms carelessly.

Is legal expertise then about knowing how to use legal language and frame issues? How does a legal expert frame and shape the issues she is dealing with? These questions are at the core of Windsor's theoretical account of framing and its relevance for legal expertise. He argues that frames are important to formulating legal advice, and legal experts are not always adequately trained in critically assessing the frames they use, of which algorithmic decision-making is a topical example. The empirical chapters in this book provide unique glimpses into the way in which legal experts think and frame the world around themselves. The picture that emerges is a complex one and difficult to synthesise into one or two legal experts' mindsets. Yet, what seems to unite legal experts across various contexts in this volume is that experts are – to a varying degree – conscious of risks involved in the expert position.

For the contributors to this collection, and for us, the observation that law and lawyers are everywhere is not a harmless joke. As international law scholars – Duncan Kennedy among others – have long reminded us: law frames, limits and empowers. Law delegates power, choices and control to experts by maintaining the idea that legal expertise is neutral. EU legal scholarship has been slow in thinking about these issues. EU policy-making has been explained (indeed, framed) far too long as a technical agenda that benefits us all, with law operating as its key tool. Contrary to this, the debate on expert governance – in particular in the area of international law – has more or less explicitly focused on agenda, power and elite tendencies. For international law, experts are representatives of a (transnational) elite. This aspect is, interestingly, mostly missing among the contributions to the volume, with the exception of Bradford's chapter. Very few interviewed legal experts reflected on the elitist nature of legal expertise or whether it has exclusionary effects, pushing others to the sidelines of policy-making. One interviewed NGO legal advisor in Korkea-aho's chapter, however, challenged the idea of increasing legal capacities in NGOs, noting that 'if we have this elitist idea that only people who have a legal background can contribute to the definition and the adoption of laws, then we won't reach the people who are furthest behind and that's not an inclusive way of making law'.

Legal experts also position themselves differently in relation to political decision-making. Some of the legal experts interviewed by Leino-Sandberg openly took an active role in formulating policy objectives. Other legal experts maintained that they take a purely enabling role, thus distancing themselves from their client's political agenda. Such distance often proves difficult to sustain in practice as some legal experts working in the European Parliament argue. Yet, maintaining this distance is relevant even in the case of legal academics, as Klabbers demonstrates in his chapter. Even academics transmit a world view, establishing frames through which matters are taught, thus setting aside alternative views of the world. In the context of NGO advocacy, legal advisors are particularly alert to how their activities frame and shape the issues of their NGO 'client', constantly asking themselves whether the activities they are engaged in end up legalising NGO advocacy.

Another issue which international lawyers have long drawn attention to is that expert governance is inescapable, and no politician can dream to succeed without an expert or two on her side. Legal experts working for NGOs acknowledge the role they have in guaranteeing the credibility of NGO activities. Both chapters (Korkea-aho, Lee and Abbot) on NGO legal advocacy zoom in on environmental NGOs where competition for influence is intense, and it is no surprise that NGOs wish for 'high-calibre' senior lawyers. Even Members of the European Parliament – who generally find law and legal experts something of a nuisance and a hindrance to the realisation of their political visions – admit that law matters for their credibility. Drafting proposals that are deemed legally impossible hampers one's credibility as a politician.

Legal advisers are also concerned about their performance. How a legal adviser manages to assist their clients in achieving their goals also matters. NGO legal advisors and legal advisors in parliaments (EU, national) articulate fears about disappointing their clients (NGOs, parliamentarians). They understand that their clients are disappointed at the 'solutions' offered by law, but often legal experts – as the medium of law and legal expertise – feel the disappointment of the unmet need or inability to deliver the agenda defined by the client. Particularly for legal advisers working in the European Parliament, this underlines the need to be helpful and identify legally imaginable and politically suitable solutions. Imagination is indeed a key requirement of a good legal expert.

The identification of legally imaginable and politically suitable solutions is rarely one person's job. How does a legal expert interact with competing legal experts, that is, in the situation of 'hybridisation' of legal expertise? The chapters show that legal experts are everywhere, and they have made – what

Avril calls – new 'jurisdictional claims' on new territories. In this work, they are bound to meet other legal experts and need to work with them. The credibility and usefulness of legal experts is evaluated by other legal experts who assess it based on the internal logic of law and legal professionals. However, in the EU policy-making contexts that we have studied, the performance of legal experts is continuously assessed by non-lawyers and their clients for whom the main measurement of credibility might be how well the advice coincides with their own political ambitions. This puts additional pressure on lawyers to be helpful and find solutions. A legal expert who is 'too much of a lawyer' is quickly found redundant and to be replaced by another more creative lawyer.

What surprised us was how certain areas of law stood out. When we began working on the volume we envisaged how there might be turf wars between, for instance, government legal advisors and NGO lawyers, or how legal experts from different contexts would come together to pool their epistemic resources. We anticipated, as Windsor writes, that 'in a legal environment characterised by regime proliferation, expert advisers are typically engaged in a competition for semantic authority'. To a certain extent competition and collaboration both happened. Brexit managed to bring different environmental NGOs together, resulting in deepened and shared legal expertise. NGO legal advisors also commented on how they are not fixated on thinking in traditional legal ways about law, and are able to creatively strategise, unlike those in traditional legal jobs (in governments). However, in many chapters it was emphasised that there is a sense of competition between specialist legal experts (EU law, constitutional law, trade law) and non-specialist lawyers. Particularly fascinating is the role of constitutional law in making legal experts. Steinbeis notes that

> twenty years ago, constitutional law was considered mostly boring, nerdy stuff for people with weird intellectual predilections ... Constitutional law exists to enable politics, to provide a framework of procedures and institutions to come to collectively binding decisions and maintain diversity at the same time. If that works properly, you do not have to care much about how and why it works unless you are an expert.

While constitutional lawyers may have become the elite of legal scholars, more broadly the sudden 'coolness' of constitutional law is a sign of concern, as it points out that things are not working properly.

Does this then mean that legal experts work in silos of their specific expertise, or employer with paths rarely, if ever, crossing? Certainly not. Bradford notes how the Commission's expertise is wide-ranging, blending legal expertise with scientific and economic expertise in particular. In this context, she predicts that 'legal expertise is likely to become more generalised regulatory expertise over time, as legal questions intersect with questions of scientific or economic nature'. In the Commission, blending occurs inside the institution. Yet, many of the other chapters contain evidence of how legal experts frequently rotate between institutions and sectors, moving from the position of a corporate lawyer to lobbying, from a director to a civil servant, from a manager to a corporate lawyer crossing at the same time the international and domestic institutional divide. France and Vauchez posit that here we see the birth of a 'third sector', a hybrid space 'at the edges of the public and private sectors that is becoming increasingly autonomous'. The recognition of this new hybrid space allows us to appreciate the legal expert – introduced to us by France and Vauchez – who argue that their role is to 'defend the public interest in the private sector'. It also makes us more aware of how silos of expertise are not necessarily being broken down but are reproduced according to the new order emerging.

How is the legal expert different, if at all, from other professionals providing policy expertise? Of the questions we posed to our authors this was probably the trickiest one. Professional literature generally starts from the assumption that expertise is evaluated against the interpretative practices of the relevant professional community – its governing law, the way legal arguments are made and analysed – and assessed based on the 'tacit norms of acceptability to the professional community'.[2] Due to this inwardness, there is a risk of overemphasising the special nature of expertise of this particular profession. This risk is not confined to law and the legal profession, but is a familiar one to all scholars of the sociology of professions.

Yong writes that a profession is marked by its claim to possess a particular expertise, which laypeople do not and cannot share. The possession of this expertise points to an important marker of a profession: autonomy from the client. The research on the sociology of legal professions has argued that the client's perception of expertise matters, and scholarship on the legal profession has emphasised the importance of the client in understanding the work of lawyers and their claims to expertise. As Yong points out, literature on the legal profession and professionalism more generally argues that since the client lacks this particular expertise, they are in a position of weakness relative to the profession. The context in which the client's perspective has been brought to bear has been that of an attorney and an individual seeking to receive advice on their personal matter. In these instances, legal assistance and representation might often be a mandatory requirement.

[2] W. Bradley Wendel, 'Government Lawyers, Democracy, and the Rule of Law' (2009) 77 *Fordham Law Review* 1333–62 at 1361.

The relationship is different in the context of policy-making. The clients of legal advisors we have studied in this volume are in some sense experts or professionals themselves – parliamentarians, NGO staff, legal academics, civil servants, lobbyists and so on. They often have the choice to consult or not to consult. An interviewed MEP, for example, argued that she would not check everything with legal experts; after all, she often knows herself what the law says. Yong's parliamentarians at Westminster would 'shop around' for opinions and advice around before entering into what he calls, borrowing from Eliot Friedson, a 'professional referral system'. For this more experienced type of a client, legal expertise may appear as some form of common knowledge – anyone knows this! – which in the eyes of legal advisors fails to properly appreciate the complexity and significance of legal expertise.

The interviews of NGO legal advisors and their communities show how the law does not translate into 'commonly' knowing something but has 'a certain authority' or 'mystique', and cc'ing a legal advisor in an email works as a 'threatening card'. The same hunger for the law's unambiguous authority shows in the European Parliament, where clients often specifically ask for one solution, not several. For some of them, 'what the law says' should dictate one solution, not a full range of them. However, what we have learned from many of these chapters is that there often is no single solution, and this is the unhappy message our legal experts deliver to their clients. Instead, various solutions are possible, and constructing them is a matter of (legal) expertise. Antoine Vauchez has elsewhere endorsed a holistic appraisal of the space in which a 'case has been debated and framed',[3] and the identification and appraisal of this space should be taught in law schools.

In this respect, we could also make a difference between legal scholars, who might find the application of the legal scientific method more relevant, and legal experts whose expertise might be more practical than scientific. However, this distinction might be more artificial than real. The role of method in legal scholarship tends to be modest. The method of reaching the conclusion is more commonly opened and debated in the social sciences than in law, where legal dogmatics often serve as the only method ('the law is what the law says it is'). The method is in this respect hardly distinguishable from the toolbox of legal experts working in a policy-making context. In the EU policy-making context, legal experts frequently rely on teleological

[3] Antoine Vauchez, 'EU Law Classics in the Making' in Fernanda Nicola and Bill Davies (eds.), *EU Law Stories: Contextual and Critical Histories of European Jurisprudence* (Cambridge: Cambridge University Press, 2017), p. 21, p. 31.

interpretations where the law is more about enabling what we think should be done and less about what the law prevents us from doing.

In his chapter, Micklitz emphasises that in the administrative state, the lawyer competes with other disciplines for the authoritative position that was earlier allocated to professionals more or less automatically. In the EU governance structures, there is often no differentiation between expertise and legal expertise but the latter counts as just one possible competence that is integrated into the information-based processing approach. He argues that this leads to a downgrading of the legal profession. But is this always a bad thing?

For us, legal expertise is not a special case, and its uses in policy-making processes should be studied like any form of expertise. This does not mean that we would close our eyes to the particularities of legal expertise and legal experts, but rather that their role should be subjected to scrutiny. This is particularly important in the policy-making context, where the spectrum of legally possible solutions should be subjected to political scrutiny and made understandable to a broader audience. We agree with Klabbers who writes that 'lawyers are often excluded from scrutiny on the ground that their work is mostly hermeneutic in nature, rather than having a direct social relevance – lawyers are mostly seen to affect the social world through advising their clients: governments, criminal suspects, corporations, rather than directly and immediately'. This volume has hopefully banished any lingering ideas of 'mere' hermeneutic relevance, and shown that lawyers have a direct and immediate social relevance.

Are we circling back to where we started? We began the work towards this volume to amend the situation where studies on expertise and experts rarely mention legal experts, and if they do, they only look at legal experts in contexts of litigation. If we now deny the special character of legal expertise, do we acquiesce to the fact that legal experts do not merit attention? Our answer – the one we referred to in the title – is 'no', and we hope that this collection manages to convince that both the political role of legal experts and what Klabbers calls the 'legal effects' of legal experts should no longer escape scrutiny. The first step – which we have strived to have taken here – is to make the political role and legal effects visible. Once they are visible enough we can venture to ask whether they are subject to (political) control. We should not, however, be singularly focused on how accountability mechanisms work. Instead, we should push further, asking for instance what kind of ideas lawyers working as legal advisors have about the policy process; do they see issues through technocratic lenses, as questions that are best answered by competent scientists, economists or lawyers or as questions best answered by involving societal actors as broadly as possible? In doing so we should keep in mind the warning that France and Vauchez voice in their chapter. Any individualised analysis of legal experts should not lose sight of the fact that whatever we have discovered and will discover about legal experts should be seen as underscoring the systemic rather than the individual nature of legal expert activities. Discussions of legal experts and legal expertise 'must be founded on a solidly political reflection on the conditions of the proper functioning of democracy'.

As indicated in the beginning of the book, we have dedicated it to the legal experts that we have studied. We have been impressed by their commitment to their work. For them, work is seldom just 'work', but a means of contributing to a better world, which they pursue rigorously and with pride and high integrity. We hope that the book does justice to their work and numerous discussions we were lucky enough to have with them. We also hope that it 'returns a favour' by providing opportunities for self-reflection of their role and impact in a word of conflicting objectives, by placing their individual experiences in a broader framework of European policy-making.

# Index

For EU product safety concerns, contact us at Calle de José Abascal, 56–1°, 28003 Madrid, Spain or eugpsr@cambridge.org.

www.ingramcontent.com/pod-product-compliance
Ingram Content Group UK Ltd.
Pitfield, Milton Keynes, MK11 3LW, UK
UKHW021943180726
473460UK00010B/172
* 9 7 8 1 1 0 8 8 2 1 6 4 3 *